Hitler's *Mein Kampf* and the Holocaust

PERSPECTIVES ON THE HOLOCAUST

A series of books designed to help students further their understanding of key topics within the field of Holocaust studies.

Published:

Holocaust Representations in History (2nd edition), Daniel H. Magilow and Lisa Silverman

Postwar Germany and the Holocaust, Caroline Sharples

Anti-Semitism and the Holocaust, Beth A. Griech-Polelle

The Holocaust in Eastern Europe, Waitman Wade Beorn

The United States and the Nazi Holocaust, Barry Trachtenberg

Witnessing the Holocaust, Judith M. Hughes

Hitler's Mein Kampf *and the Holocaust: A Prelude to Genocide*, John J. Michalczyk, Michael S. Bryant, and Susan A. Michalczyk (eds.)

Forthcoming:

Sites of Holocaust Memory, Janet Ward

Hitler's *Mein Kampf* and the Holocaust

A Prelude to Genocide

Edited by
John J. Michalczyk,
Michael S. Bryant, and
Susan A. Michalczyk

BLOOMSBURY ACADEMIC
LONDON • NEW YORK • OXFORD • NEW DELHI • SYDNEY

BLOOMSBURY ACADEMIC
Bloomsbury Publishing Plc
50 Bedford Square, London, WC1B 3DP, UK
1385 Broadway, New York, NY 10018, USA
29 Earlsfort Terrace, Dublin 2, Ireland

BLOOMSBURY, BLOOMSBURY ACADEMIC and the Diana logo are trademarks of Bloomsbury Publishing Plc

First published in Great Britain 2022

Cover design by Design Holborn
Cover Image: Picture taken on January 1945 at Auschwitz, after the liberation of the extermination camp by te Soviet troops, showing the entrance of the camp. (© /AFP via Getty Images)

A catalogue record for this book is available from the British Library.

A catalog record for this book is available from the Library of Congress.

ISBN: HB: 978-1-3501-8545-6
PB: 978-1-3501-8544-9
ePDF: 978-1-3501-8546-3
eBook: 978-1-3501-8547-0

Typeset by Deanta Global Publishing Services, Chennai, India

Dedicated to Jacques Salmanowitz (1884–1966)

Jacques Salmanowitz, a Swiss businessman, was instrumental in bringing to safety in Switzerland many individuals trapped behind German lines in the Second World War.

CONTENTS

FIGURES

FOREWORD

"When a person gives, he needs to take," Adolf Hitler once said, "and I take what I need from books." Hitler was a voracious reader. By the time of his suicide in April 1945, he owned an estimated 16,000 volumes in 3 private libraries, at the Reich Chancellery in Berlin, at his Prinzregentenplatz apartment in Munich, and at the Berghof, his alpine retreat on the Obersalzberg. His private secretary, Traudl Junge, once told me that she remembered Hitler reading a book a night, which he invariably and tediously reprised for her the following morning at breakfast. "Books, always more books! I can never remember Adolf without books," a Hitler associate from his teenage years recalled. "They were his world."

There was no book more central to Hitler's life and identity than *Mein Kampf*. There is no event more central to his legacy than the Holocaust. For these reasons, this volume represents a welcome and important addition to the vast literature on the former Nazi leader and the Holocaust, in particular. While *Mein Kampf* is often discussed as a self-serving and unreliable autobiography or an impossibly ponderous and impenetrable political manifesto, and frequently referenced as a source for understanding the nature of Hitler's anti-Semitism, this volume represents the first systematic examination of *Mein Kampf* with specific focus on the Holocaust.

The editors, John J. Michalczyk, Michael S. Bryant, and Susan A. Michalczyk, have enlisted an impressive range of scholars and researchers, indeed some of the world's leading authorities on *Mein Kampf*, to consider the origins, sources, impacts, and implications of this infamous treatise, from the nineteenth century to our own day. Through the individual chapters we come to understand the place of *Mein Kampf* not only within the personal life and career of its author but equally important within the broader context of German society. The contributors trace the origins of European racial theories more broadly and examine how these theories found their most extreme expression in Hitler's words and policies. These chapters help illuminate Hitler's personal manifesto, a work that can be as impenetrable as it is repulsive, with the advantage of allowing one to explore *Mein Kampf* without subjecting oneself to the punishing experience of reading the original.

Timothy W. Ryback
Author, *Hitler's Private Library: The Books That Shaped His Life*
Berlin, Spring 2021

ACKNOWLEDGMENTS

As a collective effort of many individuals, our text reflects not only the ideas and extensive scholarship of our contributors but also the work of other individuals who understood the importance of coming to terms with the evolution of Hitler's mindset in the early 1920s as a prelude to the Holocaust. In hosting the Boston College conference at which our contributors offered a lecture and an interview for our accompanying documentary on the subject, Boston College, Bryant University, and Brandeis University provided funding for both travel and lodging. Monetta Edwards of the Carroll School of Management assisted significantly with financial details at Boston College, while Michael Bryant of Bryant University and Sabine von Mering did the same for their part of the sponsorship. To document the conference Robert Heim filmed the interviews while Michael Resler and Susan Michalczyk conducted them for our companion documentary, *Hitler's* Mein Kampf*: Prelude to the Holocaust.*

Andrew Wilson was an integral part of the *Mein Kampf* project, providing assistance with both textual and photographic matters. The Boston College library staff, primarily Eugenie M'Polo and Nina Bogdanovsky, furnished support with materials for the text and documentary. The Jacques Salmanowitz Program for Moral Courage in Documentary Film offered significant assistance with student support and financial backing. At the same time, Christopher Stoldt of the Graphics section of Media Technology Services and his student assistants have continued to offer their guidance and skills with the superior quality of the photographs. Richard Koenigsberg and his rich files in the Library of Social Science have provided significant resources about *Mein Kampf.* Extensive bibliographical assistance came from Amanda Ross, whose editorial eye has been greatly valued. We are further grateful to Djuna Carlton for providing the complex index to our work. Through the many and diverse projects over the years, colleague Jeffery Howe has been a constant technical and personal Michalczyk guide whose assistance has been most invaluable. John Michalczyk III provided further technical assistance through the editing process. With their significant contributions to the recent publication of the text of focus here, *Hitler,* Mein Kampf*: Eine kritische Edition* (2016), Magnus Brechtken and Othmar Plöckinger have added a rich dimension to this work.

Lastly, we are most appreciative of the continued support and guidance of Rhodri Mogford, Laura Reeves, and the editorial staff at Bloomsbury.

Introduction

The greatest riddle of the Third Reich [is] how Mein Kampf could be disseminated in public and how Hitler's dominion and the 12-year period of this dominion could come about, although the Bible of National Socialism circulated for years prior to their assumption of power.

VIKTOR KLEMPERER, *LTI (Lingua Tertia Imperii)*

When the Bavarian government's copyright to Adolf Hitler's *Mein Kampf* lapsed on January 1, 2016, the opportunity to reissue the book in German arose for the first time since 1945. One week after the copyright expired, *Mein Kampf* appeared on the shelves of German bookstores in a prosaic, two-volume edition bound in plain gray cloth. The editor and publisher was the Institute for Contemporary History (*Institut für Zeitgeschichte*, IfZ) in Munich, a research center founded after the Second World War and dedicated to the study of modern German history with an emphasis on National Socialism. Together amounting to some 1,950 pages, the two volumes consisted of not only the text of *Mein Kampf* itself but also substantial annotated footnotes prepared by six professional historians from the Institute. (The editors' Introduction to volume I alone runs to eighty-four pages.) The extensive commentary was intended to balance out the countless falsehoods, distortions, and misrepresentations of Hitler's memoir-cum-manifesto. "We don't let any of Hitler's claims pass without our interpretation in our footnotes," one of the lead editors of the *Mein Kampf* project, Christian Hartmann, stated in a media interview.[1]

The cautious approach of the editors notwithstanding, critics voiced their opposition to republishing Hitler's notorious book. When the national teachers' union supported the integration of the new edition into German public school curricula, the Bavarians balked. "This book still causes deep pain for a lot of people and we're not going to have a simple reprint of it going into our schools," the Bavarian education minister declared in a newspaper interview. The head of the Jewish community in Munich expressed skepticism about the pedagogical value of *Mein Kampf*, characterizing it as "irresponsible to include such libelous invective against Jews in schools."

In her view, teaching young Germans about the Nazi period could be accomplished without exposing them to Hitler's scurrilous text.[2]

Why republish *Mein Kampf* today? And why should anyone read it? The reasons weighing against both questions are formidable. Simply put, it's a badly written, internally inconsistent, and poorly constructed book. By his own admission, Hitler had little aptitude for writing. "I'm no writer and write badly," he confessed, "all the more as I believe I owe my people works rather than words." Hitler's surprisingly negative view of his own prose style was shared by many of his readers both then and in the decades since *Mein Kampf*'s first publication. One of his leading biographers, Joachim Fest, described Hitler's prose as combining "middle-class pretentiousness and Austrian chancery clerk bombast."[3] A notable German scholar of *Mein Kampf*, Peter Beyersdorf, accused Hitler in 1974 of deploying "absolutely unintelligent, vapid, and primitive arguments."[4] German literary scholar Dietrich Schwanitz adjudged the book an "unreadable concoction of anti-semitism, racism, militarism, chauvinism, Lebensraum theory, historical interpretation, and political propaganda, which, on account of its obvious idiocy, no one took seriously."[5] The editors of the Institute for Contemporary History sum up the consensus view of *Mein Kampf* as a literary work:

> *Mein Kampf* is today widely considered a half-baked, chaotic, scarcely readable text, the brutal and misanthropic messages of which repeatedly and sharply contrast with passages that are involuntarily comical. . . . And in point of fact Hitler's writing abounds with so many gaffes—not only biased and false formulations but numerous grammatical errors, which, despite multiple revisions of the text until 1944, were by no means all identified and corrected.[6]

For the editors, *Mein Kampf* suffers from an "enormous redundancy: the repetitions as well as the length, digressions, and breaks as generally the disparate character of the whole, which sometimes presented a challenge to its most well-meaning readers." Other pejoratives the editors apply to the book are "disorderly," "vague," "erratic," "contradictory," "disjointed," and "illogical."[7] No less a Hitler fanboy than Joseph Goebbels conceded the many faults of *Mein Kampf*, writing in his diary entry for May 10, 1931, that "the style [of *Mein Kampf*] is sometimes insufferable. . . . He writes like he talks. That has of course an immediate effect, but it is often unskillful."[8]

Clearly, *Mein Kampf* is of dubious literary value. Readers would not turn to it for its engaging artistry as they would the memoirs of other wartime leaders such as Julius Caesar, Winston Churchill, or Ulysses S. Grant, all of whose books continue to find audiences long after their deaths. Nor does *Mein Kampf* provide special insight into Hitler's childhood or his allegedly formative years in Vienna. Most scholars do not believe the biographical elements in *Mein Kampf* are accurate; rather, they serve the purpose of Hitler's self-stylization as the brilliant, misunderstood child of destiny, anointed to someday lead the Germans back to national greatness. Likewise, scholars have universally rejected his claim that he acquired the "granite foundation" (as he called it) of his ideology during his Vienna years.[9] Rather, many experts think Hitler projected onto the past his current beliefs *c* 1924–5. In short, Hitler's memoir was as deficient in historical truth as it was in literary merit.

If *Mein Kampf* is as bad as so many critics assert, however, why then republish it today and toward what end? One argument in favor of reading the book was suggested by the late German historian Eberhard Jäckel, who said that rarely if ever had a ruler written down beforehand what he would later do the way Hitler did in *Mein Kampf*. The editors from the Institute for Contemporary History pick up on this theme, documenting the many harbingers of Nazi excess in *Mein Kampf* that eventually came to pass. These include his rant against the "wailing letters from home" (*Jammerbriefe aus der Heimat*), which Hitler contended had demoralized the soldiers receiving them and which he would later address through draconian wartime laws that criminalized "treachery"; Hitler's accusation that "our people can't keep a secret," leading to his secrecy order issued in January 1940; his charge against the "ne'er-do-wells" in parliament for their supposed failure in the First World War to fully exploit the manpower available to them, a blunder Hitler would rectify in the waning months of the Second World War by mobilizing elderly men and young children to fight as *Volkssturm* soldiers; and his aphorism that "you can die on the front, but as a deserter you must die," converted during the war into murderous retaliation against soldiers accused of desertion, who were executed in the tens of thousands. The editors glimpse in the pages of *Mein Kampf* the outline of a dictatorship that would radicalize during the war years, plunging Germany into the abyss.[10]

In spite of its many distortions, lies, and fabrications, the candor with which Hitler related his intentions in *Mein Kampf* can be deeply impressive for readers today. It should be recalled that he wrote the book for his most fervent followers. Accordingly, he pitched his discussion of the Nazi political program to suit their zeal, writing with such a frankness that Victor Klemperer, a German Romance language scholar, commented after the war that never before had a work of propaganda been composed "with the shameless honesty" of *Mein Kampf*.[11] In fact, after the seizure of power, Hitler would come to regret this candor. More than once he was confronted with the incendiary statements he had made a decade before his breakthrough, and each time the Führer had to walk back the clear meaning of his earlier assertions. Thus in November 1933 he assured a French journalist he only wanted peace with France. When the journalist pointed out the contradiction of this avowal with his plain words in *Mein Kampf*, Hitler countered that it was "a book full of maledictions, written in a prison cell with the raging passion of a persecuted apostle."[12] Throughout the decade of the 1930s Hitler continued to soft-pedal the anti-French outbursts contained in *Mein Kampf*. To another French journalist in 1936 he waved off the asperity of his language, claiming that France's military occupation of the Ruhr Valley had been the reason for his tough words.[13] In his effort to defuse the adversarial tone of his book, Hitler was successful. Rarely did the outside world comprehend that his goal to unite Germans within a single ethnic state and expand its borders through war was a calculated, long-term plan.

The tendency among many observers was to accept Hitler's chicane and historicize *Mein Kampf*, attributing its extreme statements to the unique geopolitical conditions in Europe in 1924. Among Hitler's followers in the 1930s, however, the interpretation was considerably different. They looked upon *Mein Kampf* as the sacred scripture of the Nazi movement. To them it was not an artifact of a bygone time but Nazism's inspirational and authoritative program.[14] Their interpretation of Hitler's book, and not that of observers misled by Hitler's bunkum, proved to be the correct one.

If this is so—if *Mein Kampf* forebode the actions of the Nazi government more than a decade before they were carried out—what might it reveal about the worst of Hitler's crimes, the Holocaust? This is the central question of this volume of collected chapters you are holding in your hands. As we will explore more fully later in the book, scholarly opinion about the origins of the Final Solution has wavered between two poles, "intentionalism" and "functionalism." Intentionalists stress the central role of Hitler in the Final Solution, portraying the final decision to murder the Jews of Europe as the result of his premeditation and conscious planning. The closer a scholar is to pure intentionalism, the more he or she will stress the formation of Hitler's genocidal purpose at the early stages of his career. Functionalists by contrast de-emphasize Hitler's role or the idea that the Final Solution arose from advance planning. Instead, they place in the foreground the contingent nature of Nazi policy, which evolved gradually at local levels in occupied Europe, driven by on-the-ground German officials responding to perceived demographic crises. The closer a scholar is to pure functionalism, the more he or she will deny a preexisting intention to commit genocide on the Jews, focusing instead on the emergence of the Final Solution from the play of circumstances at lower levels of the Nazi command structure. As the editors of the present volume, we would suggest that a fresh look at *Mein Kampf* may shed light on, and perhaps even reinvigorate, this debate. Although none of the contributors argue that a clear plan of extermination emerges from the pages of *Mein Kampf*, a dire, violent, and hateful anti-Semitism pervades Hitler's book. If this attitude arguably reflects a murderous intention, actual or potential, then that intention, no matter how embryonic, should inform the debate over Hitler's role in the destruction of the Jews.

Whether or not it was unique as a preview of a dictator's future plans before he seized power, as Eberhard Jäckel believed, *Mein Kampf* was certainly not novel in its contents. The editors from the Institute for Contemporary History demonstrate that *Mein Kampf* was one of a multitude of right-wing and folk-national works that circulated in pre– and post–First World War Germany. Further, they show that many of Hitler's obsessive themes in *Mein*

Kampf were shared with other right-wing authors of his era. If it were only a period piece like so many of these other writings, *Mein Kampf* would be of little interest to anyone. What elevates the book above the throng of its submediocre companions is the simple fact that its author became the totalitarian ruler of Germany, provoked a world war, and presided over the murders of, among many others, nearly six million Jews. The extent to which the Holocaust lurks within the dense semantic wilderness of Hitler's prose is an issue for scholarly investigation—an investigation that cannot be undertaken without a deep reading of *Mein Kampf*. The contributors to our work have drawn their own conclusions about the concepts and themes in the book.

Karla Schönebeck, author, journalist, and resident of Landsberg, in Chapter 1 "Focus Landsberg: A Bavarian Town and Its Historical Ties to Hitler," sets the geographical and historical stage for Hitler's writing of *Mein Kampf*. Here she describes Hitler's incarceration in "the Fortress," as the Landsberg prison was called. Her chapter further captures the spa-like ambiance of the prison during Hitler's writing of *Mein Kampf* as well as the importance of the location of Landsberg as a pilgrimage site after 1933. Then, during the Second World War, she reveals a darker side of Landsberg with its concentration camp and later the venue for the imprisonment of Nazi war criminals following the Nuremberg trials and the Dachau and Shanghai war crimes trials.

As one of the coeditors of the critical edition of *Mein Kampf*, Othmar Plöckinger, in Chapter 2, "*Mein Kampf*: Part of the Right-Wing German Postwar Literature," provides the historical publishing context of the work in light of prevalent themes in earlier literature. He situates Hitler's text in the right-wing political and literary scene of post–First World War Germany in order to improve the overall understanding of the book and its history. Plöckinger shows that *Mein Kampf* was perfectly integrated into the right-wing, anti-Semitic, and nationalist literature of the day.

In Chapter 3, "*Mein Kampf:* The Critical Edition in Its Historical Perspective," Magnus Brechtken, deputy director of the Munich/Berlin Institute for Contemporary History, provides the background of the recent publication of the Critical Edition of *Mein Kampf* (2016). He describes succinctly the origins and development as well as the meaning of Hitler's text at the outset of National Socialism. He also puts the work into the wider historiographical context of discussions about Germany's coming to terms with the past after 1945. Brechtken's chapter further explains why the furore over whether or not the book should be republished as a critical edition was often rather artificial and regularly based on a lack of knowledge about the actual availability of the text. The chapter also shows the meaning of *Mein Kampf* for the ideological development and political practice of the Third Reich until 1945 and thus contributes to both academic and historiographical discussions.

In prison, Hitler concerned himself with maintaining his leadership in the National Socialist German Workers' Party. He vowed that in order to preserve a leadership role, power and violence would have to go hand in hand. Historian Paul Bookbinder in Chapter 4, "Hitler, Leadership, and the Holocaust," sketches out Hitler's notion of a leader who would make Germany once again a great nation after its defeat in the First World War. Hitler believed that the *Volk* wanted someone strong and charismatic who could command the loyalty of the people. However, he also recognized that the leader would be most effective if he tapped into deeply held beliefs and prejudices of the people, especially their anti-Semitism.

In Chapter 5, "Violence in *Mein Kampf*: Tactic and Political Communication," coauthored by Nathan Stoltzfus and J. Ryan Stackhouse, the authors argue that Hitler chose to use discriminate violence, changing tactics at opportune times, in order to sell the ideals and goals set out in *Mein Kampf* to the German people.

John J. Michalczyk, in Chapter 6, "*Mein Kampf*: Race, Blood, and the Holocaust," spells out how Hitler absorbed the ideas of late nineteenth- and early twentieth-century German authors on race as well as American and German writers on eugenics and casts them in his own voice. No citations indicate his sources as he describes at length the apocalyptic battle of the Aryan race to maintain its purity against the onslaught of the Jews attempting to infiltrate and destroy it. *Mein Kampf* lays out the struggle not as a blueprint for genocide but as a fertile racial ground from which it can eventually spring.

Chapter 7 by Ralf Yusuf Gawlick and Barbara S. Gawlick, "Degeneracy—Attack on Modern Art and Music," paints a clear picture of the parallels between Hitler's perspective on degenerate art and music and his attitudes toward the disabled. In an organically pure Germany, there was no room for either one. *Mein Kampf* reflects the need to eliminate both, one in the somewhat blasphemous art exhibit of 1937 (*Entatarte Kunst* and later *Entartete Musik*), the other by means of a euthanasia policy to exterminate the disabled in 1940.

Historian Michael S. Bryant, in Chapter 8, "The Auroras of the Final Solution: Intimations of Genocide in *Mein Kampf*," maintains that Hitler's desire to destroy the Jewish threat appeared even prior to writing *Mein Kampf*. However, as a shrewd politician, he feared any backlash to discussing an outright mass murder of the Jews until he felt that conditions were supportive of it. Following the implosion of Jewish emigration schemes in the late 1930s, in 1941 he made his genocidal move with some confidence.

David M. Crowe demonstrates in Chapter 9, "Pathway to the Shoah: The Protocols, 'Jewish Bolshevism,' Rosenberg, Goebbels, Ford, and Hitler," that the writings of American automobile mogul Henry Ford in *International Jew* and the apocryphal *Protocols of the Elders of Zion* dominated Hitler's thinking as he composed *Mein Kampf*. His attacks in *Mein Kampf* on Marxists and Jews, as well as his territorial intentions for conquering Russia, eventually merged in the Nazi plan to invade the country in June 1941 in Operation Barbarossa.

Chapter 10, "Marxism—Enemy of the People in the Political Party and Military System," by Melanie Murphy, continues the discussion of the political peril of Marxism to the German nation. Deprived of any intellectual substance, Hitler's notion of Marxism is swallowed up in generalities. Ironically, the specter of Marxism for Hitler can be viewed as both a threat and a model: the ideology contrasts with Nazi principles yet could be admired for its success in winning the support of the masses.

In her description of the gradual intensity of Hitler's diatribes against the Jews, Susannah Heschel in Chapter 11, "Being Adolf Hitler: *Mein Kampf* as Anti-Semitic Bildungsroman," points out the seductive quality of Hitler's style. In his vivid and horrific description of the Jews he paints a picture of an ugly, destructive force that will engulf Germany unless action is taken against it.

Martin Menke addresses Hitler's notions of the relationship of Christianity to Judaism in the lead-up to the Holocaust in Chapter 12, "*Mein Kampf*: Catholic Authority and the Holocaust." Hitler craved the Church's magisterial authority for himself. The failure of the National Socialist Party to fully achieve such authority complicated the Holocaust much more by requiring a gradual approach.

David Redles regards Hitler's text as an amalgam of diverse traditions. "The Apocalypse of Adolf Hitler: *Mein Kampf* and the Eschatological Origins of the Holocaust" (Chapter 13) takes a focused look at Hitler's millenarian worldview as evidenced in *Mein Kampf*. Hitler's work reveals an eclectic mix of Christian apocalyptic belief, German racial occultism, and a pantheistic Social Darwinism, expressive of a worldview that envisioned an eschatological war between the forces of order and chaos, Aryan and Jew. Hitler's messianic complex placed himself in the role of Aryan world savior.

In the Epilogue to our work, "Holocaust Education and (Early) Signs of the Erosion of Democracy," Tetyana Hoggan-Kloubert places *Mein Kampf* in the context of its use in Holocaust education. The chapter argues that Hitler's text can be employed as a pedagogical tool to address global and universal issues today. The emphasis of such an approach is based on critically attaching meaning to given historical documents.

The Appendix expands our knowledge of Hitler's text with an essay on its reception in the two decades before the demise of the Third Reich. Here, Othmar Plöckinger, one of the coeditors of the recent *Hitler*, Mein Kampf: *Eine kritische Edition*, shows the evolution of the work's popularity. Anson Rabinbach, Philip and Beulah Rollins professor of history, Emeritus at Princeton University, in his review of the new edition of *Mein Kampf*, "Struggles with *Mein Kampf*," originally published in the *Times Literary Supplement*, provides an extensive assessment of the 2016 republication.

PART I

The Mise-en-Scène of *Mein Kampf*, 1924–2016

In a 1946 letter to Karl Jaspers, Hannah Arendt complained that the crimes of the Nazis were so unprecedented, so far beyond the ordinary human categories of sin, guilt, and accountability, that they "explode the limits of the law; this guilt, in contrast to all criminal guilt, oversteps and shatters any and all legal systems." Jaspers would have none of it, chiding Arendt that such an attitude invested Nazi crimes with "satanic greatness." Jaspers's view that Nazi villainy was not truly original applies equally to many, and perhaps all, of the half-baked ideas presented in *Mein Kampf*, which Hitler adopted from the hard central European right of the *fin de siècle* and the fetid intellectual sewer of the postwar years in Germany.

At one time, Hitler's party was just one of a hundred folk-national groups in the country against whom the Nazis competed for support. In Munich alone, between 1925 and 1928, Hitler had to contend for mastery with seventy extreme right-wing groups. In aggregate, they formed a taproot of imperialist, anti-Semitic, and anti-Republican notions that Hitler drew on when writing *Mein Kampf*. Some of them, like the belief that the Jews were dirty and malodorous, were centuries-old stereotypes dating back to the Middle Ages. Others were the excrescences of nineteenth-century German Romanticism, such as the idea that war strengthened and renewed a population. The concept of the Führer, a charismatic "strong man" mentioned in connection with Hitler's leadership for the first time in December 1921, likewise had its origins in Romanticism as a backlash against mass democratic politics and, during the Wilhelmine period, disappointment with Wilhelm II's *Weltpolitik*. By the 1920s, the Führer conceit had come to underlie a prevalent convention of the German far-right, the dichotomy between democracy/the mass and the "personality." From Romanticism, the German folk-nationalists also borrowed the notion of the state as a "living organism," reinterpreted by Hitler and other right-wing leaders as a body devoted exclusively to preserving the German race.

Nearly every anti-Semitic cliché in *Mein Kampf* is derived from other sources. The myth that the Jews had "Judaized" German culture, the equation of Jews with disease and leftist political groups, the claim that the Jew was an inveterate liar, the charge that the Jews dominated the press, the stereotype that the Jews were materialistic and incapable of higher spiritual values, the assertion that race, not language, is the determinant of German nationality, the belief that the Jews had enslaved the German government—these and dozens of other themes expressed in *Mein Kampf* were well-worn coins in the anti-Semite's purse long before Hitler.

Hitler's theory of race in *Mein Kampf*, too, was derivative. The foundation appears to be Joseph Arthur de Gobineau (1816–82), a French aristocrat who argued in his *Essay on the Inequality of the Human Races* (1853, translated into German as *Versuch ueber die Ungleichheit der Menschenracen*, 1898–1902) that humanity consisted of three races—the yellow, black, and white—and that of these three, only the white race, due to its "Aryan" elements, possessed the ability to achieve high culture. The decline and fall of every civilization in history were due to racial interbreeding between these three groups, wherein the culture-producing vitality of the Aryan was eroded. The German translation of Gobineau's book gained traction in the Bayreuth Circle around Richard Wagner, whence his ideas sifted into Houston Stewart Chamberlain's treatise *Die Grundlagen des neunzehnten Jahrhunderts* (The Foundations of the Nineteenth Century, 1899). Wagner and Chamberlain, then, transmitted these ideas to Hitler and the German folk-national right. Hitler's additive was to see in the Jews not only a threat of cultural decay but an actual conspiracy to destroy the higher culture of the Aryan.

In the end, none of Hitler's ideas was particularly new. What *was* new, however, was Hitler's willingness to implement them once he stood astride Europe as the supreme warlord, pursuing them with a dogged fanaticism unto the gas chambers of the death camps.

1

Focus Landsberg

A Bavarian Town and Its Historical Ties to Hitler

Karla Schönebeck

The ties and connections between Landsberg and Adolf Hitler are the story of a relationship that is characterized by sober calculation, as well as highest expectations and unrequited love. It is a story with far-reaching consequences up to the present day.

At the time of his writing *Mein Kampf* in the Landsberg prison, Hitler was as relatively unknown as the provincial town itself, little known in Upper Bavaria as elsewhere in Germany. Still, on the evening of November 11, 1923, the consignment to the Landsberg prison of a man who had tried to put himself in power represented legal justice.

Was Hitler only a small revolutionary, perhaps a lunatic, who, once sent to the Landsberg prison, simply described himself as a pompous and meaningless writer?[1] Or perhaps the future protector of salvation, promising the Landsbergers, the Bavarians, and even the Germans freedom from economic, social, and political burdens, escape from all the traumas they had suffered every day as a result of the loss of the Great War and the humiliation of the Treaty of Versailles?

The end of the Great War heralded an epoch of unprecedented trials for the German people. With the slaughter at the battles of Ypres, before Verdun, or at the Somme, the history of industrial killing had begun.[2] All those who returned, defeated from battle, found a completely changed world. This became quite clear in the small towns with few inhabitants, such as Landsberg, that felt the casualties and deaths in the extreme. Landsberg, at that time, had only about 7,000 inhabitants.

The small town on the river Lech was known for its natural beauty, a humble hamlet-like idyll characterized by schools, Catholicism, public administrations, handicrafts, as well as its economic achievements, with a number of small and medium-sized industrial enterprises. Above all, Landsberg was familiar to everyone as a garrison town and had since 1908 one of the most modern prison buildings in Bavaria, a visible symbol of law and order.

Social and political conflicts accompanied the economic and thus existential hardship caused by the war, exacerbated by a Bavarian phenomenon. The Bavarian municipal constitution, dating back to the prewar period of 1908, linked municipal voting rights to civil rights. Since most of Landsberg's workers were not part of the long-established population, only a few of them were recognized as having the right to vote.[3] With a privileged minority dominating municipal politics, eventually an unbridgeable gap opened up between the traditional upper and lower classes, and it was against this backdrop that the revolutionary events of 1918–19 took place.

Only 50 kilometers away, in Munich, Kurt Eisner of the Independent Social Democratic Party of Germany (USPD) had proclaimed the Bavarian Republic as a "Free State" after the unspectacular fall of the last Bavarian king Ludwig III on November 8, 1918. Eisner was elected prime minister by the Assembly of Workers' and Soldiers' Councils, and only one day later, on November 9, 1918, a workers' and soldiers' council was formed in Landsberg, similar to those in Augsburg and Ingolstadt. Compared to the civil war–like conditions in Munich, the Landsberg revolution seemed moderate and non-threatening. Although thousands of supportive citizens gathered on the main square, when the acting mayor, Dr. Hermann Straßer, took the floor, and not the chairman of the Workers' and Soldiers' Council, it was seen as a sign of constructive cooperation.[4]

The fact that Munich mutated into the epicenter of the Central European Counterrevolution for a short period of time did not leave Landsberg unaffected; however, apart from a few harsh fisticuffs, there was no bloody confrontation between white and red. Red cells, Spartacists or communists, on the other hand, were found by chance at the neighboring Ammersee (Riederau/Dießen), where, among others, a son of Karl Liebknecht, Helmi Liebknecht, had fled after the murder of his father at the beginning of 1919.

Even though the fear of left-wing radical revolutionaries outside Munich was unfounded, fears of an overthrow of the social order, as elsewhere in Landsberg, encouraged the formation of Freikorps associations and local defenses. It was in this context that the name of Felix Danner,[5] a native of Franconia, appeared for the first time. While at the Landsberg railway station, he had succeeded in carrying 2 box cars destined for the Red Army in Munich, including 56 machine guns, 500,000 rounds of ammunition and hand grenades. The weapons remained hidden and were never used.

One month later, on February 21, 1919, Bavarian prime minister Kurt Eisner was murdered on his way to the Bavarian Parliament where he was planning to abdicate. The assassin, Arco Graf von Valley,[6] sympathized with the anti-Semitic Thule Society and was sentenced to life imprisonment in a fortress, which was seen as an honor, and transferred to Landsberg.

After Eisner's assassination, the disputes between the supporters of a parliamentary democracy and those of a socialist Soviet republic in Bavaria intensified. The revolutionary counterforces were never used in Landsberg itself; however, they were put to good use outside the city. The Liftl Group operated in Munich, as did the Freikorps Landsberg, in association with the Bavarian corps of shooters, Schützenkorps, under the leadership of Colonel Franz Ritter von Epp. The Freikorps Landsberg, consisting of approximately 1,000 men, had been originally founded by former officers of the 9th Field Artillery Regiment stationed in Landsberg and eventually dissolved after the First World War, following the terms of the Treaty of Versailles. These troops, the Freikorps Landsberg, had hidden their weapons in the Benedictine abbey of St. Ottilien, forever known in history for their participation in "Operation Munich" and the associated violent suppression of the dictatorship of the councils.

With the municipal and district elections of June 15, 1919, the Bavarian council movement (*Räterepublik*) was defeated and politically destroyed. In Bavaria, as in the entire Reich, the civil defense forces were combined to form a statewide self-defense association, the so-called *Einwohnerwehren*. From then on, they presented themselves not only as a security instrument but also as a means of enriching social life with concert evenings in Landsberg.[7]

And Adolf Hitler? He had experienced the revolution more or less as a spectator, facing political uncertainty, and yet he learned much from these events. He identified with and understood the small soldiers returning home as defeated and damaged losers. In prison, Hitler knew that others saw him as a nobody without a graduation certificate, humiliated once again at the Beer Hall Putsch Trial, painfully similar to his humiliation in Vienna, where he had twice been rejected by the Academy of Fine Arts. The catastrophes of the postwar period, the fall of the monarchy, the civil war, and the provisions of the Treaty of Versailles had obviously affected his mental health, pushing him toward a crisis.

Hitler directed his intense experiences of loss outward, turning his frustration and anger into intense delusional hatred of the Jews that would become the driving force for his future plans. Munich, a city of countless emigrants from the former tsarist empire, fleeing the Russian Revolution, was the ideal place and breeding ground, providing a toxic connection to the losers of the First World War. The myth of Jewish Bolshevism combined with anti-Semitism naturally and smoothly linked thoughts of both émigrés and local folk. This ominous mélange spread as quickly and destructively as an epidemic.

In the spring of 1920, Felix Danner from Landsberg met Adolf Hitler in Munich's Sterneckerbräu, the pub and founding location of the National Socialist German Workers Party (NSDAP), under whose guidance Danner founded the Landsberg local group (the NSDAP) shortly afterwards. The Bavarian People's Party (BVP), which had emerged from the Catholic Centre Party, was strongly represented. In the state elections between 1919 and 1933, the BVP, also susceptible to nationalist and anti-Semitic tendencies, received between 31 and 39 percent of the vote. The Landsberg BVP participated almost vehemently in the propaganda against Weimar foreign policy, while all other bourgeois parties played only subordinate roles. The radical right, on the other hand, had already firmly established itself in Landsberg, chanting the slogan, "November criminals, the Jews, the Communists and all the other enemies of the people." In addition, SA stormtrooper units had quickly formed in Landsberg and the surrounding area.

Their zeal was tempered when an SA unit from Dießen at Lake Ammersee after Hitler's committal on November 11, 1923, hoping to participate in his liberation following the failed Beer Hall Putsch, was recalled from Munich.[8] In contrast, nothing took place when after being convicted of treason by the Munich People's Court on the same day, April 1, 1924, Hitler began his prison sentence in the Landsberg "Fortress."

Among the approximately 500 visitors to Hitler from all over Germany were some Landsbergers and of course Felix Danner. When Hitler was released prematurely from prison on December 20, 1924, after only five months of his sentence, this Landsberg chapter of history was closed temporarily.

FIGURE 1.1 *Hitler, released from prison, poses in front of the Bavarian Tower in Landsberg. Courtesy of the Hitler Archive.*

Interestingly enough, only after the NSDAP had been readmitted did Hitler return once again, and in fact, several times, to Landsberg to promote himself and his movement. With the arrival of 1933, nothing would ever be as it had been before, as Hitler became Reich Chancellor in the Reichstag elections of March 5, 1933, with the Landsbergers casting 44.9 percent,[9] the most votes in the Reich, for Hitler (Figure 1.1).

The former Hitler cell soon became a place of pilgrimage of international importance. Tourism boomed and new hostels and restaurants were overwhelmed by Nazi sympathizers from all over the world. Visitors' arrivals took on an atmosphere of extravagant splendor, some accompanied from the train station by music bands. The people of Landsberg certainly did not lack imagination and ideas when in 1937 Reich Youth Leader Baldur von Schirach, at the height of his power and following the suggestion of the city council, proclaimed Landsberg the "City of Youth." The local politicians enjoyed his visions at a major rally on the main square and Nazi local group leader Wilhelm Nieberle agreed with von Schirach, affirming political support for Hitler in his statement that "Landsberg will thus become a new

FIGURE 1.2 *Hitler returns to Landsberg in 1934. Courtesy of the United States Holocaust Memorial.*

great educational factor for our people, and no other place than Nuremberg will exert such power on the youth of our people. It has become a national sanctuary for us through Adolf Hitler."[10] What a triumph: the self-proclaimed Hitler city believed itself to be on a par with Munich, Nuremberg, and even Berlin! (Figure 1.2)

And Hitler? He had intended to give the city a completely different role, and as a result, he never officially entered the "site of his shame" again. Unofficially, however, his prison experience became part of his propaganda plan, as, for example, in 1937, when he brought the cinematic superstar Leni Riefenstahl to Landsberg prison to show her the place of his "disgrace." When the Lord Mayor became aware of Hitler's visit, he hurried from his official residence to the main square, hoping to meet Hitler and his entourage, who were scheduled to be at the Café Deibl. The mayor experienced another missed opportunity, as by the time he reached the Café, he was too late; Hitler had already left the city again.

The Landsbergers wanted to donate the former prison to the Führer with plans to convert it into the largest youth hostel in the Reich. There had even been plans for the youth of the world to join the loyal Landsbergers. Hitler never seriously considered personally accepting the honorary citizenship he had been offered several times and eventually his Landsberg supporters resigned themselves to sending the honorary document to Munich, leaving their plans unfulfilled. Devoted and disappointed Landsbergers found some consolation in theatrical performances by Hitler Youth, with marches under operetta-like staging on the main square, after the Nuremberg Reich Party Congress had concluded. In closing ceremonies at the visit to Hitler's cell, each of the 1,500 participants received a copy of *Mein Kampf*. With the outbreak of the Second World War, this chapter was also closed, and the chaos and tyranny finally came to an end on April 27, 1945, when the Americans liberated Landsberg.

As a self-proclaimed former "Hitler city," Landsberg faced challenges from its willingness to identify itself with Hitler's time spent in Landsberg prison. With renewed energy, the people of Landsberg tried to distance themselves from the connections and all that had transpired since Hitler's arrival in their city, to focus on leaving the past behind them.[11] The Americans, however, unintentionally perpetuated these connections when the Allies decided to convert the former Hitler prison into War Criminal Prison No. 1 (WCPL). Now housing convicted war criminals of the ongoing Nuremberg trials and the Dachau trials, Landsberg prison remained a constant reminder of the past, bringing together guilt and atonement in one and the same place.

In addition, the former barracks area had become a camp for displaced persons, exclusively reserved for Jewish Holocaust survivors. Under these conditions, Landsberg grappled with the complexities of its past, once accommodating Hitler and now, in its new role, both his victims and co-perpetrators. As with the initial sentence to the Fortress at Landsberg, justice was once again served. Some felt that they were wrongly labeled as perpetrators and found a sympathetic audience, as in the case of Oswald Pohl, a former Waffen-SS officer sentenced to death, who was seen as a martyr by Hitler's supporters. Most considered the 1,600 inmates guilty, though some documents from the trials reflect a pro-Nazi atmosphere, declaring the prisoners innocent and wrongly imprisoned in the WCPL, as seen in the support of the Catholic chaplain Karl Morgenschweis (Figure 1.3).[12]

On January 7, 1951, approximately 4,000 Landsbergers demonstrated on the Hauptplatz, the town's main square, against the threatening executions of convicted war criminals by the American occupying forces. They no longer wanted to be associated with the war or with the trials, fearing that they would bring more shame upon Landsbergers and tarnish their city's history and legacy. Their justification for not wanting executions of war criminals in Landsberg stemmed from the 1949 Federal Republic law that had abolished the death penalty. Justification and justice can take many sides. After interventions against these death sentences by President Harry S. Truman and Pope Pius XII, among others, some sentences were reversed. With others, the American High Commissioner John McCloy was able to assert:[13] "Then the cloak of silence lay over the complex recent past.

FIGURE 1.3 *Father Karl Morgenschweis prays for condemned prisoners on the gallows in the Landsberg prison. Courtesy of Wikimedia Commons.*

Committed citizens took the initiative and tried to shed light on the darkness while the official Landsberg continued to establish itself in defense mode." To this day, there are no information boards in the city or an information center. Nearly 100 years after Hitler's imprisonment in Landsberg, the town has begun to set up a website that will also deal with this dark chapter in its history.

2

Mein Kampf

Part of the Right-Wing German Postwar Literature

Othmar Plöckinger

It is not unusual that politicians publish an autobiography. Sometimes they do it after their career, sometimes they do it to advance it. It is not unusual that they try to present themselves in a favorable light. In the years after the First World War many leading figures of the German army or the government did precisely this. For example, in 1919 General Erich Ludendorff, who was a political partner of Hitler for a few years, published his *Meine Kriegserinnerungen* (*My War Memoirs*). So did Gustav Noske, a Social Democrat and Minister for Military Affairs,[1] who published his revolutionary memoirs *Von Kiel bis Kapp* (From Kiel to Kapp) in 1920. Especially in Bavaria, which soon after the war had both left- and right-wing and even short-term communist governments, memoirs from every political direction were very popular.[2] One of them was Ernst Röhm, the later chief of Hitler's SA killed in 1934, who published his memoirs *Die Geschichte eines Hochverräters* (The History of a High Traitor) in 1928. In this respect, then, Hitler's book was nothing special.

Even in 1925, within a few weeks of *Mein Kampf*'s publication, two other famous politicians and former prisoners published their memoirs: Anton Graf Arco-Valley, the murderer of the Bavarian prime minister Kurt Eisner, and Felix Fechenbach, the former secretary of Kurt Eisner, whose books attracted the attention of the public and press. In this respect, *Mein Kampf* was published under very unfavorable circumstances, but until today authors and publishing houses have no influence over what their competitors do.

So far there is nothing special about *Mein Kampf*. But there is much more—Hitler exploits his biography not only to champion his ideology but also to present himself as a genius who created National Socialism single-handedly, or as Hitler would have said, he "struggled" hard to find his ideology. There is a good deal of the genius-cult of German Romanticism in this kind of Hitler's self-dramatization, which had laid a foundation of anti-Semitism one hundred years earlier. But it is far from the historical truth as we know it today. Even Karl Harrer, one of the founders of the Nazi Party in 1919, in his review of *Mein Kampf* in 1925 criticized Hitler for his dishonest mischaracterization that reduced the early party history to his own person.[3]

Considering his extreme tendency to exaggerate his accomplishments, it is not surprising that hardly any names of writers or authors can be found in *Mein Kampf* from whom Hitler borrowed ideas or inspiration. Even his mentor Dietrich Eckart, who promoted him strongly and exerted considerable influence on his ideological, propagandistic, and also literary development, is mentioned only once at the end of the second volume.[4] Contrary to other national-socialist and völkisch[5] authors like Eckart himself or Alfred Rosenberg, who name-dropped in order to present themselves as educated and well-read, Hitler nearly always avoids reference to other authors, books, or publishing houses. And to some extent we still follow his example when we focus on *Mein Kampf* without reflecting on the considerable amount of literary, journalistic, and propagandistic publications that were published and widely read within the right-wing scene in the years before *Mein Kampf*.

There are of course the usual suspects—starting with Arthur de Gobineau, who paved the way to a racist interpretation of history, and Richard Wagner, who became the doyen of cultural anti-Semitism for decades. They were followed by prewar authors like Houston Stewart Chamberlain, Paul de Lagarde, Julius Langbehn, and figures like Artur Dinter, Oswald Spengler, and Arthur Moeller van den Bruck, who became famous during and after the war. But as soon as one inspects them more closely, problems arise. Chamberlain criticized Gobineau harshly for his feeble anti-Semitism, Langbehn drifted away into a mystical form of Catholicism, and Richard Wagner despised politics in general. Dinter had sharp political rows with Hitler beginning in the mid-1920s, climaxing in his expulsion from the party in 1928, while Moeller van den Bruck killed himself in 1925 and Spengler was categorically rejected by leading Nazi ideologues like Alfred Rosenberg.

Therefore, the question of how and to what extent all of these authors influenced Nazi ideology in general and Hitler in particular is not easy to answer. But undoubtedly they laid the groundwork for other writers who formed and influenced the radical *völkish* and anti-Semitic ideology in a much more direct way.

Going back a few years before *Mein Kampf* was written, we find an early pattern of Hitler's belief system. On behalf of a military propaganda officer in September 1919, he wrote a letter in which he for the first time developed his anti-Semitic views.[6] There are no references or sources whatsoever mentioned in his letter, but nevertheless Hitler was very familiar with all the themes of contemporary anti-Semitic literature.[7] He emphasizes that the Jews are a race and not a religion, rejects pogroms, demands a "rational" and not an emotional anti-Semitism, and avoids any hint of Bolshevism. While the first aspects were central elements of anti-Semitism since the late nineteenth century, the last one is crucial for the interpretation of anti-Semitism at that time: texts designed for propagandistic purposes used anti-Bolshevism with great frequency. But texts with a theoretical approach, however, had little interest in this topic. They always interpreted Bolshevism as a creation of liberal Jewish capitalism, a part of the Jewish "Golden International" and its quest for world domination.[8]

The fact that Hitler was au courant in his grasp of anti-Semitic literature shows how interested he was in the topic. In autumn 1919, he was reassigned from his original regiment in the old Bavarian army to a regiment in the new Reichswehr.[9] There is not much information about what Hitler did during this time. But we know that, on the one hand, he was in charge of the library of his regiment[10] and on the other, he started and increased his activities in the NSDAP,[11] becoming in this way a kind of personnel support by the military authorities for the young party. Thus, he had ample time to read all of the more than forty political books and brochures which were officially distributed among the German troops by the military authorities in 1919–20 in Bavaria. They dealt mostly negatively with the political developments in Germany after the Revolution of 1918, with the situation in the eastern provinces of Germany, and with communism and Bolshevism. But apart from a few exceptions, anti-Semitism was a side issue and in many of the officially distributed texts Jews were not even mentioned.[12] From these facts it is clear that when talking about right-wing literature in Germany after the First World War, we should be precise and pay close attention to this kind of literature. Although it may not have had and did not have a significant influence on anti-Semitism, it formed and pushed the negative political image of democracy, parliamentarism, and civil society within the paramilitary environment of the radical right-wing groups.

The military authorities behaved in an ambivalent way. They quickly intervened to stop *völkish* and anti-Semitic activities when such activities became conspicuous or threatened to damage the public image of the troops. Nevertheless, the military authorities tolerated, in addition to the official material, the informal distribution of *völkish* and anti-Semitic literature in general (although there were considerable differences between the various units throughout Bavaria).

A plethora of *völkish* leaflets, brochures, pamphlets, and books was quite influential not only in national-conservative circles but also "non-officially" within the German troops, warping the minds of postwar Germans with anti-Semitic and racist notions as we have noticed in Hitler's case. Especially in 1919, a great number of anti-Semitic books were published. One of them was the notorious *Protokolle der Weisen von Zion* (the Protocols of the Elders of Zion), published by Ludwig Müller von Hausen. It became one of the most infamous anti-Semitic books of the twentieth century. Hitler did not ignore the book and, at least in the early days of his political career, he occasionally referred to it. But overall he remained much more reserved than other *völkish* and anti-Semitic authors.[13] Müller von Hausen also published the anti-Semitic journal *Auf Vorposten* (On Outpost) in his publishing house of the same name in Berlin. Several other anti-Semitic publishing houses also published both books and magazines; they included the *Hammer-Verlag* of Theodor Fritsch, the *Hoheneichen-Verlag* of Dietrich Eckart, and the *Eher-Verlag*, the later party publisher of the NSDAP.[14] Some of the publishing houses only had a short lifespan, while others were active for years. A second wave of *völkish* publishing houses developed in 1924 in the course of the trial of Hitler and Erich Ludendorff after their failed putsch in autumn 1923.[15]

Furthermore, a strict distinction between *völkish* and anti-Semitic publications on the one side and national-conservative publications on the other is difficult to make. An example is the important Munich-based magazine *Deutschlands Erneuerung* (Germany's Renewal). It was founded in 1917 by Houston Stewart Chamberlain and several other influential right-wing authors and politicians and lasted until 1944. The magazine was a reaction to the so-called Peace Resolution adopted by the German Reichstag in the summer of 1917, calling for an end to the First World War. Right-wing politicians and authors condemned the Resolution as a betrayal of Germany and its war aims. After the war, the magazine became even more radical and formulated four central objectives that were typical for this kind of publication. The objectives were: "The moral and state construction of Germany, the liberation from racial-alien internationalism, the unification of all Germans, the liberation from Marxism."[16] In their articles anti-Semitism was an important and integral element, but it was not the key topic. Hitler himself published his first comprehensive text about German foreign policy in this journal in April 1924.[17] There were a significant number of journals and newspapers of this kind in Germany, and their number and importance increased in the context of the "conservative revolution" beginning in the mid-1920s. They included *Die Tat* (The Deed),[18] *Der Ring* (The Ring), and *Der Reichswart* (The Warden of the Reich). The last journal was edited and mostly written by Ernst von Reventlow, who joined Hitler in 1927, becoming an important supporter of the Nazi Party within the völkisch movement.

Especially in Bavaria, in addition to short-lived anti-Semitic newspapers, we should mention newspapers linked to the Nazi Party, primarily the *Völkischer Beobachter* (*Völkish* Observer) and the journal *Auf Gut Deutsch* (In Plain German). The *Völkischer Beobachter* evolved from the *Münchener Beobachter* (Munich Observer), which, serving originally in 1918 as the mouthpiece of various radical *völkish* groups in Munich, was acquired by the young NSDAP at the end of 1920.[19] *Auf Gut Deutsch* was first published in 1919 by the author and journalist Dietrich Eckart and contained mainly comprehensive texts and lyrics. Eckart soon became not only a central figure in the rising NSDAP but also the personal mentor of Hitler and Alfred Rosenberg.[20] Rosenberg himself again founded in 1924 his notorious magazine *Der Weltkampf* (The World Struggle) and beginning in 1925 Gregor Strasser and Joseph Goebbels published the *Nationalsozialistische Briefe* (National Socialist Letters). Most of the named journals did not only have propagandistic purposes but saw themselves as ideological-theoretical papers with the purpose of forming and discussing the ideological and political basis of the NSDAP.[21]

Publishing houses developed along lines similar to the newspapers and journals. Publications with more or less clear anti-Semitic and racist positions were found in several publishing houses, which had a much wider reach than the decidedly *völkish* ones. But there these positions were mostly scientifically or literarily altered. Despite this, or perhaps because of it, they contributed in their own way to the spread and popularization of anti-Semitic and racist attitudes.[22] However, the ideological, political, and propagandistic focus on these attitudes was centered in the national publishing houses. In 1921 the *Vereinigung völkischer Verleger* (Union of *Völkish* Publishers) was founded. Every year it published a catalog titled *Das Deutsch Buch* (The German Book), which pursued the goal of "opening up ever wider circles of the population to literature and suppressing foreign spiritual influences."[23] It presented the newest publications of more than twenty publishing houses that defined themselves as *völkish* and therefore provides a good overview of the current topics and publications.[24]

In Munich and its surroundings there were several *völkish* publishing houses[25] like the *Deutscher Volksverlag* (German People's Publishing House), led by Ernst Boepple,[26] and the publishing house of Joseph Carl Huber. In 1920, the *Deutscher Volksverlag* published Alfred Rosenberg's first book, *Die Spur des Juden im Wandel der Zeiten* (The Trace of the Jew in the Course of Time), while Huber published the first edition of Gottfried Feder's famous pamphlet *Manifest zur Brechung der Zinsknechtschaft* (The Manifesto for Breaking the Slavery of Interest) in 1919. But one of the most influential right-wing publishers, not only in Bavaria but in all of Germany, was Julius Friedrich Lehmann. Not only did he edit the right-wing magazine *Deutschlands Erneuerung* and books with *völkish* tendencies, but he also produced very successful medical books and publications on race. He became an early supporter of the NSDAP and later provided Hitler with all his political and racial publications for free.[27]

Beginning in 1926, Gregor Strasser's *Kampf Verlag* (Struggle Publishing House) in Berlin made northern Germany quite important for the propaganda of the NSDAP.[28] Nevertheless, for the publications of the party the *Eher-Verlag* was crucial. Acquired by the party in 1921, it developed after 1933 into one of the largest publishing houses not only in Germany but all over Europe. It soon started to publish both the *Völkische Beobachter* and books and brochures of the NSDAP, including the main publication series *Nationalsozialistische Bibliothek* (National Socialist Library), the chief editor of which was Gottfried Feder. In dozens of books it tried to cover all main ideological and political topics, starting with the party program and extending to questions of economics and school policy. In 1941, a comprehensive overview of the books and brochures of *Eher-Verlag* since 1923 was published. By 1926, it had issued twenty titles (including Hitler's *Mein Kampf*) with a total number of 169,000 copies, and over the next several years the numbers doubled almost every year.[29] *Mein Kampf* therefore was an important title in the program of the *Eher-Verlag*, but it was only one among many others.

As we have seen, there was clearly a massive amount of right-wing and *völkish* newspapers, magazines, leaflets, brochures, and books both before and during the time *Mein Kampf* was written. And these materials achieved wide distribution, as the two main organizations that tried to fight the anti-Semitic "wave" after the First World War indicated: the *Central-Verein deutscher Staatsbürger jüdischen Glaubens* (Central Association of German Citizens of Jewish Faith) and the *Verein zur Abwehr des Antisemitismus* (Association for the Defense against Anti-Semitism). Both organizations repeatedly referred to the countless journals, pamphlets, leaflets, and anti-Semitic books published since 1919.

In 1922, in an article for the *CV-Zeitung*, the magazine of the *Central-Verein*, the journalist, philosopher, and sociologist Julius Goldstein from Darmstadt wrote about the methods of anti-Semitic propaganda: "Year in, year out, its newspapers and magazines collect everything that is somehow and sometime done badly by Jews in the wide world. Wherever there has

FIGURE 2.1 *Theodor Fritsch,* Handbuch der Judenfrage *(The Handbook of the Jewish Question). Courtesy of Wikimedia Commons.*

FIGURE 2.2 *Theodor Fritsch (1852–1933) was a journalist and publisher of anti-Semitic writings such as* The Protocols of the Elders of Zion *and Henry Ford's* International Jew, *besides* The Handbook of the Jewish Question. *Courtesy of Wikimedia Commons.*

been an outrage, it is suggested that Jews could at least be their intellectual originators."[30] He especially dealt in detail with the method of anti-Semitic collections of quotations of well-known German and international artists, scientists, and politicians, and especially of Jews.[31] In addition to citing quotations from the Talmud,[32] this was the modus operandi of Theodor Fritsch in his *Handbuch der Judenfrage* (The Handbook of the Jewish Question), one of the most popular anti-Semitic books of the late nineteenth and early twentieth century. As the first of three books, it will be discussed here in order to understand better the role and relevance of Hitler's *Mein Kampf* as part of this kind of literature (Figures 2.1 and 2.2).

The *Handbuch* was edited by Theodor Fritsch, one of the most influential radical anti-Semites of the Kaiserreich. Beginning in 1881, he published several magazines and journals, the most important of which was *Hammer. Blätter für deutschen Sinn* (Hammer. Pages for German Meaning).[33] Furthermore, in 1921 Fritsch edited through his own publishing house the first German translation of Henry Ford's book *The International Jew*. From 1929 until his death in 1933, Fritsch supported Hitler and the rising NSDAP.[34] His *Handbuch* was first published in 1887 with the title *Antisemiten-Katechismus. Eine Zusammenstellung des wichtigsten Materials zum Verständnis der Judenfrage* (Anti-Semite Catechism. A Compilation of the Most Important Material for Understanding the Jewish Question). By 1944, the book had gone through 49 editions, appearing in constantly revised and expanded versions that sold as many as 300,000 copies.[35] Among them were the twenty-eighth and twenty-ninth editions published in 1919 and 1923, which became important for the propagandistic and ideological formation of the emerging National Socialism. Nevertheless, as Hitler claimed in a letter to Fritsch, he had already read an older edition during his time in Vienna. In November 1930, Hitler addressed Frisch: "I had already studied the 'Handbook of the Jewish Question' in detail in Vienna in my early youth. I am convinced that it was precisely this that contributed in a special way to preparing the ground for the National Socialist anti-Semitic movement."[36] And Heinrich Himmler, later the chief of the SS, noted in autumn 1923 after reading the *Handbuch*: "It is a manual in which you can find everything relevant. Even an insider shudders when he reads all this with understanding. If only some of the eternally unteachable could get that in front of their eyes."[37]

The book was probably the most important source for anti-Semites as it presented hundreds of anti-Semitic quotations throughout history, from ancient historians up to Fichte, Schopenhauer, and Bismarck. Whenever an anti-Semite referred to an anti-Semitic quotation, it was often found in Fritsch's *Handbuch*. He wanted his book to be a counterpart to the public opinion that he and other anti-Semites regarded as dominated by Jews. He stated: "The great mass of our people—as well as the educated—has been thoroughly deceived about the nature of anti-Semitism to this day."[38] In his preface to his collection Fritsch wrote about the "core of the Jewish question" and summarized his purpose:

> It is further of interest to see from the collected utterances how the insight into the true nature of Judaism only very gradually deepens, how it gradually progresses from the superficial idea of the religious and usurious Jew to the recognition of the special nationality and racial nature, and finally to the presentiment of the psychological riddle of the moral perversity of Hebrews, a problem which has not yet been recognized in its ultimate consequences.[39]

Theodor Fritsch saw his *Handbuch* as a kind of sourcebook for anti-Semites for their political and journalistic agitation, and it was used extensively in this form. "Analytical" approaches were of secondary importance for Fritsch.[40]

This claim was also made by another influential book with the title *Judas Schuldbuch* (Judas' Book of Debt).[41] First published in 1919 by the publishing house *Deutscher Volksverlag*, it went through eight constantly revised and expanded editions until 1921.[42] Its author, Wilhelm Meister—a pseudonym for the *völkish* journalist Paul Bang—claimed to give an overview and analysis of the worldwide efforts of the Jews to destroy Germany and to gain world dominance.[43]

Paul Bang was very active in the right-wing and *völkish* movement, at both a political and propagandistic level.[44] He was a member of the radical nationalistic *Deutschnationale Volkspartei* (German National People's Party) and took part in the so-called Kapp-Putsch in 1920, which tried to overthrow the young parliamentary democracy in Germany. In 1928, he became a member of the German Reichstag and state secretary in the Ministry of Economics in 1933. He was one of the editors of the previously mentioned *völkish* magazine *Deutschlands Erneuerung*. Additionally, he published many articles in several nationalistic and *völkish* newspapers (often under changing pseudonyms) and several anti-Semitic books and brochures.[45] Soon after its publication, his *Judas Schuldbuch* became very popular. It was used and discussed widely within the *völkish* movement and became one of its most valued books. It was reviewed and extensively quoted, not only in *völkish* newspapers like the *Völkische Beobachter* but also in nationalistic Protestant papers.[46] It was distributed at meetings of the NSDAP,[47] and Rudolf Heß, Hitler's future deputy, recommended the book and gave it as a gift to his friends for Christmas in 1920.[48]

Bang explained his perspective at the beginning of his book: "The German question of existence, the question of renewal for the body and the soul of the German people, is the Jewish question par excellence. Whoever continues to elude it is either a pitiful weakling or a conscious traitor to the people and a seller of souls and thus becomes a Judas Iscariot himself."[49] For Bang the "re-establishment of the national spirit" was the solution to this question.[50] In particular, he dealt with the money economy and the press, which for anti-Semites were two of the most important "means of power" wielded by the Jews.

In the early 1920s, the books of Theodor Fritsch and Paul Bang were often described by Jewish journals and magazines as typical anti-Semitic texts and as examples of the growing influence of this kind of literature.[51] And a third book became very important, especially for anti-Semites like Alfred Rosenberg, who focused on Freemasonry as well as anti-Semitism (anti-Semitic and anti-Masonic attitudes often went hand in hand). Erich Ludendorff regarded the fight against Freemasonry as one of his most important goals.[52] In 1919, the Austrian politician and anti-Semitic author Friedrich Wichtl published *Weltfreimaurerei, Weltrevolution, Weltrepublik* (World Freemasonry, World Revolution, World Republic) through the publishing house of Julius Lehmann. Before the First World War, Wichtl was a member of the Reichsrat, the Austrian Parliament, and afterwards became a member of the first Provisional National Assembly in 1918–19. He was a member of the *Deutschen Nationalpartei* (German National Party) in Vienna, which had a *völkish* ideology inspired by Georg von Schoenerer calling for annexation of Austria to Germany.[53] When he died in the summer of 1921, a Jewish Vienna newspaper stated about Wichtl: "He was one of the most productive anti-Semites, who sought to explain everything that happened from a mysterious connection between Judaism and Freemasonry."[54]

Wichtl's book was first published in 1919 and had gone through eleven editions by 1928.[55] Like the book of Paul Bang it soon became famous within the *völkish* movement. It was discussed and reviewed in several newspapers,[56] and references and quotations from his book in *völkish* books and brochures are numerous.[57] Heinrich Himmler noted after reading the book in the summer of 1919: "A book that explains everything and tells us whom we have to fight first."[58] And Anton Drexler, one of the founders of the Nazi Party, used Wichtl's book for his first pamphlet "Politisches Erwachen" ("Political Awakening") in the spring of 1920.[59] At the same time Wichtl started to hold speeches all over Bavaria and even northern Germany and cooperated with anti-Semites like Dietrich Eckart or Gottfried Feder, as well as with several *völkish* organizations, including the newly founded Nazi Party.[60] In this connection he was involved in the increasing attacks against Jews. Concerning a meeting in January 1920 in Bamberg at which Wichtl spoke, the police reported: "In the meeting one could hear for the first time threats of violence against the life of the Jews."[61]

Wichtl's book had the subtitle "A Study on the Origins and Ultimate Goals of the World War." He stated that the assassination of the Austrian prince Franz Ferdinand in Sarajevo in 1914 and, therefore, the outbreak of the First World War were planned by Freemasons. But Freemasonry would be only one of the instruments the Jews use to gain world dominion; the other instruments would be communist revolutions and liberal-democratic ideas. Wichtl stated that the "Jewish" revolution in Germany in autumn 1918 was part of an overall plan:

> The Jewish revolution was to begin with a reign of terror in order to force blind and unconditional obedience. Violence and backstabbing, bribery, betrayal and fraud would be suitable means to this end. Chaos would result from the Jewish revolution, a state of complete lawlessness. Finally, the nations would be forced to voluntarily offer them—the Jews—world domination.[62]

In this respect for Wichtl the Fourteen Points of Woodrow Wilson's peace program from January 1918 turned into a part of the Freemasonic plan to start the World War in order to bring about the world revolution that would end in a world republic.[63]

These three books mentioned previously give an impression of the fecund anti-Semitic literary scene, which, especially in the first years after the war, produced numerous writings that exerted influence over many years. The three books made a fundamental ideological claim and were accompanied by many other writings and pamphlets, which, while staking similar ideological claims, often had more propagandistic aims. This distinction between ideological and propagandistic claims in anti-Semitic texts is important inasmuch as their treatment of topics could be very different.

Misinterpretations are therefore inevitable if this aspect is not taken into account. This applies, for example, in their approaches to Bolshevism. In the course of the 1920s it was central to propagandist writings; in more ideologically oriented texts, on the other hand, its significance was considerably less.

When Hitler began *Mein Kampf* he was deeply embedded in the right-wing, *völkish*, and anti-Semitic literary scene. He was also a latecomer within the Nazi Party. In the first few years after its foundation, the NSDAP saw itself as a part of the *völkish* movement despite all the competition and conflicts within this movement. The party's ideology was essentially based on demands that were also supported by other groups, in particular those that, like the Nazis, made a "German-social" claim. Only in the fields of political agitation did the NSDAP prove to be more radical (though by no means more successful). In spring 1921 the party leadership even initiated a merger with other parties against Hitler's will. As a consequence, Hitler resigned from the party in protest and, on his return, ensured that the merger was stopped and he was given full powers.[64] Until 1921–2 other radical right-wing groups such as the *Deutschvölkish Schutz- und Trutzbund* (German-völkish Protection and Defense League) were considerably larger and more influential than the NSDAP.[65]

But from autumn 1922, the party became more and more dominant within the *völkish* movement, at least in Bavaria.[66] Only on a political level did the NSDAP become more independent and influential. At the same time, steps were taken to develop a clearer and more independent ideological profile.

For a rather long time it was not Hitler who played an essential role in this development. In November 1921, a party library was established. Until the putsch in November 1923, when the library was confiscated and dissolved by the police, it had grown to some 400 items.[67] Furthermore, Alfred Rosenberg's anti-Semitic magazine *Weltkampf*, from its origin in May 1924, collected book titles as a basis for a bibliography of anti-Semitic literature. In 1925, more than 200 titles were listed.

Especially in 1923, the attempt of several party members to position themselves as ideological leaders became obvious. They tried to consolidate and expand their political and ideological influence in the developing party. In January 1923, Alfred Rosenberg published his first comprehensive commentary on the party program. In his commentary, revealing the new approach of the NSDAP, he wrote:

> Not so much new thoughts are needed as new thinking in general. If this has been achieved, if the nationalist state-view and ideology has triumphed, then the National-Socialist German Worker's Party has fulfilled its mission and can step down from the scene. What is today's battle cry against all powers of this time will then become the basis for all new forms of the eternally pulsating life.[68]

A few months later, Anton Drexler—one of the founders of the NSDAP—republished a considerably extended version of his *Mein politisches Erwachen* (My Political Awakening). It is one of the few books Hitler mentions in *Mein Kampf*.[69] For several years it was the only extensive text from its own members that the party had at its disposal. Nazi leaders tried to distribute a short version of it as a leaflet, but of course it could not come close to the importance of the many other writings on the right-wing scene. In a newly written epilogue, Drexler talked about the German mission in the world and warned the German people against its enemies: "You cannot go on living, you will be wiped out, as other great nations have been wiped out before you, if you do not find the will to create the power to defend yourself against those who seek to kill you."[70]

And again a few months later Gottfried Feder published his *Der Deutsche Staat auf nationaler und sozialer Grundlage* (The German State on a National and Social Basis). The book came onto the market in the fall of 1923, just before the putsch. Feder was one of many amateur financial theorists after the First World War who saw all economic and social problems caused by money and combined it with an anti-Semitic ideology. He became famous in right-wing circles for his call for "Breaking the Slavery of Interest."[71] His book would possibly have become a principal basis of national-socialist ideology if Hitler had not written *Mein Kampf*. In 1924, Hitler himself wrote a dedication for the second edition and stated: "The hope and longing of millions have found form and powerful expression in it. The literature of our movement has found its catechism in it."[72]

And finally, also in 1923, Dietrich Eckart wrote his book *Der Bolschewismus von Moses bis Lenin* (Bolshevism from Moses to Lenin). Although it was published posthumously in 1924 after Eckart's death in December 1923, the large number of quotations and sources in Eckart's text provides an informative overview of the foundations of *völkish* ideology and its political and cultural references.[73] As the subtitle "Zwiegespräch zwischen Adolf Hitler und mir" ("Dialogue between Adolf Hitler and Myself") already suggests, it was written in the form of a fictitious dialogue, which of course never took place in this form.

In view of these numerous attempts by various party leaders to influence the political and ideological course of the party through their publications, it is clear that Hitler's *Mein Kampf* was not the beginning but the end of a development. For him as a party leader, who had to both strengthen the party internally and set it apart from ideological competitors externally, it was extremely urgent to underline his claim to the leadership role with his own writing. This is one of the reasons why *Mein Kampf* is not only an autobiography and party history but also a political pamphlet and an ideological manifesto all in one.

Not a single statement in Hitler's published work cannot be found in other *völkish* publications. As has become clear, when Hitler started to work on *Mein Kampf* he had to compete with numerous writings and books that had already covered all aspects of his ideology and political ideas. Therefore, it is not surprising that one of the most detailed and influential reviews of Hitler's book commented on this very point. The *Deutsche Zeitung* (German Newspaper) in Berlin, one of the leading German nationalist newspapers, wrote in September 1925:

> It can be taken as certain that, as in other places, the author himself is firmly convinced that he gained all knowledge so early and far before the majority of his contemporaries. This faith then gives such a self-confidence that many people believe to have pronounced things and thoughts for the first time, which were only new to them, but in reality have already been pronounced long ago, often even better and more sharply.[74]

There was only one field in which Hitler was granted some originality by critics—that is, his comments on propaganda. But even there, Hitler moved largely along the lines already laid down by other authors.[75] Indeed, several of Hitler's political anti-Semitic claims can be found, for example, in the book *Wenn ich der Kaiser wär'* (If I Were the Emperor). It was published in 1912 for the first time by the well-known *alldeutschen* (pan-German) politician and author Heinrich Class and became quite influential in the *völkish* movement even before the First World War.[76] Another example, the core elements of Hitler's remarks about the history of the Jews, can be found in anti-Semitic books of the nineteenth century as well as in leaflets and newspapers since 1918.[77] Much more radical positions and future plans were formulated by his early comrades. In May 1920, Hans Knodn, a soldier from Hitler's inner circle who like Hitler joined the NSDAP in the autumn of 1919, wrote a paper concerning the "Solution of the Jewish question." How serious he was about it is proven by the fact that he submitted his essay to the Bavarian government. In it he demanded:

> 1. Within 24 hours, 48 hours at the latest, the majority of the Jews should be registered, i.e., they should have arrived at certain collection points. From these places the transport to the concentration camps would then have to take place. Only the most essential items of clothing should be allowed to be taken along. 2. Jews who try to escape internment by flight or who have lost their lives through bribery should forfeit their property to the state and [their property] must be confiscated. 3. Germans who assist Jews to escape, who are persuaded to do so and who accept bribes, must suffer the same fate.[78]

It is necessary to look at *Mein Kampf* from different perspectives to understand its meaning and its relevance. On the one hand it is of course an important source for the ideology and history of National Socialism. However, on the other hand, Hitler's book is a part of the anti-Semitic literature of its time and therefore should not be interpreted with a too-narrow focus on its author and the history after 1933. That would overlook important parts of the history and the dynamics of anti-Semitism in Germany, leading to misinterpretations as befell Hitler's contemporaries with very different attitudes. In 1924, Carl Christian Bry, a young conservative Catholic and a short-time member of the NSDAP,[79] wrote after his separation from the party in his book *Verkappte Religionen* (Disguised Religions):

> That anti-Semitism is not a political movement with exaggerations and with a wrong aim, but actually a religion in disguise, can be seen from the fact that almost all of its followers give different and usually quite unclear answers to the question of what should actually happen to the Jews according to an anti-Semitic recipe. Up to the grim, but in any case clear wisdom of the patriarch: anyway, the Jew will be burned, only a few dare to go forward, certainly not because they back off from the roughness of the pogrom, but because they are basically less interested in the Jew than in the easily won self-intoxication.[80]

And even more misguided in its assessment of National Socialism was the statement of Stanjek in 1925. He was chief editor of the *Abwehr-Blätter*, which had been committed to the fight against anti-Semitism since 1891.[81] In one of the best reviews of *Mein Kampf* ever written, Stanjek revealed all the lies, distortions, and ideological contradictions of the book. In the end, however, he came to the conclusion: "All in all, one puts Hitler's book aside with a feeling of satisfaction: as long as the völkish movement does not know how to put other leaders at its head, many waters will continue to flow into the sea until it wins in the land of poets and thinkers."[82]

3

Mein Kampf

The Critical Edition in Historical Perspective

Magnus Brechtken

When the Institute for Contemporary History/*Institut für Zeitgeschichte* (IfZ) issued its critical edition of *Mein Kampf* in January 2016, such a publication was long overdue. For decades, scholars of twentieth-century history had advocated that a research-based scholarly edition should be produced and that it should preferably be done by the IfZ. Why this seemed obvious to so many, why such a publication was not only appropriate but necessary, and why the goal of reissuing a critical edition of *Mein Kampf* could nonetheless not be reached until 2016 shall be described in the following overview.

Introduction and Historical Context

To explain the long-term background, we have to take a quick look at the very origin of Germany's dealing with the National Socialist past in the immediate aftermath of the Second World War. The IfZ was founded to collect material on the history of the Third Reich and to obtain, analyze, and present research-based information. Its goal would be to develop knowledge of the reasons why National Socialism became a political force in Germany in the 1920s and to explain how the movement gained momentum from the seizure of power after January 1933 to its downfall in May 1945.

The IfZ's key architects, while hailing from different German political traditions, were all driven by a similar desire: to establish an institution that would be able to focus on the material of the immediate past rather than to wait for time to pass to achieve a more objective perspective. Rather, the planned institution should immediately develop tools for research-based knowledge on contemporary history as a contribution to defending democracy.

The Institute's creation developed over three years, from 1947 to 1950. When its first structures were created in 1947,[1] its financing collapsed due to the currency reform of June 1948.[2] With great difficulties a new structure was set up by the end of 1948, which again faced serious financial obstacles until the federal minister of the Interior, Gustav Heinemann, signed the IfZ's constitution on September 8, 1950 (Figure 3.1).[3]

The Institute's most important supporters during the foundation period were Hermann Brill, Anton Pfeiffer, Dieter Sattler, Walter Strauß, and Gerhard Kroll. There are several other personalities—civil servants, politicians, and historians—who played a role in this process, but in an overall view it was the dedication and persistence of these four personalities that finally led to the permanent establishment of the Institute. To appreciate the wider context, it is worth stressing that many individuals who played a role in the foundation process were influential on several political levels. A central link between these personalities was promulgation of the German *Grundgesetz* (the Constitution of the Federal Republic). Hermann Brill was a member of the Constitutional Assembly (*Verfassungskonvent*) at Herrenchiemsee that played a decisive role in shaping the material for the Parliamentary Council in Bonn. In Bonn, Gerhard Kroll, Anton Pfeiffer, and Walter Strauß

FIGURE 3.1 *Institut für Zeitgeschichte (Institute of Contemporary History), Munich, Germany: staff members at a cabinet with building plans from the Third Reich,* c. *1950.*

were members of Parliamentary Council. So were Ludwig Bergsträsser, who became the first chairman of the Institute's Academic Advisory Board, and Theodor Heuss, the first president of the Federal Republic. It was Heuss who convened the IfZ's constituting meeting of the ministerial control body (*Kuratorium*) and the Academic Advisory Board (*Wissenschaftlicher Beirat*) on September 11, 1950, in Bad Godesberg near Bonn. Heuss also became an honorary member of the Advisory Board. All these men with their backgrounds in politics were involved during the Institute's first decade.[4]

With hindsight the four most influential men were Brill, Kroll, Pfeiffer, and Strauß. Their backgrounds were remarkably different. Hermann Brill was a seasoned Social Democrat who had been imprisoned during the Third Reich. After liberation from Buchenwald he quickly became secretary of state and head of the Hessian State Chancellor's Office. In 1949, Brill became a member of the German *Bundestag*, the new Federal German Parliament. Walter Strauß had also been a victim of the National Socialists and their racial policies. After the war he became secretary of state, first in Hesse and later in the Federal Ministry of Justice. His influence grew over time and lasted until the 1960s. Anton Pfeiffer had been an influential figure in the Bavarian People's Party before 1933. He had a close relationship with the English-speaking world (his PhD dealt with Lord Byron), particularly with the United States. Already as a student he had worked for the "Coit School for American Boys" in Munich from 1907 until its closure in 1916. In 1927, Pfeiffer founded an "American Institute" as a successor institution, which was shut down in 1935.[5] As a politician and intellectual, Pfeiffer had analyzed National Socialism since the early 1920s and had written about the dangers of its ideology even before Hitler's attempted coup in 1923.[6]

After the war Pfeiffer became a powerful representative for the newly founded conservative Bavarian *Christlich Soziale Union* (CSU) and head of the CDU/CSU group (*Fraktion*) of the Parliamentary Council. Here he was regarded "after Adenauer" as "the leading personality of the CDU/CSU."[7] A "polished and diplomatic conversationalist with an excellent knowledge of English and French,"[8] as a British observer put it, Pfeiffer had extensive contacts with the Allies. Since the 1920s he had been a friend of Robert D. Murphy, who at the time was a representative of the State Department in Germany and political adviser to General Dwight D. Eisenhower and General Lucius D. Clay. The fourth decisive person was Gerhard Kroll, who became the Institute's first "director" (at this stage called *Geschäftsführer*/chief executive officer). Kroll was among the founders of the CSU and a member of both the Parliamentary Council and later the Bavarian Parliament. Kroll's image is somewhat blurred to this day since the sources about him are contradictory. Kroll was a staunch Catholic and was especially interested in British political structures. He particularly advocated the majority electoral system. Due to this hyper-focus on one issue, which he failed to establish in the *Grundgesetz*, Rolland Chaput de Saintonge, the British liaison officer to the Parliamentary Council, described Kroll as "a fanatic."[9] According to some documents Kroll's demeanor was sometimes overbearing. At the same time, he was decisive in shielding the Institute from long-established nationalistic and historiographical influences.

Despite their differing political roots, all these founders of the Institute agreed that historical research as it had been practiced at universities and by professors of history in the decades before could hardly be expected to investigate the origins of National Socialism with impartiality. The majority of German historians had always been close to the state, identified with legitimizing the national cause by writing in a fervently nationalistic manner. Many of the younger generation (those born after 1900) had been supporters of National Socialism.[10] It seemed highly unlikely that whoever reestablished the historical profession at German universities would be able and willing to produce independent research and self-critical appraisals of the Nazi past. When several highly influential historians voiced disagreement and sought confrontation over this issue (to which we can only refer here in passing), it was the politicians and high-level civil servants who were crucial for ensuring the Institute's independence of nationalist bias, rather than the designing representatives of the historical profession.

The role of the Allied Occupation Forces remained more or less passive. A story in the magazine *Der Spiegel* in April 1949 appears to have conveyed the mistaken interpretation that the American government ("the Americans," as the *Spiegel* writes) had conceived the idea for the Institute and had met with a positive response from historians ("circles of specialists").[11] Both of these interpretations are misleading. Neither "the Americans" nor German historians played a significant role in the foundation of the Institute. *Der Spiegel* added that "the Americans promised" to pay the costs of running the Institute from the profits of the "Neue Zeitung."[12] While it is correct that the difficulties of financing the Institute led to attempts to ask the Americans for funding, this was not supported. As the Cultural Affairs Advisor to General Clark wrote, the Americans had "reluctantly come to the conclusion that it would be improper for military government to finance the Institute. Both Col. Textor and Dr. Wells feel that this is a most important undertaking, and for this very reason should not be jeopardized by any subsidy which might leave it open to the charge that it was part of American propaganda."[13] Instead, the Americans wanted to maintain their distance and avoid undermining the credibility of the efforts by the German architects of the IfZ. To a question by the Bavarian minister-president, the Office of Military Government for Bavaria (Charles D. Winning) replied on November 30, 1948:

> It is not necessary for your institute to have a license or even approval from Military Government. As far as this division [Office of Military Government for Bavaria, Education and Cultural Relations Division, MB] is concerned there is no objection to the institute undertaking an objective and systematic study of German History during the period of the National Socialistic [!] Reich. In view of the fact that Military

> Government has no objection to your study, you should find no difficulty in gaining access to such material as may now be under the control of Monuments, Fine Arts, and Archives Section, Restitution Branch.[14]

As an act to support its research, the American Military Government delivered twenty-eight boxes with material from the Nuremberg trials in May 1949, which became the basis of the IfZ's archives.[15]

Thus the *Spiegel* summary stands as a mix of well-informed background knowledge with fantasy-filled speculation, fueling inaccurate anecdotes that circulated for decades.[16]

Historians: Reluctance and Ambitions

The Institute's formation was very obviously part of West Germany's first tentative attempts to come to terms with the National Socialist past. But this was by no means generally welcome. The public was reluctant for a variety of reasons. Most important was the unease over confronting a recent past in which so many Germans had been both supporters of the National Socialist regime and bystanders to its crimes.

There was reluctance among historians, too. Prominent representatives like Gerhard Ritter, who in these years wielded a powerful influence among German scholars of history, aimed for a controlling position and guidance through university chairs like his own. Ritter was a leading member of the influential Historical Commission of the Bavarian Academy of Sciences. He repeatedly sought to present himself as an international figurehead of German historiography. In 1948, Ritter published a book on *Europe and the German Question*.[17] Instead of analyzing the specific and concrete reasons and motivations of German politics, culture, and society, he referred to the "age of the masses" and the "international state of affairs." Ritter saw National Socialism as the consequence of "the general decline of culture, a lack of religious faith and moral nihilism"[18]—all by no means German but global trends. For him National Socialism was thus not something specific to German national history but a "phenomenon" that had unexpectedly gained power in Germany. "The Germans themselves were more surprised than anyone else by the rapid rise of the National Socialist Party to a position in which overall power in the state was at its disposal," he claimed.[19] Ritter's stance of blaming external powers rather than looking for domestic reasons provoked sharp backlash. Geoffrey Barraclough called Ritter's book on Europe "the coolest piece of propaganda yet to come from Germany." He saw Ritter representing "those in Germany who are still fighting, not of course for Hitler, but for the ideas and ideals of those who, from Hindenburg downwards, backed Hitler."[20]

Barraclough's observations had some substance. At the first national historians' conference (*Historikertag*) after the war, which took place from

September 12 to 15, 1949, in Munich, Ritter claimed with respect to research institutions on the Third Reich (avoiding a direct reference to the parallel process by which the Institute for Contemporary History was established):

> But how careful, how prudent must the organization of such an institute be if it is to avoid becoming a center of political defamation! Without the guiding hand of an experienced historical specialist who knows how to separate the essential from the incidental and how to focus all resources on the crucial problems, and who is supported by a team of selected specialists, it will fail.

Ritter claimed to speak for "the entire body of German historians."[21] Ritter's worldview was well known, as was his self-image as a Protestant Prussian state historian legitimized by connections to the resistance movement against Hitler. Thus those who heard him might gather the justified impression that Ritter wanted a research institute with a focus that propagated his own view of history.

Even one of Ritter's opponents, Munich historian Franz Schnabel, who had been a critic of National Socialism and whose career had been blocked after 1933, argued against "dealing with the 'most recent' history"[22]—by which he meant contemporary history. Schnabel believed that these events were still too close to be researched and evaluated objectively: "If this material is systematically collected and made easily accessible at this point in time, when 'contamination' by the past plays such a major role in political struggle and in the competition for the few positions available, then this places scholarship over life in a way that completely contradicts common sense."[23] Today, Schnabel's arguments sound strange, even disconcerting, since the aim should be not to "preserve" the past but to analyze it, understand it, and (it is hoped) learn from it. The fact that Schnabel called for "covering up," that is, consciously looking the other way, suggests that while he was aware how fundamental National Socialism was to German society, he did not wish to acknowledge this truth during his lifetime.[24]

Such "covering up"—if it would have even been possible, which is doubtful—would have fundamentally differed from what Hermann Lübbe characterized as "communicative silencing" (*kommunikatives Beschweigen*) as the main feature of German society's preferred behavior in the 1950s.[25] For "silencing" implies that all persons involved are conscious of the dimensions of the past as well as their responsibilities yet actively avoid communicating about it in order to keep the troubled past out of present dealings. The aim was not to cover up but to avoid mentioning something that was nevertheless constantly present, even when it was not expressed in words.

When the Institute was created, Ritter's standing was considered too important not to be included. He became a prominent member of the first Academic Advisory Board (*Wissenschaftlicher Beirat*) in 1950.[26] Ludwig

Bergsträsser, like Brill a Member of the German Parliament (*Bundestag*) for the Social Democratic Party (SPD), was elected chairman.[27] Ritter made his mark by threatening to resign if the then head of the Institute, Gerhard Kroll, who was an economist by profession, were to be elected general secretary of the fully established Institute. The high-level civil servants in the ministries concerned did not want to offend the historians for whom Ritter claimed to speak. Kroll gave in and agreed to step down once a replacement was found from the historical profession. Thus Hermann Mau became general secretary in 1951. Although Mau had a background in medieval history, he was academically qualified and proved to be clearheaded about the challenges he and his colleagues would face. Remarkably straightforward, he stated that the Institute could not "deal with the National Socialist past intellectually . . . on its own and in others' stead." In other words, there was no "kind of shortcut" that would relieve members of society in general "of the effort required to engage and deal with this past."[28] Mau's tenure ended prematurely in October 1952 when he was killed in a traffic accident.[29]

The Institute was still on a challenging path. University historians like Ritter sought to shape the new institution in accordance with their views. But it was Ritter himself who triggered the first major scandal that ended his association with the IfZ. In 1951, Ritter published *Hitler's Table Talks* as the first book connected to the Institute.[30] He did so without any critical commentary. Ritter claimed he just wanted to "show [it] as it actually was," a reference to Leopold von Ranke immediately recognizable to every German interested in history. Excerpts were even published in the tabloid magazine *Quick*. Thus, through Ritter's ignorance and indolence, Adolf Hitler became indirectly the author of the first publication of the Institute.[31]

Further difficulties arose through attempts by other institutions to gain influence within the IfZ. The Secret Service organization "Organization Gehlen" (OG) in the first two years tried to establish links to the Institute as well. The OG was working as the German "Foreign Secret News Service" (*Auslandsnachrichtendienst*) for the US Central Intelligence Agency (CIA).[32] Gerhard Kroll as the IfZ's first head forged a relationship with Wolfgang Langkau, a former Wehrmacht officer. Kroll and Langkau came into contact in 1949 through Hans Speidel,[33] an ex-Wehrmacht general and historian who became a member of the Academic Advisory Board. Speidel was convinced (as were several others involved in planning the Institute's structure) that it was in need of a person who could produce publications on military history. Instead of working for the Institute, Langkau joined the OG and in later years became a central figure of the German Secret Service. He remained a friend of Kroll's who met Gehlen several times during his tenure at the helm of the Institute in 1950. The first meeting took place in Pullach on February 8, 1950; Langkau took extensive notes.[34] Since Langkau was no longer available for the Institute, Speidel recommended another former general, Hermann Foertsch, for a study on military history. Foertsch received a short-term contract and produced an account of the crisis of military leadership in

1938 when Hitler replaced the War Minister Werner von Blomberg and the head of the army Colonel-General Fritsch. The story of this crisis, written by a former Wehrmacht officer rather than an historian, became the Institute's first "official" publication.[35]

It is obvious that the period 1949–51 was shaped by dubious attempts to mold what the Institute might yet become. With hindsight it is clear that these attempts more or less faded when Hermann Mau took over and the personnel of the Institute were recruited from among professional historians rather than former Wehrmacht generals. It is important to note that only two academics of the first generation of researchers, recruited in 1950 and 1951, remained at the Institute—Anton Hoch as the head of the Institute's archives and Thilo Vogelsang as the head of the library.[36] By the time that Helmut Krausnick joined the Institute in 1952, all former academic staff had either left the Institute or were on their way out.[37] The challenges—how to deal with the conflicting interests of the many stakeholders from universities to ministries and intriguants—remained. But what really shaped the years to come were the challenges of fundamental research on a subject that was still vividly remembered by many Germans.

Expert Reports

From the very beginning, the Institute's staff provided all kinds of commentaries and evaluations. Since the early 1950s the Institute's researchers have written several thousand expert assessments for courts and public institutions. The *Vierteljahrshefte* (quarterly) stated as early as its second issue that the Institute "is often used for information requests and expert reports."[38] This production of numerous *Gutachten* was by no means the result of a strategic plan but emerged from the everyday practice of a society confronted with its past. Research for judicial and public administrative use, as well as applications in a variety of other institutions, thus became an essential element of the IfZ's profile. A brief description of the range of this work illustrates the multifunctionality of the IfZ.

The records begin on January 2, 1953, with an enquiry by a person named D. C. Riede from Iowa City, United States. He or she was searching for information on the topic of "German cardinals and National Socialism." This was an unusual start because the question was from the United States and from a private individual. Typically, requests for expert opinions came from German courts, offices, federal ministries, and district presidents, as well as from newspapers and journals. Of the first twenty reports, seven were produced for district courts (*Landgerichte*), one for the Bavarian State Compensation Office, one for the Federal Ministry of the Interior, and a further one for a district president.[39] No systematic statistical analysis is available yet, but an informal review suggests that this pattern is quite representative of the 1950s and 1960s. Drawing up these evaluations consumed a significant part of the Institute's workload and dominated its staff's everyday activities to a large extent.[40]

Two volumes containing such expert opinions and assessments are available from the early years of the Institute. In 1958 the Institute self-published sixty-nine of these reports[41] with an explicit statement that these texts hitherto had "only become known to the circles involved in the hearing rooms."[42] In his introduction, Paul Kluke, head of the Institute from 1953 to 1959, asked readers for "additions or corrections in the interest of the matter itself (. . .) Any such support for its work will be gratefully received."[43] It is safe to say that this self-understanding, which focused upon public communication and alluded to the inclusion of readers as part of the discourse, was highly unusual. It stood in marked contrast to the views of professors of history at universities. It is hard to imagine that someone like Gerhard Ritter or other grandees of the field would think about asking their listeners and readers to correct their insights and theories. Kluke's request can be interpreted as an attempt to address the minefield of contemporary witness testimonies. By issuing this invitation the IfZ also embraced a new style of public scholarly discourse that explicitly understood itself as serving society. It thus became part of a new discourse culture about the Third Reich.[44]

Looking at the numbers we understand that there were just about 1,100 working days between the 1,000th report of January 1959 and the 3,000th (which not only those with an interest in statistics will find striking).[45] This means that roughly every day two expert opinions were sent to courts, offices, administrations, other institutions, and private individuals. In 1961 alone, the number of enquiries and reports rose to 600—around 12 per week on average. The productivity of IfZ staff is eye-popping when we consider the context: at the time, the Institute had twelve positions "for academically fully qualified staff," including the director and the heads of the archives and library.[46]

The most influential and best-known reports are without any doubt those produced for the Frankfurt Auschwitz trials. The authors Hans Buchheim, Martin Broszat, Hans-Adolf Jacobsen, and Helmut Krausnick first published their texts in 1965. These books first came out with established but not widely known publishers.[47] But publications soon moved to the more popular and widely circulated *Deutscher Taschenbuch Verlag* in December 1967.[48]

In his preface, Hans Buchheim wrote about the evaluators' role and their own understanding of their task: "The concentration camp crimes and the mass murder of the Jews were specific components of National Socialist rule. Many people have forgotten this connection."[49] Buchheim's formulation, written in the early 1960s, is instructive in several ways. In Buchheim's sense central aspects of National Socialism had already been "forgotten." But in fact, if one looks at German society of these years, these topics had actually not yet become part of public discourse. They certainly had not been discussed in any differentiated, research-based manner. Furthermore, these were matters on which empirical analyses were scarcely available.[50]

Research was still in its infancy and scholars were not yet fully conscious of the task in all its dimensions.

It was in this context that Buchheim formulated the supposedly neutral stance that later became known in Martin Broszat's words as the "pathos of soberness":

> Discussing the history of the National Socialist period within the framework of a criminal trial requires a particularly high level of rationality and soberness, as the facts identified . . . enter into the decision on the defendant's future fate. In public debate, the due rigor applied by the courts constitutes a beneficial counterweight to a widespread emotional style of "dealing with the past" that . . . takes liberties with the reality of historical facts and contexts. As it is clear that Hitler's dictatorship should be judged negatively in all regards, it is tempting to not think about it enough. For this reason, we already have a plethora of literature on the Third Reich,

thus Buchheim's view in 1965:

> but only comparatively few real insights that are genuinely useful. There is a trend to move away from a historic, rational perspective to a moral and emotional one. (. . .) In Germany, however, what we need in order to engage with National Socialism and its time is not emotions, not a moral revival, but sober, level-headed work involving sense and reason.[51]

Similar self-descriptions can be encountered repeatedly in later historiographic discourse, too, claiming that the moral question of how to evaluate National Socialism had already been decided and that the focus should be on "sober analysis." The extent to which such arguments reveal conscious exoneration strategies requires further discussion. Dismissing the past in such a wholesale manner did at least discourage thorough enquiries into the individual involvement and responsibility of the millions of *Volksgenossen*. Buchheim's statements were written at a time when, for example, Raul Hilberg was told that his 1,000-page sober and rational account of the Holocaust—and particularly of the many minor and major perpetrators involved in this process—had been blocked by his German publisher Droemer Knaur, even though 300 pages had already been translated.[52]

Critical Editions

Apart from research publications, the Institute produced a wide variety of critical editions of historical documents.[53] An early example is Kurt Gerstein's report on the mass shootings, which was published in the second volume of the *Vierteljahrshefte für Zeitgeschichte* in 1953.[54] In 1980 the Institute supported the publication of Hitler's complete writings for the period 1905–24, edited by Eberhard Jäckel and Axel Kuhn.[55] These include the surviving correspondence, notes, and other primary documents written by Hitler during that time.[56] Over the decades numerous texts by Hitler from the entire span of his political activity have been published and edited in a scholarly critical form.[57] Also among the important recent editions was *Die Tagebücher von Joseph Goebbels* (Diaries of Joseph Goebbels).[58] From 1992 to 2003, the Institute edited twelve volumes comprising Adolf Hitler's speeches, writings, and decrees for the period 1925–33 (*Reden, Schriften und Anordnungen*).[59] Hitler's so-called *Zweites Buch* (Second Book), written in 1928 but not published at the time and only rediscovered after the Second World War, has been available since 1961.[60] In 1995 it was updated and republished by the Institute in cooperation with its original editor Gerhard Weinberg as part of the new critical edition of all of Hitler's writings before 1933.[61] This text provides an example of how public perception and awareness regarding Hitler's texts had changed. For in 1995 it was decided that "Hitler's Second Book" should no longer appear under that heading. Instead the text got the less eye-catching title *Außenpolitische Standortbestimmung nach der Reichstagswahl Juni-Juli 1928* (Foreign Policy Clarification after the Parliamentary Election June/July 1928). One consequence of this renaming is that the edition of 1961 is still widely used because even many scholars have not realized its replacement by an updated version due to its different title.

This brief overview illustrates that for many years all relevant writings by Hitler up to 1933, and indeed many texts from the years thereafter, are available in scholarly editions. For the period before 1933, there had been just one single notable text left unedited: *Mein Kampf*. This text had originally been published in 1925–6 in two volumes by the publishing house *Franz Eher Nachfolger* in Munich. From 1930 onward, the parts were combined and offered in a single volume as a so-called popular edition. Hence when we speak of *Mein Kampf* today, people usually think of a one-volume book.

The reason why no academic critical edition could be achieved for decades was copyright. Upon Hitler's death he was considered to be a citizen of Munich, where he had owned a flat and officially lived since the 1920s. As with the rest of Hitler's property, US Occupation Authorities seized the rights of his book that lay with his publisher, *Eher-Verlag*. In 1948, the rights were transferred to the Free State of Bavaria; the Ministry of Finance took over responsibility. With reference to the copyright the Ministry consistently refused to allow any republication of the text. All arguments by the historical profession to permit a critical edition in alignment with all other texts published by Hitler met with rejection.

According to German law, any copyright expires seventy years after the author's death. The same principle applied to Adolf Hitler. Thus the rights to publish *Mein Kampf* came into the public domain on January 1, 2016. This was the principal reason why so much attention was focused on that date and the question of what might happen with Hitler's historical text afterward.

It is essential to note that regardless of the reprint restrictions due to copyright laws, *Mein Kampf* was never forbidden. The book was readily available ever since its first publication in 1925. Until the end of the Second World War, some 12.4 million copies had been published in the German language in at least 1,122 print runs.[62] We can assume that at least several hundred thousand copies survived the war and its aftermath. Copies remained available, shelved in private households, kept in libraries, offered in antiquarian bookshops, and traded in flea markets.

In the decades after 1945 there were no judicial or practical difficulties in getting access to *Mein Kampf*. Whoever wanted to purchase a copy could easily do so. Until a few years ago, numerous antiquarian online booksellers offered copies for sale.[63] For quite a few years it has also been available on the internet. It could be read or downloaded as a PDF file by anyone wishing to do so. In sum: the German version of *Mein Kampf*, regardless of the ban on its reprinting, was always present in the public sphere for anyone interested in it.

For audiences of the English-reading market, access was even easier. The *Eher-Verlag* had sold the English-language copyright in 1933. At least three translations of *Mein Kampf* have been produced since. The English versions were never out of print and have continuously been available across the globe.

With the copyright expiration date approaching, the question arose how research institutions like the Institute for Contemporary History should prepare for it. Obviously, one could imagine reprints, devoid of any commentary, on bookstore shelves early in 2016. And equally obviously this was not a prospect attractive to anyone interested in research-based historical discourse. Thus, one could immediately see the need of an appropriate scholarly critical edition. These considerations lay at the heart of the decision of the Institute to produce an edited version of the text based on an intensive analysis of decades of research. The critical edition was mapped out to inform, explain, and provide references to research and literature, as well as to offer an apparatus of critical commentary. The Institute's team of researchers and editors started their work in August 2012, and finished it by the end of 2015. In January 2016, the edition was published as *Hitler, Mein Kampf: Eine kritische Edition*.

Historical Relevance and Current Topicality

To illustrate why the call for a historical-critical edition of *Mein Kampf* had been voiced repeatedly over the years we need to examine more closely the text's relevance for understanding Hitler's worldview and the political practice of National Socialism.[64] Hitler had been active in the Munich political sphere for just over three years when he attempted a coup in November 1923. Although it failed, this endeavor made Hitler a widely known representative of the extreme right. He was treated leniently by the Bavarian judiciary. Sentenced to five years in 1924, he only served a few months in Landsberg prison. Upon his incarceration in June 1924, Hitler commenced writing the first volume. He had time on his hands and aimed at a narrative that enabled him to present himself to his followers. When he was released in December, the volume had progressed to the point where it was about to be published. At this stage it was entitled *4 ½ Jahre Kampf gegen Lüge, Dummheit und Feigheit* (4½ Years of Struggle against Lies, Stupidity and Cowardice). In spring 1925, Hitler thoroughly reworked the text, completing this revision in June 1925. The book appeared in July with the now-familiar title of *Mein Kampf*, subtitled *Eine Abrechnung* (A Reckoning). Hitler quickly began writing a second volume, working on it in several phases until autumn 1926, mostly in Berchtesgaden and at the nearby Obersalzberg. It appeared in December that year, entitled *Die nationalsozialistische Bewegung* (The National Socialist Movement). The two volumes were published together, as mentioned, from May 1930 onward. Initially this was meant as a "popular edition" followed by numerous other editions as a single volume. Combining the two volumes into one has led to the misperception that *Mein Kampf* had been a single tome right from the start.

The first print run of the two volumes comprised some 10,000 copies. Volume I enjoyed considerable sales, and at the end of 1925, a second print run was in preparation; for the second volume, a new run became necessary in 1929. It should be noted that the two volumes, costing 12 Reichsmarks each, were comparatively expensive at the time. Given the price and the regional focus of Hitler's actions at this stage, the sales until 1930 were quite considerable. It is important not to interpret the exorbitant later total number of copies printed—in 1933 alone, more than a million copies were sold—as the benchmark for the earlier period.

What does Hitler present to his readers? What are the purpose and the general aim of his text? Larger sections of the first volume of *Mein Kampf* provide a fabricated personal autobiography. It is a tendentious self-portrait, styled in a manner to communicate to his followers. He insinuates being engaged in a historical mission and claims a messianic role in German politics. All the material is arranged according to his preferences in 1924 rather than to historical facts. The first volume also contains extensive programmatic sections that are further elaborated in the second volume. Any reader of the approximately 780 pages of both texts combined will note numerous tedious repetitions, as well as a plethora of odd formulations and stylistic peculiarities. Many contemporaries perceived it as turgid and intermingled with passages of involuntary humor. But—and this marks its historical importance—there is a constant ideological chord resounding throughout the text. In its consistency and coherence this ideological construction is central and decisive for analyzing Hitler's dogmatic stance as a politician and for the National Socialists' use of power after 1933.[65]

Scholarly discussions of Hitler's role and influence have gone through several phases. In the 1950s the dominant view was that Hitler had no real philosophy of governance but was rather a Machiavellian and nihilistic politician.[66] As for National Socialism in general, it was interpreted with the background of the Cold War: Hitler had established a totalitarian rule and the majority of the German people were victims of this system—as were the people under Stalin's reign at the same time. Thus people felt no need to have a closer look at the ideological elements undergirding the actions of those millions of Germans who had actively made the National Socialist rule such a brutal reality for its victims. In the following decades, particularly the 1960s and 1970s, alternative interpretations gained support stressing that National Socialist rule had been a process of structural radicalization. Anonymous stakeholders rather than individuals were regarded as driving the process. From the NSDAP to the army, from the SS to the bureaucracy and administration—the dynamics were perceived to be rooted in permanent competition for power. Once more, these interpretations regarded the ideological aspects as *quantité negligeable*. When the research on the peoples' community (*Volksgemeinschaft*) gained momentum in the 1990s, the focus moved to the role of the many "ordinary Germans" that had in one form or another helped to shape the development of the dynamics after 1933. Although ideological motivations were foregrounded, there was little interest in relating the overall motivations from top to bottom to the ideological fundamentals.

This is where *Mein Kampf*—which always must be analyzed and interpreted in light of Hitler's speeches[67]—demonstrates the constant intertwining of ideology and political practice in National Socialist policy. The text also shows how Hitler remained the source of inspiration for millions of individuals until the very end. Hitler's core conviction and his springboard for all further reflections on history, politics, and society are his belief to have identified the law of human existence and its determining principle: Hitler is convinced that all history is nothing but a sequence of racial struggles. With his concept Hitler stood in a tradition of "theories of race" which had developed since the mid-nineteenth century. Essentially they derived from a combination of publications which went back to Joseph Arthur de Gobineau and Charles Darwin. Gobineau published his four-volume *Essai sur l'inégalité des races humaines* (Essay on the Inequality of the Human Races) between 1853 and 1857, in which the so-called Aryan was regarded as being at the top of a hierarchy of races. A few years later Charles Darwin's theories set forth in *The Origin of Species by Means of Natural Selection*, which were based on observations in the animal world, were misused to develop theories of an unavoidable and constant natural struggle among human beings. Although this had neither been intended by Darwin nor had any foundation in his original concepts, these theories were bent into so-called Social Darwinism. In the age of imperialism these concepts served as justifications for territorial conquest and colonial rule. Through the impact of the First World War they underwent further radicalization, becoming comprehensive racist models driven by an absolutist claim. According to these models, the "cultural-creative purity of the Aryan race" and its superiority based on natural law were existentially endangered by racial mixing.[68]

Hitler adopted these theories and their categorizations not just in *Mein Kampf* but as key elements of his political belief system that he propagated constantly until his death. He claimed that Aryans (who were in his view almost identical with Germans plus a few other people from Northern Europe) were the sole creators of culture. Hitler in consequence imagined himself as the man with the key to world history in his hands, assigned by fate as the chosen leader to transpose this thinking into political reality. Hitler believed that Central Europe at this stage of the mid-1920s harbored a cohesive "racial nucleus" of at least seventy million "Aryans." He saw it as his historical task to establish a racial state and to ensure the domination of the "Aryans." It was an auto-suggestive missionary self-perception that drove him to transform his ideological faith into political practice.

The other crucial element of this ideological construct was its dichotomy. Hitler took up theories of modern anti-Semitism that had developed at the same time as the theories of Gobineau and Social Darwinism. Shaped by his interpretation of the First World War, Western democracies, and the Bolshevik Revolution in Russia, he saw "the Jews" as the driving force behind both Bolshevism in the Soviet Union and democratic parliamentarianism in Western countries. In short, for Hitler "the Jews" constituted a "counter-race." Democracy and Bolshevism were both sinister "Jewish" instruments of diversion from the "racial instinct." Hitler was convinced that the "basic racial instincts" of his imagined "German-Aryan community" were still intact but would be lost if democracy, parliamentarism, or Bolshevism had their way. Thus he saw himself in the historic role to unify the "racial core" and secure it for the future.[69]

In *Mein Kampf* Hitler described three central parameters of these imagined necessities: (a) the size of the people, (b) its space and territory, and (c) the correlated military geography. Accordingly, he deemed it necessary to increase the population and expand its territory through seizure of *Lebensraum* ("living space") in order to ensure that the military geography of the *Volksgemeinschaft* would be adequate for future conflicts. As soon as these prerequisites were safe-guarded, the "Aryan race" would have created the conditions for prevailing on a global scale. Combined with actively heightening racial consciousness and military preparation, Hitler believed that it was a central task to fight and annihilate the so-called counter-race, which primarily meant "the Jews"; however, in a wider perspective, he was fighting against all "racial competitors."[70]

Such a world in danger required the relentless striving for political power and the creation and implementation of all decisive parameters such as education, economy, and military capacities to conquer the habitat required for Aryan dominance. Of highest importance was the formation of a political party prepared to put the supposedly natural laws into practice and to establish a "racial state." The ideological absolutism necessarily included the rejection of parliamentary rule and of all institutions that promoted established humane values.

Conclusions

What do we learn through the critical analysis of *Mein Kampf* and the wide range of contextual material that the critical edition provides? First, it gives essential insight into Hitler's self-perception and political worldview. Second, we understand that *Mein Kampf* must always be put in perspective: its relationship to other texts (speeches, orders, etc.) and the nature of political practice after its publication. If we analyze these perspectives, it becomes obvious that from the very beginnings of the National Socialist movement, it was a matter of principle that once the believers in this ideology achieved power, they intended to eliminate any opposition, destroy parliamentary democracy, and establish a society along the lines of their racial conceptions. By means of permanent "education," the *Volksgemeinschaft* should identify with its assumed superiority. The Nazis made it clear that everyone had to be reeducated to appreciate their "racial consciousness" and that individuals who could not be relied on to serve the imagined *Volksgemeinschaft* were "enemies of racial unity" and excluded accordingly. This could, and would, mean their liquidation. The implementation of the authoritarian Führer state after 1933, and the organization of public, social, and cultural life according to racial principles, thus was pursued as an indisputable necessity. The new state had to embrace its historic task as an entity in global racial competition. It had to develop a foreign policy consonant with this view and prepare for military conquests to achieve its purposes.

However, this should not be taken to mean that *Mein Kampf* formulated an exact pre-determined "itinerary" as to what actions were to be applied or when and how they would be pursued. The actual political task before the seizure of power consisted in striving for opportune junctures and options for implementation, then moving on to concrete action as soon as opportunities permitted. Central to the dynamics was the self-image of Hitler and his historic role and the faith of his followers.

Hitler's speeches and texts, both before 1933 and after his ascension to office, reverberated with these themes of ideological intransigence, fanatical readiness to fight, and ruthless violence as a political tool—including clearly imagined fantasies of destruction brought upon all adversaries. *Mein Kampf* was a foundational text of this program.

Thus the analysis of *Mein Kampf*, its roots, and its impact provides historical resources to identify the construction of racialist conceptions.

Additionally, a critical study of *Mein Kampf* offers tools to identify and deconstruct political ideologies that seek to negate human liberty as a natural right as well as the universal concept of humanity and human rights. In this sense, the critically annotated edition of *Mein Kampf* offers a contribution to both of these endeavors that is relevant to continuing historiographical debates as well as to informed democratic discourse in current civil societies.

PART II

Establishing Power

In addition to seeking to mobilize Germans against the supposed existential threat of the Jews, *Mein Kampf* had another aim of coequal importance—to convince the folk-national movement to accept him as their unchallenged leader. Hitler's conception of leadership, akin to the hankerings after an authoritarian leader among the extreme folk-national right in postwar Germany, harks back to nineteenth-century Romantic notions of the "genius" or "great man." Originally conceived as an exceptional thinker or creative artist, the genius concept mutated into an image of the heroic individual who imposes his will on a recalcitrant world, pushing it in a direction of the genius' choice. In this form it would appear in the works of Arthur Schopenhauer (*The World as Will and Representation*, 1819) and Friedrich Nietzsche (*Twilight of the Idols*, 1889), two philosophers influential in Hitler's thinking. On the cusp of the First World War the yearning for a leader of extraordinary will and creativity was prominent among pan-German racists. Among them was Heinrich Claβ (1868–1953), a German right-wing politician and chairman of the anti-Semitic Pan-German League, whose 1912 work *Wenn ich der Kaiser wär': Politische Wahrheiten und Notwendigkeiten* (If I Were the Kaiser: Political Truths and Necessities) proclaimed that "the need still exists today in the best of our people to follow a strong, fit leader" because solely "through subordination to a leader" could the Germans "achieve greatness." As Othmar Plöckinger has already shown, Claβ's book was an uncited yet fruitful source for many of Hitler's ideas in *Mein Kampf*.

In the early years of the Weimar Republic, the longing for the "great man" spread throughout the folk-national right. The nascent NSDAP was not immune to this development. Both Dietrich Eckart and Rudolf Heβ longed for an authoritarian leader to guide their movement, and for both men Hitler fit the bill. For the first time, an article in the Nazi Party newspaper *Der Völkische Beobachter* published in December 1921 referred to Hitler as the "Führer." The success of Mussolini's "march on Rome" (1922) was a windfall for Hitler, helping cement his position as the leader of the Nazi Party.

Hitler's own view of leadership is set forth in volume II of *Mein Kampf*. At its core, it is a facsimile of conventional right-wing views. Influenced by Alfred Rosenberg, Hitler claims he wants to "build not on the thoughts of the majority but on the personality." This dichotomy between the "mass" and the "personality" (i.e., the ingenious, iron-willed monocrat) is fundamental to Hitler's concept of leadership. Only this figure—the man of destiny able to mold reality according to his will—is capable of truly thinking and acting creatively, not the mass of the population. The people's duty in the folk-national state is to submit to such a leader. In Hitler's eyes, democracy snubbed the critical role of the dominant man; in substituting majority rule for the monocratic leadership of the individual genius, democracy "poisons all life," committing an act of self-destruction for which Hitler blames the Jews. As with every adjunct of Hitler's thought, even his conception of leadership ultimately circles back to anti-Semitism. Jews try to negate "the paramount significance of the personality," using trade unions and other Marxist ruses to replace "the person" with "the mass." Hitler's argument that the state must be "anchored" in the "personality principle," meaning that only one man "makes decisions," would be later translated into Nazi policy as the "principle of the leader" (*Führerprinzip*). According to the principle, in the hierarchy of the Nazi state all authority flowed downward from the leader to his subordinates. The subordinates in turn owed unconditional obedience to the Führer's orders. As Hitler himself put it in *Mein Kampf*, "authority of every leader [moved] toward those below and responsibility from below toward those above."

In short, National Socialism took the Romantic fascination with the leader, implicit in all right-wing politics of the Weimar era, and fetishized it. By the late 1930s the result would be one of history's most noxious totalitarian dictatorships.

4

Hitler, Leadership, and the Holocaust

Paul Bookbinder

The Holocaust would not have taken place without the Führer, Adolf Hitler. To understand the development of the Holocaust, it is crucial to understand Hitler's concept of leadership, how entwined his anti-Semitism was with every aspect of leadership, and how obsessed he was with the need to eliminate the "Jewish menace." With this focus, he leveraged his role in everything of importance during the Nazi years with the deeply held beliefs of many Germans to build support for the mass murder programs. His ideas on leadership were crucial to his actions and are keys to understanding the Holocaust. This chapter concentrates on the ideas in *Mein Kampf* related to leadership and the Holocaust supplemented by supporting evidence from recent published work on Hitler.

In his comprehensive biography of Hitler, Peter Longerich writes, "For a systematic anti-Semitic policy to emerge out of a widespread hostility to the Jews, and for this policy to be geared to the most radical possible solution required the engagement, co-ordination, the driving force of the authoritative man at the top of the regime."[1] Longerich is clear that Hitler's obsession with the Jews and his desire to eliminate them from Europe are obvious in a reading of *Mein Kampf* and was as real in his bunker at the end of the war as it had been while he was writing the book. Longerich argues forcefully that there is no truth in the assertion that Hitler's henchmen carried out the murder of the Jews without his knowledge or even against his will. "Hitler's treatment of the Jewish question over a lengthy period," Longerich states, "makes it clear that it was always he who set the agenda for the various stages of radicalization and controlled developments."[2]

In the conclusion of his book, Longerich sums up the centrality of Hitler's role in every aspect of the Nazi regime. He writes,

> It is beyond question that no single individual was responsible for the catastrophic outcome of the twelve years of dictatorship. Millions of committed Nazis had worked tirelessly for this regime; a huge army of willing helpers and opportunistic fellow travellers had given it unquestionable support; the elites had been only too glad to put their specialized knowledge and experience at its disposal; officers and soldiers had carried out their military tasks obediently and with great commitment; the majority of the population had followed their Führer devotedly and without protest. And yet these facts on their own are not adequate to explain what happened. There had to be a political figure who knew how to exploit the preconditions and forces designed to realize his aims and ambitions. At the heart of the Third Reich there was a determined dictator who shaped this process, focused all these energies on himself as an individual, and managed to acquire such extensive powers that he enjoyed unprecedented freedom.[3]

The achievement and extent of Hitler's power were quite remarkable, and he remains one of the great enigmas of modern history. He had none of the standard prerequisites for success in the German society of his day and yet came to dominate his country, plunge most of the world into a ferocious war, and initiate genocidal campaigns that led to the murder of millions. He began his political career without wealth, without an impressive family name or connections, without academic degrees or titles, and without having achieved officer rank in the military, thus without the advantages that made the hope of power seem a realistic possibility. His accomplishment in becoming the most popular political leader of the Weimar period and propelling the National Socialist Party to achieve close to 38 percent of the vote in a field of over thirty parties on the ballot in 1932 was a colossal achievement. How Hitler managed to gain power and what he actually did when in power remain compelling questions as relevant today as they were during and in the immediate aftermath of his dictatorship.

Hitler's ideas on leadership were already being defined in the initial Weimar years. Early on in *Mein Kampf*, Hitler compared the masses to a woman whose psychic state is determined less by abstract reasoning than by an indefinable emotional longing for a force that will complement her nature and who would consequently rather bow to a strong man than dominate a weakling. He stated, "the masses love a commander more than a petitioner and feel inwardly more satisfied by a doctrine tolerating no other beside itself, than by granting liberalistic freedom with which as a rule they can do little and are prone to feel that they have been abandoned."[4]

Hitler constantly comes back to his use of the woman analogy. He argues, "The people in their overwhelming majority are so feminine by nature and attitude that sober reasoning determines their thoughts and actions far less than emotion and feeling."[5] In Hitler's terms the people do not want freedom and do not want choice. As analyzed in the 1950s by the American political scientist Erich Fromm, the people want an escape from freedom and Hitler sensed that. People find having to make their own decisions about what is right and wrong, moral and immoral anxiety provoking, and they long for someone to make these decisions for them. Intuiting what the eighteenth-century German Enlightenment philosopher Immanuel Kant had argued, Hitler believed that, out of laziness and cowardice, most men and all women do not want to challenge forceful authority out of laziness and cowardice. He believed that the people wanted a leader with a strong message and charismatic ability, and this leader could command the loyalty of the people. However, he also recognized that the leader would be most effective if he tapped into deeply held beliefs and prejudices in the people. Hitler followed these understandings that he put forth in *Mein Kampf*, and they contributed to his success.

Hitler was convinced that the insights of the masses were slight and that they would follow a leader who made shameless promises, particularly in the economic area. Hitler saw the Jew as the master of making these promises.[6] A forceful leader who could make promises that could actually be fulfilled could win over the masses.

Hitler also believed that it was easier to unify people against things than in favor of them and that a common enemy was crucial in rallying support. He saw politics, as did Carl Schmitt, the jurist who would help the Nazis to redefine German law, as based on the friend-foe principle. For Schmitt, the ideal enemy was one both within and outside the political society, and if the leader could achieve this clear identification of the enemy, the people should be willing to kill the enemy. The Jew would be this enemy for Hitler. A reading of *Mein Kampf* makes clear his obsession with the Jews and his belief that he could tap into and reinforce the anti-Semitic beliefs held by the German people. Hitler believed that a simple message constantly repeated was necessary as the majority of people responded best to simple and unequivocal messages, as he develops in chapter VI on war propaganda in volume I and chapter XI on propaganda organization in volume II. He also believed that people have an infinite capacity to forget and that could be utilized as well. The view he developed and presented in *Mein Kampf* of the Jews as the greatest menace to his goals for Germany, and his belief that he had to make the German people aware of how serious this danger was, played a role in Hitler's ordering the mass murders that characterized the Holocaust. Thus, the strong leader could dominate the people while reinforcing their prejudices with a clear and narrowly focused message delivered to them through the use of propaganda.

Hitler indicated that his views on race that would be a key to his political message had become clear to him in Vienna. He became an enemy of the Habsburg Empire of his birth and which his father had served for all his working life as a customs official. He decried the multiethnic nature of the empire that he saw in racial terms and particularly that of Vienna. "I was repelled by the conglomeration of races which the capital showed me, repelled by the mixture of Czechs, Poles, Hungarians, Ruthenians, Serbs and Croats, and everywhere, the eternal mushroom of humanity-Jews and more Jews. To me the giant city seemed the embodiment of racial desecration."[7] While the man Hitler admired the most for his political skills, Karl Lueger, mayor of Vienna, was an anti-Semite, Hitler doubted Lueger's real conviction on this issue and cast Lueger's anti-Semitism in economic rather than racial terms. For Hitler it was the racial issue that was paramount.

In the early 1920s, Hitler separated himself from those on the political right who longed for a return of the monarchy. Analyzing the monarchy's major failure, he wrote:

> Kaiser Wilhelm was the first German Emperor to hold out a conciliatory hand to the leaders of Marxism [the Jews], without suspecting that scoundrels have no honor. While they still held the imperial hand to theirs, the other hand was reaching for the dagger. There is no making pacts with Jews (Figure 4.1).[8]

FIGURE 4.1 *"One People, one Reich, one Fuhrer/Leader": Image of authority. Courtesy of the United States Holocaust Memorial Museum.*

Having rejected the idea of a return to monarchy, Hitler saw himself as leader of a *völkisch* state based on race. A new movement had to be created as he saw all the existing parties at the beginning of the Weimar years as incapable of bringing about the changes that were necessary to transform Germany. Once again for Hitler the real problem was the Jews. "What makes this [the necessary transformation] all the more impossible is that the leading elements [in these parties] are always Jews and only Jews. And the development we are going through today, if continued unobstructed, would fulfill the Jewish prophecy—the Jew would totally devour the peoples of the earth, and would become their master."[9] The true leader can reverse these developments:

> Thus confronting the millions of German "bourgeois" and "proletarians" who for the most part, from cowardice, coupled with stupidity trot toward their ruin, he [the true leader] pursues his way inexorably, in the highest consciousness of his future goal. A party which is led by him can, therefore, stand for no other interests besides his interests: The first task is the elimination of the Jewish state which with the concerns of Aryan nations have nothing in common.

Hitler's ideas of leadership were influenced by Richard Wagner, who was one of his idols. Wagnerian ideas inspired him from his early days in Linz to his end in a Berlin bunker, where he cast defeat in Wagnerian terms. Hitler, like Wagner, manipulated myth. John Adams, in a New York Times book review, writes:

> The incomparable thing about myth is that it is always true and its content through utmost compression is always true. Hitler's genius like those of Wagner was to tap our mythological subconscious in a manner that for each of us is always true and yet different from the next person. The behemoth whispers a "different secret" in each listener's ear.[10]

Hitler was also influenced by watching Mussolini use myth to create a movement that rejected all the existing political parties, energized the masses, emphasized the leader, and dramatically achieved political power. Carl Schmitt admired Mussolini's use of myth and was impressed by Hitler's understanding of the importance of myth for the true leader.

In close reading of *Mein Kampf* evidences that Hitler had a profound understanding of politics and group psychology, and he applied his understandings to his analysis of the history of his country in his own time. The Weimar Republic that was created as Hitler left military service was born in the fire of military defeat in World War I that most Germans did not expect and did not understand. The government-controlled media often did not have and could not present an accurate picture of the military situation. Plagued by economic hardships, the new republican government faced considerable obstacles in its attempt to win over a population that was not used to parliamentary government that had real power and that was the main governmental policy maker. Unlike the United States, where the legislature has real power and wheeling and dealing and some corruption are customary, the German people were unaccustomed to these political behaviors and were shocked and angered by these changes.

Hitler used the dismay of the German people and their deep reservations about parliamentary government in his strategy to dominate his own National Socialist movement and his rise to power. He argued, "It is not the aim of our present-day parliamentarianism to constitute an assembly of wise men, but rather to compose a band of mentally dependent nonentities who are the more easily led in certain directions, the greater is the limitation of the individual. That is the only way of carrying on party politics in the malodorous present-day sense."[11] He further wrote:

> Such an institution, the parliament, can only please the biggest liars and sneaks of the sort that shun the light of day, because it is inevitably hateful to an honorable straightforward man who welcomes personal responsibility, and that is why this type of democracy has become the instrument of that race which in its inner goals must shun the light of day now in all age of the future. Only the Jew can praise an institution which is as dirty and false as himself.[12]

As Hitler sees it parliamentarians only court the people during election periods when they express concerns for the problems people face and promise all kinds of dramatic solutions. After ignoring these problems for most of their four-year terms,

> an unconquerable urge suddenly comes over the gentlemen. Just as a caterpillar cannot help turning into a butterfly these parliamentary larvae leave their parliamentary cocoons and, endowed with wings, fly out among the beloved people. Again they talk to their voters, speak of the enormous work they have done and the malignant stubbornness of their opponents.[13]

When these parliamentarians receive criticism they promise more new programs to solve all the problems. The people, middle and lower classes, are often taken in by these promises. "In view of the granite stupidity of our humanity, we have no need to be surprised at the outcome. Led by their press [controlled by Jews] and dazzled by a new an alluring program, the 'bourgeois' as well as the 'proletarian' voting cattle return to the common stable and again vote for their old misleaders."[14]

Hitler has contempt for the Members of Parliament, whom he characterizes as leather merchants who in their heart of hearts know what "lamentable figures they cut."[15] He argued that the agents of the Jewish press legitimize these mediocre parliamentarians. However, for Hitler the Members of Parliament are of little ability and will be dwarfed by the true leader, who has "the power and genius of a giant." This true leader will have to battle against the political class that he calls idiotic incompetents and bigmouths who hate nothing more than a superior mind.

In *Becoming Hitler*, utilizing reception theory, Thomas Weber ascribes Hitler's growing popularity to his ability to turn himself into a canvas whose interpretation was determined by the *Weltanschauung* of the viewer. "In short, he managed to present himself in a way that insured that everybody had their own Hitler, thus empowering him to pursue his own policy goals, which for instance allowed both monarchists and their adversaries to view Hitler as one of their own."[16]

In *Mein Kampf* it is clear that Hitler's political acumen was a major factor in his leadership arsenal, which contributed to his success and complemented his charisma. Peter Longerich is one of the historians who emphasizes Hitler as politician. Throughout his biography, Longerich reiterates the pivotal nature of Hitler's political skills. "The key to Hitler's effectiveness," he observes, "did not lie in achieving overwhelming consensus by means of the power of his charisma, but rather in his ability to reshape extraordinarily complex situations through skillful, flexible, and (albeit after considerable hesitation) decisive political action."[17] While this political acumen was critical to his achieving of power, certainly his charisma did play a pivotal role.

Hitler became convinced early in the 1920s that in order to achieve a major transformation of Germany, one leader who could focus one movement on that goal was required. Hitler understood that there were a number of movements and a number of leaders who saw themselves in that role. As he wrote in *Mein Kampf*, the realization of who the true leader would be would take time to be realized:

> Here, too, assuredly, by virtue of a natural order, the strongest man is destined to fulfill the great mission: yet the realization that this *one* is the exclusively elect usually comes to the others very late. On the contrary they *all* see themselves as *Chosen* and *have equal rights* for the solution of the task, and their fellow men are usually able least of all to distinguish which among them—being solely endowed with the highest ability—deserves their sole support.[18]

For Hitler that goal was to free Germany from the Jews and their destructive effects on German society. All his political ability was going to be necessary to create the movement and convince the others that he was the one to accomplish this. He would use many slogans and messages to achieve his dominance and his goal, often cloaking it to expand his support base.

Hitler was committed to the use of propaganda to achieve his goals. He believed the message had to be clear, unequivocal, and endlessly repeated. The Germans had lost the propaganda war in the First World War to the British and the Americans who painted the Germans as barbaric, Neanderthal-like "Huns." Hitler and Joseph Goebbels, the Nazis' gifted propaganda minister, learned the First World War lesson, improved on their enemies' techniques, and used the emerging technology of the radio to spread their message.

Hitler was a student of those who he felt understood how effective propaganda worked. He believed that speeches were the most effective form of propaganda. His opinion of what made an effective speech and how it differed from the judgment of academics can be seen in his reaction to evaluations of the speeches of David Lloyd George that German academics called "hackneyed speeches." Hitler had come into possession of a book of George's speeches and disagreed:

> I had to laugh aloud that an average German Knight of the inkpot [intellectual] should possess no understanding for the psychological masterpieces in the art of mass propaganda. . . . German critics judged these speeches by the effect they had on their own blasé natures, while the Great English demagogue had set out solely to exert the greatest possible effect on the mass of his listeners, and in the broadest sense on the entire English lower class. Regarded from this standpoint, the speeches of this Englishman were the most wonderful performances, for they testified to a positively amazing knowledge of the soul of the broad mass of the people. And their effect was truly powerful.[19]

Hitler recognized that propaganda was a means and not an end, and thus he could admire the words of David Lloyd George while deploring his ends.

Hitler also believed that the true leader understood the need for others who shared his goals, possessed political skills, and recognized that he was the true leader, the prophet of a new order. These men would recognize the connection between ideology and politics.

The relationship between ideology and political objectives was an issue for the entire major Nazi leadership, prime among them Heinrich Himmler. While many historians have viewed Himmler as a rigid romantic ideologue with dreams of recreating a medieval kingdom, neither Longerich in his study of Himmler nor Robert Gerwarth in his study of Reinhard Heydrich see him that way.[20] As Longerich writes, "he [Himmler] was first and foremost a highly flexible and adaptable politician who knew how to legitimize whatever policy he adopted by dressing it up with appropriate ideology."[21] Himmler was attracted to Hitler because he responded to Hitler's charisma but also admired his political acumen.

Hitler, while critical of "bookworm" intellectuals, believed that intellect on the part of an active political leader was important. He argued that it was the intellect of the leader that was crucial not that of the followers as his arch rivals the Social Democrats believed. "They [the Social Democrats] never understood that the strength of a political party lies by no means in the greatest possible independent intellect of the individual members, but rather in the disciplined obedience with which members follow the intellectual leadership."[22] This was particularly true when the leader was a "genius." Thomas Weber described how Hitler developed as a leader in the early 1920s and that as early as 1922 he had decided that Germany needed a dictator and a dictator who was a genius. Hitler came to believe that he was that genius. He also attacks the idea of monarchy because rule through inheritance provided no guarantee of the ability of the ruler and only worked in the rare case of a ruler such as Frederick the Great who was a "heroic genius".[23] Hitler writes that the genius needs "a special cause, a positive impetus to make him shine." Explaining how such a genius could arise not only from a young ruler but also from a seemingly insignificant person, he talks of how in situations where the great majority of people lose hope the genius emerges. He writes that "The hammer of fate which throws one man to the ground suddenly strikes steel in another and when the shell of everyday life is broken, the previously hidden kernel lies open before the eyes of the astonished world."[24]

The leader had to focus on one goal, in fact only a part of that goal, to succeed. He writes:

> The great masses of people cannot see the whole road ahead without growing weary and despairing of the task. A certain number of them will keep the goal in mind, but will only be able to see the goal in small, partial stretches, like the wanderer, who likewise knows and recognizes the end of the journey, but is better able to conquer the endless highway if he divides it into sections and boldly attacks each one although it represented the desired goal itself. Only in this way does he advance without losing heart.[25]

Hitler believed that the leader had to understand that various elements of the German population saw the world differently and had to be approached differently by the leader. While recognizing that the bourgeoisie was an important element in the German state and one that would be difficult to inspire and gain as supporters, he did not see them as a problem. As he writes, "Even if the German bourgeoisie, for their well known narrow minded and short-sighted reasons, should, as they once did toward Bismarck, maintain an obstinate attitude of passive resistance in the hour of coming liberation—an active resistance, in view of their recognized and proverbial cowardice, is never to be feared."[26] The masses are a different story. He argues that in their natural primitiveness, they are more inclined to the idea of violence and, moreover, their Jewish leadership is more brutal and ruthless. Once again it is the Jews who are the enemy and threaten the rebirth of the German nation. The Jewish menace has to be dealt with. "Historically it is just not conceivable that the German people could recover its former position without settling accounts with those who were the cause and occasion of the unprecedented collapse which struck our state."[27]

Hitler saw the leader involved in every area of the people's lives, including the most private, their sexuality. In all these areas the figure of the Jew was paramount. Hitler was personally obsessed with the spread of syphilis and planned action to stem it when his movement attained power. Even here he saw the figure of the Jew as key to the prostitution that was crucial to its spread. The Jew had also intruded spiritually as well as financially in this area. "The Jewification of our spiritual life and mamonization of our mating instincts will sooner or later destroy our entire offspring."[28]

Hitler took advantage of the fact that, while the Jews had achieved legal equality in 1871 when Germany emerged as a unified nation, most Germans did not see Jews as their equals, as "true" Germans. In the early nineteenth century supernationalists such as Turnvater Jahn, organizer of a major youth movement, began to define who a German was, and Jews were not included. Biological racism represented by Wihelm Marr at the end of the nineteenth century reinforced the idea of the foreignness of the Jews. In a post–First World War play, *Friedrich*, the socialist Ernst Toller, who had been in combat in the army during the First World War, has his lead character tell his fellow combat veterans who had been in the trenches with him that he would not have survived if it weren't for his feeling of German patriotism. His fellow soldiers told him that he wasn't a German, he was a Jew. His response that his father had been born in Germany and his grandfather had been born in Germany didn't move them. For them he was a Jew and a Jew could not be a German.

Hitler, an Austrian by birth who lived in the Austrian Empire until 1913, needed the emphasis on race to argue his Germaneness. His language had an Austrian flavor to it, but he would passionately argue that Germaneness was not a product of regional accent but being racially German and particularly being committed to battling the greatest danger to the German race, the Jews. The Austrians he admired most were those who understood the dangers of the Jews.

Both of Hitler's early models of leadership, Karl Lueger and Georg von Schönerer, were committed to anti-Semitism. In *Mein Kampf*, Hitler describes how he came to his hatred of the Jews slowly. The anti-Semitic press in Vienna and the pronouncements of Lueger moved him to see that the Jew was not only religiously different but dangerous as well. Hitler came to believe that Lueger was the greatest mayor of all time and was a model of how to influence an electorate in a voting situation. His criticism of Lueger was that while a superb politician his convictions were less important to him than achieving and maintaining power.

As Hitler began his journey down the path that would culminate in the Holocaust, he needed to discredit the idea that the Jews could be loyal Germans despite the fact that many had served during the Great War. About his First World War observations in Munich, he writes, "The offices (military headquarters) were filled with Jews. Nearly every clerk was a Jew. I was amazed at the plethora of warriors of the chosen people and could not help but compare them with their representatives at the front."[29] Hitler is fostering the idea that was prevalent on the political right that most Jews avoided military service and those who served avoided frontline combat. The army had conducted their own survey as their leaders shared this belief. When the survey did not confirm their preconceived ideas and to the contrary indicated that considering their percentage of the population, Jews were overrepresented in military service, in combat roles and in casualties, they did not publish the results.

Hitler highlights the racial reasons for the defeat of Germany in the First World War to support his obsession with the Jews. "If we pass all the causes of the German collapse in review the ultimate and most decisive remains the failure to recognize, the racial problem and especially the Jewish menace."[30] While Hitler did believe the Jews were a factor in Germany's defeat, the idea of the Jew as the "major" cause of Germany's defeat in the war was put forth for public political purposes. He actually believed that the entry of the United States with its unlimited productive capacities and huge quantities of fresh manpower was the decisive element in Germany's defeat.

While Hitler did not introduce race into the German consciousness, he was the most effective leader to utilize it. Johann Chapoutot's *Law of Blood* stresses the importance of the racial factor for Germans and thus such an important weapon for Hitler.[31] Chapoutot argues that by the time German armies were marching east during the Second World War, large numbers of Germans were prepared for a war of enslavement and extermination. They accepted the portrayal of the enemy, particularly the Jews, as less than human and, in fact, as vermin. The imagery in Fritz Hippler's film, *The Eternal Jew* (1940), was a common perception. Adolf Hitler's words, SS publications, and many military communications presented Germany's enemies, particularly Jews, by mirroring the words of Paul de Lagarde, "You don't negotiate with trichina or bacilli. You exterminate them, as quickly and carefully as possible."[32] Chapoutot in a key observation writes that "What had been virulent and hate filled but still largely metaphorical discourse in the nineteenth century became literal truth in Nazi Germany."[33] By the early 1920s, Hitler had tied the scourge of syphilis to the Jews who he believed were responsible for "white slavery" that promoted the disease. He argued that, "This poison was able to penetrate the bloodstream of our people unhindered and do its work, and the state did not possess the power to master this disease."[34], , and he referred to the Jewish press as "a thousand

Jewish vipers and run by aliens and enemies [...] to divert attention from the problem and present false information to the people."[35]

Had more people read *Mein Kampf* carefully they would not have been shocked as to where he would lead Germany and what he would do to the Jews if he achieved power. Those who did this careful reading did understand. In his book about his grandfather Chemin Sasha Abramsky, Sasha Abramsky describes the man who had had one of the largest collections of books and other documents on Jewish history and the Holocaust in the world. Chemin's notes focus on his belief that Hitler had decided on mass murder for the Jews by the time he wrote *Mein Kampf*. He had underlined key passages in red ink and had written precise little notes in the margins such as "He [the Jew] lacks the most essential requirements for cultured people, the idealistic attitude." On the page where Hitler had written that Jews were stateless wanderers, Chemin comments that to Hitler they were worse than nomads. Most revealing as to Hitler's plan for the Jews he underlined Hitler's description of the Jews as parasites and most significantly as bacilli that must be destroyed to save the German nation. Sasha Abramsky writes, "Whether this finally led to the Final Solution is a separate question but there is little doubt that the germ of the extermination of the Jews is contained already in *Mein Kampf*."[36]

Hitler surrounded himself with men who had total faith in him as the leader but also saw propaganda as a key political tool and foremost among them was Joseph Goebbels. These men also had to share Hitler's obsession with the Jews. Goebbels felt himself superior to everyone in the Nazi leadership group with the exception of Hitler. His feelings for Hitler bordered on worship and the man best known as a master propagandist shared Hitler's views on Jews.

Although Toby Thacker in his study of Goebbels makes the questionable assumption that Goebbels had a conscience of sorts, he argues that Goebbels had no sympathy for Jews. "His racially centered view of the world," Thacker states, "put the Jews beyond any of this [sense of conscience]; he considered them as a whole and without exception, so fiendish and diabolical that they merited no sympathy."[37] That attitude, plus his unqualified adoration of Hitler made him a perfect underling, and he never questioned the der Fuehrer. Goebbels's dominant leadership could be counted upon to play policy roles when Hitler did not want to make certain statements or make certain decisions. One of the striking features of the book is Thacker's argument that Goebbels played a major role in the development of Nazi policy fulfilling Hitler's need for a thoroughly reliable disciple. "Although [Goebbels'] formal office as Propaganda Minister might suggest that he was involved directly only with presentation and with the manipulation of opinion," Thacker concludes, "he used his position to intervene more widely in the formation of policy."[38] Thus, Goebbels as Himmler and others could be counted upon to help realize Hitler's leadership goals and would be vital to actions against the Jews.

Hitler was politically astute, understanding that certain beliefs and goals that were important but secondary to his goal of a racially pure German society should not be stressed in the quest for power and should be targets for the future. The desire for religious transformation advocated by some right-wing groups was one of those areas. Hitler had understood this when he criticized one of his Vienna days' heroes, Georg von Schönerer, for attacking the Catholic Church. Hitler realized that such an attack was a losing issue that would limit the appeal of Schönerer's German nationalist and anti-Semitic movement. Hitler had no thought of limiting his emphasis on the Jews, the key issue through which he could connect with the German people and lead them to take drastic action.

In assessing the development and intensification of Hitler's genocidal attitude toward Jews in the early 1920s, Thomas Weber considers whether Hitler's hostility was initially motivated by radical, racist Judeophobia or by anticapitalistic anti-Semitism. He asks whether the extreme language that Hitler began using on the "Jewish question" was truly genocidal or only metaphorical. Weber concludes that wherever Hitler might have been on these questions when he emerged from the army in 1919, he moved quite early toward a genocidal conclusion. Citing an interview Hitler gave to a Catalonian journalist in 1923 in which he praised Kemal Atatürk for creating the new, homogeneous Turkish state facilitated by the Armenian genocide, Weber sees Hitler as coming to believe early on that under the right conditions, particularly during a war, carrying out a genocide was possible.[39]

As Hitler battled to create and lead a movement for transformation and renewal, he understood that he had to struggle against men who claimed that they had advocated similar ideas for decades. However, a true leader is in Hitler's terms not fighting for the right cause often for extended periods of time but being successful in implementing these ideas in a reasonable amount of time. In criticizing some of the *völkisch* leaders on the extreme right, he argues, "Anyone who fights for forty years for so-called ideas, without being able to bring about even the slightest success, in fact, without having prevented the victory of the opposite, has, with forty years of activity, provided proof of his own incapacity."[40] Carl Schmitt, who would help the Nazis reorder their legal system famously declared in 1934, "The Führer interprets the Law." Schmitt waited until Hitler showed he could succeed before becoming an enthusiastic supporter. The mark of a true leader is success. It is also being out front and taking risks, not claiming you are working quietly and behind the scenes that are in Hitler's terms an excuse for cowardice and deception. As he sees it, "Every last agitator who possesses the courage to stand on a tavern table among his adversaries, to defend his opinions with manly forthrightness, does more than a thousand of these treacherous sneaks."[41]

Hitler understood instinctively what Carl Schmitt argued intellectually that the essence of politics is the "friend-foe principle" and that the use of the foe to create political unity works best if there is only one enemy.[42] In Schmitt's view, political unity was achieved when the community of friends was willing to kill the enemy. For Schmitt it was not necessary to actually kill the enemy. The willingness to do so was sufficient. In the case of the Jews for Hitler the willingness of the people to kill the enemy was ultimately not sufficient—the enemy did have to be killed. Not only did the leader have to focus his people on the one true enemy, but he also needed to provoke that enemy and make its hostility obvious. "Anyone in this world who does not succeed in being hated by his adversaries does not seem to me to be worth much as a friend."[43] Such a person could not be an effective leader.

The true leader had to recognize, as Bismarck did, that "politics is an art of the possible," but the true leader can see within the range of the possible much more than political leaders who were active during the early years of the Weimar Republic.[44] By focusing on Germany's "real" enemy, Hitler sees the true leader as telling the truth to the German people, to forget striking out at the rest of the world and concentrate on the real enemy:

> Furthermore the German people has no right to blame the rest of the world for its conduct as long as it has not called to account the criminal who sold and betrayed their whole country. Really it is not serious for us to curse and protest from a distance, England, Italy, etc. from a distance and leave the scoundrels at large, who in the pay of enemy war propaganda, took away our arms, broke our moral backbone, and auctioned off the crippled Reich for thirty pieces of silver. [45]

In his bid to lead the new National Socialist movement he would constantly go back to the First World War years to position the Jews as the enemy. Hitler claimed in *Mein Kampf* that in the 1916–17 period the whole of production was under the control of Jewish finance and that the new leader for Germany, the "genius dictator," would have to destroy this system of control. As Hitler writes, "The spider was slowly beginning to suck the blood out of the people's pores."[46] The use of insect or rodent images to characterize the Jews became a frequent Nazi device to make the Jews repellent in the eyes of their Christian fellow citizens. For Hitler the true leader had to maintain the purity of the blood of his people. As he declares, "All great cultures of the past perished only because the originally creative race died of blood poisoning."[47]

To prevent that creative race from perishing and for German society to transform itself, Hitler believed it must become "an embodiment of the endeavor to place thinking individuals above the masses, thus subordinating the latter to the former."[48] For Hitler it was the Jews who made the masses the key to political leadership because the Jews could manipulate them. This was a rejection of the Aryan principle of leadership by a superior elite led by the genius. "Thus, the organizing principle of Aryan humanity is replaced by the destructive principle of the Jew. He becomes a ferment of decomposition among peoples and race and in the broader sense a dissolver of human culture."[49]

In order to succeed, the leader had to understand the role of the Jews and fight against it. Hitler declared, "Was there any form of filth or profligacy, particularly in cultural life, without at least one Jew involved in it. If you cut cautiously into such an abscess, you found, like a maggot in a rotting body, often dazzled by the sudden light —a kike."[50]

Utilizing a large variety of sources as the basis of his research, Chapoutot gauges the extent of public support for Hitler's ideas. He concludes that while the sources were varied in length, style, and language, "Nevertheless, the texts I investigated were all based on postulates and assumptions that followed specific paths of reasoning and formulated concepts, that either explicitly or indirectly, by imitation or quotation, were present everywhere, including newsreels, films, ideological teaching materials, tracts, posters and meeting agendas."[51] Nazi ideological education had far-reaching goals. "It must unite the entire nation to uncompromising fanaticism," Chapoutot observes, "and ensure that each person feels he is soldier and fighter for Adolf Hitler."[52] Most significant is his conclusion that most Germans, along with the Nazi leaders, were true believers.

The invasion of the Soviet Union was a key to Hitler's war aims in three ways. It was the target of his Lebensraum program, the source of oil and other resources for his ultimate battle with the United States, and his plan to murder the Jews. Drawing on Hitler's comments in *Mein Kampf*, the military historian Stephen Fritz writes, "In breathtakingly, radical fashion then Hitler not only laid out the enormous task before Germany, but explicitly linked the acquisition of living space [Lebensraum] with the destruction of Jews living there."[53]

As Fritz Stern pointed out in lectures he gave in Germany later published as *Der Traum vom Frieden und die Versuchung der Macht: Deutsche Geschichte Im 20 Jahrhundert*[54] (Dreams and Delusions: The Drama of German History), Hitler had a musician's instinctive sense of the rhythms of thought that were pulsating through his society, and he was able to tune in and focus on these themes. He played on deep wounds to the souls of German people. Hitler understood the movement he was creating as a political substitute for religion and used what Stern saw as pseudo-religious language. He talked about salvation, rebirth, and painted his enemies as godless and satanic. Clearly seeing the Jews as Satanic was within a long-established Christian tradition that Hitler could tap into and utilize in his mass murder program.

The philosophical-political-religious movement Hitler desired did require political understanding and skill for success. In analyzing how politics works, Hitler argued that Jews create political parties while he is creating a movement based on a philosophy and not merely a political program. For Hitler, the leader must never compromise. Compromises are the means to advance the narrow interest of specific groups, the Jews being the primary beneficiaries. "Political parties are inclined to compromise, philosophies never. Political parties even reckon with opponents; philosophies proclaim their infallibility."[55] The leader who embodies this philosophy is also infallible.

Infallible though he may be, there still were practical considerations that had to be faced, such as the press, and this is a major issue for Hitler that he discusses in *Mein Kampf*. He considers how the coming leader of Germany had to deal with the press. The true leader needed to destroy the liberal press. "The so-called liberal press was actively engaged in digging the grave of the German people and the German Reich."[56] Jews of course dominated this press.

The true leader must inspire and direct the cultural life as well as the political life of the people. Hitler considered himself an artist and was prepared to exercise that function. As he presents the state of German culture in *Mein Kampf*, he once again concentrates on the destructive role of the Jews. "Culturally he contaminates art, literature, the theater, makes a mockery of natural feeling, overthrows all concepts of beauty and sublimity, of the noble and the good, and instead drags men down into the sphere of his own base nature."[57]

Hitler believed that the leader must embody the gifts of intelligence and clear thinking that separate superior individuals from the masses. Writing about the party that he will lead, Hitler states, "It must itself be an embodiment of the endeavor to place thinking individuals above the masses, thus subordinating the latter to the former."[58]

Because the leader's most important function is to protect the racial purity of the people, once again Hitler invokes his obsession with the Jews: "The destructive effect of the Jew's activity in other national bodies is basically attributable only to his eternal efforts to undermine the position of the personality in the host-people and to replace it by the mass. Thus the organizing principle of Aryan humanity is replaced by the destructive principle of the Jew."[59] The greatest danger to this racial purity is the Jew. "With satanic joy in his face, the black-haired Jewish youth lurks in wait for the unsuspecting girl whom he defiles with his blood thus stealing her from her people. With every means at his disposal he tries to destroy the racial foundations of the people he has set out to subjugate."[60] This is the type of rhetoric that would lead to mass murder.

Hitler's ideal leader would usher in Germany's revival as a great power with a dynamic productive economy that would ultimately prove itself in war and would carry out the objective of freeing Europe from the Jewish menace and creating a continent dominated by racially pure Germans. This mission is described by the German military historian Dieter Müller, who, in his account, juxtaposes the impressive military achievements of the Wehrmacht—"the most combat effective regular army"—with its role as a "Marching Slaughterhouse, A Criminal Organization."[61] He highlights the fact that "The genocide of European Jews was something Hitler had always seen as a requirement for 'internal security' of his Reich and as his most important war goal."[62] While Müller is aware of the key role of the SS and the *Einsatzgruppen* he argues that recent research has made clear that the "final solution of the Jewish problem" had a close connection with military events and the military forces, and that the killing squads often worked together.[63]

In everything that Hitler did he believed that he was ultimately going to lead a crusade to free Germany and the rest of Europe from the Jews. The Jews, he believed, were a major factor in Germany's defeat in the First World War, in destroying Germany's economy, corrupting her political institutions, in contaminating Germany's youth, and by their very existence threatening Germany's racial purity. The Jews who are present in so many pages in Hitler's major treatise *Mein Kampf* are guilty of the "Crime of Being," and thus Hitler the leader would be the major factor in a step-by-step unleashing of the Holocaust.

5

Violence in *Mein Kampf*

Tactic and Political Communication

Nathan Stoltzfus and J. Ryan Stackhouse

In *Mein Kampf* violence is a tactic to suppress enemies and unite popular support for Nazism. Hitler was fully committed to using violence to reach his goals and to eradicate Marxism from Germany, but he thought that any state sustained by coercion was ultimately doomed to failure. This chapter shows how the tactical use of violence fits into Hitler's understanding of domestic politics and political strategy at the time he wrote *Mein Kampf* while exploring the place of violence in Hitler's understanding of political legitimacy. The need for an alternative belief system to replace Marxism in the hearts and minds of German workers dictated a strategy based on organization and persuasion. Violence had its place, particularly in suppressing the Marxist leadership, but it had to be presented as a defensive response. Brutal repression of Marxists would evoke sympathy for them and fuel opposition unless it was backed by what Hitler called "spiritual weapons," which provided a just cause for violence.[1] Bismarck's battle against German socialism failed, Hitler wrote, because he relied too much on coercion while "there was no new worldview to fight for" in its place (Figure 5.1).[2]

Hitler's ultimate aim in *Mein Kampf* was unifying Germans as a nation, which Hitler thought possible only by first expunging Judeo-Bolshevism. He did not expect to accomplish this before taking power, but *Mein Kampf* does envision open, narrowly focused Storm Trooper (SA) violence against

FIGURE 5.1 *SA/Sturmabteilung storm troopers in action. Courtesy of the United States Holocaust Memorial Museum.*

communist-dominated precincts. The Beer Hall Putsch, Hitler wrote, had been "injurious from the viewpoint of the movement" for turning away from activism.[3] Hitler's new plan included provoking confrontations with German Communists (KPD) to justify violence in popular opinion as a defensive response. Storm Trooper activism in contested precincts provoked conflict that Hitler presented as "self-defense" of patriotic activity to win the hearts and minds of onlookers.[4] The Nazi Party (NSDAP) focused its violent attacks on the KPD, which was about half its size according to the popular vote during the early 1930s but which represented an effective target since it was so deeply and widely loathed, particularly by President Paul von Hindenburg and his fellow Conservative (DNVP) party members.

There are limits to the utility of force in *Mein Kampf* nonetheless. Hitler thought he could not take something as important as religion from the people by mere force, for example, without offering an acceptable replacement: only "fools or criminals" would remove a people's religion before offering a substitute that was "visibly better."[5] Effective force also had to be narrowly focused and ideologically legitimized to sidestep popular backlash. Naked repression would inadvertently strengthen opposition by turning valuable "Aryans" (ethnic Germans) into sympathizers who would then have to be exterminated:

> Experience shows that such a blood sacrifice affects the best part of a people, since any persecution that takes place without mental or spiritual preconditions [*geistige Voraussetzungen*] appears as morally unjustified

> and immediately whips up the more valuable stocks of a people to protest. . . . This will occur for many simply from a feeling of opposition against the attempt to crush an idea through raw force. . . . As a result, the number of inwardly-committed followers [of the opposition] grows in step as the persecution increases . . . a so-called "inner" cleansing can only take place at the cost of general impotence.[6]

Mein Kampf therefore positioned Nazi terror as legitimate self-defense and framed political violence as essentially Marxist. This legitimized Nazi terror because, as Hitler wrote, it was imperative to overcome force through even greater force applied with strategic precision. The side that failed to "fight poison gas with poison gas" was doomed to failure "by mathematical certainty."[7] A street fight against Communists that the Nazis controlled would signal German industrial workers in Marxist-dominated towns and cities that they could safely join the Nazi Party without fear of reprisals from their old communist masters. By provoking fights that appeared defensive, the SA displayed both strength and patriotic conviction. Hitler noted the effect of these displays on observers. For example, when his men forced a gang of communists to flee "we were greeted with cheers from all the windows."[8] The crowd forming on his side against the communists was his objective. This intersection of violence and politics was widely understood at the time. The communist Red Front Fighter's League founded in 1924 used a clenched fist to symbolize "protecting the friend, fighting off the enemy" alongside slogans such as "hit the fascists wherever you meet them."[9]

Nazi violence thereby cleared space for persuasion while reassuring workers that support and curiosity would be defended against reprisal. Nazism was certainly "more intense and extravagant in its violence" against Jews and social outsiders than other modern regimes. Ominously foreshadowing the Holocaust, Hitler wrote that German war sacrifices would have been justified had 12,000–15,000 Jews been gassed.[10] *Mein Kampf* outlines manifold applications of violence in foreign relations, "racial cleansing," and politics. However, in the context of domestic politics involving "Aryans," Hitler used defensively framed violence to build popular support and suppress political alternatives. *Mein Kampf* justifies Nazi violence as defensive by characterizing political terror as essentially Marxist from the outset. Illustrative of his early encounters with political violence, or so Hitler claimed, was his work on a Vienna building site with Marxists, who pressured him to join their organizations. He declined, describing how repugnant he found the cynical worldview of his Marxist coworkers toward nation and religion. Hitler instead confronted them on the intellectual battlefield:

> I argued, better informed each day about their own learning than my adversaries themselves, until one day, that means which obviously overcomes reason was brought to bear: terror, violence.[11]

A coworker presented Hitler with an ultimatum. Either leave the building site immediately or be thrown from the scaffold. Hitler departed. The basic premise that Marxism rested upon the threat of violence was established for the benefit of the reader, while the account of the scaffolding shows that Hitler shrank back from challenging a foe with naked force if that foe had the capacity to respond with greater force. The columns of protesting socialists that Hitler would watch snaking past the city hall during his time in Vienna suddenly took on a sinister new meaning of an implicit threat.[12]

The use of force against "Aryans" (ethnic Germans) was otherwise subordinated to Hitler's goal of mass movement and national unity in *Mein Kampf*. Forcing compliance among "valuable" Germans would only fuel opposition unless "spiritual weapons"—the justification for violence grounded in the narrative of a grand ideological confrontation between Nazism and Marxism—legitimized the exercise of force. Spiritual weapons were justifications grounded in this worldview that linked highly targeted and specifically rationalized exercises of legitimized violence to restoring national unity and securing Germany against culturally alien influences.

The provision of this alternate worldview was prerequisite to dispatching the misguided influences of Christianity and Marxism. Starting with the challenge to meet German workers on their own terms after Marxism had achieved dominance among that class, Hitler aimed to provide "spiritual weapons" that would simultaneously legitimize violent attacks to destroy Marxism and establish his alternative worldview as an acceptable substitute. Force without this substitute viewpoint resulted in a counterproductive bloodbath:

> The application of force alone, without the driving force of a basic intellectual belief as a prerequisite (*geistige Grundvorstellung als Voraussetzung*), can never lead to the extermination of an idea and its spread, other than as complete extermination of the last carrier and the destruction of the last tradition.[13]

Spiritual weapons ensured the necessary consistency and popular consent to crush rivals and alien influences using force. Effective use of force required this violent repression to be one tactic among many aligned in the pursuit of larger goals. Violence would only accomplish what Hitler envisioned where it kindled "a new thought, an idea or ideology":

> Every ideology . . . fights less for the negative extermination of the opposing world of ideas than for the positive realization of its own. . . . The struggle against an intellectual power by means of force remains defense so long as the sword does not appear as the representative, herald, and propagator of a new spiritual doctrine (geistige Lehre).[14]

Hitler's concept of political legitimacy, presupposing mass support for dictatorial rule as the instrument of popular will, compelled this tactical view of violence. The use of force had to be publicly perceived as legitimate. Hitler's populism informed this understanding by differentiating "between the state as a vessel and the race as the content" to situate legitimacy not in "obedience to weak superiors . . . but obedience to the *Volksgemeinschaft*."[15]

Effective violence to break the Marxist political monopoly thus had to be "representative, herald, and propagator" of the National Socialist alternative. Just the same, the Nazis were compelled to break the powerful social structures and forces that bound workers to Marxism—namely, the foundational cohesion of conformity. By 1932, noteworthy sectors of largely unorganized blue-collar workers in small-scale manufacturing and handicrafts voted for Hitler.[16] Two years later, in 1934, Rudolf Diels estimated that 70 percent of new SA members were former communists.[17] The sustaining wind at Hitler's back was this growing movement.

Mass Movement Authority as the basis of Legitimate Use of Force

Popular mass movement politics comprised the cornerstone of Hitler's political vision, enabling him to take power by means of Weimar's democratic constitution. In 1952, Alan Bullock, following Walter Langer in 1943, identified the centrality of mass movement politics in *Mein Kampf*, along with implications for Hitler's use of political violence. Langer identified Hitler's mass movement as a "reciprocal relationship": the people "stimulates" the Führer "and vice versa," he wrote. It was a "simple fact [for Hitler] that no great idea, no matter how sublime or exalted, can be realized in practice without the effective power which resides in the popular masses," Bullock wrote. A leader was thus someone who could "move masses." The reciprocal nature of the mass movement and Hitler's efforts to keep them under his sway set some checks on his use of force within the Reich, limiting the number of Germans Hitler could alienate rather than attract. To be sure, "violence and terror have their own propaganda value," Bullock wrote, adding that according to a *Mein Kampf* credo these must be used strategically in conjunction with "spiritual weapons," so that force appeared to serve a worthy goal rather than causing the people to identify with the victims of a violence they perceived as unfair.[18] Studies since Bullock and Langer have often overlooked *Mein Kampf*'s frequent use of the words "spiritual" and "spiritual weapons" that condition Hitler's thoughts on how force could be used effectively to rule his people. The heavy emphasis on the roots of the Holocaust is always central to interpreting *Mein Kampf*, while the contemporary rise of popular dictatorships returns our attention to these earlier studies of the ways that National Socialism relied on democratic institutions to gain power and then degrade them. If Eric Hofer's observations in 1951 are correct, mass movements serve psychological needs that are widespread among peoples, although the hatreds used to mobilize them are interchangeable. While pan-Germanism and anti-Semitism were not new ideologies, Hitler did pioneer government by fascism, one example of which is Hofer's mass movements that mobilize persons who feel powerless and long for change into a collective that elevates belief and fanaticism over reason and truth.[19]

Hitler lambasted Weimar's system for allowing the stupidity of majorities to decide politics, rather than the genius who inspired his followers to fight and expand through the power of an idea. All successful leadership was the work of the "visible protest of a genius against the inertia of the masses." A brilliant idea and plan were always preferable to following a majority "of sheep and empty heads." A parliamentarian might win through flattery or bribery, but he was then beholden to the "stupidity of his fellow citizens" in contradiction with decency, honesty, and conviction.[20] For Hitler, the more a leader stood out from the majority, the better he led.[21]

The relationship between mass movement, authority, and legitimate force in this system is anticipated at the outset of the *Mein Kampf*. Hitler considers the purpose and limits of instrumental force for achieving his aims in a chapter titled "Fundamental Thoughts on the Meaning and Organization of the SA." The three-part model for achieving authority presented there is reflected throughout *Mein Kampf*. The primary emphasis falls on the construction of a mass movement of supporters. This was the basic tactic in Hitler's strategy for taking control through legal means. With a mass movement that appeared to represent the majority already in place, Hitler wrote, force could then be exercised in a way that the masses would consider legitimate. The third and final pillar of authority in Hitler's model is the alignment of social norms with national policy, so that popular will and policy were one and the same. With authority resting first on popular consent with force then deployed to "stabilize" that support, the congruence of social customs and laws would achieve an authority that was indestructible.[22]

Hitler's goal of changing German attitudes and transfiguring behavioral norms was a complex operation done in large assemblies. Hitler saw the challenge of managing the masses as a kind of violent seduction, inveigling them into their most fanatical selves while swaying them toward his goals. In the throng, the dominance of the mass crushed all nonconformity, and individuals melded into the majority under the restraints of the crowd, whether they wanted to or not.

Nazi rallies and SA violence were all in service of winning this popular acclaim since states, in *Mein Kampf*, relied "not on laws for their protection or court sentences for deterrence . . . [but] rather on the general trust that the leadership and administration will and can bring about a commonwealth of values (*Gemeinwesens*)."[23] The foundation of authority was the people's "unshakable inner conviction in the altruism and honesty of the government and administration of a country as well as the agreement of the spirit of the laws with the feeling of general moral attitudes."[24] States without this were doomed "as in the long run systems of government will not be maintained through the pressure of force, [but] rather through the . . . representation and advancement of the interests of a people."[25]

Violence disrupted existing political structures to unify Germans into this new *Volksgemeinschaft.* A "movement, which has set itself the reestablishment of a German state with its own sovereignty as a goal, [must] orient its struggle completely upon winning over (*Gewinnung*) the broad masses."[26] "The national education of the broad mass" could only occur "through an indirect route of social improvement" as an "economic precondition . . . that allows individuals to take part in the cultural goods of the nation."[27] Drawing connections to the army as an example of altruistic state authority where "the best heads of the *Volksgemeinschaft* are brought to leading significance and influence," Hitler neatly summarized "our entire concept of the state to be: Authority of each leader below (*nach unten*) and responsibility above (*nach oben*)."[28] The political expression and essential prerequisite of this authority was mass movement. The streets served as a stage for the SA to act out this script prepared at mass meetings.

Violence as Political Communication

Following the failed Beer Hall Putsch, Hitler returned to his ideas from 1920 to 1922 for building power on a firm foundation of authority grounded in the popular mass movement.[29] Prominent in Hitler's reorganization of the Nazi Party beginning in early 1925, between his writing of the two volumes of *Mein Kampf*, was the creation of regional satraps (Gauleiters), charged with winning their people to Nazism.[30] In November 1926, Hitler finally turned to the subordinate political purpose of the SA, identified in his "first order to the SA" and mirrored in volume II of *Mein Kampf*. The order identifies principles for the use of violence in domestic politics reflected throughout the book.[31] Created in 1921 to protect Nazi meetings from disruption by superior force, the SA certainly did brutalize leaders of the political Left as well as Jews. However, given that violence had to appear legitimate yet always be used to counter aggressive force, the SA was not "to establish violence as its aim" but rather to "protect the messengers of the spiritual aim against oppression by violence."[32] SA men did not only bash heads but intimidated and drew support by choreographed marching in smart uniforms, sometimes even into church pews.[33] Just as many people voted for Hitler without hearing him speak, some communist precincts during the early 1930s also went for Hitler without bruising Nazi street battles. SA brawls with communists were a relatively minor tactic within Hitler's overall strategy for gaining support as the great man who would overthrow democracy and dissolve the shackles of the Versailles Treaty to bring Germany back to its rightful place.

Hitler's reorientation of the SA following the putsch focused on combat sports and public relations. First, Storm Troopers were to pursue physical education for "party purposes." Hitler ordered the SA to avoid military exercises, poison, and the sword in favor of learning jujitsu techniques of redirecting force and the boxer's strategic counterpunch.[34] Training in "boxing and jujistsu" would "inoculate the individual with conviction of his superiority" and "serve the defense of the movement as a weapon."[35] Second, the SA were to project a uniformed public presence for purposes "useful to the movement and known to the entire public."[36] Storm Troopers had to be schooled in how to represent "the great ideas of the movement" in their tasks.[37] The concern here was to sidestep a ban by destroying "any myth of a 'secret organization'" and elevating the struggle from an "atmosphere of petty revenge and conspiratorial action against the current state to the grandeur of an ideological war of extermination against Marxism and its constructs . . . for the establishment of a new National Socialist ethno-state."[38] Third, the "organizational formation," institutional culture in other words, as well as "clothing and armament" were to reject the military as a role model.[39] Hitler went on to expound how these directives would advance the movement through propaganda of the deed.

Terror, violence, and threat of violence for political ends were key elements of Nazi communication strategy. By winning Nazism the contested monopoly of violence in public perception, terror was both a precondition and engine of mass movement. Storm Trooper street fights were political theater to suppress and demoralize adversaries while emboldening supporters. A display of Nazi force would sway some of the crowds, which Hitler characterized in *Mein Kampf* as a feminine mass that was emotional and in search of a strong leader. These views guided Hitler's actions "in 1920 and 1921" with "such success, that we already had a considerable number of centuries in uniform by late autumn of 1922."[40] These gains were grounded in public spectacles that permitted the Nazis to position a show of force as a response to political persecution.

Hitler identified five psychological effects from observing street fights as the cornerstones of mass movement. First, violence created space for Nazism as a political alternative in Marxist-dominated precincts by limiting the influence of their organizations. Second, and directly related, violence activated suppressed supporters by extending protection against retaliation for breaking ranks. Third, defeating Marxist combat leagues demoralized their supporters across the party apparatus. Fear of being in the minority cut both ways and despair would ripple through the broader organization. The SA was "a pile driver in the red districts" preparing a foundation for Nazism.[41]

Two broader considerations treated terror as political theater to sway society at large. Fourth, simple dominance swayed the "feminine mass" waiting to see who would emerge victorious. This created a bandwagon effect on political weathervanes who sided with the strongest. Fifth, couched as "self-defense," violence displayed suitability for the government during the crises of Weimar. Willingness to sacrifice for the nation was considered necessary in the face of red scares accompanying the hyperinflation and the Great Depression.

Street fights thereby disrupted structures that governed working-class political support to clear space for persuasion. Neighborhoods and factories developed political orthodoxies as they came to be dominated by partisan unions and associations during the Weimar Republic. Nationalist workers stranded in Marxist-dominated places like Coburg, a Bavarian town, or the Neukölln district of Berlin, so Hitler thought, may well have sympathized with Nazism. But they could hardly be expected to support the cause with Marxist organizations regimenting their views. The labor union movement operated in conjunction with the broader "organization of the Marxist doctrine" to prepare "the masses for the political organization, indeed it whips them in with force and pressure."[42]

The psychological utility of violence to open this space and win support echoed through practical lessons drawn from the earliest days of the party. Breaking "coercion with coercion and terror with terror" would be necessary before "a new constructive state of affairs" could be created.[43] Nazism had made itself a target by attempting to "reclaim that mass, which had stood exclusively in the service of the international Marxist-Jewish and stock exchange parties."[44] Marxism was "determined to eliminate a movement that appeared dangerous to them by any means—the most effective in these cases [of public gatherings] being the same as always, terror, violence."[45] The fledgling movement had initially avoided appearing publicly "for fear of being beaten."[46] Hitler did not want

> to avoid this struggle, rather one must prepare for it and for this reason acquire the arms which alone offer protection against violence. Terror is not broken by spirit, but by terror. The success of the first meeting strengthened my position in this direction. Soon we had the courage for a second, already grown to a somewhat larger scale.[47]

Such "self-protection" communicated suitability for leadership amid the contested monopoly of violence. Hitler emphasized that "any gathering which relies exclusively on the police for its protection discredits the organizers in the eyes of the broad masses."[48] Inability to defend meetings translated into inability to defend supporters. The same way "a brave man will conquer the hearts of women easier than a coward, so the heroic movement wins the hearts of a people before the cowardly whose lives are only preserved by police protection."[49] Similar experiences with the first mass meetings at Circus Krone, where physical confrontation with Marxists further increased membership, convinced Hitler that the "psychologically correct leadership of meetings" depended on "self-protection" to communicate suitability for political leadership amid the revolutionary currents of Weimar politics.[50]

Hitler circled back to this mutually reinforcing interrelation between mass movement and violence throughout *Mein Kampf*. The "lesson of intolerance" taught by Marxist terror was instructive to him. The psyche of the broad masses

> is not receptive for anything halfhearted and weak.
>
> The same as women . . . [who] would rather bow to the strong than rule the weak, so too the masses love the ruler more than the supplicant, and inwardly feel more satisfied with a lesson that tolerates no others than by permissive liberal freedom.[51]

The SA brought both the positive alternative and the necessary muscle to stand their ground when they marched into red neighborhoods. Nazism was but one alternative during Weimar, and working-class men frequently changed allegiance between the SA and Proletarian Centuries as they explored options.

The information warfare around street violence translated these events into useful political narrative. Once again, Hitler presented the means to this end as essentially Marxist. The struggle to control the political narrative around violence ran up against "a creeping barrage of lies and slander" intended to sway the middle classes against Nazism. The "technical tools of social democracy" singled out "a certain symbol" until "the nerves of the attacked break and they, in order to have peace again, sacrifice the hated."[52] Any attempt to break Marxist terror with greater Nazi terror would bring

> horrible wails of bloody murder, as old disparagers of state authority shriek for it, in most cases in order to actually reach the[ir] goal in the general confusion—namely: they will find the herd [of supporters] of a senior official, who, in the stupid hope of perhaps making the feared opponent better inclined later, help break the adversaries of this world scourge (*Weltpest*).
>
> The impact of such a blow on the broad masses as well as followers and opponents can only be assessed by he who knows the soul of a people . . . from real life. As in the ranks of its followers, the victory gained counts as a triumph of the rightness of their own cause, in most cases the defeated opponent doubts in the success of further resistance entirely.[53]

Street fights were only one battlespace in the war for votes. But they were the frontline where Nazis and Marxists fought for ground, manifested guarantees of supporters' personal security, destabilized each other, projected strength to observers, and embodied altruistic claims through example.

The Law for the Protection of the Republic provided the backdrop to the first great act of political theater Hitler cited as proof of these concepts. An Article 48 state of exception beginning June 26, 1922, had suspended freedom of association, and to large extent freedom of speech, after a circle of right-wing plotters connected with *Freikorps* leaders assassinated Walter Rathenau. For ethno-nationalists, the deceased foreign minister—vilified thrice over as a Jew, industrialist, and principal architect of the reviled Fulfillment Policy normalizing relations based on Versailles—typified betrayal by cosmopolitan forces commanding the republic. The law passed on July 23, 1922, during the aftermath of his assassination, only provided ammunition to the anti-republican right.[54] Chancellor Wirth set the tone with his promulgation speech where he famously announced:

> There stands the enemy, who drips his poison into the wounds of a people. There stands the enemy, and there can be no doubt: This enemy stands to the right.[55]

Section 7, paragraph 4, of the new law was particularly thorny as it promised a jail sentence of three months to five years for "whosoever in a secret or subversive connection undertakes the effort to undermine the constitutionally established republican form of the Reich or a state, participates, or supports the undertaking in service as a member with advice and action, in particular with money."[56]

Criticism was swift from all sides. The future chancellor Wilhelm Marx had argued for an emergency decree rather than a law overriding the constitution. The minister president of Bavaria argued that invoking Article 48 was an entirely unnecessary intrusion on state rights and the statute unfairly targeted right-wing associations while ignoring the left. The German Democratic Party split from the Bavarian coalition government in response.[57] The stage was set for a "protest of all patriotic associations" on the Königsplatz in Munich.

As the patriotic associations processed onto the plaza, hundreds of Nazis bearing an array of battle standards accompanied by the pageantry of two marching bands made for "immeasurable excitement."[58] As Hitler remembered events:

> The success of the event was overwhelming, all the more so because, all red threats to the contrary, for the first time it was proven that nationalist Munich could also march on the street. Red republican defense associations, which attempted to attack the columns with terror, were routed with bloodied skulls within a few minutes by SA centuries. The nationalist movement had shown its determination for the first time from then on to make use of its right to the streets and thereby wrench this monopoly from the hands of the international traitors of the people and enemies of the fatherland.[59]

Memory of the Second Munich Soviet Republic led by a pair of Russian-born activists, not to mention the execution of bourgeois hostages as government troops crushed the insurrection, was still fresh. Hitler easily capitalized on this narrative even though the city had long been pacified by 1922 and Munich increasingly dominated by right-wing politics.[60] At any rate, the number of SA centuries doubled in short order after the event and provided the "indisputable evidence for the psychological and also organizational correctness of our conceptions about the development of the SA."[61]

The German Day in Coburg organized in October 1922 by the *Deutschvölkischer Schutz- und Trutzbund* as a protest against the same law was the second grand occasion. Coburg was considered a Marxist stronghold compared to the rest of Bavaria. The SPD had won 58.6 percent of the vote there in the first postwar Landtag election of February 1919. The Landtag elections of 1920 saw these numbers decline even as they remained above the state average. The Marxist parties captured 31 percent of the vote across Bavaria with a negligible 8.2 percent to the liberal German Democratic Party in July 1920. In Coburg the Marxist parties polled 9 percent higher at 40.1 percent while the DDP took a staggering 32.7 percent.[62] The characterization of Coburg as a "red fortress" is therefore something of an exaggeration. However, there was clear continuity in the Nazi worldview, where liberal republicans serving Jewish financiers worked hand in hand with the Marxist November Criminals.

"The Train to Coburg" confirmed lessons from the Königsplatz demonstration to become a founding myth of the Nazi Party. Hitler remembered it years later as a "landmark" in the rise of National Socialism.[63] Indeed, the Coburg Badge counted as the highest party award to outstrip even the Blood Order commemorating the putsch.[64] Hitler had seen an opportunity to expand NSDAP activity beyond Munich and negotiated a reduced registration fee for personally appearing at the event with roughly 650 men. A special train decked in swastika flags was commissioned to bear the participants north.[65] Warnings of coming "provocations" appeared in leftist newspapers leading up to the event. Veiled threats in the following days encouraged readers to give "the most effective support to the efforts of the authorities to avert provocative public rallies." Workers were to be conscious of their "historic task [as] protectors and guardians of the republican constitution."[66] When they arrived, the Nazis supposedly received "an order from the local unions as well as the Independent [Social Democratic] and Communist parties" forbidding entry to Coburg by train. The SA marched into town "with music ringing and flags waving" instead.[67]

The Nazi version of events recorded that a crowd of thousands threatened the procession with cries of "'murderers,' 'bandits,' 'robbers,' and 'criminals.'" Hounded by the mob, "fearful police organs" directed the column to the local Hofbräuhauskeller, where a brief siege saw the Nazis locked inside until the officers escorted them to their quarters on the edge of town. This time, Hitler claims, the crowd began to attack the column with cobblestones. "With that our patience was gone, and so a devastating hail fell left and right for ten minutes long, and fifteen minutes later there was nothing red to be seen on the streets."[68] Street fighting continued into the night. Once again, *Mein Kampf* records these incidents as ambushes on individual Nazis found by SA patrols "in horrible condition." Retaliation made "short process with the opponents. By the next morning the red terror which Coburg had suffered under for years was already gone."[69]

At this point, Hitler decided to force further confrontation with provocations. The leftist parties "with true Marxist-Jewish dishonesty" distributed leaflets organizing a demonstration against Nazi violence. The confrontation of the previous day had meanwhile swollen Nazi ranks to "one and a half thousand" men. Hitler, "firmly determined to deal with the red terror once and for all," decided to march out of town "over the great square where the red demonstration was supposed to occur." Crossing the square proved once again that "a few hundred" could overcome "tens of thousands."[70]

The lessons Hitler drew from his stylized retelling of Coburg are more important than any mythologized exaggeration. Crossing the square carved a memory of how "the anxious intimidated population slowly awoke, gained courage, dared to greet us with calls and in the evening at our departure broke out in spontaneous celebration in many places."[71] Subsequent events must have cemented this memory. The Socialist press certainly reinforced his impression as it reprinted headlines about "Coburg Under the Rule of Hitler: The Capitulation of State Force before the Hitler Guardsmen."[72] *Landtag* debates between the SPD opposition and BVP government pitted cries that the administration of justice had collapsed in Bavaria against a defense of equality before the law in the Nazi's right to assembly.[73] For Hitler the lessons about using political violence to build mass movement ran through Coburg like a red thread. The confrontation had sent a message to workers who had observed events:

> A portion of the Marxist working class, who in any case must only be seen as seduced themselves, learned through the fists of National Socialist workers to understand that these workers also fight for ideals, as experience shows one only fights (*schlägt*) for something that one believes and loves.

Taking back the streets had further "re-established equality of citizens before the law for the first time since 1914."[74] It legitimized the Nazi claim to the monopoly of violence since "only democracy moans that one could dare . . . to counter a brutal attack with fists and clubs instead of pacifist songs." It undermined the republican claim that "the state protects the lives of its citizens, as this was not true then at least; because the citizens had to defend themselves against the representatives of the current state at that time."[75] However, without a propaganda machine to translate events, the bourgeois press was "mean, as always, and only a few decent newspapers hailed the fact that at least someone had finally put a stop to the Marxist highwaymen."[76] Nationalist, völkisch, and veterans' groups had united behind a new *Ortsgruppe* in Coburg nonetheless persuaded that Hitler could steer Germany onto a new course.[77] Terror had broken terror and swayed the political loyalties of the onlooking masses.

The results brought home these lessons. From its founding in January 1923, the Coburg *Ortsgruppe* grew from nothing to 600 members by September to constitute 1.9 percent of the town's population.[78] Most importantly, though, the strategy was repeatable:

> We now went systematically into all places in which the red terror had prevented gatherings of dissenters, to break this, and re-establish freedom of assembly. Battalions were mustered in such places, and gradually in Bavaria one red fortress after another fell victim to National Socialist propaganda.[79]

SA ranks had meanwhile grown to 5,000 men by the end of year. Coburg had defined the Nazi strategy of political violence to build a mass movement. Only the French occupation of the Ruhr had derailed this "logical development" and forced the movement from "its track up to this point."[80]

The SA was both a primary instrument and an object lesson of "defensive" violence as political communication in *Mein Kampf*. On the one hand, Hitler was backing away from the failed strategy of a paramilitary coup and reasserting authority over the SA. On the other, he was returning to an earlier strategy of building support through street fights from before the organization had militarized in response to the French occupation of the Ruhr. Underpinning all of this was a belief that "the people always see ruthless attack on an adversary as proof of their own rightness, and perceive the abandonment of extermination of the other as insecurity in relation to their own rightness, if not as a sign of their own injustice."[81] Street violence as a public spectacle had already proven this regionally and would serve to build a national mass movement going forward.

Conclusion

Mein Kampf treats violence as a tactic to build a mass movement rather than an end unto itself essential to fascism. This was based on Hitler's understanding that authority flowed from a popular will and his concern to preserve "valuable" Germans. The state's use of violence against its own people had to be narrowly focused, publicly legitimized as a defensive response to an attack, and popularly accepted. "Spiritual weapons" grounded in the Nazi worldview of a titanic struggle against Marxism justified these highly targeted exercises of force to realize utopia. The SA did not always understand or adhere to Hitler's principles that force should be generally perceived as legitimate, but he justified their "excesses" as essentially defensive.

Following the failed Beer Hall Putsch, which Hitler considered injurious to establishing a mass movement as the primary pillar of his authority, Hitler returned with a clear focus on ideas that he had articulated from 1920 to 1922 for establishing power through popular acclaim. This is evinced in Hitler's so-called first order to the SA of November 1926, which emphasizes their role as building his movement by convincing Germans to turn to Nazism while eschewing even the appearance of another coup. Coming almost two years after he had begun reorganizing the Nazi Party with the aim of securing support and winning elections, Hitler's 1926 order to the SA emphasized the organization's subordination to the larger party framework in light of Hitler's decision to take power through legal means.

Mein Kampf posits that national unity was only attainable by expunging Judeo-Bolshevism and absorbing workers into the Nazi mass movement. Toward these ends, a calculated use of SA street fights as political theater opened access to working-class voters. Suppressed supporters could be activated, active Marxists could be suppressed, and Nazi suitability for power publicly displayed. The chains of the Marxist parties could be cast away. Workers, taking cues from their comrades, could safely express support. Middle-class voters would welcome the suppression of revolutionary threats. The apolitical would turn to the strong. The resulting mass movement would ultimately reshape social values, as throngs flocking to Nazism crushed nonconformists remaining in their midst.

The mass movement was a work in progress. Hitler monitored the popular mood to ensure its forward momentum, and the process of building it was never more complete than the construction of the *Volksgemeinschaft* itself. The struggle to construct the Nazi Reich could not be won with violence alone. *Mein Kampf* asserts that people would willingly sacrifice but only for a higher cause. Hitler thought money could never motivate total self-sacrifice, although the cause of nation could. Political violence was but one step in Hitler's overall strategy. Political violence was but one step in Hitler's overall strategy. An instrument for use within the stages of his planning to be discarded after achieving true authority. Ultimately, Hitler thought, the judiciary and its processes would be replaced by a totalitarian Nazi society with sanctions for nonconformity grounded in popular acclaim.

PART III

Eugenics and Aesthetics in *Mein Kampf*

From the beginning of Hitler's reign till its fiery end, purification of the German people was at the center of the Führer's concerns. Purification would take two forms: exclusion of alleged genetic inferiors, who would be sterilized; and exclusion of despised racial groups like the Jews and the Roma, who would be stripped of their rights and segregated. When these solutions proved unsatisfactory to the Nazis, both groups would ultimately be murdered.

Two years before his appointment as Chancellor, Hitler declared that sterilization was "the most humane act for mankind." He urged his audience to put aside their squeamishness about it. Leading German eugenicists Fritz Lenz and Ernst Rüdin applauded Hitler's view that the genetically unfit should be rendered incapable of reproducing. For them, Hitler was the only politician to stress "the importance of eugenics . . . to all intelligent Germans."

Eugenics (meaning "well-born") had been an international movement since the late nineteenth century, when the term was coined by Francis Galton. At the simplest level, eugenics aims at improving the health of the population through government policy. Historically, it has consisted of two kinds distinguished by their radicality. The milder form of eugenics, or "positive" eugenics, sought to promote the reproduction of persons with "high-value" genetics. The more extreme variant, or "negative" eugenics, focused instead on rooting out persons considered racially damaged or biologically unfit by means of sterilization and prohibiting them from marrying. Already in his two volumes of *Mein Kampf*, Hitler was a firm proponent of negative eugenics, references to which pepper its pages.

As with his grotesque anti-Semitism, hatred of democracy, anti-Slavism, imperialist urges, and similar ideas expressed in *Mein Kampf*, Hitler's eugenics was not especially new. Late nineteenth-century eugenicists throughout the world generally accepted the notion that the state should propagate the "racially valuable" elements of the population. In his award-winning treatise *Vererbung und Auslese im Lebenslauf der Völker* (Inheritance and Selection in the Life Cycle of the Peoples, 1903), Wilhelm Schallmayer, the cofounder (with Alfred Ploetz) of the eugenics movement in Germany, advocated a "qualitative population policy" aiming at the "greater procreation of the generatively more valuable elements of the population" while simultaneously reducing "to the most minimal level possible the increase of the mentally and physically weak." Writing in 1921, Fritz Lenz declared the main goal of "racial hygiene"—a synonym in Germany for eugenics—to be the "greater procreation of the genetically superior" and the restriction in the increase of the "genetically inferior." At the time of Hitler's putsch, Lenz occupied the first chair in Germany for racial hygiene at the University of Munich.

The Nazis wasted little time implementing aggressive eugenic policies once they seized power. In January 1934, a mandatory sterilization law went into effective, the "Law for the Prevention of Offspring with Hereditary Diseases," allowing the state to sterilize Germans suffering from genetic illnesses like mental retardation and schizophrenia, among others. Applications for sterilization would be received by new hereditary health courts attached to local courts of general jurisdiction. A positive finding by the courts would authorize local health authorities to institute measures to sterilize affected persons, with or without their consent. A finding of a relevant disease was not by itself sufficient to justify sterilization; the main criterion was whether the person was socially useful to the German people. In the years following passage of the sterilization law, most of its victims (52.9 percent) were considered "feeble-minded" (retarded), followed by schizophrenia (25.4 percent) and epilepsy (14 percent).

Hitler's preoccupation with eugenics is coextensive with his attitude toward art; both are firmly linked in his thought. A fascist aesthetics formed the two sides of the eugenic coin. On the one side, Hitler's ideal of beauty followed the banal standards of the folk-national right of his era, which were explicitly based on classical age Greece. The German nationalist art historian Julius Langbehn, with whose writings Hitler was likely familiar, declared as much in his influential 1890 work *Rembrandt als Erzieher* (Rembrandt as Educator): "War and art [are] a Greek, a German, slogan; it finds its most exquisite embodiment in the epos of a specific Aryan style of poetry; and Homer's *Iliad* is its earliest expression." Hans F. K. Günther, a prominent eugenicist influential among Nazi race theorists, wrote in *Rassenkunde des deutschen Volkes* (Racial Science of the German People, 1922) that the Nordic person was "the measure of beauty." This ideal exuded health, strength, balance, proportion, and clarity.

On the other side of the eugenic coin was inscribed Hitler's conception of ugliness, which he associated with mental and physical disease. Inspired by Hitler's aesthetics, the Nazis would condemn much of modern art as "degenerate," a label that, once applied, qualified a work of art for censure and destruction. Dadaism, Cubism, Impressionism, Expressionism—all are singled out for vilification in *Mein Kampf*. Were these movements and their misbegotten products to gain traction with the public at large, Hitler writes, it would signify a "degeneration of the human mind."

Who was to be blamed for the hideous deformations of modern art? The Jews, of course. "[The Jew] contaminates art, literature, theater, besots natural feeling, overthrows all ideas of beauty and grandeur, nobility and goodness, and drags downwards human beings under the influence of his swinish mentality," Hitler wrote in volume II of *Mein Kampf*. The charge that the Jews strove to ruin the noblest ideals of Western culture was commonplace among the anti-Semitic right. According to Nazi Party ideologue Alfred Rosenberg, the Nordic ideal of beauty as expressed by Günther was under attack by the Jews, a group devoted to a "systematic" plan to annihilate it. By 1937 the Nazis had organized an exhibition of so-called Degenerate Art intended to hold masterpieces of modern art up to public ridicule. With their claims that modern artists were "Jewish Bolsheviks" conspiring to destroy German values of beauty and decency, the promoters of the exhibit placed themselves in rigid lockstep with *Mein Kampf*.

Mein Kampf's reflections on eugenics and aesthetics in both art and music show that Hitler, well before the start of the Second World War, was already a radical perched uneasily on the edge of a precipice. Only a push was needed to tip him over that edge into mass murder and genocide.

6

Mein Kampf

Race, Blood, and the Holocaust

John J. Michalczyk

The notion of race played a key role in scientific discussion of the nineteenth century in Europe, and in Germany in particular as *Rassenhygiene*, promoted by Alfred Ploetz and Wilhelm Schallmayer and a host of other scientists. In the early twentieth century, other Germans took up the issue such as eugenicists including Eugen Fischer, Fritz Lenz, and Erwin Baur, who published a two-volume work in 1921, *Menschliche Erblichkeitslehre und Rassenhygiene* (Principles of Human Heredity and Racial Hygiene), which became a type of doctrinal text on racial issues in 1933 when Hitler came to power as chancellor. Eugen Fischer would feature as a link between early race studies as founder of the Society of Racial Hygiene in Freiberg in 1908 and the Nazi policies of racial hygiene as director of the Kaiser Wilhelm Institute of Anthropology, Human Heredity and Eugenics.[1] While incarcerated in the Landsberg prison, "the Fortress," in 1924, Hitler had already some familiarity with the work of this trio of racial scholars who supported eugenics principles including sterilization.

Almost a century later, race has again become the political, legal, and cultural focus in Europe and especially in America, impacting both Germany and the United States with white supremacy and virulent anti-Semitism on the rise. In 2018, white supremacists in Chemnitz, Germany, attacked the Schalom Restaurant, alarming citizens with their slogan, "Get out of Germany, Jewish pigs." The country further faced the rise of white supremacist and extremist movements when the government discovered neo-Nazis in the ranks of the military in 2020 as did the United States in

2021 following an assault on the US Capitol on January 6, 2021, to reverse a legal election process. White supremacists wore tee-shirts at the insurrection bearing anti-Semitic messages such as "Camp Auschwitz: Work Brings Freedom," while earlier the Proud Boys sported shirts marked "6MWE"—Code for "Six Million Wasn't Enough."

Anti-Semitism has not disappeared almost a century after the appearance of *Mein Kampf*, and in fact it has increased dramatically since 2016. In Charlottesville, Virginia, in the summer of 2017, marching demonstrators of a "Unite the Right" gathering chanted, "Jews will not replace us!" and "Blood and Soil." Hitler supported both notions, although separately over the years, and allusions to them already existed as part of *Mein Kampf*. Hitler's belief in these ideas already existed as part of *Mein Kampf* and evoked the fear that minorities will remove those from their "rightful" status as proud individuals of a white European stock. At the same time, the white supremacists in Charlottesville carried TIKI torches not unlike those in the nighttime Hitler rallies viewed in Leni Riefenstahl's *Triumph of the Will* (1935). In *Mein Kampf*, a blatant manifesto of fear-mongering, Hitler, somewhat paranoid both on paper and in his speeches, raises the alarm in his replacement belief about the Jewish domination of the Aryans as he writes, "And the development we are going through today, if continued unobstructed, would fulfill the Jewish prophecy—the Jew would really devour the peoples of the earth, would become the master."[2] His conspiracy theory further reinforces this in his scare tactics about the "Jewish tendency of world conquest,"[3] a rampant fear dramatized earlier by the fabricated *Protocols of the Elders of Zion*.

The Charlottesville "blood and soil" slogan of the white supremacists recalls the National Socialist call for purity of blood as well as the recognition of the land as theirs. For Hitler, this land also must be geographically extended, later referred to as *Lebensraum* (Figure 6.1).[4]

The Charlottesville white supremacists' chants about "soil" (*Boden*) further evoke Hitler's view that "the soil exists for the people which possess the force to take it," alluding to the power of the dominant race, the Aryans.[5] Early on in *Mein Kampf*, Hitler already raises the issue of blood and soil: "Germany-Austria must return to the great mother country. . . . One blood demands one Reich."[6] Hitler's notion of extending German land in 1924–5 results in action at the annexation of Austria in 1938. With the removal of the Jews in a "Juden-frei" Europe as well as Aryan domination of the continent, Hitler's mindset in *Mein Kampf* serves as a major preliminary step toward the Shoah, suggesting that if the National Socialists come to power, this qualifies as a basic objective.

The concept of race and its symbolic manifestation, blood, can be best understood as a blend of physiological, cultural, and behavioral elements common to a group of people. In *Mein Kampf*, Hitler absorbs the earlier thinking on race and blood purity from a wide array of eugenicists, historians, biologists, anthropologists, and other right-wing writers, as Othmar

FIGURE 6.1 *"Blut und Boden" ("Blood and Soil") was the 1930s slogan for a program that combined racial ideals with the land. Courtesy of the United States Holocaust Memorial Museum.*

Plöckinger writes in his chapter, in order to create his own *Weltanschaung*. Few, like Schopenhauer, Ford, or Chamberlain, are even referenced as a source of his thinking.[7] The connections of race to the American eugenics movement and racial thinking in Germany were developed by various scholars like Stefan Kühl, Edwin Black, Paul Wielding, and James Q. Whitman along with a host of others. On occasion this chapter will touch upon the interflow of racial beliefs between the two countries to show the communality of racist attitudes and laws, as Isabel Wilkerson poignantly indicates in her masterful work *Caste: The Origins of Our Discontents*[8] with striking similarities in India, Nazi Germany, and Jim Crow America.

For Hitler, the time spent in the Landsberg prison was a period of serious reflection, reading and writing. He utilized this time as well to follow the eugenics movement in Germany and America. According to Franz Hemmrich, a guard at "the Fortress," Hitler had access to many volumes of works offered by his guests, some listed by Timothy Ryback in *Hitler's Private Library*, including eugenics writings and current literature on political and ideological philosophies.[9] At the turn of the twentieth century approximately thirty countries focused on eugenics as a solution to the social ills of society. Germany already established its own eugenics approach to race in the studies of *Rassenhygiene*, promoted by Alfred Ploetz from 1895 in his writing about the fear of degeneration of society if the country did not adhere to eugenics principles. The Americans soon appeared to be taking a lead in the movement at one point, and Hitler admired the mandatory state sterilization laws in America, according to Benno Mueller-Hill.[10] Hitler scoured texts in German that quoted eugenicists like Paul Bowman Popenoe, author of *Applied Eugenics* (1918) and a dynamic advocate for the obligatory sterilization of the mentally disabled. Hitler later admired Leon Whitney, president of the American Eugenics Society, who further promoted mandatory sterilization of the mentally disabled. Hitler, like Whitney, decried the mixture of the races. It was the racial ideas of Madison Grant's *Passing of the Great Race or The Racial Basis of European History* (1916) that had an impact later on Hitler, ideas already seriously discussed by the *völkish* movement, although the German translation of Grant came out too late to be influential in the writing of *Mein Kampf*. In his Thiersch Street apartment Hitler had a 1916 copy of Grant's text in German translation published by Julius Lehmann in 1925. The fourth edition of the book had an inscription to Hitler by Lehmann.

Some of the earlier studies of race go as far back as Arthur de Gobineau (1816–62), the author of *Essai sur l'inégalité des races humaines* (Essay on the Inequality of the Human Races, 1853), who believed Germans were the best examples of the Aryan race. For him, they stood out as the finest example of human development. Gobineau also believed that blood was at the core of civilization, something Hitler believes and interprets in anti-Semitic terms in *Mein Kampf*—the general notion that the threat of the presence of Jews hinders the progress of civilization. John Nale writes,

> Analyzing the notion of race deployed in Arthur de Gobineau's *Essai sur l'inégalité des races humaines*, I argue that Gobineau's notion of racial types goes well beyond physical characteristics. In particular, his understanding of racial blood is not that of a physical substance one might analyze empirically. Instead, Gobineau understands "blood" to be the common bond that unifies a civilization, a substance that is best studied historically and discursively rather than biologically. In this context, blood refers to the common values, spirit, and history Gobineau feels are essential to any civilization.[11]

In referring to the purity of blood, Hitler may have both the physical and more metaphorical notion in mind in his thinking and writing.

Othmar Plöckinger, one of the coeditors of *Hitler, Mein Kampf: Eine kritische Edition* (2016), offers some nuance to Gobineau's reasoning:

> In my opinion Gobineau is a complicated case—he was seen as an early and important promotor of a race-based interpretation of history. For this he received general recognition in the volkish movement. But in detail he was criticised harshly by other volkish authors like Houston Stewart Chamberlain, e. g., because of a false/weak concept of "races" or a lack of (racial) anti-Semitism. Hitler certainly knew his name and the main ideas of his work, but it seems questionable if he took the time to

> read it as it had four volumes. Furthermore, Gobineau is not mentioned in any of Hitler's speeches or writings.[12]

Timothy Ryback's *Hitler's Private Library* does not include a Gobineau citation; however, Ryback does indicate that Houston Stewart Chamberlain (1855–1927) read with a passion the work of Gobineau on race. Ryback nonetheless does point out that Hitler borrowed Chamberlain's *Foundations of the Nineteenth Century*, published in German in 1889 as *Die Grundlagen des neunzehnten Jahrhunderts*, from Friedrich Krohn's lending library in Munich.[13] Chamberlain's monumental work sets in opposition in an epic struggle the white Christian European world to the Semitic world, reflected in part in *Mein Kampf*, dedicated to the anti-Semitic Dietrich Eckart.[14] Eckart, early Nazi Party philosopher prior to Alfred Rosenberg and mentor to Hitler, provided him with a solid understanding of Chamberlain's thinking.

In Hitler's view, post–First World War Germany serves as a battleground for an apocalyptic conflict between the Aryan and Jewish races. Bolshevik Jews, the physically and mentally disabled, the Slavs, and the Afro-Germans would soon be added to the ranks of the destroyers of the purity of the Aryan race. Hitler considers above all the Aryan race as superior and perceives a significant threat from the inferior Jews who have "polluted" or "contaminated" the Volk with their very being, as he fears, "the poison of the international world Jew."[15] His prewar exposure to Jews with their kaftans in Vienna, where he looked at them as filthy and disgusting, results in his view of them in *Mein Kampf* as "scum,"[16] as well as "dirty and false."[17]

In 1934, Rudolph Hess, who spent prison time with Hitler in Landsberg, said that "National Socialism is nothing but applied biology," alluding to the fact that Nazi Germany is in essence a racial state. A decade prior, in this battleground of Germany we see the embryo of this racial state as an apocalyptic racial conflict which transpires between Aryan and Jew, as David Redles writes in our work. In the racial scheme of things, Hitler advances earlier notions of degrees of racial value to its peoples, placing the Nordic Aryan at the top, and the Jew, Roma/Sinti, Slav, and African-German at the bottom. He reinforces the notion of the Aryan as one of pure blood, although the concept of "Aryan" is more complex.[18] For Hitler, "Aryan" lies in direct correlation with the concept of a Northern European of pure stock, who aided in the progress of civilization. The Aryan in Hitler's mind has come to be endangered on all fronts and must confront the invasive forces—the religious and cultural elements of the Jews and political machinations of the Marxists. The notion of Aryanism further implies racial separatism echoing some of the ideas of Gustaf Kossinna (1858–1931), a German archaeologist and ethnohistorian, a proponent of *Nordische Gedanke* (Nordic Thought). Some adherents of this notion of Nordicism include Houston Stewart Chamberlain, Madison Grant, and Karl Penka, an Austrian anthropologist.[19]

A September-October 1932 *Eugenical News* article praised Hitler for the eugenics principles he advocated. The article notes, "The Hitler movement sooner or later promises to give him full power [and] will bring the Nordic movement general recognition and promotion by the state."[20] This Nordic movement reflects the Aryan at the pinnacle of the evolutionary process. Hitler writes:

> It is idle to argue which race or races were the original representative of human culture and hence the real founders that we sum up under the word "humanity." It is simpler to raise this question with regard to the present, and here an easy, clear answer results. All the human culture, all the results of art, science, and technology that we see before us today, are almost exclusively the creative product of the Aryan.[21]

Hitler continues by calling the Aryan "the Prometheus of mankind," whose genius helps Man "to climb the path to mastery over the other beings of the earth."[22] Hitler often claims in a Social Darwinian sense that the Aryan over the centuries, due to various challenges and trying conditions, has been able to rise above them, survive racially, and improve society. The Aryan thus has been and is "the bearer of human cultural development."[23] In his continued development, the Aryan has encountered lower peoples and "subjugated them and bent them to his will."[24] He "regulated their practical activity under his command,"[25] indicating that the Aryan was destined to be the superior, dominant species. Hitler goes further than a focus on the individual Aryan and views his nobility through his self-sacrifice for the greater good, the community, and, if the hour demands, even sacrifices his life. "In him the instinct of self-preservation has reached the noblest form. Since he willingly subordinates his own ego to the life of the community."[26]

In this racial, political, and cultural struggle, Hitler judges the Jews as subhuman, thereby oversimplifying the concept of "Jew" throughout *Mein Kampf* by denying its individual characteristics of nationality, faith, culture, ethnicity, heritage, or language. In the early days of the Nazi Party, on September 16, 1919, he already addressed the Jewish Question in a letter to Adolph Gemlich in racial and anti-Semitic terms. He characterized the Jews in his letter absolutely as a race and not a religious association and referred to the Jews as "race-tuberculosis of the peoples," a kind of disease-related language he would use in *Mein Kampf*. He further wrote about eliminating the Jewish people from Germany through legal means: "The ultimate objective [of such legislation] must, however, be the irrevocable removal of the Jews in general."[27] A year before he began drafting *Mein Kampf*, in an interview with German-American National Socialist sympathizer George Sylvester Vierek, for the *American Monthly*, Hitler remarked that it was necessary to "disenfranchise" the Jew in order "to protect the integrity of our race." He called Jews "destructive," "an alien people," and referred to them as a "mixed breed" that is "a worthless product."[28]

Hitler soon after reiterated this goal of the removal of Jews from the nation in an address to a massive crowd in the Munich Hofbrauhaus on

February 24, 1920. The political meeting also marked the birth of the National Socialist German Workers' Party (NADSP). At this gathering of approximately 2,000 people, the 25 Points of the Nazi Party of Anton Drexler and Hitler set out a potential blueprint or political program for the movement, including Germany's defiance of the Versailles Treaty and German citizenship based on blood. One reads in Point 4 that no Jew may be a citizen of the nation, already marginalizing the Jews: "Only a member of the race can be a citizen. A member of the race can only be one who is of German blood, without consideration of creed. Consequently, no Jew can be a member of the race." In the following point those noncitizens must be considered as foreigners and aliens. Once in power, Third Reich legislation would soon deprive the Jews of German citizenship.

In two instances in *Mein Kampf* Hitler goes even further by wishing for the elimination of "the vermin" and "corrupters," at this point only metaphorically. Recalling his wartime experiences, he compares the deaths of German soldiers to the removal of Jews: "If the best men were dying at the front, the least we could do was wipe out the vermin."[29] Near the close of *Mein Kampf*, almost as if were prophetic, Hitler suggests that if the German soldiers at the front were being gassed by the Allies and dying, it would have redeemed their deaths if the Jews were similarly gassed: "If at the beginning of the War and during the War, twelve or fifteen thousand of these Hebrew corrupters of the people had been held under poison gas, as happened to hundreds of thousands of our very best German workers in the field, the sacrifice of millions at the front would not have been in vain."[30] Hitler's logic is skewed in seeing that the gassing of Jews would redeem the deaths of German soldiers on the battlefields of the First World War. At this point he may not reflect genocidal beliefs but he does hold that the Jewish peril must be seriously confronted. Richard Weikart indicates that Darwinian followers believed that even up to the First World War, respected members of society like Rudolf Cronau, the German-American painter and journalist, and others believed that "lower races," for Hitler the Jews, should be eliminated to improve humanity, since the goal of applying eugenics was for the betterment of society:

> [Rudolf] Cronau-along with a host of leading scientists, physicians, and social thinkers who embraced Darwinian social explanations and eugenics in the late nineteenth and early twentieth centuries thus argued that the key to progress was the annihilation of the "lower races," who stood in the way of advanced culture and civilization. Some social Darwinist thinkers went further, arguing that racial extermination, even if carried out by bloody means, would result in moral progress for humanity.[31]

Joachm Fest cites Hitler's speech in 1942, which echoes the need to rid Germany of the *Untermenschen*:

> Nature is cruel; therefore we are also entitled to be cruel. When I send the flower of German youth into the steel hail of the next war without feeling the slightest regret over the precious German blood that is being spilled, should I not also have the right to eliminate millions of an inferior race that multiplies like vermin?[32]

The roots of Hitler's anti-Semitism running deeply into Germany's history and politics prior to his incarceration and the writing of *Mein Kampf* brought about the tragedy of the Shoah. Hitler often irrationally considers Jews as a menacing race attempting global domination in all spheres of human life, and with Joseph Goebbels later, he promoted this rabid anti-Semitism through highly focused propaganda. Ideologue Alfred Rosenberg's 1930 bestseller *Der Mythus des 20. Jahrhunderts* (The Myth of the Twentieth Century) later captured key racial beliefs of Houston Stewart Chamberlain, which promoted the racial dominance over the inferior Jewish Bolsheviks. Julius Streicher, through his perverse publication *Der Stürmer*, further reinforced these notions in racial ideology and imagery. The stage was set for the extermination of the imminent subhuman threat to Aryan purity and the protection of the well-being of the nation.

Germany as a National and Human Body

In terms of purity of blood, throughout *Mein Kampf* Hitler conceives of Germany as a human body or organism with blood pulsating through it. Furthermore, he conceives of the country as a "national organism: A Germanic State of the German Nation."[33] The health of this "national body" or organism is imperiled by germs, tumors, parasites, and viruses coming from outside into the once healthy body of Germany. The purity of blood must be maintained so a healthy Germany can survive. When Hitler assumed power as chancellor, he undertook steps to create a healthy national body that he perceived in *Mein Kampf* as suffering from a world sickness caused by the Jews in all sectors of society. The Jewish doctors and other professionals were soon eliminated from the profession through the April 1933 Law for the Restoration of the Professional Civil Service; the Jewish doctors were further not allowed to administer to Aryans. The Aryan doctors of pure blood could then take on the chief role of healing the German nation-body.[34] Bringing up the sickened nature of an ailing Germany in post–First World War Germany, Hitler views himself as the potential healer of a diseased Germany. On July 10, 1941, Hitler mentioned to his confidant, diplomat, and liaison officer from the Reich Foreign Office Walter Hewel, "I feel like I am the Robert Koch of politics. He discovered the bacillus and thereby ushered medical science onto new paths. I discovered the Jew as the bacillus and fermenting agent of all social decomposition." Robert Koch (1843–1910), the late nineteenth-century microbiologist and physician, discovered bacterial causes of tuberculosis and cholera. Hitler made the parallel of discovering the Jew that caused the unhealthy state of Germany, for "his existence is as bad as the plague."[35] As with Albert Camus's allegorical novel *La Peste* (The Plague, 1947), the plague must be first detected, understood, and confronted.[36] "The cure of a sickness can only be achieved if its cause is known, and the same is true of curing political evils."[37] The following year, on February 22, 1942, Hitler enjoyed a dinner with Himmler and a Danish Sturmbannfuehrer from the Viking Division. Hitler continued this obsession with Koch, claiming that he had discovered the Jew as the virus plaguing society and demanding that the Jew must be removed:

> The discovery of the Jewish virus is one of the greatest revolutions that has taken place in the world. The battle in which we are engaged today is of the same sort as the battle waged by Pasteur and Koch. How many diseases have their origin in the Jewish virus!. . . . We shall regain our health only by eliminating the Jew.[38]

Roman Töppel, in his essay "Volk und Rasse," indicates that Hitler is hardly original in the assertion of his discovering the Jew as the bacillus destroying German society. "The defamation of Jews as 'bacillus' and 'germs' was likewise nothing new among antisemites, any more than the belief that 'solving the Jewish question' was the key to society's 'return to health.'"[39] Töppel further mentions that Theodor Fritsch (1852–1933), a rabid anti-Semitic political scientist, gathered nineteenth-century anti-Semitic conspiratorial quotes for his 1893 publication *Handbuch der Judenfrage* (Handbook on the Jewish Question), a work Hitler recalls reading during his early years in Vienna.[40]

In his work on Nazi medicine, Paul Weindling illustrates Hitler's thinking by showing how the imagery of the Jew represents "alien bacteria" and "racial poison."[41] Hitler's mission in the Third Reich will be to offer an antidote, which restores the health of the country that he views as "sick and rotten,"[42] affirming that he alone can heal the nation and make Germany superior again.

Hitler etched these themes of purity of blood and the ostracizing of plague-ridden Jews into *Mein Kampf* and into the hearts and minds of his followers in the National Socialist Party through a racial perspective. This was followed by anti-Semitic laws, as in the Nuremberg Laws of September 1935, and political violence that led to the extermination of Jews, Roma/ Sinti, homosexuals, Jehovah's Witnesses, and others in the Shoah. The demonstrators in Charlottesville believed, as did Hitler and his followers, that they fight in the struggle for survival as Aryan descendants of early white Europeans who are threatened by the Jew, who is a pollutant to society. The Charlottesville white supremacists and the adherents of National Socialism both abide by a territorial imperative that will try to protect them from this onslaught. In their minds, the white race must be protected at all costs!

Beyond Darwin

In 1859, little did Charles Darwin (1809–82) know that the publication of *The Origins of Species: By Means of Natural Selection or the Preservation of Favoured Species in the Struggle for Life* would lay the foundation for a discussion of the preservation of a species by his half-cousin Sir Francis Galton (1822–1911), the originator of the eugenics movement. Nor would he have fully realized that his work on the nonhuman world of nature would pave the way for a belief in a superior human race, the Aryan, and an inferior race, the Jew. Later, Blacks, Roma/Sinti, and mixed races would fall under the rubric of being a non-Aryan and therefore belonging to an inferior race or species, hence disposable. These members of the inferior race would soon be considered as "subhuman" by eugenicist Theodore Lothrop Stoddard (1883–1950), whose *The Revolt against Civilization: The Menace of the Subhuman* (1922) when translated into the German read *Der Kulturumsturz: Die Drohung des Untermenschen* (1925). The term "Untermensch" became widely used by the Nazis to label the so-called inferior species. The acclaimed paleontologist Heinrich Georg Bronn in April 1860 translated Darwin's controversial text into German. Zoologist and anthropologist Ernst Haeckel, the "German Darwin," further promoted the theories of evolution and theorized that there were superior and inferior species. The evolutionary line between Charles Darwin and Adolf Hitler is long and meandering, but the concept of a "favoured species" remains front and center in Hitler's autobiography and personal, political vision of a greater Germany.

Darwin sets this "favoured species" in a lifelong "struggle," which coincidentally Hitler employs as a title for his prison writings:

> All that we can do, is to keep steadily in mind that each organic being is striving to increase at a geometrical ration; that each at some period of its life, during some season of the year, during each generation or at intervals, has to struggle for life, and to suffer great destruction. When we reflect on this struggle, we may console ourselves with the full belief, that the war of nature is not incessant, that no fear is felt, that death is generally prompt, and that the vigorous, the healthy and the happy survive and multiply.[43]

As Hitler writes *Mein Kampf* in his eclectic manner, he creates, in Timothy Ryback's words, "an odd patchwork that seems to have been cut from the cloth of the likes of Charles Darwin and Max Weber."[44] In *Mein Kampf*, Hitler transfers the Darwinian concept of "the survival of the fittest," coined by Herbert Spencer in 1864, from the nonhuman world to the state, *Volk/Gemeinschaft*, community, nation, species, and above all, the Aryan race. He writes, "A stronger race will drive out the weak, for the vital urge in its ultimate form will, time and time again, burst all the absurd fetters of the so-called humanity of individuals, in order to replace it by the humanity of Nature which destroys the weak to give his place to the strong."[45] In July 1932, in Kempten, Germany, Hitler reinforces the use of strength and power: "I do not believe in any law in the world that is not protected by power." ("Ich glaube an kein recht in der welt das nicht von einer Macht beschirmt ist.") This power will be unleashed through the Reich's later use of Gestapo and S.S. tactics, the threats of imprisonment or the concentration camp, as well as violence as viewed in Kristallnacht of November 9–10, 1938.

Drawing from Darwin's idea of the preservation of the species and basic eugenics principles, Hitler relies on the notion of the struggle to survive, a problem for the earlier nation which ignored the importance of racial distinctions: "The deepest and ultimate reason for the decline of the old Reich lay in its failure to recognize the racial problem and its importance for the historical development of peoples. For events in the lives of peoples are not expressions of chance, but processes related to the self-preservation of the species."[46] While Hitler considers this racial concern significant for the nation, it is even more important for all mankind, and he views it as a primary objective: "In general it should not be forgotten that the highest aim of human existence is not the preservation of a state, let alone a government, but the preservation of a species."[47] He generalizes and believes that "All who are not of good race in the world are chaff. And all occurrences in world history are only the expressions of the races' instinct of self-preservation, in the good or bad sense."[48]

Hitler acknowledges that humans can defy the casual forces of Nature and alter the destiny of a race in order to better it. He applies this notion to the nation-state especially as the Nazi Party develops in the 1920s: "The question of regaining our people's political power is primarily a question of recovering our national instinct of self-preservation."[49] He further elaborates on this application to a political institution by emphasizing the role race can play in the development of a civilization: "Thus, the highest purpose of a folkish state is concern for the preservation of those original racial elements which bestow culture and create the beauty and dignity of a higher mankind."[50] This empowerment through race alludes to a preeminent race that will become a Master race: "The German Reich as a state must embrace all Germans and has the task, not only of assembling and reserving the most valuable stocks of basic racial elements in this people, but slowly and surely of raising them to a dominant position."[51]

A German biology textbook in 1942 by Marie Harm and Hermann Wiehle maintains a Social Darwinian perspective in the section "The Laws of Nature and Mankind." According to Yuval Noah Harari in *Sapiens*, the text observes "that the supreme law of nature is that all beings are locked in a remorseless struggle for survival." Harari quotes the authors' view: "Biology not only tells us about animals and plants, but also shows us the laws we must follow in our lives, and steels our wills to live and fight according to these laws. The meaning of life is struggle. Woe to him who sins against these laws."[52] Harm and Wiehle further include a quote from *Mein Kampf:* "The person who attempts to fight the iron logic of nature thereby fights the principles he must thank for his life as a human being. To fight against nature is to bring about one's own destruction."[53]

Reproduction

In order to dominate other species, namely Jews, Slavs, and Roma, it is necessary to control the reproduction of the species. In Social Darwinism, one central goal is to improve society by a direct intervention in natural processes such as reproduction. In his 1919 letter to Adolph Gemlich, Hitler describes "the danger of Jewry" and also includes a major subject of the American and German eugenicists, reproduction: "He [the Jew] destroys the character of princes with byzantine flattery, national pride (the strength of the people), with ridicule and shameless breeding to depravity."[54] As with many eugenicists who believed in the over-population theory as it relates to reproduction, Hitler stresses that Germany must become more concerned about a viable future and create a more limited and purer race. In the late eighteenth and nineteenth century, believers in the Malthusian theory that population growth far outpaces food supply voiced their opinions on the measures required to restrict population increase. Hitler cites the statistics for population growth at the time of his writing, stating that the annual German population is increased by 900,000 births (actually closer to 500,000). He envisions "the difficulty in feeding this army of new citizens" and fears this increase will result in a "catastrophe."[55] He proposes a solution in citing the example of the French management of the birth rate by artificially restricting it.[56] In this way Hitler believes the nation can further civilization. At the same time, he further focuses on promoting a more elite race in the survival of the fittest offering his ideas about survival throughout Nature's challenges: "By thus brutally proceeding against the individual and immediately calling him back to herself [Nature] as soon as he shows himself unequal to the storm of life, she keeps the race and species strong, in fact, raises them to the highest accomplishments."[57]

Reproduction of the species takes on a significant position in Hitler's mindset that Germans must protect the longevity of the Aryan race. "What we must fight for is to safeguard the existence and reproduction of our race and our people, the sustenance of our children and the purity of our blood."[58] Furthermore, in his most significant racial tenets in chapter XI ("Nation and Race"), Hitler emphasizes racial purity through essential survival in hostile Nature through reproduction of the healthiest:

> In the struggle for daily bread all those who are weak and sickly or less determined succumb, while the struggle of the males for the female grants the right or opportunity to propagate only to the healthiest. And struggle

> is always a means for improving a species' health and power of resistance, and therefore, a cause of its higher development.[59]

The higher element will be the Aryan. Along with the omnipresent and perilous Jew who infects the race as "the germ within the body politic," "the bacillus," and the "parasite," the disabled jeopardize the health and growth of the species and the German nation as a collective body. The "immune response" occurs because the object is experienced as a force operating within one's body. Later Hitler will claim to be the savior and healer of a nation diseased by these "foreign" bodies, as he discusses the parasitic nature of the Jew: "He [the Jew] is and remains the typical parasite, a sponger who like a toxic bacillus keeps spreading as soon as a favorable medium invites him. And the effect of his existence is also like that of spongers: wherever he appears, the host people dies out after a shorter or longer period."[60] The diseased portions must be kept in check, first by sterilization, and then later, excising the unhealthy ones through elimination, read euthanasia or annihilation. Once Hitler became chancellor in January 1933, the seminal ideas in *Mein Kampf* of keeping the Aryan race "pure" through the concept of sterilization became law six months later, on July 14, 1933. With the passage of the "Law for the Prevention of Offspring with Hereditary Diseases" (*Gesetz zur Verhütung erbkranken Nachwuchses*), this step helped assure this purity of the race. The obligatory sterilization of the "impure," those with mental and physical disabilities, would lower the reproductive rates of those who threatened the advancement of the Aryan race. The list of hereditary diseases affecting the targeted group includes schizophrenia, epilepsy, physical deformity, blindness, deafness, and other disabilities. Section 1 of the Law for the Prevention of Offspring with Hereditary Diseases reads: "§1. Anyone suffering from a hereditary disease can be sterilized by a surgical operation if, according to the experience of medical science, there is a high probability that his offspring will suffer from serious physical or mental defects of a hereditary nature."[61] American eugenicist Paul Popenoe in his 1934 article "The German Sterilization Law" praises Hitler's wisdom in highlighting the importance of sterilization, citing several quotes from *Mein Kampf*. In general, Popenoe observes that Hitler "bases his hopes of national regeneration solidly on the application of biological principles to human society."[62]

Sterilization of the Disabled

With respect to how a nation or species considers its racial identity, Hitler early on views disability as a weakness, both a "crime" and a "disgrace" to the community, and this evolves from the sterilization law to the establishment of the euthanasia program.[63] It is therefore an obligation to educate about the necessity of purifying the Aryan race: "Those who are physically and mentally unhealthy and unworthy must not perpetuate their suffering in the body of their children. In this the folkish state must perform the most gigantic educational task."[64] Sterilization would be a significant step to prevent a contamination of the body of the nation. Hitler further writes, "If the fertility of the healthiest bearers of the nationality is thus consciously and systematically promoted, the result will be a race which at least will have eliminated the germs of our present physical and hence spiritual decay."[65] This elimination will later occur with the belief that the disabled represent "life unworthy of life" ("Lebensunwertes Leben"), a principle that Madison Grant already proposed in 1916: "The laws of nature require the obliteration of the unfit and human life is only valuable when it is of use to the community."[66] The child euthanasia policy in Germany followed in 1939 with the adult program ensuing the next year.

In *Mein Kampf*, Hitler believes that this form of scientific sterilization comprises the most humane and rational approach to keeping the Aryan race devoid of racial impurity and to promoting the soundness of mind and body of the species: "The demand that defective people be prevented from propagating equally defective offspring is a demand of the clearest reason and if systematically executed represents the most humane act of mankind."[67] Basic eugenics principles have been linked to this reasoning since 1907 in the United States, and the German eugenicists followed America's "progress." In 1922, American eugenicist Harry Laughlin wrote a major work on the subject of sterilization, *Eugenical Sterilization in the United States*. While positive eugenics adhered to the principles of promoting the Aryan race through marriage and the like, the negative prevented defective offspring from reproducing.[68]

In her enlightening comparative study on class or racial status in India, Jim Crow America, and Nazi Germany, *Caste*, Isabel Wilkerson writes that the Lothrop Stoddard text on the "under-man" mentioned earlier became a staple in Nazi Germany's school curriculum, and that Stoddard himself participated in Nazi sterilization trials. Stoddard admired the Nazis for their elimination of the worst elements of German society in a humanitarian manner, although he felt that they did not go far enough in their work.[69] Eventually they did, the sterilization of the unfit in Hitler's notion of purifying the Aryan race would result in the sterilization of between 200,000 and 400,000 Germans. Following the same eugenics policies, in 1927, the US Supreme Court ruling of 8 to 1 in the infamous eugenics case of *Buck v. Bell*, resulted in the involuntarily sterilization of approximately 70,000 allegedly "unfit" Americans.

Blood Mixing

Isabel Wilkerson further sets the stage for us with her study of the fear of pollution of a dominant race in her international parallels:

> The fourth pillar of caste rests upon the fundamental belief in the purity of the dominant caste and the fear of pollution from the castes deemed beneath it. Over the centuries, the dominant caste has taken extreme measures to protect its sanctity from the perceived taint of the lower castes. Both India and the United States at the zenith of their respective caste systems, and the short-lived but heinous regime of the Nazis, raised the obsession with purity to a high, if absurdist, art.[70]

To preserve the purity of Aryan blood, the community must beware of contaminating their white Nordic stock with the polluted blood of subhuman beings. Timothy Ryback notes that Hitler owned a "well-thumbed copy of *Racial Typology of the German People* by Hans F. K. Günther, known as 'Racial Günther' for his fanatical views on racial purity."[71] Günther believed that Jews were so racially mixed over the centuries that they had become peoples of a second racial order. Houston Stewart Chamberlain, whose general ideas Hitler knew, in his *Foundation of the Nineteenth Century* decries the fact that "half-breeds" and "blood mixing" have increased in Germany, indicating a decline in Nordic vitality.[72] Chamberlain further views this as a great "struggle" in civilization. "But this struggle, silent though it be, is above all others, a struggle for life and death."

To preserve the Aryan race, in Hitler's mind, it is important to forcibly resist an attempt to mix it with any "inferior blood," which could pollute the Aryan. In *Mein Kampf*, Hitler commented on the perils of intermarriage with respect to the Jew: "He poisons the blood of others, but preserves his own. The Jew almost never marries a Christian woman; it is the Christian who marries a Jewess."[73] Miscegenation, a term coined in the nineteenth century about race mixing, hindered the development of the purer breed in Hitler's perspective. However, the concept of race mixing preceded the German racial hygienists by several centuries for one of the first laws came into existence in the New World colonies, when a law in Virginia in 1691 prohibited a white settler to marry a member of a lesser race such as a Negro, mulatto, or Native American. Hitler praised the ability of North Americans to keep their stock pure by not mixing it "with the lower colored peoples."[74]

Hitler understood the power of blood laws in Jim Crow America that extended through several generations. The Florida Constitution regulated this racial mixing through marriage: "All courtships between a white person and a Negro person, or between a white person and a person of Negro descent to the fourth generation inclusive, are hereby forever prohibited."[75] Racial laws such as this common one in Florida and throughout America will echo in part the two basic tenets of the Nuremberg Laws with respect to marriage and Jewish lineage, namely citizenship. Already in 1916 eugenicist Madison Grant in his *Passing of a Great Race* discussed in detail how racial mixing, for example with a Negro, would result in the lowering of the quality of the white race (Figure 6.2).

FIGURE 6.2 *In 1933, Jewish businessman Oskar Danker and his girlfriend, a Christian woman, were forced to carry signs discouraging Jewish-German integration. Intimate relationships between "true Germans" and Jews were outlawed by 1935. Courtesy of Yad Vashem.*

In *Mein Kampf*, Hitler stresses: "The result of all racial crossing is therefore in brief always the following:

(a) Lowering of the level of the higher race
(b) Physical and intellectual regression and hence the beginning of a slowly, but surely progressing sickness."[76]

In general, in Hitler's thinking, one must follow racial principles and counteract Nature since in this manner a racially united society thrives and develops into a prosperous and noble civilization. Failing to ignore the real reasons for a collapse of a noble civilization such as epidemics, migrations, climate change, hostile invasions, and the like, he naively and falsely acknowledges the decline of earlier societies solely from the intermingling of the races. "All great cultures of the past perished *only* (author's emphasis) because the original creative race died out from blood poisoning."[77]A culture does not vanish due to a lost war, he writes, "but by the loss of that force of resistance which is contained only in pure blood."[78] Such resistance can overpower the desire to allow racial mixing.

On January 30, 1937, four years to the day when Hitler became chancellor, he marked the occasion by a lengthy Reichstag speech about "National Socialism and World Relations." As in *Mein Kampf*, the Führer reinforced the notion of the significance of race as being at the heart of the movement:

> The greatest revolution which National Socialism has brought about is that it has rent asunder the veil which hid from us the knowledge that all human failures and mistakes are due to the conditions of the time and therefore can be remedied, but that there is one error which cannot be remedied once men have made it, namely the failure to recognize the importance of conserving the blood and the race free from intermixture and thereby the racial aspect and character which are God's gift and God's handiwork. It is not for men to discuss the question of why Providence created different races, but rather to recognize the fact that it punishes those who disregard its work of creation.[79]

"Rhineland Bastards"

Among the targets of Hitler's observations concerning race mixing were the Afro-Germans. The "Rhineland bastards," a derogatory term used from the 1920s referring to children of African-German parents, indicated individuals of a mixed race who also became victimized by the Third Reich's sterilization policies. In 1913, anthropologist and professor of medicine and eugenics Eugen Fischer published a work on the concept of bastardization and in the early 1920s studied the mixed races in a German colony in West Africa. He arrived at the conclusion that children there born with racially different parents were the cause of the impurity of the white race. He applied his studies in Germany to the situation of an African colonial father wedded to a German woman and felt that the parents should be sterilized to prevent the continuation of impure blood. As an early advocate for the application of eugenics to societal issues, Fischer promoted sterilization as a preventive measure for keeping Germany pure-blooded. From 1927 to 1942 the influential Fischer served as director of the Kaiser Wilhelm Institute of Anthropology, Human Heredity, and Eugenics. Taking cues from the policies of the Kaiser Wilhelm Institute, in 1937, the Gestapo secretly rounded up 800 Afro-German children and compulsorily sterilized them (Figure 6.3).

The issue of the intermingling of races had created a stir in Germany prior to *Mein Kampf* and certainly influenced racial thinking. Just a few years before Hitler arrived at "the Fortress" in Landsberg, political tensions between France and Germany in 1920 escalated. French African soldiers from Senegal and Madagascar soon occupied the Rhineland, with troops numbering 250,000 at its peak in 1920, a fact that Hitler was aware of in

1924. Iris Wigger writes about this racial threat and the various campaigns in both the United States and Germany about the occupying forces. She describes the stereotypes of the African-born soldiers, not unlike those racial images of Blacks in America during the Jim Crow era:

> The colonial soldiers were construed as an alien element to European civilization, and an instinctive and uncontrollable sex drive was attributed to them. In their supposed "racial" and "sexual" otherness, they were perceived as a horrible "racial threat" to "white women," and defamed as "Black Shame," "Black Disgrace," "Black Horror," or "Black Pest."[80]

Robert C. Reinders details this "onslaught" of race mixing in the region by describing the article in the *British Daily Herald* for April 10, 1920, by so-called liberal Edmund D. Morel:

> Edmund Dene Morel under banner leads: BLACK SCOURGE IN EUROPE SEXUAL HORROR LET LOOSE BY FRANCE ON RHINE DISAPPEARANCE OF YOUNG GERMAN GIRLS. France, Morel wrote, "is thrusting her black savages . . . into the heart of Germany." There "primitive African barbarians", carriers of syphilis, have become a "terror and a horror" to the Palatinate countryside.[81]

Morel further comments on the backwardness of the African occupiers as "not so advanced in the forms of civilisation as ourselves,"[82] referring to a white "civilized" population. These racist beliefs are held by Hitler in *Mein Kampf* as he writes it would be "criminal lunacy" to believe one can drill into such an "inferior" being the makings of a lawyer, for example, an echo of Madison Grant's racist notions: "It has taken us fifty years to learn that

FIGURE 6.3 *Photo of biracial girl used in lectures at Germany's State Academy for Race and Health. Courtesy of the Library of Congress.*

speaking English, wearing good clothes and going to school and to church does not transform a Negro into a white man."[83]

Referred to as "Die schwarze Schmach" ("The Black Disgrace") or "Die schwarze Schande" ("The Black Shame"), the race mixing by African-French soldiers had already been discussed in German newspapers during the close of the First World War. President von Hindenburg also wrote an appeal in September of 1918 about the French sending Blacks and other colored people to attack the Germans. The French occupation of the area from 1920 until 1930 commonly engendered racist attitudes among the German population toward children born of an African parent. Iris Wiggers points out that German women were also stigmatized for marrying an African soldier since it was a stain on the honor of womanhood, the race, and the nation.[84] In *Mein Kampf*, Hitler reiterates the biases of everyday Germans, who felt that the human remnants of Germany's colonial past in Africa would be viewed as outsiders and therefore treated with deserved hostility. This was reinforced during the French occupation of the Rhineland. German citizens' fears, like Eugen Fischer's, were that the dark-skinned Africans would dilute the pure whiteness of the German population, an alarm that American eugenicists spread when the influx of Southern Europeans like the Italians entered America. The concern was already fostered in the United States by the Immigration Restriction League, founded in 1894. Two decades later and expressing eugenics beliefs, Madison Grant wrote in 1916:

> We Americans must realize that the altruistic ideals which have controlled our social development during the past century and the maudlin sentimentalism that has made America "an asylum for the oppressed," are sweeping the nation toward a racial abyss. If the Melting Pot is allowed to boil without control and we continue to follow our national motto and deliberately blind ourselves to "all distinctions of race, creed or color," the type of native American of Colonial descent will become as extinct as the Athenian of the age of Pericles, and the Viking of the days of Rollo.[85]

National immigration quotas were further developed in the Immigration Act of 1924, which Hitler admired.[86]

Raising his common conspiracy theories, Hitler partially lays the blame for the race mixing and lowering of the white identity of the Aryan with the Jewish handling of "Negroes" in Germany. "It was and it is the Jews who bring the Negroes into the Rhineland, always with the same secret thought and clear aim of ruining the hated white race by the necessarily resulting bastardization, throwing it down from its cultural and political height, and himself rising to be its master."[87] Later on he further decries the adulteration of the Aryan race by the Negro:

> For the contamination by Negro blood on the Rhine in the heart of Europe is just as much in keeping with the perverted sadistic thirst for vengeance

> of this hereditary enemy of our people as is the ice-cold calculation of the Jew thus to begin bastardizing the European continent at its core and to deprive the white race of the foundations for a sovereign existence through infection with lower humanity.[88]

For Hitler, the African is a "half-born ape" even though the Jewish bourgeois speaks of "his theory about the *equality of men.*"[89]

A Munich folk-national organization, *Deutsche Notbund gegen die Schwarze Schmach*, published an article by Bruno Stehle, describing an analogy that former Italian prime minister, economist, and journalist Francesco Nitti makes regarding America. Nitti asks the American United Press interviewer what America would do if it lost the First World War and Germany positioned "Negro" troops in the country and further demanded 100 or 150 billion dollars, alluding to the reparations Germany was to pay stated by the Treaty of Versailles.

> "And remember," says Nitti, "that these African regiments are composed of savages for the most part untouched by any contact with civilization, and if the victorious Germans had then demanded after all this formal humiliation, that American women and American girls must in one form or the other be supplied to the carnal lust of these Africans, Africans barely removed from the practices of voodoo and cannibalism, all America would have resounded with horror at this barbarity."[90]

Nitti's words certainly are in line with Hitler's and other racially minded individuals who stereotype the Black population whether in Germany or America.

Nuremberg Laws: Ideology into Law

In the Third Reich until 1935, the racial mixing through intermarriage and the legality of citizenship for Jews did not appear as part of Reich law. Seeing the importance of a legal statute in a racial state, seventeen businessmen and legal scholars met in June 1934 with the intention of creating blood laws. Already in *Mein Kampf*, Hitler promoted the significance of pure Aryan blood endlessly, and his beliefs developed into an ideology over the next decade. Those gathered in June 1934 had some familiarity already with blood purity in American legal documents on the subject, but it was only on September 13, 1935, two days prior to the Nuremberg Congress, that a hastily drawn set of laws would start to take shape. They provided the basis for the two tenets of intermarriage and citizenship. Racial categories were introduced for a pure German, Jew, half-Jew (*Mischling*), and quarter-Jew. Racial restrictions hindered the Jews in all sectors of society with the promulgation of the Nuremberg Laws—the "Law for the Protection of German Blood and

Honor and the Reich Citizenship Law"—at the September 1935 Nuremberg Party Congress in "the City of the Reich Party." These laws, evolving from an ideology or a mindset about marginalizing Jews, were enacted legally and brought serious consequences if transgressed. The Nuremberg Laws further isolated the Jews from the Aryans:

Article 1 of the "Law for the Protection of German Blood and Honor" reads:

> 1. Marriages between Jews and citizens of German or related blood are forbidden.
>
> Marriages nevertheless concluded are invalid, even if concluded abroad to circumvent this law.

Article 2 of the Reich Citizenship Law states:

> A Reich citizen is a subject of the state who is of German or related blood, and proves by his conduct that he is willing and fit to faithfully serve the German people and Reich.

Certain technicalities and nuances, nevertheless, had to be determined, so on November 14, 1935, a supplement created categories similar to American Jim Crow blood laws, especially the legal and social racial classification with the "one drop law." The harsh racial blood laws through careful classification become yet another step in keeping with the Jim Crow statutes in a eugenics-focused America; both deprived their disfavored minorities (Jews and Blacks) of education, voting rights, and above all, human rights. For Germany, the Nazi legalization of racial attitudes serves as a further step closer to the Shoah (Figure 6.4).

Conclusion

Hitler's writings in 1924–5 evolved into concrete actions step by step, concluding in the historical tragedy of the Shoah. His racist ideology developed into practice almost immediately at achieving power as chancellor, especially in 1933 as the Third Reich subsequently enacted law after law to eliminate Jews from their professional careers, their citizenship, then their personal and commercial property, and eventually their lives. How could the malevolent government attempt to justify later the near destruction of the Jewish community? At the Nuremberg Doctors' Trial of 1946–7, the defense of Hitler's personal physician, Karl Brandt, by Dr. Robert Servatius, later defense counsel for Adolf Eichmann in Jerusalem in 1961, revealed its strategy by pointing to America. Servatius indicated that those in the medical profession on trial followed in the footsteps of American eugenicists

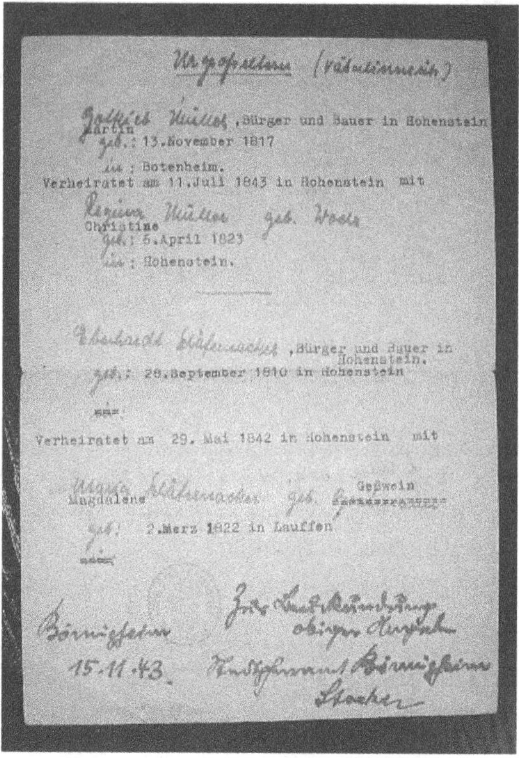

Martin ,Bürger und Bauer in Hohenstein
13.November 1817
: Botenheim.
Verheiratet am 11.Juli 1843 in Hohenstein mit

Christine
: 5.April 1823
: Hohenstein.

,Bürger und Bauer in Hohenstein.
: 28.September 1810 in Hohenstein

Verheiratet am 29. Mai 1842 in Hohenstein mit

Magdalene Geßwein
2.Merz 1822 in Lauffen

15.11.43.

FIGURE 6.4 *Aryan certificate (*Ariernachweis*) stating that one is of Aryan bloodline. Public domain.*

and others, who helped pass laws about blood mixing, sterilization, and human experimentation for the betterment of society. For the Nazis on trial at Nuremberg, the justification for the unethical treatment of prisoners (Jewish and non-Jewish) focused on a "service to humanity," "consequences of 'total war,'" and "following state orders." Medical historian and neuropsychiatrist Dr. Werner Leibbrandt on the stand for the prosecution at the Nuremberg Doctors' Trial rejected (although falsely as we now know) the defense position that Americans had used unethical principles in their experimentation on prisoners. At the trial Dr. Servatius maintained: "The German doctor who acted in conformity with the German regulations can no more be punished than the American doctor who complied with the requests of his state in the way which is customary there."[91] Most likely unknown to the prosecution, US health officials in the Tuskegee syphilis experiments until the 1970s and the US-sponsored STD experiments on prisoners in Guatemala viewed the marginalized Blacks, prostitutes, and prisoners in their studies as *Untermenschen.* Using standard eugenics principles of the ends justifying the means of improving society, as the Nazi doctors did, the health officials were willing to act unethically in the name of medicine and the betterment of society.

To document his legal defense of Brandt, who was given responsibility for the adult euthanasia program with Philipp Bouhler, Servatius placed on exhibit the work of chairman of the New York Zoological Society Madison Grant in *The Passing of the Great Race* (1916) dealing with sterilization.[92]

> A misunderstood conception of laws that are supposed to be divine, and false faith in the sanctity of humane life will result in preventing the extermination of inferior children as well as the sterilization of such adults who are worthless or detrimental to the community. Natural law requires extermination of the incapable, and human life is only valuable, if it is of use to the community or the race.[93]

Servatius supplemented that document for the exhibit with a second quote from Grant referring to euthanasia: "A strict selection by exterminating the insane or incapable—in other words, the scum of society—would solve the whole problem in one century, and would enable us to get rid of the undesirable elements who people our prisons, hospitals and lunatic asylums."[94] The defense lawyer's last quote referred to Grant's urgency about the need for sterilization:

> The individual may be supported, brought up, and protected by the community during his lifetime, but the state must see to it by sterilization, that he is the last individual of his line of descent, otherwise future generations too, will be burdened with the curse of an over increasing number of victims of misguided sentimentality.[95]

The exhibit reinforces the Nazi rationale that American eugenicists encouraged sterilization and even euthanasia almost two decades prior to the establishment of the Third Reich.[96]

At the fall of the Third Reich's racial state, the Nazis still sought to rationalize their actions based on eugenic principles that circulated in America, Germany, and other countries. However, following the Doctors' Trial, the Nuremberg Code provided an ethical guide to the humane treatment of the individual, focused especially on human experimentation. What began with Hitler's utopian vision in *Mein Kampf* of creating a Huxleyan brave new Aryan world turned into a dystopian world of death and destruction in the Shoah.

7

Degeneracy—Attack on Modern Art and Music

Ralf Yusuf Gawlick and Barbara S. Gawlick

On April 1 (April Fool's Day), 1924, Adolf Hitler was admitted to the Landsberg penal facility—located in the town of Landsberg am Lech, 40 miles west of Munich—to start his five-year prison sentence for leading the Nazis' unsuccessful "Beer Hall Putsch" in Bavaria the previous year. Five weeks earlier, on February 25, Arnold Schoenberg's *Suite for Piano op.25* was premièred 250 miles away in Vienna. This artist and composer represented and embodied significant traits that Hitler loathed and associated with degeneracy, feelings of disgust, and anti-Semitism that he would put to paper during his incarceration: Schoenberg was Jewish, wrote atonal music, and had been a member of the avant-garde Munich-based *Der Blaue Reiter* (The Blue Rider) group, which drew parallels between art and music. They dabbled in the phenomenon of synesthesia whereby an experience of one art form leads to subliminal sensations of another, and in this case, music. Charles Baudelaire and John Keats both introduced *synesthetic* effects in their literary work.

Schoenberg's *Suite* is a serial work, a seminal example of organized atonality in which dissonance—or rather degrees of dissonance—replaces the core equilibrium of consonance and dissonance that had defined Western music since the Middle Ages. Tonal and harmonic deviations were soon labeled deviant, just as modern art was pronounced by traditionalists/antimodernists to be aesthetically repellent and politically subversive. Schoenberg's radicalism musically is mirrored visually in his 1910 self-portrait *Der rote*

Blick (The Red Gaze): in efforts to "express" and "evoke" unconscious emotion and meaning rather than—as Adorno writes—"the harmonious, affirmative nature of art."[1] The *Gestalt* of both art and composition exhibits distortion and exaggeration: *musically* through dissonant harmonic pitch collections, angular melodies, irregular phrases, extremes in dynamic contrasts, and changing texture; and *artistically* through distortions of forms, strong and bold colors, exaggeratedly executed brushstrokes generating a sense of frenetic intensity. In 1937, Hitler's concepts of purity in the arts earlier expressed in 1924 come to fruition in the condemnation of modern art in the Degenerate Art Exhibition (*Die Ausstellung "Entartete Kunst"*) and the exaltation of pure German, read Aryan, art in the Great German Art Exhibition (*Große Deutsche Kunstausstellung*). Included in the attempt at the purification of the arts was the Third Reich's denunciation of modern music, *Entartete Musik*.

Of course, it is well known that Hitler served only a rather cozy and accommodating nine months of his sentence during which time he penned his political manifesto *Mein Kampf*, a perverse autobiography in which he expressed hatred of what he considered the world's twin evils—Marxism and Judaism. These threats permeated his *Weltanschauung* (worldview), philosophy, and goals in all matters of politics, society, and the arts. This chapter intends to first present a brief survey of Hitler's views on art and by extension music by quoting extensively from *Mein Kampf* within a sociopolitical and cultural context—in particular his conceptions of "degenerate" art. It will further trace the path these views metastasized into during the 1937 Degenerate Art Exhibition in Munich and the 1938 Degenerate Music Exhibition in Düsseldorf, exhibitions signifying the final, total purging of modern art by the National Socialists.

The disdain of modern art and architecture—described by Hitler as the "queens of art"[2]—by the general public, press, and officialdom prevailed in the early twentieth century well into the Weimar period. The Dresden group *Die Brücke* (The Bridge)—including such painters as Ernst Kirchner and Max Pechstein—were accused of cultivating a sense of the insane. One element of the Munich press in all seriousness called for the arrest of *Der Blaue Reiter* painters—Kandinsky, Klee, Marc, and Macke. Opposition to modern art was a common cause to many segments of the population—in particular, the antimodernists who reflected the political fortunes and attitudes of the far-right. Hitler laments the state of the arts in pre–First World War Germany: "In nearly all fields of art, especially in the theater and literature, we began around the turn of the century to produce less that was new and significant, but to disparage the best of the old work and represent it as inferior and surpassed."[3] He viewed the "old work" as "healthy," a concept he frequently used to describe the ideal, pure status of Germany now threatened by the pollution and degeneracy of criminals, Jews, Bolsheviks, and soon homosexuals, Roma/Sinti, Jehovah's Witnesses, and others in the lead-up to the Shoah.

In *Mein Kampf*, which the Jewish-German novelist Lion Feuchtwanger called a "collection of 164,000 offences against German grammar and syntax,"[4] Hitler taps into the conservative, traditionalist view of the *Volk* that bemoans the decline of high culture. He speaks of a "spiritual degeneration" that no longer has anything to do with art: "To be sure, even in earlier times there were occasional aberrations of taste, but such cases were rather artistic derailments, to which posterity could attribute at least a certain historical value, than products no longer of an artistic degeneration, but of a spiritual degeneration that had reached the point of destroying the spirit."[5] Hitler's words appear ironic, since Wassily Kandinsky and other members of *Der Blaue Reiter* praised the "spiritual value" of art, and the artist himself wrote a treatise in 1910, *Über Das Geistige in Der Kunst* (Concerning the Spiritual in Art).

Hitler's taste reflected his late Victorian small-town origins in Austria. He extols the work of such facile romantic painters as Moritz von Schwind and Arnold Boecklin.[6] His ideas on art and architecture follow his own failure to gain admittance into the Vienna Academy of Fine Arts, instead becoming an illustrator and "working independently as a small draftsman and painter of watercolors."[7]

In *Mein Kampf*, Hitler radicalizes an ideology that reaches back, ironically, to the influential work of the Jewish doctor Max Nordau. This ideology was taken up by conservative, nationalistic cultural critics and involved the pathologizing of modern art: this modern/"degenerate" art was understood as a pathological, sick deviation from an original type.[8] According to Nordau, "Degenerates are not always criminals, prostitutes, anarchists and declared madmen. They are also sometimes authors and artists."[9] Nordau defamed and attacked modern art and cultural life authoritatively in his 1892 publication *Entartung* (Degeneration). The term "degenerate art" gained a status of common currency and was applied to various different directions of modern art including impressionism, expressionism, cubism, and after the First World War, especially against Dadaism and New Objectivity.[10] In *Mein Kampf*, Hitler refers in a racist aside to this style of modern art as "trash of the modern artistic development, which a nation of Negroes might just as well as have produced."[11] Later, the NSDAP was fundamentally against all forms of the avant-garde, including music, film, and theater. For Nordau initially, the paragon of "degenerate" art was Richard Wagner; and in his estimation, the composer contained more degeneracy than all degenerates combined: "The 'Disease State of Degeneracy' reveals itself in the composer in eerie completeness and lush display."[12] Again, there is a twisted irony with the choice of Wagner—and in clear contrast to Hitler—because of Hitler's idolization of the composer's music and surely also his notorious and perverse 1858 essay, *Das Judenthum in der Musik* (Judaism in Music). The text was an influential anti-Semitic work that denies Jews the ability to produce cultural achievements, which will be echoed in *Mein Kampf*. Nevertheless, Hitler's association of modern art with brain damage is already present and finds potent stimuli in Nordau's study, in which "new tendencies in art and literature, as expressions of Mysticism and re-addiction can be traced back organically to the brain's cell structure and misdirected neurological stimuli."[13]

Hitler next associates spiritual pestilence and brain damage with the Jew, carriers of disease "worse than the Black Death of olden times, and the people was being infected with it!"[14] And elsewhere:

> Everywhere we encounter seeds which represent the beginnings of parasitic growths which must sooner or later be the ruin of our culture. In them, too, we can recognize the symptoms of decay of a slowly rotting world. Woe to the peoples who can no longer master this disease! Such diseases could be seen in Germany in nearly every field of art and culture.[15]

According to Hitler, the Jewish "infiltration" into German culture results from the fact that Jews never possessed a state—therefore never called or could call a culture their own. There exists only a Jewish sham culture:

> With all appearances of intellectual characteristics . . . never has there been a Jewish art and accordingly there is none today either. . . . The two queens of all the arts, architecture and music, owe nothing original to the Jews. What they do accomplish in the field of art is either patchwork or intellectual theft . . . instead culturally contaminates art, literature, the theater, makes a mockery of natural feeling, overthrows all concepts of beauty and sublimity, of the noble and good, and instead drags everything that is truly great into the gutter. . . . Not because or through him, but in spite of him does humanity develop.[16]

The "supposed" destruction of everything "noble," "good," and "beautiful" by Jews was a common anti-Semitic topos propagated substantially by authors such as Theodor Fritsch. Fritsch, a serious influence on Hitler, was viewed as a prophet of National Socialist anti-Semitic thinking, especially in his 1916 *Der falsche Gott* (The False God) and earlier 1893 *Handbuch der Judenfrage* (Handbook of the Jewish Question). In the latter, he decries the rise of urbanization and industrialization, anything that was "modern." The cover of a publication of the *Handbuch* reveals a serpent marked with Jewish stars swirling around a swastika.[17]

This Jewish "infiltration" serves their larger goal of working toward a twofold revolution in economic and political spheres by thousands of agitators:

> The democratic people's Jew becomes the blood-Jew and tyrant over peoples . . . the most frightful example of this kind is offered by Russia, where he killed or starved about thirty million people with positively fanatical savagery, in part amid inhuman tortures, in order to give a gang

> of Jewish journalists and stock exchange bandits domination over a great people.[18]

Hitler rants that the "evil intent of the apostles of the future" is clear: the destruction of all culture to pave the way for the "spiritual preparation of political Bolshevism"[19]—along with Judaism, a menacing threat to the German body.

It is at this point in his ideological thinking that Hitler lays the abstract foundations for policies that later turn genocidal as he assumes power in the Third Reich government. With respect to his, the Aryan's, moral and existential responsibility and justification to combat the spreading of cultural and political pestilence, clear suggestions of extermination and sterilization prevail, as Hitler writes: "It is the business of the state, in other words, of its leaders, to prevent a people from being driven into the arms of spiritual madness."[20] Hence, he argues,

> the cleansing of our culture must be extended to nearly all fields. Theater, art, literature, cinema, press, posters, and window displays must be cleansed of all manifestations of our rotting world and placed in the service of a moral, political, and cultural idea. . . . Only after these measures are carried out can the medical struggle against the plague itself be carried through with any prospect of success. But here, too, there must be no half-measures; the gravest and most ruthless decisions will have to be made. It is a half-measure to let incurably sick people steadily contaminate the remaining healthy ones. This is in keeping with the humanitarianism which, to avoid hurting one individual, lets a hundred others perish. The demand that defective people be prevented from propagating equally defective offspring is a demand of the clearest reason and if systematically executed represents the most humane act of mankind. . . . The right of personal freedom recedes before the duty to preserve the race. . . . Anyone who refuses to see these things supports them, and thereby makes himself an accomplice in the slow prostitution of our future.[21]

Hitler's words here reflect his belief that "degenerate" opposed the concept of "pure," which he promoted throughout *Mein Kampf* whether in terms of blood or art. Besides the Jews, seen as degenerate, diseased, and impure, he viewed the disabled as weak and inferior. In order to maintain a purer race, the disabled must be prevented from reproducing an inferior species as he suggests with sterilization, but also with extermination, at least metaphorically at this point. Within two decades a metaphor evolves into action.

Hitler makes an encompassing sociopolitical, cultural, and ethnic pronunciation that justifies persecutive measures against not only deviant cultural "parasites" but anyone who sympathizes with them: in essence, these statements constitute nothing less than a sweeping ideological decree that finds guilty the perpetrators as well as those guilty by association, any and all people and ideas contrary to Aryan ideals. These are foundational ideals rooted in Hitler's Aryan-centric definition of culture: "What today is regarded as human culture, as the result of art, science and technology, is almost without exception the creative product of the Aryan. He is the Prometheus of humanity from whose bright forehead the divine spark of genius protrudes at all times."[22]

As the Nazi Party became a mass political body in the late 1920s and early 1930s, gaining strength and popularity, thanks to an unprecedented and innovative use of propaganda and ideology, the topos of Judaization of art, theater, literature, film, and press continued to be omnipresent in anti-Semitic literature.

Then, in 1933, Hitler became chancellor and the following year, upon President Paul von Hindenburg's death, Führer, the all-powerful totalitarian leader of the Third Reich. When the *Reichstag*, the German Parliament, was deliberately burned down and blamed on the communists, Hitler began his stranglehold on the country over the communists and Jews. Through a series of laws, over 400 aimed primarily at the Jews, the Reich controlled every aspect of society, including art. Division VI of Joseph Goebbels's Reich Ministry of Public Enlightenment and Propaganda had jurisdiction over art, music, and theater, creating extensive policies of censorship as well as patronage.[23] The Reich Culture Chamber established paradigms of art that supported the Nazi ideal of *Volk*, purity, and glorified Hitler, the failed artist, now proclaimed as the new architect and healer of a pure aesthetic Germany. Melanie Murphy, in her essay "*The Architecture of Doom* (1991): Blueprint for Annihilation," indicates how the film reveals the aesthetic drive of the Third Reich involved making beauty, cleanliness, and splendor as Nazi ideals, especially in the arts: "the *Architecture of Doom* presents Hitler as artist and Hitler as ruler as indeed one, and contends that to understand Hitler as artist-prince, who did not, in fact, could not, step outside this role, is to understand genocide."[24]

Hitler and Goebbels also wanted to create a "Greater Germany by changing the modern cultural landscape and returning the country to traditional 'German,' 'Aryan' and 'Nordic' values. Pastoral scenes and large imposing sculptures became the hallmark of approved art. The Nazis promoted paintings and sculptures that were traditional in manner and that exalted the 'blood and soil' values of racial purity, militarism, and obedience to the *Führer*."[25] Racial purity and return to the land became integral elements of Nazi ideology, especially after Richard Darré's 1930 book *Neuadel aus Blut und Boden* (A New Nobility Based on Blood and Soil). Darré promoted a eugenics program for selective breeding in the development of a "master race," including a return to the land and avoidance of the moral swamp of urban life.

Very much in line with the then-current eugenics movement, ideas of which were already present in embryonic form in *Mein Kampf*, Hitler wished to purge the Jewish, "foreign," and "degenerate" influences in Germany, and shape a racially pure community (*Volksgemeinschaft*) which aligned with the Nazi Party political platform. Hitler saw Germany as an organic unit, and before he fully undertook to contain the diseased part of the country—the disabled, Jews, and homosexuals—he targeted the artists. Given its prominent place in public ceremony and propaganda, a high social value was placed on the visual arts. The National Socialist leadership gave the visual arts four years from the assumption of power in 1933 to the opening of the House of German Art in 1937 to adjust to the cultural policy of the new government. In those years in particular, a campaign was mounted against "degenerate" art and artists—a war on culture, against the Jewish Bolsheviks and their ilk, in the minds of the government, even though only several were Jewish. In fact, German and non-Germans, Jews and non-Jews, were targeted.[26]

So, what actually constituted "degenerate" art?

Recurring ideas and labels denoted a political position, not qualities readily evident in paintings; the term was used as a means of orientation to cover vast forms taken by art. Although there may have been some controversy over what was *acceptable*, there were hardly any differences in consensus on what was *objectionable*. This is actually surprising given the diversity of prohibited art styles and programs. Thus, "degenerate" art would include (1) socially and politically committed artists such as Käthe Kollwitz, Otto Dix, and Georg Grosz, (2) communist artists as well as (3) artists who were convinced National Socialists such as Emil Nolde. In essence, the National Socialists attacked and rejected almost everything that existed on the art scene prior to 1933 and compared modern art to deviant and disfigured figures.[27]

In 1937, Adolph Ziegler, Reich politician and Hitler's favorite painter, oversaw the purge of art that was deemed "un-Deutsch" (Un-German) and did not live up to the vision of Hitler's and Goebbels's standards. Already in April 1933, the government passed the Law for the Restoration of the Professional Civil Service and eliminated all non-Aryan museum directors from their posts. They comprised some of the best directors in Germany. Ziegler's crew stripped German museums of modern German Expressionist art as well as foreign Expressionist works.[28] Exhibitions of "infamous" art with such titles as the "Government Art from 1918–1933" and "The Spirit of November: Art in the Service of Social Decay" were meant to discredit the Weimar Republic by associating it with both deviant modern art and art with desperate social conditions.[29] Per Nazi aesthetic canon, all depictions and evocations of human anguish, distress, pain, and ugliness were banished.

In the cleansing of the country of these "depraved" artists, Ziegler was charged to organize the mock exhibition of "Degenerate Art" that would be a blockbuster in Munich and then throughout twelve cities in Germany as part of a most popular tour. As noted earlier, this was the final attack on, the last purge of, modern art in the Third Reich.[30] Under Ziegler's direction, there were plundered artworks from over 35 collections and museums in over 30 cities with the total number of confiscated art estimated at close to 16,000 pieces! The campaign against "degenerate" art took in works of 1,400 artists, including, but not limited to, Beckmann, Dix, Corinth, Barlach, Grosz, Kirchner, Klee, Kokoshka, Kollwitz, Marc, and Pechstein. From these, 112 by the above artists were selected to exhibit to the public in a 1937 free exhibition entitled *Entartete Kunst* (Degenerate Art). This degradation of modern art was to be shown *in contrast* to the concurrent Great German Art Exhibition, in which 900 works revealed the pure Aryanism described in *Mein Kampf*: idealized pastoral landscapes with allusions to "Blut und Boden" policies (*Young Farmers*), Ziegler's seductive nudes in *Four Elements*, a classic mythological representation of *Prometheus*, and heroic Aryan heroes, as in *This Was the SA* (Stormtroopers) (Figure 7.1).

The officially unacceptable art in the "Degenerate" exhibition, shown to the German public as a mockery of modern art, intended to showcase the monstrosities, madness, insolence, incompetence, and degeneracy of modern art. The original exhibit, housed in few halls located in an old gallery building of the *Hofgarten* arcades, drew over two million visitors in its four and a half month duration, more than three times the number that attended the "German" exhibition.[31] The exhibited works were later sold by auction to benefit the Nazi coffers or to be eventually burned. The visual memory of the exhibit has been preserved at the United States Holocaust Memorial

FIGURE 7.1 *Publicity for the* Entartete Kunst/*Degenerate Art exhibition: Otto Freundlich's sculpture "Der Neue Mensch". Courtesy of the United States Holocaust Memorial Museum.*

Museum in the form of a short four-minute film by American documentary filmmaker Julien Bryan.

The selected works were crowded together in narrowly partitioned, claustrophobic rooms, where spectators were pressed against each other and had to crane their necks in order to view the exhibit, for example to read the swirling script about Dada high above the visitors. Since the primary goal was to ridicule the modern art, modes of display were adapted that were deliberately detrimental to the works. These measures included terrible lighting, paintings hung helter-skelter, and without frames and subjugating works with inflammatory labels, commentaries, and obscene jokes.[32]

Speaking from Munich's Institute of Archeology in the *Hofgarten* to open the Degenerate Art Exhibition on July 17, 1937, Ziegler declaims:

> We now stand in an exhibition that contains only a fraction of what was bought with the hard-earned savings of the German people and exhibited as art by a large number of museums all over Germany. All around us you see the monstrous offspring of insanity, impudence, ineptitude and sheer degeneracy. What this exhibition offers inspires horror and disgust in us all.[33]

Ziegler's words provide the essence of "degeneracy," which became a threat to a pure-blooded Aryan nation interested in preserving all aspects of society and especially its culture.

The exhibit was "organized"—if such a term is even permissible to be used in this context—into nine groups listed in the exhibition guide. Groups ranged from "a general survey of barbarous methods of organization," to "hocus-pocus art," to "art as a tool of Marxist propaganda," to the "world as a whorehouse," to "Negro" art representing the racial "ideal" of a modern art that worships "idiots, cretins and the paralytic." The latter racially charged indications can be found in *Mein Kampf* as Hitler believes nothing can make a Negro civilized, and the disabled and marginalized are simply *Untermenschen* (subhumans). Further classifications include "representative selections from the endless supply of Jewish trash," the "total madness reflecting the height of degeneracy" and comparing a number of modern art works with superficially similar products of the mentally ill, further allusions to Hitler's view of the mentally challenged as inferior.[34]

Entartete Musik

Some confiscated and "appropriated" works continued to be displayed in the Reich in traveling exhibits;[35] the concurrent Degenerate Music exhibition proved less "successful" and smaller/quieter in scale as to not incite protest, music being a more "sensitive" subject in Nazi Germany. The exhibits—which included compositions by Hindemith, Berg, Eisler, Weill,

FIGURE 7.2 *Exhibition poster for the 1938* Entartete Musik *exhibition. Courtesy of Wikimedia Commons.*

Schreker, Stravinsky, and Webern—were boycotted by significant numbers of musicians and composers in Germany, including committed party members (Figure 7.2).[36.]

Unlike trends in the history of the visual arts, in which French, Italian, Spanish, Dutch, and even English traditions prominently shaped aesthetic movements, German visual art played a much less significant role. It is rather in the field of the musical arts that German-speaking composers defined the evolution of the Western music canon since the seventeenth century: unbroken branches and lines exist from Bach, Handel, Mozart, Beethoven, Schubert, Mendelsohn, Brahms, Mahler, Wagner, Strauss, among many others. Sadly, several of these illustrious composers and their music were censured once the National Socialists assumed power in 1933: Mendelsohn and Mahler because of their Jewish racial background, Handel because of his oratorios based on Jewish themes and subjects from the Old Testament.

By the time the Nazis took control of the arts, Germany and Austria had been beacons for already more than a century of creating and supporting the very music institutions necessary for the widespread public consumption of music. For example, such venerable institutions as the *Leipzig Gewandhausorchester* (1781), the oldest civic orchestra in the world, the *Musikverein* (1870), founded by the *Gesellschaft der Musikfreunde* in Vienna (1812), and the *Berlin Philharmoniker* (1882), to mention just a few, provided not only among the first modern concert hall venues but also a social welfare network for musicians and their families. Increasingly in the nineteenth century, the role of music in German-speaking culture became associated with engendering an ideal and edifying moral character. The German philosopher Arthur Schopenhauer elevates music to a truly exceptional status. In his *Die Welt als Wille und Vorstellung* (The World as Will and Representation), he states that "music is by no means like the other arts, namely a *copy* of the ideas, but a *copy of the will itself*, the objectivity of which are the ideas. For this reason the effect of music is so very much more powerful and penetrating than is that of the other arts, for these others speak only of the shadow, but music of the essence."[37]

Running in parallel to the creation and performance of "serious" art music, the last quarter of the nineteenth- and early decades of the twentieth centuries also witnessed a widespread blossoming of lighter musical genres and venues throughout many European cities, most notably in Paris and Berlin. *Fin de siècle* Europe reflected an unprecedented melting pot of ideas, aesthetics, and styles in all the arts. In music, such avant-garde trends as impressionism, neoclassicism, atonal expressionism, and serialism thrived alongside jazz, swing, cabaret, vaudeville, operetta, and music and dance clubs.

Tragically and with brutal consequence, the NSDAP's prioritized assault in the 1930s on all these forms of musical expression put composers, performers, and audiences in immediate danger. The radical and defining moment of Nazi cultural policy occurred after Socialists seized power and established, in September 1933, the *Reichsmusikkammer* (Reich Music Chamber), a branch of both the *Reichskulturkammer* (Reich Chamber of Culture) and the *Reichskulturkammergesetz* (Reich Culture Chamber Law), and Goebbels's *Propaganda Ministerium* (Ministry of Propaganda).[38] The RMK functioned as a "corporate body of public law of and for musicians, which was to promote and administer German music, offer guidance, and regulate economic and social affairs of and for professional musicians, while also providing for the means to purge and control its membership more systematically than before via the notorious questionnaire about ancestry and political reliability."[39]

Such preeminent and internationally famous composers/conductors as Richard Strauss, Wilhelm Furtwängler, and Paul Hindemith were appointed to pave the way for a new, "purified" German music, built upon and upholding intrinsic German values.[40] Strauss, the first elected president of RMK, in his opening address at the first RMK convention in 1934, glowingly praised Hitler's and Goebbels's commitment to the restructuring of German musical life in light of the poor economic situation plaguing many music institutions and exacerbated by the high unemployment among musicians.[41] Thus, it comes as no surprise that Furtwängler initially welcomed Nazi financial support, when in 1932–3, the most esteemed of all German musical institutions, the Berlin Philharmonic Orchestra, was on the brink of shameful bankruptcy. Strauss's and Furtwängler's initial enthusiasm was, however, soon curbed when they realized that the evil intents of Nazi cultural machinations collided with their artistic and human ideals. In 1935, Strauss resigned because RMK had excluded Jews from membership[42] while Furtwängler walked a precarious, often, dangerous tightrope in his efforts to resist and circumvent policies of Nazi officialdom.[43] Hindemith's carrot and stick relationship with the authorities led to his profound disillusionment with the regime and resulted in his self-exile in 1938.[44]

Notwithstanding objections and criticisms by leading German musicians, and in line with Nazi racial ideology, the RMK's role was also to purge "unsuitable" elements in the professional body.[45] These "unsuitable" elements were defined on the basis of race, sexual preference, political affiliation, and artistic orientation. As a result, Jewish, Roma, and other minority musicians were denied membership and consequently removed from official posts, banned from publishing and composing music, performing, and being performed.[46]

Hideous accusations elevated Jewish and avant-garde music to an almost universal embodiment of evil and the arch enemy of the German people. Allegations ranged from calling Jewish and other non-Aryan composers "imitators and distorters" of the great music masters, economic opportunists, whose compositions poisoned the musical tastes of German culture.[47] The music of Kurt Weill, whose *Die Dreigroschenoper* (The Threepenny Opera) to a libretto by Bertolt Brecht was one of the most popular pieces in the late 1920s (translated into 18 languages and performed over 10,000 times in 5 years throughout Europe alone), was banned because of his "dirty street song talent" and Marxist leanings; his characters were all antiheroes and represented the human societal filth so despised by the Nazis: corrupt officials in league with a sleuth of degenerate societal outcasts that included prostitutes, murderers, beggars, and pimps acting in the London underworld of Victorian England. The work's mass(ive) appeal lay as much in the catchy and hypnotic rapture with which the melodies wrapped themselves around Brecht's irreverent texts, as in the "unmoralizing" moralizing nature of the texts themselves, spoken and sung by unsavory characters: to a country riddled with and suffering from staggering unemployment and astronomical inflation, a 1920s Germany going hungry, Brecht's iconic phrase from the ballad "Wovon lebt der Mensch" (What keeps a man alive?) must have been met by nodding winks, a collective approval shared by all audience members fully aware of its biting (pardon the irony) irony: "Erst kommt das Fressen, dann kommt die Moral" (First food, then morals).

Schoenberg, on the other hand, was accused of destroying the natural order of tones in music by turning to atonality and inventing his own twelve-tone system, which constituted "the Jewish principle of reducing everything to the same level."[48] Schoenberg's modernist pupil Alban Berg, who, along with his fellow student Anton Webern, formed the core group of composers comprising the Second Viennese School, suffered state-supported public indignation and ridicule for groundbreaking achievements in atonal expressionism and dodecaphony. His 1925 opera *Wozzeck*, based on Georg Büchner's fragmentary and incomplete stage play *Woyzeck* (1836–7), achieved undisputed success and was considered the first great atonal opera. Yet despite its seminal musical achievement, the Nazi government uncompromisingly censored performances of the work throughout Germany and German-occupied/annexed countries. Of course, the work was an easy target given both its musical language and subject matter: *Wozzeck* deals with the dehumanizing effects of doctors and the military establishment on a lonely, lowly, and abused soldier living in the barracks in a small provincial military town. Wozzeck's mental instability and perception of events around him distorted through debilitating schizophrenia find perfect expression in Berg's atonal musical landscapes and a variety of singing employed that ranges from traditional operatic singing to high-pitched neurotic vocalizations to speaking to *Sprechstimme*, a Schoenbergian invention that crosses between speaking and singing.

Wozzeck embodied everything the Aryan man was not—and should never be! The witch hunt did not limit itself to living composers but extended back to Mahler, Mendelsohn, and Meyerbeer as well. Mahler's talent was reduced to a capable technical proficiency insufficient to the achievement of true German expression. Instead, he produced kitsch, negative expression, and "hypnotic nirvana." Similarly, Mendelsohn was also denied the ability to reach German depth. His most popular pieces were harshly criticized and deemed to lack "the German soul."[49]

In 1935, jazz was banned from the *Reichs-Rundfunk-Gesellschaft* (Reich Broadcasting Corporation) and derogatorily dismissed as "Nigger music." While modernity and atonality were associated with the Jews, jazz was the product of another inferior race, namely the American Negro. Nazis regarded jazz as representative of a corrupt, capitalist America. Jazz's musical freedom and individualism, improvisation, and syncopated, "primitive" rhythms offended the German sensibilities of high musical art. Furthermore, the Nazi leadership considered the influx of foreign musicians as undesirable and economically threatening.[50]

In *Mein Kampf*, Hitler expressed his racist notions of the "Negro" in America during the Jim Crow era. In several instances he criticized Americans for allowing intermarriage and felt that a "Negro" is inferior and primitive. This reflects in the German mind that his music, jazz in particular, is not cultured.

Although lighter and more popular genres were viciously targeted by Nazi arts policies between 1933 and 1945, the various styles of music performed in nightclubs (jazz, swing, etc.) were sometimes tolerated and unofficially condoned because party members and officials and members of the *Wehrmacht* frequented these venues. Goebbels understood that banning jazz all together would result in Germans listening to foreign radio programs and that would of course involve direct exposure to broadcasts of Allied propaganda.[51]

No work drew the opprobrium of the Nazi Party more than the jazz-influenced opera *Jonny spielt auf* (Jonny Strikes Up) by the "Aryan" composer Ernst Krenek, in which the title character is a Black jazz musician involved in scheming and shady activities. The distorted caricature of Jonny became the iconic image for the 1938 *Entartete Musik* exhibition in Düsseldorf. The exhibit poster image portraying Jonny as an ape, playing saxophone, with a Jewish star on its tuxedo lapel, offensively groups together three enemies of the state: Jew, Negro, jazz; for good measure, a fourth *Untermensch* is included by suggestion: the Gypsy vagabond represented by the prominent gold earring. The exhibit was part of the Reich Music Days, a propaganda festival of "good" and "bad" German music. The "good side" events included performances by the Berlin Philharmonic in concert halls and factories, conducting appearances by Richard Strauss, and new compositions ranging from party hymns, marches, fanfares, secular cantatas, and operas. The "bad" music was featured in the *Entartete Musik* exhibit modeled on the *Entartete Kunst* exhibit from 1937. However, given the performing nature of music which does not lend itself to exhibitions, Nazi organizers struggled with the exhibit format. Pamela Potter describes it as "a confusing mixture of all music that was construed as alienating, overly intellectual, sarcastic, socialist, capitalist or American"[52] and created by Jews or Bolsheviks. Among the composers presented as degenerate were Schoenberg, Weill, and several non-Jewish composers such as Krenek, Berg, Hindemith, and Stravinsky. She further continues to show that the exhibit's heavy reliance on the imagery and devices used in the Degenerate Art exhibit only "highlighted the difficulties in pinning labels on music."[53] To heighten the shock value, degenerate art images were used in connection to musical pieces with the inscription "degenerate art and degenerated music hand in hand."[54] In addition to looking at pictures and reading information about degenerate styles and composers, the participants could sample the "forbidden fruit" in the listening booths, which constituted the most popular feature for curious music listeners, many of whom returned multiple times until denied reentry.

Neither Goebbels nor Ziegler, the exhibit curator and visual artist, had any musical skills or knowledge on how to precisely define the superior features of German music and offered rather vague remarks that "the nature of music lies in melody," that it should be rooted in the folk and reflect German origin (nationalism) and appeal to the masses (socialism).[55] Consequently, any music that did not conform to Nazi ideology was deemed un-German and thus subversive. The speed and force of persecution cannot be overemphasized: by the time the exhibit opened in 1938, "only" five years had elapsed since the NSDAP seized power, and yet, most of the composers "heard" the proverbial music and managed to emigrate, making them easy targets. The exhibit received considerably less publicity than the 1937 *Entartete Kunst* exhibit and within a week or so was hurriedly closed—much earlier than planned.

The Munich exhibition of "Degenerate Art" has gone down in history as the most potent symbol of Nazi cultural barbarism and brutality, the climax in the development of a totalitarian ideology.[37] Ironically, Goebbels, Hitler, and especially Göring collected the works of modern artists or had them sold on the international market to enrich the coffers of the Reich.[56]

An ominous and foreboding excerpt from Hitler's address opens the Great German Art Exhibition from July 18, 1937, held a day before the launch of the Degenerate Art Exhibition. Hitler leaves no doubt as to the final reckoning awaiting denounced artists;[57] this rhetorical downbeat to the "German" exhibition can also be regarded as the ideological upbeat to the genocide that follows—from canvas to concentration camp:

> From now on we will wage an inexorable purge of war against the last elements of our cultural breakdown. But now—I assure you—all the mutually supportive and thus, holding cliques, of babblers, amateurs and art swindlers will be dug up and eliminated.[58]

PART IV

Mein Kampf and the Crusade against Germany's "Enemies"

In turning to the specific connections between *Mein Kampf* and the Holocaust, we launch our boat onto deep and stormy waters. Nowhere in *Mein Kampf* does Hitler clearly declare his intentions to murder the Jews. Even his bizarre assertion in volume II (viz., "had twelve or fifteen thousand of these Hebrew spoilers of the people been held under poison gas as the hundreds of thousands of our very best German workers from all classes and professions had to endure on the battlefield, then the sacrifice of millions at the front would not have been in vain") is too vague as a wild-eyed subjunctive to prove the existence of a coherent murder plan. The tone of brutal indifference toward the Jews evinced in the previous statement was fully consistent with Hitler's public addresses of the early 1920s. In Munich's Bürgerbräukeller in July 1920, he called for the "removal of the Jews from the *Volkskörper* [people's body]," demanding that "no humanity" be shown them. Intimates of Hitler's attested to his violent malice toward the Jews at this time. Hitler's biographer Georg Schott described his position on the Jewish Question in 1924 as follows: "'Until they're all hanged from lampposts, there won't be any peace.' Certainly, dear friend, Adolf Hitler said that."

These and other threats against the lives of Jews aside, Nazi Jewish policy after Hitler seized power endeavored to "solve" the Jewish Question through revocation of their civil rights and forced emigration. As the editors of the critical edition observe, nothing in any of Hitler's anti-Jewish measures of the 1930s foreshadows the genocide of European Jews through mass shooting and gas chambers. The critical step toward mass murder evolved from a string of interrelated events, beginning with the invasion and occupation of Poland in 1939 followed by the attack on the USSR in the summer of 1941. Complications related to the mass shooting of Eastern European Jewish civilians during that fateful summer led to experiments in August and early September. Their object was to find alternative methods of killing that would spare the shooters the trauma of killing hundreds of thousands of men, women, and children. By the latter half of September 1941, the Nazis had arrived at gassing as the preferred technique for achieving the aims of the "Final Solution."

In their interpretations of the decisions culminating in the Final Solution, scholars have differed over Hitler's role. Some emphasize the centrality of his influence, portraying him as acting like a Mafia don ordering his henchmen to carry out his dirty work. Others, while conceding that Hitler's anti-Semitism formed the general context for genocide, argue that the actual plan to gas the Jews and the steps toward its execution were largely undertaken by Nazi officials in occupied Eastern Europe with little input from Hitler. These steps involved the deportation of Jews from every corner of Europe to the death camps of Auschwitz-Birkenau, Majdanek, Sobibor, Treblinka, Belzec, and Chelmno, all of them located in Poland.

The notion of a Jewish conspiracy to overthrow or sabotage an established authority provided the ideological cover for killing operations targeting Jews. This idea was a fixture of the postwar folk-national right in Germany, as Othmar Plöckinger describes in our text. No document of the Weimar era electrified the Jewish conspiracy myth more than the fraudulent *Protocols of the Elders of Zion*, published in Russia in 1903 and purporting to be the record of a conspiracy of Jews and Freemasons to subvert world civilization. The conspirators, it claimed, would weaponize leftist politics as a means of toppling world governments, thereafter erecting in their place a vast Judeo-Masonic tyranny. Despite the exposure of *The Protocols* as a forgery in 1921, anti-Semites across the globe propagated the legend of a Jewish cabal to subvert Western cultures. In his *Handbuch der Judenfrage* Theodor Fritsch, whose writing exerted an important and lasting influence on Hitler, wrote that "all the revolutions of the previous centuries . . . predominately served the interests of the Jews." According to Fritsch, World Jewry was both the cause and the leader of these revolutions, which included the French Revolution, the Revolutions of 1848, and the 1917 Bolshevik Revolution. To achieve Jewish dominion the conspirators employed socialism and Marxism as well as liberalism, capitalism, and Bolshevism. *Mein Kampf* is studded with similar allegations, as in this passage from volume I: "only in the brain of such a monster—not a human being—could the plan of an organization assume sensible form, the activity of which must lead as the final result to the collapse of human culture and with it the devastation of the world."

The United States was not immune to this pernicious myth of Jewish treachery. Its main American exponent was the industrialist Henry Ford, whose anti-Semitism preexisted *The Protocols* yet received a fillip from it when Ford encountered the forgery in the early 1920s. Under *The Protocols*' spell Ford's newspaper, *The Dearborn Independent*, claimed that Jews used both the national debt and the Federal Reserve System to enslave Americans. They perpetrated such crimes as members of an international Jewish conspiracy, one that conferred significant advantages on Jews in their dealings with upright Gentiles handicapped by their individualism.

Mein Kampf reveals a septic anti-Semitism so radical in both its contents and implications that it dwarfs the half-measures taken against the German Jews by the early Nazi regime (disemancipation, emigration). Although no concrete plan for their systematic murder is visible in *Mein Kampf*, clouds of homicidal intent billow around its baleful language. Genocide is in the air that *Mein Kampf* breathes, just as it would be on the soil of Eastern Europe by the summer of 1941.

8

The Auroras of the Final Solution

Intimations of Genocide in *Mein Kampf*

Michael S. Bryant

We defy augury. There's a special providence in the fall of a sparrow. If it be now, 'tis not to come. If it be not to come, it will be now. If it be not now, yet it will come—the readiness is all.

(HAM 5.2.165-68)

The year was 1923, and Adolf Hitler, a demobilized army corporal, failed artist, and head of a rising, Munich-based, folk-national political party, was becoming an idol of the extreme Weimar right wing. Such was his growing fame that by the fall of that year he had become an object of international journalistic attention. In September, just two months before he would try to overthrow the Weimar government, Hitler was interviewed by a Catalonian journalist, Eugeni Xammar. In the course of their interview he told him:

> A pogrom is a splendid thing, but nowadays it has lost a good deal of its Medieval effectiveness. . . . How would it profit us to eradicate the Jewish population of Munich when the Jews in the remainder of the country, as it is now, still control money and politics? In all of Germany there

> are more than a million Jews. What do you want to do? Kill all of them during the night? That would of course be the best solution, and if that were to be done then Germany would be saved. But that isn't possible. I have examined the problem from all sides: it isn't possible. The world would attack us instead of thanking us as they really should do. The world has not understood the importance of the Jewish Question for the simple reason that they are ruled by the Jews. Do you understand now? The Jewish Question is a chain, and Germany must tear this chain if it doesn't want to die. We've already seen that pogroms don't work. Therefore there only remains expulsion: mass expulsion.[1]

All of the elements of Hitler's "anti-semitism of reason,"[2] as it would later unfold, are imbedded in the earlier statement: Hitler's desire to get rid of the Jews through emigration, his belief that the world fails to comprehend the gravity of the "Jewish Question" because it is "controlled by Jews," the myth of the Jewish domination of international finance and politics, and the crotchet that will pulse like a heartbeat throughout his memoir *Mein Kampf*—the notion that Germany is pitted in a life-and-death struggle against the Jews. But there is another aspect of his statement to Xammar that stops the reader cold in her tracks. This is Hitler's reference to "killing the Jews during the night." Hitler's meaning, accepted on its face, is plain: he is saying the best solution would be to murder the Jews at one fell stroke. This could not be done, however, because the rest of the world would condemn Germany. Hence, the only real solution was mass expulsion.

I will leave it to readers of this chapter whether they are as startled by Hitler's words as I was when I first read them. For me the shock—this is not too strong a word to describe my reaction—was sharpened in no small degree by late twentieth-century debates over when Hitler and the Nazis determined to murder all European Jews within their reach. The battle lines were drawn between two opposing camps: the so-called intentionalists, who argued that Hitler formed the intention to destroy the Jews early in his career (as early as 1918 for a leading intentionalist, Lucy Dawidowycz),[3] and the "functionalists," who contended that the Nazis arrived at genocide late and through an improvised sequence of decisions by local German officials.[4] The intentionalists tended to stress the role of Hitler in the decision-making process; the functionalists by contrast de-emphasized Hitler's role, stressing instead the initiative of Nazi satraps in occupied Eastern Europe acting without explicit orders from Hitler but in a manner they thought he would approve.

The focus of analysis in this debate has nearly always been on Nazi Jewish policy of the 1930s and the war years—that is, on what the Nazis did once they had power to shape Jewish policy. Rarely was *Mein Kampf* (published in two volumes, 1925–7) considered relevant to this question. With the recent critical edition of *Mein Kampf* published by the Institute for Contemporary History, it may be timely to revisit the intentionalist-functionalist controversy in light of Hitler's autobiography. If we do, we might find ourselves reassessing Hitler's thinking about the fate of the Jews long before the official launching of the Final Solution.

Mein Kampf contains no direct statement of Hitler's intention to murder the Jews of Europe. It is not my position that the issues raised in the intentionalist-functionalist debate can be decided with recourse to passages in Hitler's text. However, serious engagement with it will reveal that it is laden with genocidal implications. My aim here is not to convince the reader that Hitler planned to kill all the Jews of Europe already in the mid-1920s. Rather, I would like to convey how my reading of the critical edition of *Mein Kampf* has forced me to reexamine Hitler's thinking about the Jewish Question. Such reexamination has persuaded me that mass murder was on Hitler's mind at this time, and while he likely discounted it for the reasons he imprudently shared with Eugeni Xammar—that is, the opposition of the world community—murder never disappeared from his thinking as a possible option for dealing with the Jews and, indeed, as perhaps the best option of them all.

The Sitz im Leben of *Mein Kampf*

Mein Kampf is a prison memoir. This simple fact should not be lost sight of. It was not the first time that Hitler had been imprisoned: on January 12, 1922, he was convicted of a public order offense (*Landfriedensbruch*) for disrupting the meeting of a rival group held in Munich's Löwenbräukeller. He served thirty-three days of his three-month sentence in the Munich-Stadelheim prison before release on probation. Needless to say, his conviction for high treason after the debacle of the Beerhall Putsch, a revolt aimed, in Hitler's own words, at overthrowing the "Berlin Jew government and the November criminals of 1918,"[5] was far graver than his previous offense, carrying with it the real possibility of drastically more serious consequences. Sentenced on April 1, 1924, to five years in Landsberg prison, he ultimately served only thirteen months. (He was given credit for the months he spent in pre-trial confinement.) These thirteen months, moreover, were a privileged form of incarceration known in German as *Festungshaft*, or "fortress detention." The favorable conditions afforded him the opportunity to write the first volume of *Mein Kampf*, the manuscript of which was, according to Nazi legend, smuggled out of prison in a hollowed-out gramophone.[6]

During Hitler's imprisonment, he had no idea precisely when he would be released. American readers might be incredulous given the seriousness of his crimes, but Hitler could look forward to the possibility of parole on October 1, 1924—a mere six months after pronouncement of his sentence. (In the United States, treason is a capital offense, and the occurrence of several deaths in connection with Hitler's putsch would have supported his being charged with multiple felony murders under American law today.)

Right-wing elements pressured the Bavarian government to parole Hitler at the first opportunity. These circumstances to the contrary, there was no guarantee that Hitler would be paroled sooner rather than later or that he would be released from prison at all until he had finished his full term.

The obstacles to his release were considerable. In his report opposing Hitler's parole, dated September 23, 1924, the deputy police president of Munich warned that Hitler would likely resume his subversive activities if granted parole and thus posed "a constant danger for the internal and external security of the state." Furthermore, he noted that evidence had surfaced of Hitler's involvement while in prison with plans to reorganize the paramilitary units officially dissolved after the putsch. The report went on to advise that in the event Hitler was nonetheless released on parole, he should be deported to his home country of Austria (Hitler had not at this time become a German citizen). In his recommendation against Hitler's early release, the Munich police president was joined by the original chief prosecutor in Hitler's trial.[7]

Balanced in the scales against the police president's and chief prosecutor's arguments was the glowing assessment of Otto Leybold, the governor of Landsberg prison. Leybold portrayed Hitler as an innocuous, even courtly, figure completely absorbed in writing his book. "[Hitler] will not return to liberty with threats and thoughts of revenge against those in public office who oppose him and frustrated his plans in November 1923," Leybold wrote. "He will be no agitator against the government. . . . He emphasizes how convinced he is that a state cannot exist without firm internal order and firm government." Leybold's endorsement of Hitler carried the day, and on September 25 his parole was approved. The decision to release Hitler did not, however, fully resolve the issue of his expulsion from Germany to Austria. The Bavarians sought to convince the Austrian government to accept Hitler's deportation from Germany right after he left Landsberg prison. Vienna's initial receptivity to this idea some months earlier had changed by late September, and the portcullis abruptly clanged shut on the plan to send Hitler back to Austria, never to be revived. In April 1925 Hitler would be notified that his Austrian citizenship had been terminated, forever ending the prospect of his deportation to that country.[8]

Thus, during the time he was writing volume I of *Mein Kampf*, Hitler knew that he had to remain on the good side of the prison authorities. Without their support, his bid for parole would surely fail. Moreover, he must have understood that even if he were to be paroled, he might be deported from Germany back to Austria. Either of these possibilities—his failure to secure parole or his expulsion from Germany after release from prison—would be his ruin. They would consign to the rubbish heap his plans to revive the now-illegal Nazi Party, fashion it into the spearhead of the folk-national movement in Germany, and consolidate his own position as its unchallenged leader. Not only must the worries associated with parole and/or deportation have weighed on him through the fall of 1924; Hitler also faced the double challenge of lifting the ban on his public speaking (the

Redeverbot, which extended to most of the German states from the fall of 1925 until 1927) and reversing the prohibition of the Nazi Party. In short, he had to be on his best behavior for any of these dominos to fall. These concerns crept into his composition of *Mein Kampf* and affected the book's overall structure (Figure 8.1).

For starters, the original title of the book was ungainly and provocative: *4½ Years of Struggle against Lies, Stupidity, and Cowardice: A Reckoning.* Hitler would eventually reduce it to the simpler *Mein Kampf* (My Struggle). The dates for the book's publication as advertised in *Eher-Verlag*'s brochures during the summer of 1924 all fell through. Concerns about a too-caustic tone in a book centered on score-settling with his adversaries likely induced Hitler to restructure it. He decided to de-emphasize the "reckoning" of the book's original title and place in the foreground his political autobiography.[9] The reformulated book would be a classic bildungsroman with Hitler playing the role of a pure-hearted naïf from the provinces who developed into the canny, iron-willed leader of the hard German right.[10]

FIGURE 8.1 *Rare dust jacket cover of the first edition of* Mein Kampf. *As the editors of the critical edition observe, the portrayal of Nazism's enemies as serpents directly evokes the coarse anti-Semitic imagery of the German folk-national movement. Subsequent editions of* Mein Kampf *would discard such cartoonish graphics in favor of more solemn motifs associated with the Bible and Christian hymnals. See the critical edition commentary in MKII 1753, Bild 5. Courtesy of Wikimedia Commons.*

Hitler's reorientation of his memoir may account for why we encounter no unequivocal references in *Mein Kampf* to "murder fantasies," as the editors of the new edition call them,[11] specifically focused on the Jews. Given his goals both during and immediately after his release from prison, Hitler would have avoided open threats of mass murder even if such thoughts were on his mind at the time. Nonetheless, we have persuasive evidence that such "murder fantasies" toward the Jews occupied his thoughts both before and during his thirteen months in Landsberg.

In an interview with a Munich law student in August 1920, Hitler addressed himself to the "Jewish Question," declaring that the "Jewish bacillus" had to be "eradicated" because of the threat it posed to the "body." According to the student, Hitler related that the Jews were inassimilable; the Germans simply could not abide their presence in Germany. In a situation in which the very existence of the Germans was at stake, not even the life of a *Volksgenossen* (a folk comrade) could be spared, "much less the life of a maliciously inclined, dangerous foreign stock" (by which he meant the Jews).[12]

Two years later, the journalist and retired military officer Josef Hell asked Hitler what would be done with the Jews if he gained "full discretionary powers." Hell reported the future German dictator's reaction:

> His eyes no longer saw me but instead bore past me and off into empty space; . . . he fell into a kind of paroxysm that ended with his shouting, as if to a whole public gathering: "Once I really am in power, my first and foremost task will be the annihilation of the Jews. As soon as I have the power to do so, I will have gallows built in rows—at the Marienplatz in Munich, for example—as many as traffic allows. Then the Jews will be hanged indiscriminately, and they will remain hanging until they stink; they will hang there as long as the principles of hygiene permit. As soon as they have been untied, the next batch will be strung up, and so on down the line, until the last Jew in Munich has been exterminated. Other cities will follow suit, precisely in this fashion, until all Germany has been completely cleansed of Jews."

Hell expressed the view that Hitler in this interview had "abruptly cast off the mask that I had taken for his true face."[13]

Two months before his putsch, as we have seen, Hitler told Eugeni Xammar that the best solution to the Jewish Question would be to "murder them in the night," a solution rendered unviable because of expected international reactions. Finally, in July 1924, Hitler was visited in his prison cell by a Bohemian Nazi named Kugler, who pressed him to submit an article on the Jewish Question to the Nazi newspaper *The National Socialist*. This was Hitler's reply:

> Yes, it's entirely correct that I've altered my view about the tactics used to combat the Jews. I've come to realize that previously I was far too

> mild! While writing my book I came to the realization that in the future the harshest means of combat must be employed if we want to achieve success. I am convinced that not only for our people but also for all peoples this is an existential question. Because the Jew is the plague of the world.[14]

It hardly requires pointing out that "the harshest means of combat" in a struggle for existence is killing.

As we pivot in the next section to the text of *Mein Kampf* itself, what might we conclude about Hitler's intentions toward the Jews in the first half of the 1920s? On one hand, the editors of the critical edition caution that we need to approach Hitler's demands for the eradication of the Jews with caution.[15] Othmar Plöckinger in particular has argued that Hitler's declamations against the Jews were not unique but may be readily found in other folk-national writings of the era. On the other, there is no getting around the fact (conceded by the editors) that Hitler asserted the need to physically eliminate at the very least some Jews, and that on two occasions—his interviews with the Munich law student and Eugeni Xammar—he used explicitly homicidal language to describe what should ideally be done with them. (This is true as well for Hitler's interview with Josef Hell.) In *Mein Kampf* the lowering skies of Hitler's anti-Semitism displayed in these incidents become even darker with a storm.

Predominant Themes in *Mein Kampf* and Their Implications for the Holocaust

Secularized Apocalypticism: The "Either-Or"

If there is a thematic center to *Mein Kampf*, it is the binary character of Hitler's thinking. For Hitler the Germans are in the grip of an existential crisis, a literal struggle for life and death. The failure to respond to this crisis appropriately—that is, in a manner Hitler demands—will lead to the destruction of the German people. *Mein Kampf* is written in an apocalyptic key, and the choices the Germans face are all or nothing, national flourishing or national ruin, the life of their country or its death. There is no in-between here, no reconciliation of opposites. Following in the rhetorical footsteps of his hard-right forebear Paul de Lagarde and mentor Dietrich Eckart,[16] Hitler insists "there is no making pacts with Jews: there can only be the hard: either-or."[17] The Germans will either preserve themselves by following his counsel or they will perish utterly from the face of the earth. This, says Hitler, is what his folk-national movement is all about—it seeks to create the conditions that will allow Germany to avoid its death sentence.

The apocalyptic quality of Hitler's text requires further examination because it is intimately linked to the dire threat he claims the Jews posed to Germany (and, as we will see, to all of human civilization). It has become a trope of scholarship on *Mein Kampf* that an apocalyptic mentality grounded in a distinctive Nazi "eschatology" (a theory about the end of the world) pervaded Hitler's thinking from his entry into politics in 1920 until his suicide in April 1945.[18] These of course are religious concepts. According to scholars of religion, most religions have an eschatology consisting of two parallel types: the self ("personal eschatology"), focused on the salvation of the individual soul, and the cosmos ("cosmic eschatology"), focused on the end of time. Significantly, eschatologies are often accompanied by violence. They are especially attractive to communities of people who have undergone persecution or are gripped by paranoia. Such communities are prone to demonizing their alleged oppressors or enemies. As one scholar of comparative religion, Jeffrey Kripal, has described this tendency in the New Testament Book of Revelation (a *locus classicus* of Christian apocalypticism), "[Revelation] advances a most violent logic, which involves the demonization of the outgroup or enemy, the sanctification of revenge as an act of God, and the conviction that history must end in spectacular violence."[19]

In calling Hitler's tone in *Mein Kampf* "apocalyptic," one need not accept the view that National Socialism was a "political religion," as some have advocated. However, in a modified form, religious terminology like the "apocalypse" and "eschatology" seems relevant to Hitler's attitudes toward the Jews. Some advocates of the political religions concept (e.g., Eric Voegelin and the historian Michael Burleigh) do not hold that Nazism was a religion per se—only that it "caricatured fundamental patterns of religious belief."[20] Similarly, German scholar Klaus Vondung contends that "modern apocalyptic world views" have cut away the religious underpinnings of the apocalyptic belief system. What remains is the propensity to divide the world between the "evil enemy" and "the chosen ones," between whom no rapprochement is possible.[21] Destruction of the evil enemy will lead to the earth's purification, but this is no salvation effected by God as it is in mainstream religions, nor is it located beyond time. Instead, human beings—for Hitler, the racially pure Germans led by the Nazi Party—are the agents of apocalyptic change here and now, combating a monstrous opponent in order to save the world. Vondung writes that "this apocalyptic scenario is completely worldly. It suggests that . . . violence must be used to achieve the envisioned goal."[22]

A secularized apocalypticism, then, conditions Hitler's thought in *Mein Kampf*. Religion is not the cause of Hitler's malice toward the Jews; the real cause is Hitler's belief that the Jews were behind Germany's defeat in the First World War and were scheming to overthrow the government and replace it with a Soviet system. His hatred of the Jews is political and cultural, not religious.[23] Yet, the rhetoric of apocalypticism is a vehicle for Hitler's denunciation of the Jews: his is a secularized appropriation of a theological idea. He uses the husk of a religious concept, drained of its theological content, to envision a war to the death against the Jews as the archenemy of the human race.

Having painted a stark portrait of future calamity, what then according to Hitler are the conditions necessary to the survival of Germany? He makes clear that the German population must grow, and growth is possible only if the Germans acquire more land. Already in volume I (written in 1924), Hitler admits that Germany cannot acquire more land, and thus preserve itself, without military conflict. He insists, therefore, that the Germans must prepare for war.[24] Since the land Germany needs is in the east, war with Russia will be inevitable. Only in this way can Germany avoid a "Malthusian catastrophe" (a phrase Hitler actually uses in *Mein Kampf*).[25] Thus, Hitler foretold in 1924 his invasion of the USSR in June 1941, a war that would be fought on the German side beyond the restraints of legality.

War in the east is only one condition essential to seizing land and eluding national destruction. Another is an effective reckoning with Germany's alleged internal enemies—the socialists, Marxists, and Jews. Hitler repeatedly identifies the political left with the Jews. He claims that during his Vienna years he had an epiphany when he realized that the Jews were the "leaders of social democracy" and that the social democratic press was controlled by the Jews.[26] The victory of either group—it mattered not which one because they were identical in his thinking—would mean the end of the human race. The equation of leftist politics and Jewry inspires Hitler to bombastic oratory: the triumph of Jewish Marxism would be the "funeral wreath of the human race," causing "the earth [to] . . . revolve unpeopled through the ether."[27] For Hitler the struggle against social democracy and the Jews was existential. Hanging in the balance was the survival now, not only of Germany but of the earth's entire population. With this infamous paragraph of *Mein Kampf*, the enemies of the Nazis loom as a menace not only to Germany but to the human race as a whole. The threat is not just national; it is planetary.

Jews as the Source of All Evil in the World

An enemy this nefarious must possess attributes that are uniquely and ultimately evil. Unsurprisingly, then, Hitler portrays the Jews in terms that go far beyond the garden-variety invective of political language.[28] On the surface, it would appear that Hitler uses metaphors to talk about the Jews. At various points they are likened to the Black Death, vermin, bacilli, bacteria, poison, vipers, adders, vampires, parasites, and devils. So intemperate and bitter are Hitler's words, however, that the reader gradually realizes the author is not speaking figuratively but literally: he is affirming that the Jews are not just *like* a deadly disease or a poisonous snake, but are *in fact* the Black Death and vipers in human form. Both the socialists and the Jews are "poisoners" of the German people who had to be destroyed, much as vermin noxious to human beings must be exterminated. Hitler refers to the socialists and Jews as "assassins of the nation" responsible for plotting Germany's defeat in November 1918 and laments that the military was not used back then to "eradicate this plague."[29] He uncritically accepts the self-serving canard of Jewish perfidy invented by Paul von Hindenburg in an interview given in November 1919, which blamed the left and the government for "stabbing Germany in the back" and causing its defeat. To this hoax Hitler adds his wildly chimerical fantasy of the Jews as pathogens. They didn't just betray the German people by causing the monarchy's collapse. Rather, the Jews were "disease agents" that had sapped Germany's "capacity for self-preservation."[30] They "poison the blood stream" of the German people, rendering them incapable of national self-defense.[31]

Hitler's diatribe against the Jews reaches a crescendo in the central chapter of *Mein Kampf*, chapter 11, entitled "Volk and Race." Here Hitler accuses the Jews of being "parasites in the bodies of other people."[32] A couple pages later he portrays them as parasitic vampires preying on host cultures, draining them of their life force.[33] The image of the Jew as a parasite is quite arresting in its implications. The parasite inhabits the body of the host and flourishes at its expense by imitating the body's cellular structure. The parasite is successful because it convinces the host that it poses no threat to the health of the body. Hitler draws on this concept later in the chapter as he derides the Jews as impostors mimicking the forms of German culture. In reality they are not racially German, Hitler insists. A Jew who presents himself as German because he speaks the language is hiding behind a mere *Gewand*, a disguise that can be readily changed for another. For Hitler the Jews are linguistic masters capable of speaking a thousand languages. Their mastery of languages, however, did not change their essential nature—they were still Jews.[34]

Chapter 11 of *Mein Kampf* claims the Jews are bent on enslaving and destroying all non-Jews. They've already ruined Germany's economy by means of labor unions. They prey on innocent German girls with the intent of despoiling them. He also blames the so-called Rhineland bastards on the Jews (i.e., the Afro-German children of German women and French North African troops during the French occupation of the Rhineland). Elsewhere in *Mein Kampf* Hitler has already told us that race mixing is the cause of every civilization's decay and collapse. Thus, in promoting miscegenation the Jews were a direct threat to Germany's very existence. Toward the end of the chapter, Hitler prophesies that a price will be paid for these outrages. There will come a day of reckoning for the "treason against the fatherland" of November 1918.[35]

Glorious Ends Justify Every Means: Hitler's View of Necessity

In dealing with the existential menace to Germany posed by its enemies, particularly the Jews, Hitler writes that all means of defense are justified.

This idea would become a mainstay of Nazi rhetoric through the 1930s and into the war years. Deriving from a social Darwinist viewpoint, the notion holds that the individual's "highest aim" is "preservation of its own kind." Curiously for a man allergic to the human rights language of Enlightenment *philosophes*, Hitler depicts the "preservation" of one's race as a kind of human right—a right that is superior to the state's law, summed up in the pithy phrase, "Human rights break state law" (*Menschenrecht bricht Staatsrecht*).[36] The editors of the critical edition comment that the Nazi "right to self-preservation" effectively abrogates legality and replaces it with the slogan of "whatever serves the German people is law."[37] Much later in the text, Hitler returns to the theme of a higher good served by dubious actions, affirming that all considerations of decency and humanity are abolished by war and the struggle for existence.[38] In jurisprudence the justification of criminal acts for the sake of a higher good is called the doctrine of "necessity." Within the Weimar-era far right, Hitler was not alone in citing necessity as a justification for committing crimes; other folk-national figures portrayed the Jews as harmful to Germany, arguing that all countermeasures against them were permissible in "self-defense."[39] Along with the life-and-death struggle against the Jews, necessity is a leitmotif of *Mein Kampf*. In chapter 9 of volume II Hitler returns to it in his discussion of the "organic folk-national state," proclaiming that in the state's defense all means were allowable and that "no victim was too great."[40]

Let's take a moment to reflect on what Hitler has been telling us. He believes Germany is beset by enemies like the socialists, Marxists, and Jews who are corroding Germany from within, sapping its vitality and hastening its collapse. The Jews in particular are insidious vampirish microbes that infest society in order to destroy it, mimicking the forms of German culture while remaining racially Jewish. If Germany does not rid itself of them, then it will perish from the earth. In combating the Jewish scourge all means are permissible because the right to self-preservation prevails over ethical and legal norms. Germany's very existence hangs in the balance in this struggle, as does the future of the human race. If the Jews win, everyone faces annihilation and the world will cycle unpeopled through the void of space. This is his diagnosis of Germany's predicament.

To whom, according to Hitler, should Germany look for deliverance from these straits? To Hitler's folk-national political party, quite obviously, but more narrowly the Germans should place their trust in Nazi "party members," that is, zealots who will act in strict conformity to Hitler's ideology. In volume II (completed in 1926), he distinguishes between "party members" and "party followers." The critical difference between the two resides in their attitude toward the goals of the Nazi movement. Mere followers agree with these goals while members fight for them.[41] The members should be young men whose zeal and unconditional obedience set them apart as a distinct minority within the movement. As children future

Nazi Party members would learn the virtue of "discretion." Through their military training they would be instilled with an ethic of absolute obedience and the capacity to "endure silently" the "injustice" that they witness.[42] The latter is an enigmatic sentence; what does it mean? We can interpret Hitler's words in view of his earlier pronouncement that the struggle for self-preservation justifies every countermeasure. The cause of Germany's distress are the Jews and the political left. In extricating Germany from its peril, all means are permitted. To move against this threat, then, the Nazis in power will need an ideologically reliable cadre of true believers—young men inculcated with an ethic of unswerving obedience, loyalty, and the ability to keep a secret. These "party members" will do whatever is necessary and avoid talking about it in public.

As it turns out, the SS would become these hard-core members dedicated to achieve the Nazi goal of the *Volksstaat*—a Germany under the rule of one party, strengthened by its racial homogeneity and prepared to expand its borders through armed conquest. Hitler tells us, in type italicized to emphasize its importance, that "*the larger and more inwardly revolutionary an idea, the more activistic its membership will become*." In this fashion, an organization "preserves only the most active of the followers gained by propaganda to the membership [of the organization]." For Hitler, in the cultivation of its membership "guaranteed through natural selection" lies the "prerequisite . . . for the successful fight to realize the idea [of the movement]."[43] The editors of the critical edition regard this passage as presaging the rise of Heinrich Himmler's SS as an elite vanguard of the Nazi Party.[44] Much later, in October 1943, Himmler will praise their "toughness" and discretion in an infamous address to SS officers in Posen. In his speech Himmler evoked the difference between party members and party followers when he distinguished between the SS, who knew what it meant to see thousands of corpses lying on the ground, and the eighty million Germans unprepared to commit genocide. Himmler continued: "To have endured this and—with the exception of human weaknesses—to have remained decent has made us tough. It is a glorious chapter that has never been mentioned and never will be mentioned."[45] For Himmler the "glory" of the SS was to have murdered Jewish men, women, and children by the millions because it was a necessary act required by Nazi ideology. They have carried out their orders loyally, decently, and with the utmost discretion. However, due to their silence, history would never recall their glorious exploits.

Himmler does not stop there. He goes on in his Posen speech to acclaim the murderers of Jews as a "racial elite of the Germanic people," one that in the future would form "the ruling class for all of Europe."[46] If we follow the editors' thesis, Himmler's "racial elite" was the antitype of Hitler's party members mentioned in volume II of *Mein Kampf*, sharpened on the whetting stone of constant propaganda into knife-edged fanatics who will fight, kill, and die for the racist ideology of National Socialism.

The Cagey Hitler: The Führer as Master Dissembler

At no point in *Mein Kampf* does Hitler ever declare his intention to exterminate the Jews through mass killing. The absence of such language, along with the Nazi government's efforts until 1941 to "solve" the Jewish Question through emigration and expulsion, has led many historians to accept the view that the Final Solution only emerged as an option of last resort in late 1941/early 1942. Yet, as we have already seen, there is evidence that killing Jews was on Hitler's mind as early as 1920, appearing again in his interviews with Josef Hell in 1922 and Eugeni Xammar in 1923. We will recall Hitler's statement to Xammar that it would "of course" be best to kill the Jews off during the night. If that were done, however, the rest of the world would attack Germany. Hitler then remarked that "mass expulsion" was the only alternative. The ambiguity of Hitler's thinking on display here—in this episode, his approval of murder even as he rejects it on utilitarian grounds—is also discernible in *Mein Kampf*. Early in volume I Hitler says that he learned from studying the SPD how to "conceal" his true goals. He won't talk about them publicly and certainly won't reduce them to writing in his autobiography. Instead, he will bide his time until the moment is ripe. His real thoughts, he implies, are concealed "between the lines."[47]

A report of the Supreme Court of the Nazi Party helps elucidate Hitler's habit of self-concealment and the expectation that his underlings would have to divine his secret meaning. The court inquired into allegations of murder, plunder, and rape during the Night of Broken Glass pogrom in 1938. Its purpose was not to verify the commission of these crimes nor to apportion blame for them—the party leadership had encouraged the violence unleashed by the pogrom—but to retroactively justify them. Nonetheless, its report is revealing of the Nazis' modus operandi in communicating illegal orders for execution by its rank and file, a tactic already adumbrated in *Mein Kampf*:

> The Nazi leaders had learned during the time of struggle before 1933 how to shield the Party from the legal consequences of illegal demonstrations and other actions—namely, by issuing orders so vague and imprecise that the Party could always invoke plausible deniability whenever it called on its members to commit illegal acts. The members in the lower echelons of the Party had learned on their part to read between the lines of their instructions and knew that the wishes of the party leadership did not necessarily correspond with the wording of their orders.[48]

Officially desired criminality wrapped in a skein of misdirection and subterfuge became a high art in Nazi governance. It characterized Hitler's approach to two of his most egregious programs of mass murder: the Final Solution and the T-4 operation (targeting the mentally disabled).

A meeting between Hitler and his *Kreisleiters* (Nazi district leaders) in April 1937 lends credence to the portrait drawn here of Hitler as a master dissembler, presenting different masks to the public that hid his real intent. At the meeting Hitler responded to a newspaper editorial asking that Jewish firms be identified by special markings. He bristled at the suggestion and told his listeners the following:

> From whom is he [the editor] demanding this? Who can give the necessary orders? Only I can give them. . . . My point is then this: the aim of our policy is crystal clear to all of us. All that concerns me is never to take a step that I might later have to retrace and never to take a step that could damage us in any way. You must understand that I always go as far as I dare and never further. . . . Even in a struggle with an adversary it is not my way to issue a direct challenge to a trial of strength. I do not say "Come on and fight, because I want a fight." Instead I shout at him (and I shout louder and louder): "I mean to destroy you." And then I use my intelligence to help me to maneuver him into a tight corner so that he cannot strike back, and then I deliver the fatal blow.[49]

Hitler's own self-portrait as a wily prevaricator, giving the glad hand and biding his time until the opportune moment, is a recurrent feature of his political career. In 1938 he advised General Franz Halder, on the verge of his installation as Army Chief of Staff, that "you will never be able to discover my thoughts and intentions until I give them out as orders." When Halder rejoined that military men were "accustomed to forming our ideas collectively," Hitler shot back:

> No, in politics things are entirely different. You will never learn what is going on in my head. As for those who boast of being privy to my thoughts—to them I lie all the more.[50]

For the late Holocaust historian Gerald Fleming, this aspect of Hitler's thinking—his conscious effort to mislead others about his real intentions—is central to understanding his involvement in the Final Solution:

> Although no one can pierce Hitler's mind, it is absolutely essential to establish the centrality of this aspect of deceptiveness, his cunning and his lies, particularly with reference to the enactment of the Final Solution that Hitler conceived for the Jewish question.[51]

Every liar eventually betrays himself. Did that moment occur for Hitler in his address to the *Kreisleiters* quoted earlier? Did the veil of legality fall away and Hitler's malignance for one nanosecond peer forth from the spinning kaleidoscope of false faces to announce its true intentions? Holocaust historian Saul Friedlander believes this was the case; dubbing Hitler's speech "of major significance," he considers it evidence of an exterminatory mindset visible already in 1937.[52]

When read in light of *Mein Kampf*, this and other episodes reveal Hitler's inner attitude toward the Jews well before the outbreak of the Second World War. Someday, perhaps sooner than anyone thinks, he will avenge himself on the "November criminals" who caused Germany's loss in the First World War and remained a clear and present danger to all higher culture. No concrete plan of genocide existed at this time anymore than a fully articulated murder plot guided the thinking of Henry II in his dealings with the archbishop of Canterbury, Thomas Beckett. Even in the absence of a detailed blueprint, malicious minds will drift toward death, gathering disguises of various kinds in the meantime to hide their intention. In Hitler's case evidence exists, should we heed it, that he strove to conceal his intentions until the moment for action had arrived. For Hitler, the readiness was all.

* * * *

Without directly mentioning biological killing, Hitler infused *Mein Kampf* with intimations of genocide. To carry out the illegal but necessary acts essential to Germany's survival, a dedicated inner circle of loyal and discreet troops would be needed. These ideologically reliable persons would often have to read between the lines of Hitler's orders to gather his true meaning. The cagey Hitler did not openly advocate mass murder in his autobiography, yet his text is redolent of it. One could argue that genocide is the inescapable conclusion entailed in Hitler's premises. His apocalyptic tone, Germany's very existence as a country, the danger the Jews pose not only to the Germans but also to the human race, the supreme right to self-preservation that cancels all legal or ethical restraint—from these premises will grow the Final Solution as an extreme yet not altogether unforeseeable conclusion.

That he did not explicitly declare his murderous designs may be explained by the circumstances he was facing after the failure of his putsch—namely, the need to obtain parole, avoid deportation to Austria, and lift the bans that both he and the NSDAP were facing. To attain these goals, Hitler had to walk a legal line. None was achievable if he were to espouse mass murder programs targeting German citizens. Hitler continued to dissemble his real intentions through the 1930s, falsely assuring the world of his peaceful inclinations toward countries he had rashly threatened in his memoir. His lies would be exposed to the world when Germany invaded Poland, France, and then the USSR. Long implied in *Mein Kampf* and his promises to destroy the Jews, he would eventually draw the fatal inference from their malevolent logic, ordering the Final Solution in 1941. By then, the trap had been fully loaded and the moment for springing it was at hand.

9

Pathway to the Shoah

The Protocols, "Jewish Bolshevism," Rosenberg, Goebbels, Ford, and Hitler

David M. Crowe

In the dark months after the defeat at Stalingrad in 1943, Joseph Goebbels, the Nazi Party's strident, virulently anti-Semitic propaganda minister, wrote in his diary that he had "devoted exhaustive study to *The Protocols of the Elders of Zion*" despite the fact that some argued that "they were not suited to present-day propaganda." After rereading them, he concluded that "we can use them very well," since *The Protocols* were "as modern today as they were when published for the first time." The same day, May 13, 1943, he met with Hitler, who told his propaganda minister that he thought they were "absolutely genuine." He added that regardless of a Jew's circumstances, whether it be in a ghetto or Wall Street, "they will always pursue the same aims and . . . use the same methods." Why, he went on, were "there any Jews in the world order?"

> That would be like asking why there are potato bugs? Nature is dominated by the law of struggle. There will always be parasites who will spur this struggle on and intensify the process of selection between the strong and the weak. The principle of struggle dominates also in human life. One must merely know the laws of this struggle to be able to face it. The

> intellectual does not have the natural means of resisting the Jewish peril because his instincts have been totally blunted. Because of this fact the nations with a high standard of civilization are exposed to this peril first and foremost. In nature life always takes measures against parasites; In the life of nations that is not always the case. From this fact the Jewish peril actually stems. There is therefore no other recourse left for modern nations except to exterminate the Jew.[1]

He added that there was no hope of "leading the Jews back into the fold of civilized humanity" regardless of how you punished them because they would "forever remain Jews." He saw the Jew as an "absolutely intellectual creature," who has mastered the art of lying and disguising his "innermost thoughts." The Jew, Hitler concluded, was the "inventor of the lie among human beings." The English, he told Goebbels, because of their strong materialistic traits, acted very much like Jews and had "acquired most of the Jewish characteristics." But it was only those countries that "see through the Jew and have been the first to fight him" that are "going to take his place in the domination of the world."[2] This was essentially the Nazi message that had driven much of its propaganda since the early days of Hitler's movement.

By this time, the Nazi "extermination" campaign of Europe's Jews—the *Endlösung* or Final Solution—was so successful that Heinrich Himmler, the head of the SS, began to close the temporary *Aktion Reinhard* death camps (Belzec, Sobibor, and Treblinka), where 2.3 million Jews were gassed to death.[3] Goebbels considered the mass murder of Jews to be an important part of the Nazi Party's mission to save the Aryan world from the Jewish threat laid out in *The Protocols*. Goebbels, the head of the Berlin *Gau* (administrative district), bragged about his effort to make the district *Judenfrei* in his diary entry of April 18, 1943. He considered his campaign against Berlin's Jews to be the "greatest political achievement of my career."[4]

One of Goebbels's principal ideological rivals, Alfred Rosenberg, who oversaw the "intellectual and ideological training and education" of the Nazi Party, played an important, early role in promoting *The Protocols* as a blueprint for an alleged Jewish plot to take over the world.[5] Goebbels always thought *The Protocols*, as a weapon in the Nazi propaganda arsenal, had limited usage, given its questionable Russian origins. In 1939 Rosenberg sent Rudolf Hess a copy of *The Protocols* but warned him not to make any use of them because to do so would result in "a long series of debates, which are not to be desired and could in any case lead to no result."[6] Yet despite their misgivings about the authenticity of *The Protocols*, Rosenberg and Goebbels thought their central message, particularly when linked to alleged Jewish ties to communism and other leftist movements, provided them with just the propagandistic weapons they needed to create a new mythology about links between Jews and Soviet Bolshevism. This was an international concept that predated the Nazi era and was promoted by conservative ideologues such as Henry Ford, who became one of the foremost advocates of the idea of Jewish Bolshevism.

Hitler addressed the question of *The Protocols*' origins in *Mein Kampf* and said the fact they were considered a forgery proved their authenticity. In fact, it was *The Protocols*, he argued, that proved Jewish history was based on lies, which they revealed for all to see. He added that once people understood this, the global Jewish threat would be "broken."[7] Hitler's ideas about Jews were not particularly unique insofar as a number of other German writers had been discussing the "Jewish Question" for some time. But what did make Hitler's early ideas about the Jews so important, whether it be what he wrote in *Mein Kampf* or in other works, speeches, and directives, was that they provided the core ideological basis for their mass murder during the Second World War.

Adolf Hitler was an intellectual dilettante who sought to use his time in Landsberg prison, where he was incarcerated in 1924 for his involvement in the Beer Hall Putsch, to develop a new theoretical and political ideology to guide the party in the future. By this time the idea of "Jewish Bolshevism"—a concept drawn from the earlier writings of Dietrich Eckart, Alfred Rosenberg, and Henry Ford—had matured. Hitler considered Eckart, who died in 1923, one of his early political mentors and dedicated *Mein Kampf* to him. On the other hand, he was distrustful of Rosenberg, whom he put in charge of the party while he was imprisoned. Though Eckart and Rosenberg played key roles in developing early Nazi ideas about the threat of "Jewish Bolshevism," Hitler, who strongly believed in its core tenets about the Jewish global threat and ties to Soviet Russia, cast it in a Marxist-Jewish context in *Mein Kampf*. This would strengthen his own credentials as the party's foremost theoretician and link "Jewish Bolshevism" to its German roots—Karl Marx and the Soviet-inspired German communist movement.

Wilhelm Marr set the stage for new sociopolitical concepts about Jews in *Der Sieg des Judenthums über das Germanenthum* (The Victory of Judaism over Germanism, 1879). He explained in the preface that he wrote *Der Sieg* to draw attention to the "oppressed's *chmerzensschrei* (cry or scream of pain)."[8] Marr's principal goal was to draw attention to the "historical triumph of Judaism throughout the world (*den weltgeschichtlichen Triumph des Judenthums*)."[9] He attacked the religious basis for millennia-old anti-Judaic prejudice[10] and wrote that after being driven out of their homeland, the Semites, or Jews, used age-old skills to create a "state within a state" in Germany, which resulted in the absorption of "Germanism into Judaism."[11] This began, he argued, in the Middle Ages when the Jews took control of German trade. This strengthened the German economy but also led to the transformation of Germany into the "new promised land for Semites."[12] The reason for this was simple—"Germanism did not have the mental strength to resist its Jewification."[13]

Marr wrote that this had nothing to do with religion but the obsessive cultural development of the Semite, something Germans seemed incapable of resisting. In the end, Germans had become slaves in a feudalistic society dominated by Judaic legal and political ideals,[14] while today "Judenthum is the social-political dictator in Germany."[15] This meant the death of Germany because Germanism was now too weak to resist this cultural onslaught.[16] He concluded that "'DieGötterdämmerung' ist für uns angebrochen. Ihr seid die Herren, wir die Knechte . . . **Finis Germanie**" ("The 'twilight of the god' had begun for us. You [the Jews] are the masters, we the servants . . . **The End of Germany**").[17]

Marr's treatise as well as Heinrich von Treitschke's *Ein Wort über unser Judeten* (A Word about Our Jews)[18] were written in the midst of the debate about the place of Jews in a new, Christian Germany and other parts of Western Europe. Treitschke disagreed with Marr when it came to the Jewish domination of "germandom," writing that there were far too few Jews in Western Europe to have any serious impact on "national mores." But he predicted that in light of the "inexhaustible" stream of Jews out of the "Polish cradle" in the East, they would, in future, "command Germany's stock exchanges and newspapers." The contemporary German response to the negative role that Jews played in the German press and economy, Treitschke argued, was "a natural reaction of German racial feeling against an alien element that has assumed too large a space in our life." The Jews, he concluded, were "*unser Unglück* (Our Misfortune)," a phrase that Julius Streicher began to use in 1927 on the front page of *Der Stürmer*, one of the Nazis' vilest anti-Semitic newspapers.[19]

Hitler shared Treitschke's ideas about the dangers of the "Polish cradle," in the context of not only the Jews but also Polish Christians. On the eve of the invasion of Poland in 1939, the Führer said that he considered ethnic Poles to be "dreadful racial material" who stood in the way of a greater Aryan-pure Germany. Poland's Jews, he added, were "the most horrible thing imaginable." A week before the invasion, Hitler ordered the Wehrmacht to kill "without pity or mercy all men, women, and children of Polish descent or language—only in this way can we obtain the living space (*Lebensraum*) we need." He added that once the invasion of Poland began, "the way of a Polish ruling class must be liquidated; whatever grows again we might take into our safekeeping and eliminate in due course."[20]

The works by Marr, Treitschke, and others helped create the growing anti-Semitic climate throughout Germany, which led to the creation of a number of anti-Semitic organizations and parties such as the *Deutsche Partei* (DSP, German Social Party) and the *Antisemitische Völkspartei* (ASVP, Anti-Semitic People's Party). They blamed most of Germany's problems on the Jews, who, they claimed, used socialism and liberalism to spread "national self-doubt."[21] Between 1890 and 1893, the ASVP and DSP won a handful of seats in parliamentary elections. In 1894, their leaders created a new party—the *Antisemitische Deutschsoziale Reformpartei* (ASDSRP, Anti-Semitic German Social Reform Party)—which called for new restrictions on Russian-Jewish emigration and Zionist ideology. Over time, these parties proved politically ineffective but succeeded in spreading their anti-Semitic ideas throughout Germany. According to Richard S. Levy, this helped "poison German-Jewish relations and promoted an atmosphere of ready tolerance for anti-Semitism which the National Socialists were able to use effectively" after the First World War.[22]

The question of Jewish emigration from imperial Russia and the rise of Zionism are extremely important because of the significance of these issues to later Nazi ideologues. They are also the reason for the tsarist fabrication of the *Protokoly sionskikh mydretsov* (Protocols of the Elders of Zion). *The Protocols* and the rise of Zionism, of course, can only be understood in the context of the dreadful crisis that faced Russian Jews in the vast Pale of Permanent Jewish Settlement (*Cherta postoiannoi evreeskoi osldedosti*) after the assassination of Tsar Alexander II in 1881. The Pale, that vast stretch of territory in western Russia that spread from the Baltic to the Black seas, was created by Catherine the Great during partitions of Poland from 1772 to 1795. Though Jews made up no more than 11–12 percent of the Pale's population, tsarist officials, who considered Jews "immoral and culturally decadent exploiters,"[23] did what they could to restrict their rights in what Simon Dubnow called the "dark continent."[24] But what officials could not restrict was the dramatic growth of the Jewish population in the Pale, which grew from 1.5 million in 1825 to over 5 million at the end of the nineteenth century.[25]

The same was true when it came to the vibrancy of Jewish life and culture in the Pale, particularly during the more enlightened reign of Alexander II. Jews now began to play a more active role in the Pale's economy, society, and culture. This led to growing resentment among Orthodox Christians and Greek Catholics, who considered Jews the "killers of Christ." Russian writers like Yakov Brafman, Ippolit Liutostanskii, and Fyodor Dostoevsky wrote disparaging works that accused Jews of things similar to those found in the works of Marr and Treitschke. Konstantine Podedonostsev, an influential minister in the governments of Alexander III and Nicholas II, claimed that "the Jews have won ownership of everything. Even our press is becoming Jewish."[26] Dostoevsky wrote that Jews wanted "to exterminate or enslave the non-Jewish populations of the world," while Liutostanskii revived the age-old charge of "blood libel" in *Concerning the Use of Christian Blood by the Jews* (*Ob upotreblenii evreiami kristianskoi krovi dlia religioznykh tseli*).[27]

A few days after the murder of Alexander II in 1881, several newspapers blamed Jews for his death, even though only one Jew, Gesya Gelfman, was involved in the assassination plot. What followed was a rising tide of *pogroms* (Russian, *progomit*, to break or smash) that caused widespread damage to Jewish property. An investigation by the government claimed the *pogroms* were driven by peasant reactions to "Jewish exploitation." In 1882, authorities issued a series of May Laws that forbade Jews from living in towns and villages, followed by various decrees and restrictions that seriously affected the economic and professional well-being of the 5.2–

5.3 million Jews who lived in Russia (94 percent in the Pale).[28] This new assault against Jews intensified under Nicholas II, a virulent anti-Semite, and led to a new wave of *pogroms* in 1903–6. Russia's large, diverse Jewish community reacted in several different ways. Over two million Jews fled abroad to escape the oppressive political, economic, and social environment in the country, while others decided to remain and assert their national identity in Russia. Some became involved in various political parties that "positioned themselves ideologically between Zionists and Bundists by synthesizing nationalist and socialist thought" as the "dominant ideological force" among "Russian-Jewish activists." There was also an emphasis on the use of the Yiddish language to develop a new, stronger "Jewish national culture."[29]

In 1903, the Russian anti-Semitic newspaper *Znamya* (The Banner) serialized *The Protocols of the Elders of Zion* just months after a widely criticized, violent pogrom in Kishinev. Two years later, in the midst of the 1905 Revolution, Nicholas II's government approved the publication of *The Protocols* in the final chapter of the third edition of Sergei Nilus's *The Great within the Small and Antichrist, An Imminent Possibility. Notes of an Orthodox Believer* (*Velikoe v malomi antikhrist, kak blizkaya politicheskaya vozmozhnost Zapiski pravoslavnogoh*). The tsar was particularly drawn to *The Protocols* and Nilus's ideas about the threat of Jewish conspirators throughout Russia.[30] A staunch supporter of the tsarist autocracy, Nilus was also sympathetic to the anti-Semitic policies of the Union of Russian People (*Soyuz russkogo naroda*), which was founded by Alexander Dubrovin in 1905, and its "black hundreds" (*chornaya sotnya*) that instigated violent *pogroms* throughout the country. Shlomo Lambroza called the "black hundreds" "terrorists of the right, the enforcement agents of reactionary [tsarist] politics."[31]

The Protocols were based on Édouard Drumont's *La France Juive* (1886), a massive, best-selling anti-Semitic diatribe that blamed all of France's problems on Jews. They were, Drumont wrote, "agents of capitalistic exploitation" and "were responsible for Marxism." According to Jean-Louis Bredin, Drumont "was able to reconcile anti-Semitism's counter-revolutionary thought, the Catholic tradition, and a populist anticapitalism of socialist tendency. Thanks to anti-Semitism, class conflicts were dissolved."[32] What made all of this worse, he added, was that "hundreds of millions of Aryans are so naïve that they cannot see that they have been duped by a handful of Jews." The great danger for France, he wrote, was the large influx of Jews from Russia, who threatened to overrun the country.[33]

Drumont drew on earlier German anti-Semitic works and Catholic anti-Judaic ideas, particularly the charge that Jews were "Christ killers" who practiced "ritual murder." The ultimate goal of the Jews, he argued, was to take over the world. His principal theme was that "All comes from the Jew, all returns to the Jew." Physically, Drumont thought that the Jew was the "essence of ugliness, a badly smelling creature, with a bloodless face, greenish skin, claw-like hands, the sign of Cain on his forehead. The Jew does not talk, he screams, he bites, he licks, he barks and he scratches."[34]

Drumont began *La France Juive* with a lengthy discussion of the Jews in the West, followed by their history in France. The result was a political diatribe that mocked all things Jewish, especially Judaism. According to Frederick Busi, *La France Juive* was a racial treatise that "presented an Semitic-Aryan struggle of cosmic proportions, of distinct races irremediably hostile to one another, whose antagonism has filled the world in the past and will still trouble it in the future."[35] Aryans, Drumont wrote, possessed "the virtue of justice, the feeling of liberty, and conception of beauty." They were also "enthusiastic, heroic, chivalrous, disinterested, forthright, confiding to a fault." On the other hand, the Semite was "mercantile, greedy, intriguing, subtle, tricky."[36] He was also a "cryptic . . . slippery" figure who was "difficult to notice." Jews, he went on, preyed on the Aryan's "paranoia and sense of helplessness in understanding the working of the modern world."[37] This was also a prominent theme in *The Protocols*.

The assimilated French Jew, Drumont wrote, was part of a Semitic plot to take over France, something "treasonous to God, race, and country." France, he went on, had lost its way because of the decline of traditional values, something he blamed partially on Freemasonry and Protestantism, which had introduced "Jewish practices into Christianity." What was tragic about this, he added, was that Judaism was nothing more than "a form of occult devil worship." The only way to turn the country around, he concluded, was to drive the Jews out of France. [38]

Yet despite the French origins of some of its ideas, *The Protocols* were intimately tied to the deep strains of anti-Semitism that coursed through the veins of Russian Orthodox teachings in the late imperial period. The First World War and the revolutions that swept through Russia in 1917 gave new life to *The Protocols* with its charges of a Jewish conspiracy to take over the world. The Bolshevik victories later that year and during the revolutionary wars that followed gave birth to a new idea—"Jewish Bolshevism"—that centered around the idea that Bolshevism was a Jewish movement seeking world domination.

When the war broke out in the summer of 1914, the Russian government tried to rally Jewish support by issuing a proclamation, "To Our Dear Jews" ("Nashim dogorim yevreyan"), that reminded them of all the "benefits" they had enjoyed under the Romanovs.[39] The Germans responded with a propaganda leaflet in Yiddish and Hebrew, "To the Jews of Poland" ("An die Juden in Poland"), that promised their liberation from "Russian Oppression."[40]

Initial Jewish support for the Russian war effort was widespread, although this soon changed as the Russians struggled to retain control over Congress Poland and northwestern Russia. Age-old anti-Semitic policies were revived by the Russian military, which claimed Jews were a German fifth column. As German victories mounted, Jews became the principal scapegoats for Russian losses. In 1915, as the Germans pushed Russian troops eastward, the latter began to attack Jews, steal their property, and deport many into the Russian interior.[41]

The Germans occupied Congress Poland and northwestern Russia in the summer of 1915 and created the *OberOst* in the latter. They tried to bring order to both regions and encouraged the development of local cultural and religious institutions for Jews and others. Initially, the Germans tolerated the Jews because they thought they would be useful middlemen who could help transform the *OberOst* into a breadbasket for Germany. But, over time, traditional German anti-Semitism took root and German authorities began to place severe restrictions on Jewish business activities that, according to Raphael Lemkin, caused widespread "hunger, want, and privation" among *OberOst* Jews.[42]

German anti-Semites also began to link Jews to Bolshevism, something Bogislav von Sechow, a German naval officer, noted as he entered the Reich Navy Office in Berlin on November 11, 1918, the day the war ended. He remembered seeing a red flag atop the building and a "Jewish Bolshevik" in civilian clothes standing guard. A few days later he wrote that "Jews and deserters, a mob that is nothing more than the gutter in the worst sense of the word, now rule Germany. But the hour will come to the Jews, and then woe unto them."[43] Some of the German soldiers who remained in northwestern Russia until the spring of 1919 shared this idea about Jewish ties to Bolshevism. They flowed from a sense throughout Germany during the war that Jews had profited from it and did everything they could to avoid military service.[44] This, coupled with traditional strains of German anti-Semitism, helped set the stage for the linkage of Jews to Bolshevism in the Weimar Republic.[45]

This new concept would come to haunt Jews during the two wars between Poland and Soviet Russia in 1919 and 1920. In the spring of 1920, Polish-Ukrainian forces unsuccessfully invaded Soviet territory but were gradually driven back as part of Vladimir Lenin's campaign to recapture lands lost to the Germans and the Poles during and after the First World War. By late summer, the Bolsheviks reached the outskirts of Warsaw, only to be driven back by the Poles, who began to retake lands under Bolshevik control. As they swept into northwestern Russia and Ukraine, Polish forces attacked Jewish communities, arguing that they had staunchly supported the Bolsheviks. According to Irina Astashkevich, the Poles and their allies fervently believed "that all Jews were Bolsheviks and were responsible for the [Bolshevik] Revolution, the Civil War, the fall of the Russian Empire, and the decline of the independent Ukrainian republic, and 'none entertained the idea that the Ukrainians could be Bolsheviks, even though this was undoubtedly the case.'" What she called the "Judeo-Bolshevik canard" later helped form the nucleus of the Nazi idea of Jewish Bolshevism.[46]

As Polish forces drove the Red Army back into Russia in 1920, two books were published in London that revived this "canard." The first, George Gustav Telberg and Robert Wilton's *The Last Days of the Romanovs*, claimed that

Jews, not the Bolsheviks, murdered Nicholas II and his family in the summer of 1918.[47] This was followed by Victor E. Marsden's translation of *The Protocols of the Learned Elders of Zion*. Marsden, a virulent anti-Semite who had been a correspondent in Moscow for London's *Morning Post* just after the Bolsheviks seized power in late 1917, firmly believed it was a Jewish blueprint for world domination. He argued that *The Protocols* were based on a series of meetings of the highly secretive Learned Elders of Zion, who updated a "plan of action" of the "Jewish Nation . . . developed through the ages."[48]

Protocol I had three subheadings that characterized many of the major points of the other twenty-three protocols—"Right is Might, We Are Despots, and We Shall End Liberty." *Protocol III* discussed how the Jewish Nation used different political movements, including communism, anarchism, and socialism, to destroy the aristocracy and take control of the global economy. This class struggle would be orchestrated in such a way to protect Jews and ensure that the *Goyim* would embrace a "sovereignty of reason. Our despotism will be precisely that; for it will know how, by wise severities, to pacificate all unrest, to cauterize liberalism out of all institutions." *Protocol IV* declared that one of the Elders' goals was to "undermine all faith" to "tear out of the mind of the '*Goyim*'" while *Protocol VII* stated that Jewish leaders would work "to create ferments, discords and hostility" throughout Europe.[49]

Protocol VIII stated that Jewish elders would use "the very finest shades of expression" and the "knotty points of the lexicon of law justification" to deal with international leaders. They would also surround themselves with prominent *Goyim* bankers, industrialists, and capitalists who would be used to defend Jewish interests. According to *Protocol IX*, the end result would be the creation of a Jewish "Super-State" using the "weapons" of "limitless ambitions, burning greediness, merciless vengeance, hatreds and malice." *Protocol X* argued that all of this would result in the Jewish acquisition of the "throne of the world" and the creation of a Jewish super-state that would "transform every form of government into 'Our Despotism.'"[50]

Protocol XI argued that the "Goyim . . . [were] a flock of sheep, and we are their wolves. And you know what happens when the wolves get hold of the flock?" *Protocol XII* added that once the Jews acquired global power, they would use the press to control public opinion, which *Protocol XIII* said was meant to distract the public. These policies would succeed because of the "brainless heads of the '*Goyim*.'" *Protocol XIV* stated that once "we come into our kingdom" it would be essential to "sweep away all other forms of belief." Independent thought and open education would be proscribed, which *Protocol XVI* proclaimed would help "turn the *Goyim* into unthinking submissive brutes." *Protocols XXI–XXII* dealt with vague financial matters, while *Protocols XXIII–XIV* discussed the final stages of the creation of the new Jewish kingdom. It would be led by the "Chosen One of God" who came from the "dynastic roots of King David." The last *Protocol*—XXIV—ended with the proclamation that "Our supreme lord must be of an exemplary irreproachability."[51]

The social and economic chaos in Germany and other parts of postwar Europe played into these fears, which revived interest in *The Protocols*. For some on the right, the Bolshevik victory in Russia was, in reality, a Jewish plot to take over the world. Some pointed to the fact that Karl Marx, the ideological touchstone for the Bolsheviks, was Jewish, as were some in Lenin's inner circle. Alfred Rosenberg, one of Nazi Germany's foremost racial theorists, wrote in *Die Spur des Juden im Wandel der Zeiten* (The Track of the Jew Through the Ages, 1920) that Bolshevism was "a predominantly Jewish undertaking."[52]

A Russianized Baltic German, Rosenberg was born in Reval (today Tallinn, capital of Estonia) and spent his youth in Russia. He lived in Moscow in 1917 as a student but took little interest in the upheavals that led to the abdication of Nicholas II and Lenin's seizure of power later that year. He came across a copy of *The Protocols* in Russian, which he later edited and published. He returned to Reval later that year to escape the chaos in Moscow and tried unsuccessfully to join the German army after it occupied Reval in the spring of 1918.[53]

A few weeks after the war ended, Rosenberg went to Berlin and later settled in Munich, where he met Fyodor Vinberg, a Russian aristocrat, who had served as Nicholas II's court equerry. A staunch monarchist, Vinberg was briefly imprisoned by the Bolsheviks and later fought against them in the Russian Civil War. He settled in Munich[54] and became actively involved with other pro-Russian monarchists and anti-Semites and started a newspaper, *Prizyv* (The Call), to promote his ideas. Vinberg worked closely with Ludwig Müller von Hausen, whose newspaper *Auf Vorposten* (On Outpost Duty) published *The Zunder Document* in 1920. A forged letter, it claimed that Jews were on the verge of taking "command of the world" by bringing "the Russian people under the yoke of Jewish power." A year earlier, Hausen published the first German edition of *The Protocols*, which Vinberg later used as evidence in his *Der Kreuzesweg Russlands* (Russia's Via Dolorosa) to prove his contention that Jews planned to take over the world.[55]

Rosenberg was quite taken by Vinberg and other Russians' fascination with Fyodor Dostoevsky's views on Jews. Rosenberg wrote in *Die Spur* that Jews were motivated principally by the idea of exploiting other people and made note of Dostoevsky's comment in his *Diary of a Writer* that "The Jewish idea is that of profiteering." Rosenberg praised the famed Russian writer in *Pest in Russland! Der Bolschewismus, seine Häupter, Handlanger und Opfer* (Plague in Russia! Bolshevism, Its Heads, Henchmen, and Victims), while Dietrich Eckart, the editor of the Nazi Party newspaper, published an article on Dostoevsky in early 1923 that called him "still the poet and admonisher for today, for perhaps already tomorrow 'may the Anti-Christ come and anarchy rule.'"[56] Joseph Frank wrote in his masterful biography of Dostoevsky that he was indeed a virulent anti-Semite who took every opportunity he could to blame Russia's Jews for everything wrong in

Russia. In his mind, Jews were "ruthless batteners on the misery of others and concealed masters and manipulators of world politics."[57]

Dietrich Eckart was a writer and playwright who edited an anti-Semitic, anti-Bolshevik journal, *Auf Gut Deutsch* (In Plain German), from 1918 to 1920. He was also Hitler's mentor during his early postwar years in Munich. Eckart devoted the first seven issues of *Auf Gut Deutsch* to a discussion of the contrast between what he considered the "highest expression" of the *Volksseele* (*Völkish* soul or soul of the people)—the German—and its lowest—the Jew. He saw this as an eternal conflict that went back to biblical times. Eckart argued that Jews stained everything they touched and were the cause of all things wrong in Germany. He also thought "that Jewry would be condemned to death for its crimes."[58] In 1920 he argued in *Jewry über alles* (Jewry above everything) that there were close ties between Jews, "finance capitalism," and Bolshevism. Collectively, this would lead to "a Jewish world dictatorship."[59]

Eckart published Rosenberg's first article, "Die russich-juedische Revolution," in *Auf Gut Deutsch* in February 1919. Rosenberg wrote that the February Revolution in 1917 began as a democratic revolution but was soon transformed by the "Tatar Lenin" and Jews like Leon "Braunstein" Trotsky into a "racial revolution." In the following issue of *Auf Gut Deutsch*, Rosenberg urged the German government to do everything it could to overthrow the Bolsheviks, which would lead to the destruction of Russian Jewry and a rapprochement between Berlin and Moscow.[60]

In 1920, Rosenberg published *Der Totengräber Russlands* (Russia's Gravedigger) in response to the creation of the short-lived Bavarian Soviet Republic that spring. He discussed Jewish plans to foment revolution in Russia, which he called *Judenbolschewismus* (Jewish Bolshevism) and considered Christian leaders who supported Jews as *Judentzer*, who were "outside of the pale of the Christian community."[61] He also went into great detail about the number of Jews with important roles in Lenin's Bolshevik government and military and cited Henry Ford's *Internationale Jude* (The International Jew) as evidence of the international Jewish-Bolshevik threat.[62] Rosenberg did the same in a later edition of *Die Protokolle der Weisen von Zion.*

Rosenberg's ideas were shared by some powerful leaders in other countries such as Winston Churchill, Britain's secretary of state for War and Air. The British politician was given a copy of *The Protocols* and though it is difficult to say if he read it, he certainly agreed with some of its ideas about a worldwide Jewish conspiracy, particularly when it came to the idea of Jewish Bolshevism. He considered the Bolsheviks "an illegitimate minority consisting mainly of Jews over the 'real' Russians," a point he reiterated in a speech in 1921. A staunch anticommunist, he used the idea of the Jewish Bolshevik ties in Soviet Russia to try to convince British Jews to "denounce the renegades in Russia and Poland who are dishonouring their race and religion."[63] In a rambling article in the *Illustrated Sunday Herald* in early 1920, "Zionism versus Bolshevism," Churchill depicted "Jews as historic international evil doers" yet praised "national [British]" Jews for their contributions to

British society. He wrote that Jews were the "most formidable and the most remarkable race which has ever appeared in the world" and praised Jewish contributions to Christianity. He saw Zionism as an "antidote to Bolshevism" and argued that good Jews had a responsibility to do everything they could to denounce Bolshevism and make "clear to all the world that the Bolshevik movement is not a Jewish movement."[64] London's *Jewish Chronicle* called Churchill's article "reckless and scandalous."[65]

Rosenberg argued a year later in *Die Staatsfeindliche Zionismus* (Zionism: The Enemy of the State, 1921) that Zionists in Britain had become powerful enough to successfully convince the British government to issue the Balfour Declaration in late 1917, which promised that Britain would "view with favour the establishment in [Ottoman] Palestine of a national home for the Jewish people."[66] He added in a later edition of his 1923 *Die Protokolle der Weísen von Zíon und díe jüdische Weltpolítík* (The Protocols of the Elders of Zion and Jewish World Politics) that the British promise underscored the fact that Jews played a major role in instigating the war in 1914 as a step toward achieving their ultimate goal of world domination.[67]

Eckart, Rosenberg, and Hitler admired Henry Ford because, as Hitler noted in *Mein Kampf*, the American industrial giant maintained his independence in a country, where Jews controlled industry and the stock exchange.[68] In late 1918, Ford bought *The Dearborn Independent*, which quickly became his soapbox for a variety of issues, particularly Jews and Bolshevism. Over time, he became obsessed with the idea that Jews had caused the war and agreed with Thomas Edison about the place of Jews in American society.[69] In 1920, spurred by what he thought were US government efforts to strike out against "the radical seeds that have entangled American ideas in their poisonous theories,"[70] Ford decided to launch an "educational" series on the "Jewish Question" that hopefully would force the Jews "to clean up their own house."[71]

What followed were a series of lengthy articles that appeared in the *Independent* from the spring of 1920 through early 1922 that were later published in four volumes as *The International Jew: The World's Foremost Problem*. Ford's ideas were particularly important because they carried the *imprimatur* of one of the world's foremost industrialists and were published at a time of considerable instability in the United States and Europe. Ford did not write these articles, though he is listed as the author of all of them. They were written by Billy Cameron, who was able to "make sense of the abrupt, enigmatic remarks of his employer." He also wrote Ford's column in the *Independent*, "Mr. Ford's Own Page."[72]

Ford made the connection between Jews and Bolshevism on the first page of his first article (May 2, 1920), "The Jew in Character and Business," which is included in volume I of *The International Jew*. He wrote that the Jew "is charged with being the source of Bolshevism, an accusation which is serious or not according to the circle in which it is made."[73] He added that a substantial body of literature in Germany blamed Jews for the collapse of the Second Reich, while in England the Jew "is charged with being the real world ruler, who rules as a super-nation over the nations, ruled by the power of gold, and who plays nation against nation for his own purposes."[74] The Jew, Ford wrote, is the "world's enigma,"[75] an idea that mirrors some of those expressed by Eckart.

Ford devoted his next article to the "Jewish Question" in Germany and again mentioned Bolshevism, which, masquerading as German socialism, was one of the means Jews used to bring about the "downfall of the German order."[76] The rest of the article discussed *The Protocols* followed by a series of articles on Jewish Bolshevism. He accepted *The Protocols* as factual and discussed each of them in detail. Ford's well-written explanation of *The Protocols*, particularly their threat to the United States and Europe, is far better than what was written by Nicholas II's secret police. This is doubly so because he not only explains each of *The Protocols* in considerable detail but also details how the Jews planned to achieve each of its goals. He considered Germany the "most Jew-controlled country in the world," followed by the United States.[77]

Volume II of *The International Jew: Jewish Activity in the United States* focused principally on Jewish interference in public education, religion, theatre, the film industry, and the New York Stock Exchange. Ford looked more deeply at the negative influence of Jews on American life in volume III, *Jewish Influence in American Life*, and in chapter 49, "Jewish Hot-Beds of Bolshevism in the U.S.,"[78] he claimed that Jews were using the same methods in the United States that they used in Russia to spread Bolshevism, particularly among trade unions.[79] What amazed him was that the United States "stupidly . . . permitted Jewish Bolshevism to flaunt itself so openly during the past few years."[80] He also discussed political Zionism and its broad support among some Jews and Christians in the West. He expressed some sympathy for Jews in pre-Zionist Palestine but warned that Bolshevik Jews flowing into Palestine were creating a "situation out of which many believe the next war will come."[81] Moreover, he wrote,

> The Zionist movement, with its intentional development of race consciousness and race peculiarity on the part of the Jew, is an additional obstacle against the efforts of those Jews and Christians who are seeking to break down prejudice and to bring Jews and Christians together within a common recognition of the Golden Rule: that each should treat the other as he, in like instance, would wish to be treated by him.[82]

The articles in volume IV, *Aspects of Jewish Power in the United States*, addressed the question of Jewish "self-cleansing," the idea that only Jews could stop "certain abuses" and accept responsibility for what Ford thought were "competitive forces of society."[83] But first they had to deal truthfully with *The Protocols* and its goals. Ford was also extremely critical of what he called the myth of Jewish patriotism "in the wars of the United States."[84] To counter this, he wrote a series of articles that dealt with Jewish support of the treasonous activities of Benedict Arnold during the American Revolution.[85]

Ford also discussed Jewish "concealment and misrepresentation," particularly when it came to Zionism, the American Jewish Committee, and the Jewish adoption of Christian-sounding surnames.[86] His final articles addressed growing Jewish criticism of the articles in *The Dearborn Independent* and his attacks on Jewish religious practices.[87] He also discussed what he called the Great Crime—the Jewish "introduction of corruptive and anti-American ideas into American life."[88] He tied this to the idea that "*Bolshevism is Jewish in its origin, its methods, its personnel and its purposes*,"[89] and linked this to what he considered the principal message of *The Protocols*—a description of "how the Jewish World Power plans to run thing [s] when the time comes."[90]

In his final chapter in volume IV, "Candid Address to Jews on the Jewish Problem," Ford stated that the purpose of his articles was to "let in the light—to show the Jews generally that the stench had become too great, and to show the rest of the people where the stench came from."[91] The greatest obstacle to changing the nature of the "stench," he went on, was the Jew himself. Ford had no problem with the Jew keeping "all his traditions." They are not objectionable in any way; the slightest regard for them can only hold them as romantic. But the Jew, he insisted, had to "shed his false notion of 'the Jew against the world.'"[92] The same was true when it came to "his false program of breaking down Christendom by the infiltration of Orientalism into business, entertainment and the professions."[93] For Gentiles, he concluded, the best way to deal with the Jewish "stench" was to "erect again our own moral landmarks, which the Oriental Jewish invasion has broken down."[94]

Theodor Fritsch translated and published an abridged, two-volume edition of *The International Jew* in 1921. Hitler displayed copies of it in his new Nazi Party offices in Munich and had a large portrait of Ford on the wall behind his desk. Fritsch "lauded Henry Ford for the 'great service' he had provided to America and the world by attacking the Jews"[95] in the preface of *Die international Jude: ein Weltproblem: Das erste amerikanische Buch über die Judenfrage, herausgegeben von Henry Ford*, and in multiple editions of *Handbuch der Judenfragen*, which Eckart called "our complete spiritual arsenal."[96]

Adolf Hitler's interest in Henry Ford went beyond his racial ideas, particularly after Gottfried Feder, one of the Nazi Party's early racial theorists, told him that he should read a recent article in Fritsch's journal, *Der Hammer*,[97] "Henry Ford und die industrielle Zunkunft" ("Ford and the Industrial Future"). He praised Ford for his visionary, prophetic willingness to stand up against "purely parasitical entrepreneurship." Feder also praised Ford in *Der deutsche Staat auf nationaler und sozialer Grundlage* (The

German State on National and Social Foundations, 1923) and called him the "finest and most universally known example" of the Nazi view of the goal and purpose of the national economy.[98]

By this time, Ford had been forced to apologize for his articles after growing outcries from Jewish leaders. This, coupled with a widely publicized trial that charged Ford with defamation of character, convinced him that it was time to "stop this *Dearborn Independent!*" This had more to do with economics than any change in heart when it came to the "Jewish Question." His "apology" on June 30, 1927, blamed others for the contents of his anti-Semitic publications. He stated that he was now aware that *The Protocols* were "gross forgeries" and, while praising the "virtues of the Jewish people as a whole," added that this "very flock" had its "black sheep." He asked forgiveness for the unintentional harm that he had caused and pledged to withdraw all of his anti-Semitic publications in the United States and abroad.[99] In reality, Henry Ford remained a virulent anti-Semite for the rest of his life.[100]

This did little to dampen the Nazi fascination with Henry Ford, although some questions did arise about the efficacy of what he had to say, namely Nazi propaganda. In his diary entry of April 8, 1924, Joseph Goebbels wrote that though he found Ford's works "extremely interesting . . . wholesome, and enlightening" when it came to the "Jewish Question" outside of Germany, and that it was important "not to be overly captivated by the author's intriguing evidence."[101] Four days earlier, Goebbels wrote that at the first meeting of an illegal Nazi Party cell in Rheydt, Germany, all "we basically talked about [was] antisemitism." It was, Goebbels said, a "world idea" that "brings together Germans and Russians."[102] Consequently, though he had doubts about some of Ford's ideas, he thought *The International Jew* provided him with a literary pathway to other works about "the burning question of the hour . . . the Jewish question." This included *The Protocols*, which he found "seductive" but an "anti-Semitic forgery." On the other hand, Goebbels accepted the "'inner' authenticity of the protocols," which fortified his own ideas about the "Jewish Question" and the idea that "Lenin, Trotsky, [Georgy] Chicherin are Jews."[103]

But Alfred Rosenberg was the real standard bearer for the concept of "Jewish Bolshevism" in the Nazi Party. In 1922, he published a small piece on the Jewish influence over British politics, *Der Staatsfeindliche Zionismus* (Subversive Zionism),[104] followed a year later by his commentary on *The Protocols—Die Protokoller der Weisen von Zion und die jüdische Weltpolitik* (The Protocols of the Wise Men of Zion and Jewish World Politics). In the introduction, he traced the history of *The Protocols* and noted the successes of the Zionist movement and the dominant role played by Jews in countries like the United States and Great Britain. He also mentioned Henry Ford's discussion of Bernard Baruch's success in the United States, whom Ford indirectly compared to Leon Trotsky. The United States, Rosenberg added, was now the "größte Ghetto der Welt" ("largest ghetto in the world"). He also blamed Jews for the Russian Revolution in

1917, the German defeat in the First World War, and its postwar financial crisis.[105]

His most enduring work, *Der Mythos des 20. Jahrhunderts* (The Myth of the 20th Century, 1930), would later haunt him at the Nuremberg trials. *Der Mythos* is filled with Rosenberg's bizarre ideas about race and underscored what he saw as the contrast between the ancient origins of the superior Aryans and the degenerative, corrupt nature of Semites (Jews). He also warned of the dangers of racial mixing with inferior races and partially blamed some of this on the "Judaization" of Christianity.[106] Rosenberg served as Reich minister of the Occupied Eastern Territories (*Ostland*) from 1941 to 1945 and was indicted at Nuremberg for crimes against peace, war crimes, crimes against humanity, and conspiracy.[107] In its judgment, the tribunal stated that Rosenberg was the Nazi Party's "ideologist" who spread his ideas in his newspaper, *Nationalsozialistische Monatshefte* (*National Socialist Monthly*) and *Der Mythos*, which sold over a million copies.[108]

But his principal crime was the role he played in "the formulation and execution of occupation policies" in the *Ostland* (Estonia, Latvia, Lithuania, and parts of Belorussia). This included the "policies of Germanization, exploitation, forced labor, extermination of Jews [over one million] and opponents of Nazi rule." The judges found him guilty of all four charges and cited his "knowledge of the brutal treatment and terror to which the eastern peoples were subjected" as one of the key reasons for their decision. He was sentenced to death and hanged on October 16, 1946.[109]

Der Mythos does not mention *The Protocols* because they never played a major role in Nazi propaganda once Hitler published the two volumes of *Mein Kampf* in 1925–6. But its central theme, the Jewish lust for world power, was quite influential, particularly in the context of "Jewish Bolshevism." Hitler's ideas about Jews and Bolshevism evolved in the early 1920s. In a speech in 1922, he told his audience that Jewish financiers were to blame for Germany's problems and later that year likened Lenin's New Economic Policy (NEP) in Russia to Jewish capitalism and Marxism. The "Jewification" of the Russian economy, he added, was now taking place in Germany. In a speech in early 1923, he said that the Marxist idea about class struggle was a "swindle propagated by the Jews."[110]

In *Mein Kampf*, he spoke of Jewish Bolshevism but more in the context of Marxism, which was "itself only the transference, by the Jew, Karl Marx, of a philosophical attitude and conception . . . into the form of a definite political creed."[111] Jewish Marxism, he added, devalued "the personality of man" and contested the "significance of nationality and race," which robbed "humanity of its existence and culture."

> If, with the help of his Marxist creed, the Jew is victorious over the other peoples of the world, his crown will be the funeral wreath of humanity and this planet will, as it did thousands of years ago, move through the

> ether devoid of men . . . *by defending myself against the Jew, I am fighting for the work of the Lord.*[112]

In early 1927, Hitler wrote "that the Jew is and remains the world enemy, and his weapon, Marxism, a plague of mankind."[113] He made a similar point in *Hitler's Zweites Buch: Ein Dokument aus dem jahr 1928* (Hitler's Second Book: A Document of the Year 1928), which deals with the racial dimensions of German foreign policy. Hitler argued that the "Jewish international struggle will always end in bloody Bolshevization—that is to say, in truth, the destruction of the intellectual upper classes associated with the various peoples, so that he himself will be able to rise to mastery over the now leaderless humanity."[114] Marxism, he went on, was the "intellectual father of the Bolshevik Revolution" and was now the "weapon of terror that the Jew applies ruthlessly and brutally."[115]

Yet during the 1930 Reichstag election campaign, Hitler told a reporter from *The Times* that the party rejected anti-Semitism and pogroms. But, he added, "if Jews associated themselves with Bolshevism, as many unfortunately did, they would be regarded as enemies."[116] Once in power, Hitler unleashed a torrent of decrees and laws that gradually stripped the Jews from the fabric of German society. This growing demonization of Jews culminated in the massive *Kristallnacht pogrom* on November 9, 1938, that resulted in the widespread destruction of Jewish homes, businesses, synagogues, and community centers. Hitler responded to the international outcry a few months later by telling the Reichstag that Jews never seriously took his pledge that once he took power he would "settle the Jewish problem." He added, "If the international Jewish financiers in and outside of Europe should succeed in plunging the nations once more into a world war, then the result will not be the Bolshevization of the earth, and thus the victory of Jewry, but the *annihilation of the Jewish race in Europe*!" (Figure 9.1)[117]

And he kept his word. Hitler told Wehrmacht commanders a week before the invasion of Poland on September 1, 1939, to kill all Poles "without pity or mercy."[118] This led to the creation of Nazi Germany's racial laboratory, the *General-gouvernement für die besetzten polnischen Gebiete* (General Government for the Occupied Areas of Poland), where four of the six Nazi death camps were built, along with a large network of ghettos for Poland's large Jewish population.[119]

Once war broke out, Hitler became more and more obsessed with what Goebbels now called the threats from the "Jewish plutocracy." In his New Year's address in 1940, Hitler railed against the "Jewish-international capitalists" who had "but one goal—to destroy Germany, to destroy our German Volk!"[120] A few months later he told those gathered in Munich to celebrate the twentieth anniversary of the party program that "we will eliminate this organized terror of this despicable clique of world plutocrats! We have routed these sharks of international finance in Germany, and we will not stand for others telling us what to do now. The German nation has

FIGURE 9.1 *"Behind the enemy powers: The Jew". Courtesy of the United States Holocaust Memorial Museum.*

the same right to life as other peoples do."[121] That summer, Hitler linked his dream of *Lebensraum* in the East to the "annihilation of Bolshevism, and extermination of Jewry." From his perspective, any resistance to his plans would be dealt with by the "extermination of Jewish Bolshevism."[122] He was also convinced that the destruction of Russian Jews would lead to the collapse of the Soviet Union.[123]

By late 1940, Hitler began to develop plans for Operation Barbarossa, the invasion of the Soviet Union. Specially trained killing squads, the *Einsatzgruppen*, were to move in quickly behind Wehrmacht frontline troops with broad authority to "pacify" areas under their control with *rücksichtsloser Schärfe* (ruthless severity). According to these units' *Einsatzgruppen* reports, most of their victims were Jews. In a meeting with senior military commanders on late March 1941, Hitler told them that he expected them to take the lead in this struggle against "*der bolschewistischen Komissare under der kommunistische inteligenz*" ("Bolshevik commissars and the Communist intelligentsia"). He added that what was about to take place was

> A life and death struggle between two races and two ideologies; between German and Slav; between National Socialism and the criminal code of Jewish Bolshevism, which constitutes the greatest threat to the future of civilization. . . . The ultimate objective of this war was not only the

destruction of the Red Army in the field but the final elimination of the Russian-Bolshevik menace.[124]

By this time, the concept of "Jewish Bolshevism" had become the "*bete noire* of the German officer corps," fueled by "the idea that Germany needed to counter a 'peril from the east'—Jewish Bolshevism." In the summer of 1940, Rear Admiral Kurt Fricke wrote that the Germans had to do what they could to eliminate the "chronic danger of Bolshevism," while German staff officers serving in Romania discussed at one meeting in October what they thought was a war against global finance interests and the Jews. To Colonel-General Georg von Küchler, victory would only be achieved with the total destruction of Russia.[125]

In late spring 1941, the OKW (*Oberkommando der Wehrmacht*; Armed Forces Supreme Command) issued a directive that reminded commanders that the Bolsheviks were the "deadly enemy of the National Socialist German people" and that the coming invasion would be a "struggle" that would require "ruthless and energetic actions against Bolshevik agitators, guerillas, saboteurs, and Jews, and the total elimination of all active or passible resistance."[126] On June 6 the Wehrmacht issued the Commissar Order, which freed German soldiers of any legal responsibility for their actions against an enemy that used "barbaric, Asiatic fighting methods." A week before the invasion, Heinrich Himmler, the head of the SS, ordered *Einsatzgruppen* commanders to support Wehrmacht *Selbstreiningungsbestrebungen* (self-cleansing efforts) of "anti-communist and anti-Jewish circles."[127]

Over the next six months, the *Einsatzgruppen* swept through western Russia and murdered 500,000 Jews. The SD's *Operational Situation Report USSR No. 33* of July 27, 1941, underscored what it considered the strong Jewish ties to Bolshevism in the Soviet Union, while report No. 38 of July 30 reported the execution of 200 communists and Jews in Zhitomir for arson. According to a report from *Einsatzgruppe* C, almost all of the communist leaders in Zhitomir were Jews.[128] Another report on August 5, 1941, discussed the importance of "hitting the Jewish-Bolshevik upper class [in Belorussia] as efficiently as possible,"[129] while one a few days later stated that Jews in western Belorussia were hostile toward German forces and did everything they could to "sabotage German orders."[130] Otto Ohlendorf, the commander of *Einsatzgruppe* D, testified during the *Einsatzgruppen* trial in 1947–8 that almost of all of the 90,000 Jews murdered by his unit were considered security threats to the Wehrmacht, a standard myth used by the SS, the SD, and the military to justify their murderous campaign against Jews and others in Russia from 1941 to 1944.[131]

Collectively, these units, in league with the Wehrmacht and the mass killing campaigns in ghettos and death camps in western Russia and the General Government, were responsible for the murder of millions of Jews during the Shoah. But they were never able to make Europe *Judenfrei*, something Hitler bemoaned in his April 29, 1945, "Political Testament." He blamed this on "international statesmen who are either of Jewish origin or work for Jewish interests." He hoped that the country's new leadership would adhere to Nazi racial laws and mercilessly resist the "world poisoners, international Jewry."[132]

Conclusion

Karl Schleunes described the evolution of Nazi policies toward Jews in Germany before the Second World War as a "twisted road."[133] The same could be said of the concept that the Jews of the world lusted for global power and would go to any extreme, including the embrace of Russian Bolshevism, to achieve their goals. While it could be argued that the roots for such ideas lay in the deep Western traditions of anti-Judaism and anti-Semitism, they matured in the late nineteenth and early twentieth centuries into widely accepted concepts anchored by *The Protocols of the Learned Elders of Zion* and the idea of "Jewish Bolshevism." They became an important part of early Nazi writings about the Jewish threat to Germany and would gradually provide Alfred Rosenberg, Joseph Goebbels, and Adolf Hitler with an ideological justification to argue that Jews were also an essential threat to Germany and the Aryan race. This was one of the central themes in *Mein Kampf*, which became the Nazi Bible. Henry Ford, the storied American industrialist, gave such theories credibility, while Alfred Rosenberg, one of the party's foremost ideologists, became the standard bearer for the Nazi concept of "Jewish Bolshevism." He would ultimately address his ideas about the "Jewish threat" during his years as Reichskommissar of the *Ostland*, where he oversaw the murder of over a million Jews. Goebbels and Hitler tried to do the same in other parts of Europe during the Final Solution, though once it became apparent at the end of the war that they had failed, they took their own lives in despair.

10

Marxism—Enemy of the People in the Political Party and Military System

Melanie Murphy

Hitler's expositions in *Mein Kampf* are programmatic and inflammatory, rarely simply informative, yet always nonexplanatory. The post–Great War devolution of discussion of significant public questions is exemplified by this text that does not combine fact and interpretation to persuade the reader of his point of view, yet resonated with many readers. The three main topics or issues of *Mein Kampf* are the *Volk*, the Jews, and Marxism. Marxism connects the Jews who are its bearers, using it for their goal of world domination, and that part of the people who adhere to it as an emancipatory doctrine. Marxism is an enemy, goad, and exemplar to Hitler, whose aim is to eradicate it. Attacking Marxism enables Hitler to expose and potentially punish the Jews and free the *Volk* from the grasp of evil. Commenting on these three topics, he places himself as the dominant figure in the work, with autobiographical sketches of his own development. Marxist doctrine or formations do not interest Hitler, rather how "Marxism," the extremely powerful force that almost destroyed Germany, could block his aims and the goals of any right-thinking Germans and what he could learn from the Marxist playbook.

As Hitler comments, the *Volk*, Jews, and Marxism are deeply intertwined. The *Volk* are divided and misled by Marxist leaders and ideology, and as a result endanger their group life by adhering to them. For example, toward the end of the Great War, Hitler blames a munition workers' strike for causing Germany's loss, because it had left soldiers undersupplied, and even more importantly, demoralized.[1] The January 1918 strike in Berlin lasted approximately a week, with strikers issuing demands that were largely political, although the last demand of the seven was for food, an indication of the serious privation on the home front. The workers opposed the proposed Russian annexations that later became the central feature of the Treaty of Brest-Litovsk, wanting instead a negotiated peace on the Western Front. A worker delegation representing the SPD, USPD, and Spartacus League would take part in this negotiated settlement. Chancellor Georg von Hertling was not annexationist nor enthusiastic to continue the war. Yet due to the notorious control of the government by the military during the war, the chancellor was sidelined, and the strikers punished. Some were drafted to the front, including into penal battalions, while others were imprisoned. During the strike, workers in cities and towns beyond Berlin initially stood in solidarity with the Berlin workers, before eventually deciding to return to work or being forced to do so earlier than Berlin workers.

To describe these events as "Marxist" is reductionist, and yet in Hitler's telling, everything that workers do as workers becomes subsumed under that category. Civilians, in fact the entire home front, were considered part of the war effort and all were relentlessly reminded of their duty. Expected to be unfailingly nationalistic, while also politically quiescent, they seem to prefigure civilian life in the Third Reich. These workers are indeed affiliated with parties that have a Marxist pedigree; however, their demands are political, most often including subsistence. The shop stewards became the real leaders of the strike. Contrary to Hitler's claim, the strike did not delay munitions production, rather a lack of heating materials would be keeping the factories closed at that time. Had the strikers' demands been met, German history might have been quite different.[2] Nevertheless, the military dominated the civilian government during the Great War.[3] Hitler applauds the domination of the civilian arm of the government by the military, blaming everything else for Germany's disasters. In fact, he will reproduce it when he leads Germany, with force and military priorities taking precedence over rule of law and institutions of state.[4]

As for Marxism, the Jews maintain control, along with control of parliamentary democracy, which Hitler asserts would be shut down, if Parliament excluded Socialist Parties.[5] Jewish control of two streams of political life, identified with the bourgeoisie and with the workers, shows that they are not sincere about either program, but rather only in their program of destruction, in their own favor. Hitler thus condemns Jews for doing and caring only for their own race, in a work that asserts the Aryan race must be concerned solely with the primacy of the Aryans. His canard of Jewish unrelieved self-concern builds upon other anti-Semitic discourse, and his accusations concerning the boundless self-centeredness of the Jews reinforce social prejudice and false popular ideology. What Hitler intends, a program of destruction in favor of the Aryans, is only partially understood by many of his followers (Figure 10.1).

FIGURE 10.1 *"The Eternal Jew" exhibition in Munich, November 1937. The image reflects the Bolshevik monetary and political power over the masses. Courtesy of the United States Holocaust Memorial Museum.*

Hitler does not care for any other people other than Germans, his *Volk*, and does not grant other races the right to do what he seeks for his people. In fact, his core belief builds upon a theory that all peoples cannot simultaneously protect and find prosperity themselves and, therefore, there must be a war to the death for space, resources, health, and prosperity. The very self-consciousness of the Jews on the issue of self-preservation and self-aggrandizement stands as a feature of the reasons they are the ultimate foe.[6] And yet, even as the Jews manage political life from more than one ideological orientation, they prefer Marxism, an active and potent movement quite dangerous to the German nation.

In addition to three main topics, *Mein Kampf* may be described as having three modes, philosophical, reportorial, and vicious, jarringly displaying Hitler's moods and frame of mind. Large sections discuss policy and Hitler's plans, for example his interest in having an increase in physical education in the schools. These sections are philosophical or at least tutorial and are intended to display Hitler's great knowledge. Some reportorial passages, neither vicious nor concrete, offer descriptions of the early days of the party and the like. Occasionally, there are some specific passages composed of ostensibly factual details. Two that can be considered relevant to his discussion of Marxism are his claims to have worked on a construction site while living in Vienna and his experience serving with a battalion.

At the construction site, he saw how trade unionists gang up on honest workers to force their conformity to union policy. In fact, as Brigette Hamann shows in her study of Hitler's days in Vienna, this never happened to Hitler.[7] He fabricated this life experience to make his point. The second scene occurs in chapter seven of Book One, when upon leaving the hospital where he had recovered from his gas attack, Hitler is transferred to a replacement battalion in Munich. Here he notes, "the offices were filled with Jews. Nearly every clerk was a Jew, and every Jew was a clerk. I was amazed at this plethora of warriors of the chosen people and could not help but compare them with their rare representatives at the front."[8] He continues on, mentioning the increased economic centralization in the later years of the war, stating that this was all controlled by Jewish finance. His calumny of German-Jewish wartime service is followed by a partly true assertion, with one of his relatively few mentions of economic policy.

As with other belligerents during the war, the German state did increasingly control economic life, including production quotas, wages, work hours, and more. Hitler connects the image and the economic fact to assert that the German Jew did not fight, but rather spent the war years taking control of German production and finance. This is insidious, though not a pure example of vicious descriptions and attacks, including threats of violence. Such examples flare up in the text as the third rhetorical mode.

One example of provocative bigotry is in his discussion of beauty, when he says that Jews cannot understand it because they are "an embodied protest against the aesthetics of the Lord's image."[9] The comments provoke feelings of deep estrangement toward Jews from Christians. Is Hitler calling up views from his past or being totally cynical? The Lord's image, which of course might well appear Semitic, is not a personal or artistic preoccupation for Hitler. The direct juxtaposition of beauty, a need and boon to every human, with a group who is damned to not know it because they rejected Christianity, resurrects a complaint against the Jews that had almost been forgotten in Germany in the 1920s. Still, Hitler will perpetuate this pejorative view in a discussion of cultural matters. Dehumanizing Jews and highlighting their disbelief in Christianity align them with Marxist atheism. Throughout the text he reworks and repeats, falsely emphasizing ideas about Jews in order to connect in a threatening or offensive way to readers from a variety of walks of life. But the ideas he is presenting are mostly quite old. For example, he will say that Christ's driving the money changers out of the Temple shows that Christ hates Jews. With German Jews highly assimilated, largely successful, and certainly loyal to the German state, there had been no real "Jewish Question" in Germany, even as Hitler is determined to promote one. Linking Jews to communism and Marxism is his most contemporary reference and alas one that—in the form of Judeo-Bolshevism—was widely feared from recent events such as the Hungarian Revolution and the Revolution in Munich and of course initially the Russian Revolution.

Paul Hanebrink concluded that "Judeo-Bolshevism made Hitler." And then eventually Hitler used it to create an exterminatory racial state.[10]

Hitler's approach to Marxism in *Mein Kampf* does not reveal much depth of knowledge, although he claimed to have engaged in serious study. For example, Hitler does not differentiate among revisionists, who renounce revolution, and other groups, although he does briefly discuss the relationship between trade unions and parliamentarians. Hitler does not admit the degree to which a Marxist perspective has become quite domesticated in Germany, with, for example, the SPD de facto evolving into a nonrevolutionary party.[11] Hitler hardly speaks about leading Marxists, scattering only a few references to "the Jew Karl Marx" throughout the text and citing Lenin only at the end. *Mein Kampf* depicts "Marxism" as communism or socialism or welfare statism; in fact, it is usually all these combined. Hitler does not object specifically to one Marxist thinker or another; rather, he presents Marxism as including all class-centered struggle and advocacy for the German worker. Such a big tent approach to the subject results not in an accurate, stable, informative picture of Marxism but rather a somewhat impressionistic view of a political formation which Hitler finds both disgraceful and attractive, compelling as an opponent and an inspiration, a threat and a model. At times, he expresses anger and disgust toward this totality Marxism, as when he notes that the Kaiser reached out his hand in a gesture of German unity toward the SPD when the Great War had begun. Hitler says he would not have embraced them; he would have rounded them up and executed them.[12] In fact, in the spring of 1933 when he is in power, Hitler does round up communists and men of the left. He is as good as his word on this point.

Yet, although Hitler wants to and eventually will kill Marxists, he also admires them. How is Marxism a model for Hitler, who in private spoke of himself as a socialist? His party was the National Socialist German Workers' Party, and this was not a misnomer, for, in *Mein Kampf*, he asserts that workers should be paid a living wage, although they should not expect the end of wage differentiation. Workers maintain the right to fight or protest for better working conditions, believing there should be equal respect for both artisan and professional. Education, as well, should be available to all, although it will become a much different system when Hitler rises to power. Hitler wants to increase every German's prosperity, unlike what he states had been occurring in Russia since the 1917 Revolution, with people brought down to a near poverty level.[13] He has concern for the German working class, as a numerically large element of the *Volk*, and yet the fondness he claims to have for them is not based upon his desire for justice for them, but rather is based upon his hatred for the Jews. In his ideological apprenticeship, he comes to realize that the more he understood the Jew, the more he forgave the worker, since the worker is always dominated by Jewish interests.[14] Workers forming unions or voting for their own parties, however, does not enable them to escape victimization, because Jewish interests ultimately control workers' parties. Despite Hitler's purported care for workers, when they act collectively, as trade unionists or "Marxists," his views in *Mein Kampf* demonstrate anger toward them, because he sees them as ultimately giving themselves over to Jewish domination while also choosing to care for themselves as a group within the whole, rather than for the whole *Volk*.

As Hitler writes *Mein Kampf*, Marxism still speaks to and for the German worker. In fact, much of the industrial working class accepted some variant of socialism, derived from Marxism. Hitler feels Marxists are misleading the German workers by associating them with the workers of the world, struggling "to unite." Marxism proclaims its eventual fulfillment, its victory, as inevitable, with the proletariat as the dominant class in a world of economic fairness, dedicated to a decent life for all. Hitler also wanted a decent life, a prosperous and even glorious life, for the German workers, as Germans, rather than as workers. His people or *Volk* were a race, not a class. To many in Western and Central Europe, a good life was one where "consumer durables . . . mass produced items with reduced prices would be affordable to strata of society who had been spending their income on daily necessities. They might be able to buy a glass of beer, or a cigar, or go to a dance hall or cinema."[15] This is a life common to many Americans who also had the possibility, unthinkable to all but a few Germans, of buying an automobile, most likely a Ford. Hitler's own pride meant that he wanted these same possibilities of a comfortable life for Germans as well. Social commentators, overtly, and populations, implicitly, accepted a life of work tempered with some comforts and presumed that individuals could provide their own transcendent meaning. Hitler could not let such a sociopolitical contract stand. He wrote with near certainty that his plans would include war on a wide scale, to provide a life for Aryans for millennia to come. A generation or more would potentially sacrifice the precious human satisfactions of their average lives to pay for Hitler's bio-political vision. And *Mein Kampf* leaves no doubt that Hitler was inspired by such sacrifice.

His plan meant that all Germans, particularly the *Volk* he valued, as well as the rather contemptible bourgeoisie, needed to assert their own rights to food and living space. Their victory is literally necessary for their survival, but it is not inevitable. They will eat or be eaten. This view is primitive, not in the sense of looking back to very early days but in that it shows Hitler's philosophic and psychological brute simplicity. For Hitler, Marxism is an enemy of the *Volk* primarily because of its concern for international as well as national growth and development that envisions a fairer distributive equilibrium in the future. Hitler does not share the Marxist attitude choosing instead to focus solely upon the national growth and development of Germans. To Hitler the bourgeoisie are weak-willed, selfish, and concerned only with their own pocket, not with their race. He finds them cowed during the Weimar years by socialist groups and the working class in general, and he thinks they are stupid and blind not to realize that the working class is not inextricably wedded to the SPD or other socialist groups.[16] Hitler sees that it is possible to win over great numbers of the working class to

National Socialism, since they will admire the National Socialist propensity to act and the willingness to engage in physical confrontations. The working class experiences a visceral reaction to National Socialism over bourgeois politicians and parties that fail to grasp how unattractive and pusillanimous they are. Hitler observes that if the working class comes for the show, they will gradually be convinced of the belief system of the party. Liking the combative part of National Socialism, the working class may, we can observe, be less attracted to the dying part, which is fundamental to Nazism.

Hitler believes that Nazis demonstrate real vigor, attractive to working men and uncharacteristic of the respectable German bourgeoisie. Nazi ideology stresses physical fitness, not unlike communist regimes which include a strong strain of intolerance for the differently abled not explicitly attributable to Marxism.[17] Hitler pushes boxing as a fitting sport for Germans, with strength more overtly on display and a less effete affect than in fencing or perhaps tennis.[18] He was known as an admirer of the famous German boxer Max Schmelling. In fact, interest in physical fitness was widespread in Weimar Germany, as it had been a significant interest in the Reich and did not correlate with one social group. The Nazi movement is hardly unique in caring for exercise, strength, and pure and robust health, but does differ in its emphasis on fitness as a preparation for terror and violence.

The Weimar years saw men and women focused on competitive sport, the healthy and efficient body, and exercise. One stream of interest was among men who wanted to surreptitiously practice military preparation contrary to the terms of the Versailles settlement. More widespread was a wish to have a body fit for the modern world, a body that seemed to have left behind the injury and weakness of the Great War, that could meet and conquer the demands of a competitive society and economy, and that eschewed traditional German communal exercise, such as group hiking, for activities where individual achievement could be registered. Expressions of modern individuality, however, are a tendency that is contrary to National Socialist interests howsoever much they approve of athleticism in Germans.[19] Hitler's citation of Schmelling has racial meanings, namely that Aryans should admire and emulate the ability to beat opponents into submission, but it also resonates with a strong enthusiasm for the sports hero that exists in far less pernicious form in the society at large.

Worker-oriented parties offer an opportunity for personal financial betterment, including higher wages, secure benefits, and job protection. Potentially, at least in the view of some workers, it promised a revolutionary transformation of the German economy, which would further elevate their material circumstances and add to their sense of being masters of their own lives. Hitler's frequent description of himself as the "master" of a meeting, of the Nazi Party, indicates that increased autonomy and feeling of authority among members of the German working class is not the transformation he wants. Although German workers can feel good because they are German/Aryan rather than Jewish or some other "lower race," they are expected to be followers. And working-class self-assertion merely redistributes the pie, which will result in Germany's falling further behind with productive capabilities than it had been by the disastrous end of the Great War. Redistributing the pie is counterproductive; what is needed is *Lebensraum*. The German workers' wholly inadequate perspective, in thrall to the Marxist worldview, means they seek to succeed at the expense of the German *Volk*, ostensibly to the benefit of the international working class, but in reality to the benefit of international Jewish power.

Rather than serve international communism, Germans, and in particular young Germans, should follow the example of the youth of Langemark, who marched straight into English fire in November 1914. The Langemark myth was cherished by many, including Hitler, who speaks of it in *Mein Kampf*.[20] The death of beautiful youth is to him something worth honoring. Sacrifice, especially blood sacrifice, remains the bedrock of his ideology, something to be celebrated, not mourned. When he discusses the young "monitors" at his party meetings protecting him in hand-to-hand combat, the combination of their strength, courage and youth, and the danger and risk they face, is profoundly pleasing to Hitler. His project is further validated and elevated by young German men being injured or even dying for the cause. [21]

As for the *Volk*, they have aficionados, admirers, and scholars of their heritage in many small political parties and cultural groups. Hitler, lukewarm to the *völkish* program that venerated the early Germans, seemed to regard them as antiquarians more comfortable on a study tour than in a military invasion. They were content to celebrate culture, though they did not understand power politics. Tacitus's *Germania* excited interest among many Germans and, in important Nazis, serious reverence. Hitler, although a Wagner/Bayreuth acolyte, was not enthralled or inspired by German barbarians. He requested the *Codex Aesinas* from Mussolini, perhaps to placate the Tacitus fans in his inner circle.[22] In *Mein Kampf* he argues against small *völkish* parties combining their strength to form a larger party, compromising on disagreements to reach political viability. He asserts that by staying separate and competing with one another, the stronger one will win out, to the good of all.[23] This advice appears in the latter part of Book II. At that point, a reader might suspect that Hitler is at least as much pleased to see many *völkish* groups collapse, as he is to see one emerge as the strongest, because such political formations, standing up for German pride and heroic history, have as their essence what is merely a part of the NSDAP program, but nonetheless could capture some of the National Socialists' potential membership.

There was a tendency in some *völkish* thinkers to admire, along with the diversity of the Holy Roman Empire, the varying lifeways and geography of the constituent parts of the empire. Writing just before German unification, "folklorist Wilhelm Heinrich Riehl wrote . . . [T]he very nature of the German community precludes attempts at homogenization, whether social or political."[24] The celebration of different ways of being German was potentially threatening and at the very least not appealing to National

Socialism. Furthermore, Hitler did not like the *völkish* "look." Stylistically Hitler gravitated toward elegant bourgeoisie interiors over antlers and runes, as evidenced by the interior decoration of his residences.[25] *Völkish* culture and politics interested many Germans before Hitler's entrance on the public stage. As he progressed through his career, Hitler continued to be admired by Germany's folk. Hitler believed that they entirely failed to realize what saving the *Volk* required. Stefan George may be mentioned here; although he is not particularly *völkish*, he represents a literary circle of those secretly seeking to bring back Germany's aristocratic identity. They too had found the Reich degenerate, and some were on the fringes of Nazism. Hitler would not insult George, but neither would he particularly value his literary building blocks of a potential new German Reich. He looks to Lenin more than to Stefan George. Anyone who wants a new, true German culture must be willing to resurrect "another" Germany.

The Marxist constituency or "base," as well as their aims, are different from Hitler's. However, Marxist techniques, their vigor, belief in themselves, and will to shape their future inspired Hitler. At times, he refers to Marxists as shock troops and storm troops, and he can offer no higher praise. When Hitler first plans his opening event to reveal the German Workers' Party, he happily announces that the flag will be red, an exciting color that will infuriate the communists and generate not only their anger and opposition but also that which he desperately craves most: their attention. Hitler's authentic joy at planning "happenings" is evident in these descriptions, offering a striking contrast, which could suggest that a less damaged, less vicious Hitler, in another, better political context, would have had a more benign career.[26] After the war, he admires Marxist parades since they have trucks, red banners, and red scarves. The uniformity and power of effect impresses Hitler greatly and he achieves his dream of matching this when he and his party issue forth a similar display of trucks with banners for his Circus Krone meeting.[27] This is beautiful in itself and especially as a provocation to Marxists.

Not only Marxist spectacle but also Marxist categories are embedded in Hitler's consciousness. For example, his summary description of Jewish history echoes the Marxist description of the dialectic of history as the feudal phase moves to the bourgeois and then to the proletarian phase. Hitler asserts that Jews first arrive in various European countries as advisors to monarchs, calling them "court Jews." The people, the *Volk*, become critical of the Jews' insinuating and self-enriching practices; however, before they can be expelled or punished, the Jews become involved in, and somewhat disguised by, the struggle for the rights of the bourgeoisie. They cloak their privilege and intent with advocacy for democratic rights and religious tolerance, measures which would secure their own social and financial safety and enable them to continue their nefarious work of undermining their host nations. Finally, Jews develop a social justice agenda and align with the proletariat under the banner of Marxism.

Although these are categories of history available to anyone, given Hitler's intense focus on Judeo-Bolshevism, it is reasonable to interpret his discussion of Jewish history as a demonstration that at each point of the dialectic of history, the Jewish people have come out on top. In fact, the history that Hitler describes as one of Jewish shape-shifting domination was characterized by struggle and innovation for Jews to survive with humanity intact in environments of varying degrees of hostility. As with Marxism, there is no actual Jewish history, no Jewish lived experience in *Mein Kampf*. Hitler's book falls under the heading of "dictator literature," in fact hate literature. While historical denial should come as no surprise to us, we still need to consider the actual history in contrast to the elisions.[28] Even more than with the doctrine of Marxism and its adherents, specific Jewish people, living and working, are almost entirely absent from the text.

Calumny against Jews described them as usurers, unfair bankers, rent gougers, and harsh employers. For much of their history, Jews were lenders, small tradespeople, commercial travelers, or peddlers. In the early modern Polish-Lithuanian Commonwealth, Jews were hired as estate managers, overseers, bankers, and financial advisors to nobles and their households. Many achieved a comfortable life under these conditions. Innkeeping and leather working were other jobs open to Jews, but many un- or underemployed struggled to make ends meet. In Spain and Italy, the Sephardim even when ghettoized and restricted in employment could invest in direct commercial ventures with European-wide trading and lending. However, many Sephardic Jews were also quite poor. Although some of the Sephardim who left Spain for Amsterdam became prominent in the stock market, large numbers were on the public dole.

In the seventeenth and most notably eighteenth and nineteenth centuries, Jewish disabilities were removed, and degrees of citizenship allowed them in several European countries and German city-states. Jews engaged in self-debate about proper and possible paths to make a living and the means to provide for their own poor. Should substantial numbers of Jews engage in agriculture and crafts? This was one question which was entertained especially in German territories in the early nineteenth century but did not result in a significant shift in Jewish vocational patterns. A few major names such as Rothschild achieved prominence by the 1830s as extremely wealthy international bankers. Wealthy Jewish families, be they Rothschilds of renown or other prosperous families, had access and connections to non-Jewish notables and were considered responsible for charity to fellow Jews and others, which sometimes inspired envy and even fear. Much of the nineteenth century was a comparative golden age for Jews in Western and Central Europe, as they lived in ideological harmony with Christian bourgeoisie, most of them, on the desirability of liberal nationalism and their skills and experience suited them to capitalism as it emerged and grew. Opportunities for professional education increased for Jews, although not all professions were open to them.[29]

In Eastern Europe, Jewish life was different. When Russia assumed control of the Pale of Settlement in the late eighteenth century, the majority of Jews practiced traditional religion, and most were very poor. The growth of the professional Jewish middle class was minimal. The Russian middle class was also small, with opportunities for Jews few and far between. Many tried to emigrate to Central or Western Europe or to the United States. Hitler, in his defamation of all Jews, makes much of hating the look of the Eastern European Jews he sees in Vienna, offended by their presence, poverty, and seemingly menacing lack of culture. In both Russia and abroad, Russian Jews reconceptualized their views of religion and materialism. Although the stereotyping of Jews by non-Jews, with an emphasis on material goods and money, was common practice, the works of Russian Jews in the 1860s and 1870s were a cultural moment when Jews themselves consciously reconsidered how they should treat "land, labor and bodies," in the words of Eliyahu Stern.

Long accused of being materialists, Eastern European Jews, and for that matter Polish Catholics, and others, expressed their religious and spiritual identities through material forms—in social welfare organizations, political advocacy, and cultural activity. It was the spirit of the age.[30] Western Jews at the end of the nineteenth century sought to professionalize their philanthropy, directing it toward local populations, Eastern Jewish immigrants into their countries, and even settlements in Palestine.

For centuries, Jews held a complex political and economic history, attempting to modernize, sometimes along with non-Jews. Exclusions from individual rights that restricted most jobs and careers were the root of their poverty and as a result when avenues opened to them, educational or professional, they tended to work very hard. In conjunction with community critics or leaders in the Russian territories, they sought to change religious-based customs that led to poverty. Hitler affirms a long-held falsehood of Jews as dangerous and deeply nefarious, as he describes Jewish self-preservation and self-improvement as hostile actions to destroy the German people.

Despite glaring omissions, and an overly verbose, rambling narrative, *Mein Kampf* was not greeted with widespread rejection or condemnation, nor was it widely identified as a collection of specious theories and lies. From the time Hitler came to power, the book sold well, and under the Nazi regime, it was gifted by some German cities to newly married couples. Individual sources such as memoirs vary on how much *Mein Kampf* was read—some saw it as a joke, yet many others read it and considered it valuable. Othmar Plöckinger has documented empirical evidence that many people read the book; those who did not own it might have read sections of it in school, for example.[31]

The form and approach Hitler takes reflect a recognizable pattern in public discourse in Europe and throughout the Western world that becomes normalized, as a discourse appearing primarily in newspapers and also in organization reports, public petitions, and other media reporting global issues through the nineteenth century and into the twentieth century. Derek

Pensler, for example, observes that scholars have long considered the "Jewish Question" or the "Jewish problem," that is, obstacles to Jewish free and equal relations to non-Jews and in society generally, with categorization by the governments of various states. Contemporaries perhaps suggest by the phrase that Jews are a problem, while the Jewish people themselves, and some allies, seek to solve their problems. The Jewish Question has been regarded primarily as a political question, although Pensler's study comes from an economic perspective, which was a major preoccupation of the Jewish people as well as for Hitler, albeit from radically different perspectives. The "Jewish Question" was not the only question in the nineteenth century. "A hegemonic elite or dominant majority group that discriminated against a subaltern or minority group called the latter a problem." Pensler notes the constant invocation from the mid-nineteenth century of the "social question," . . . "the Negro Question," . . . as well as the "women's question," . . . and the "Irish question," all labeled with "a similar taxonomy of dysfunction."[32]

The "Jewish Question" additionally was seen as an issue of public concern, with the notable difference that "Jews were thought to be fully capable of taking care of themselves."[33] Alleged Jewish privileges more easily turned into anger and offenses against Jews, who were targeted for having resources and strengths not available to most subalterns. In fact, they were rarely regarded as entirely subaltern, privileged with choices, powers, and connections even though these options were part of a fantasy crafted by outsiders. Yet only 1 percent of the Jews of Russia around 1870 might be classified as bourgeois; the Jews of the Pale as noted were not a wealthy population and Central European Jews had climbed to a middle-class or upper-middle-class status by the nineteenth century.

In the modern era, Pensler notes that societal categories, inequities, and injustices have been conceptualized in the problem mode. Recently, the meaning of nineteenth-century problem categories has been excavated and analyzed by Holly Case in *The Age of Questions: Or a First Attempt at an Aggregate History of the Social, Woman, American, Jewish, Polish, Bullion, Tuberculosis and Many Other Questions over the Nineteenth Century and Beyond.* Her innovative study of the emergence and changes in public discourse provides a suggestive context for *Mein Kampf*. Starting in the late eighteenth century, and especially in the early nineteenth century, matters of domestic and international government policy and societal problems were posed as questions, while the formulaic iteration of "questions" (e.g., the woman question, the social question, the Eastern question) continued for decades with the ever-repeated rhetorical form creating habits in thought and routinized responses. Predecessors of the great nineteenth-century questions might be found in the questions and answers of catechisms or the questions posed in essay contests. The great catalyst for the age of questions became British parliamentary debates, as information about them was published in newspapers. British decision-makers, while ruling an empire, addressed questions with wide geographical reach. The Congress of Vienna addressed many questions, such as the Polish, the Sicilian question, the Napoleon question, and others.

With the new public sphere and the emergence of civil society of the early nineteenth century through expanded franchises, increased literacy, and press reporting, especially in Western Europe, public bodies along with private citizens who feel they have a public voice advocate solutions to various questions. Events in the 1830s, including revolutions in France, the November Uprising in Poland, and the Greek War for Independence, perpetuated the trend to question formation, internationalizing many questions. Other questions of the age emerged from nationalist predicaments, such as the Macedonian question, while emancipatory questions such as the social question and the slavery question remained extremely important, demonstrating the strong impulse of raising questions to overturn malign systems of power, as with the West Indian question.

Large gatherings of a concerned public pressing governments for better working conditions for maids or factory workers are hardly problematic, yet over time as the question form became formulaic, it became less functional. Questions led to over-defined fields of inquiry and limited creative solutions. Querists distanced themselves from the human beings who were the objects of their questions and denied them a role in the "solution" to their question. This is notable in the Eastern question. Sometimes questions would be connected, with the aim of solving them together, as with the Belgian, Polish, and Greek questions. Shall the French fight in 1831 to solve these "bundled" questions? People feel that problems cannot be solved separately, but also despair of solutions to multiple problems. They rewrite and back date assessments of problems. Audiences ponder the sincerity of advocates for a question. Also, they start to wonder if questions are perpetual, if there is any possible solution and if not, perhaps it is not worth entertaining the question. Questions become prioritized, with competitive and dire association. Frustrated, people look for "final solutions." The term, first used in English in the eighteenth century and in the second half of the nineteenth century in German, "to reference mathematical or chemical formulae or equations" evolved in the latter nineteenth century amid the great age of laboratory sciences, with biology rather than mathematics providing the metaphors for questions and their solutions. With biological metaphors, society and nations in this period are increasingly conceptualized as bodies. As a result, then, social questions began to take on human attributes, needing to be regularly fed, and as "living" issues, unsuited for a final or perfect solution. Biology assumes the explanatory field, replacing religion and mathematics, although this shift did not quell the desire to find solutions to long-standing problems. [34]

Suggestions that major long-term questions, such as the Polish or the Eastern, or the stability of Austria-Hungary, might be solved at once fed into the outlook that made the Great War possible, and some questions were even answered in light of this war as certain peoples of the former Austria-Hungary received the governments they desired, some women achieved the right to vote, France recovered Alsace-Lorraine. The Soviet Union promised to be a workers' state. "The Soviet Union was not only the first state to make solving questions part of its *raison d'etre* but may have been the first to declare a question formally and officially *solved*."[35]

Hitler, who had been formed by the Great War, believed that most questions that were answered had been answered incorrectly, provocatively, and insultingly. He saw that Germany had lost land, had been forced to pay reparations, had suffered through revolution and regime change, economic difficulties, and disgrace. Hitler's interest in public questions and intellectual awakening despite his description of it as emerging from prewar Vienna seems to have occurred during and as a result of the Great War. His views came from the news he read and heard especially that concerning the fate of the German Army that he followed assiduously. This is where Hitler's political preoccupations originate. After the Great War, the age of questions continued, and Hitler pursues his questions in *Mein Kampf*.

Holly Case characterizes Hitler's situation in the penultimate phase of the age of questions:

> After the postwar peace treaties of 1918-1920, a number of questions were considered "solved," at least in part. But the losers of World War I—dissatisfied with the status quo—became especially active querists during the interwar period. Hitler was one of them. He bundled questions together, insisting they needed to be solved together, and saw universal war and the elimination of boundaries as the path to the great omnibus solution (including but not limited to *the* Final Solution).[36]

Early in *Mein Kampf*, Hitler describes the insights he took from the pamphlet, given to him by Anton Drexler: a staple form of the age of questions that argued for converting from a workers' orientation to a nationalist one.[37] Hitler bundles his questions in *Mein Kampf* and throughout the rest of his career, believing that they cannot be understood in isolation. Acknowledging speaking as his forte, Hitler makes much of his party rallies, praising their organization and his effective speeches. Most commentators agree in fact that his writing is far less compelling than his public speaking, which he relies upon quite effectively once he becomes chancellor for enforcing solutions to Germany's problems. "The striking pattern that emerges once we view Hitler in the context of the age of questions is how the path to war and mass violence was paved with questions."[38] The language of Hitler's greatest fluency, diplomatic pleading, threat, attack, and suppression is heard when he assumes power. Preparatory to that day, *Mein Kampf* expresses his main issues which are readily recognized by querists and the public as the "questions" of the era. The people recognized the questions and much of the answer in his writing that detailed his plans for the future. In addition, *Mein Kampf* serves as a way for him to reconcile his imprisonment and the necessity of a legal route to power. Hitler recognizes and benefits from the fact that in the latter part of the age of questions, written responses to questions are useful but not decisive and that a war may be a much better solution than use of the law to resolve any questions.

The age of questions, however, did not have to end in the Final Solution. Reflective citizens who banded together as they did at the start of the age to advocate on colonial policy or Greek Independence could lead to a functioning democracy. Who would wish that John Stuart Mill had not taken up his pen to address the question of minority rights and the tyranny of the majority? Questions that seem stale and outdated, when bundled provocatively, can allow for a darker, shadowy side of the era to emerge. With the social or Jewish Question, Hitler manipulated the object of the question, using propaganda to demonize the Jews and rationalize his power and violent plan. In *Mein Kampf*, Hitler sought to present a solution of sorts to the social question for Germans, so as to convince his audience to accept his deadly goals, by distorting the Jewish Question, attacking Marxism, and exposing the effectiveness of propagandistic and bundled questions.

Hitler's work is arresting, shocking, and at times revolutionary, yet it remains deeply a work of its time, not only by virtue of its rhetoric and subject matter but also by its discourses of degeneration, questions of will and abulia, anti-Semitism, and voluntarism. H. Stuart Hughes formulated the phrase "revolt against positivism" to describe the emergence of a belief that the mind and will ("consciousness") could alter circumstances and reality in a materialist and science-obsessed era.[39] Classical or vulgar Marxism with its preconditions for revolution was quite positivistic. Hitler believed that the revolution he sought, even though it was in quest of material goods, land, and resources, was never conditioned by material facts. Instead, it was governed by a triumph of the will. This reflects similarities to Lenin's intellectual matrix. With only one reference to Lenin in *Mein Kampf*, it might appear that he is relatively unimportant. In reality, however, considering that there are relatively few names included and recognizing Hitler's jealousy of certain important people, such as Mussolini, one reference to Lenin is perhaps more telling than ten.[40]

Lenin serves as a model for Hitler in his voluntarism. Although Marxism identifies preconditions, such as a bourgeois revolution, for the proletarian revolution, Lenin does not wait for Russia to pass through each stage, choosing to establish a vanguard party to lead the revolution and push through a proletarian revolution, even in a peasant-based society. Hitler admired Lenin and convinced himself that he too could take control and push history along so that his people could achieve a *völkish* state. Indeed, there are a number of striking parallels between Lenin and Hitler. Hitler sees the National Socialists as a vanguard party in the sense that the party has a highly engaged core, ready to take dramatic action. When he criticizes the SPD for having a revolutionary goal, though lacking in ability to realize the goal, Hitler argues that a very large, established party cannot make a revolution. The postwar revolutionary actions were spearheaded by the breakaway Spartacus League and Independent Socialists. A cadre, ready to act, to fight, and to die, can succeed in a revolution according to Hitler, as he identifies his own party, with his exemplary "monitors," who will become the SA. Yet in *Mein Kampf* he is also facing the failure of his revolutionary gesture of 1924 and recalibrating his route to power. It will not be the Leninist route, but more that of Mussolini. He has the special forces to continue his party work and to, ideally, seize power legally. And then he can control the state.[41]

Hitler, like the early Bolsheviks, downplays the state, although in a different way. To Hitler, the state exists, no matter the form, for it is the content of the *Volk* that remains definitive. His numerous remarks that form is not an issue seem sincere and also intended to persuade people to accept his hoped-for exclusive dictatorial leadership. Hitler sees the state's bureaucratic apparatus and formal division of powers as insignificant. Instead he focused solely on preserving the *Volk* for the future as the primary purpose of the state. Hitler criticizes the Weimar Republic, condemning it for having disregarded and even having suppressed the well-being of the nation by pandering to Marxists, Jews, foreign demands, and republican conventions. He envisions the Nazi Party as a racial elite, a group of leaders to be followed by the good *Volk*. But followed where? As Timothy Snyder writes:

> The ceaseless strife of races was not an element of life, but its essence. . . . Struggle was life, not a means to some other end. It was not justified by the prosperity (capitalism) or justice (socialism) that it supposedly brought. Hitler's point was not at all that the desirable end justified the bloody means. There was no end, only meanness. Race was real, whereas individuals and classes were fleeting and erroneous constructions. Struggle was not a metaphor or analogy but a tangible and total truth. The weak were to be dominated by the strong, since "the world is not there for cowardly peoples." And that was all that there was to be known and believed.[42]

Propelled by a hackneyed but recognizable form, Hitler writes at great length with constant reminders of his skill for public speaking. As with the January 1918 strikers, and the youth at Langemark, Germans are to be silenced, trained to respond in an almost animal-like way. They can run, roar, and reproduce, yet never argue or articulate their views. The "monitors," for whom he had initially expressed admiration in *Mein Kampf* and who had once served as his SA, will themselves become targets in 1934 as Hitler, unable to tolerate their strong presence, silences them in the Night of the Long Knives. The bellicose language of *Mein Kampf* anticipates the destruction of free discursive speech, democratic culture, and parliamentary rule. To Hitler, Marxism was a serious threat, one that he leveraged through imitation and through instigation of fear and pugnacity in many Germans. Many followed him, as Timothy Snyder explains, into violence, pain, and death for the sake of future Aryans, who will presumably continue the struggle. Hitler's personal struggle ended in April 1945. The rhetorical strategy of the question or problem, manipulatively posed, and the associated aspirations of antidemocratic leaders continue.

PART V

Religious Overtones in *Mein Kampf*

Hitler's view of religion in *Mein Kampf* is far milder and superficially benign than it was in reality. In the opening pages of *Mein Kampf* Hitler relates that in his youth he often "became intoxicated on the solemn splendor of the outwardly splendid Church festivals." Elsewhere in *Mein Kampf* Hitler adopts a neutral tone toward Protestantism and Catholicism, stressing in volume II that members of both confessions would find a congenial home in National Socialism. In reality, Hitler was hostile toward the Christian churches in Germany. As a political tactician he knew a public campaign against them would complicate his efforts to unify the Germans behind his plans to expand Germany's borders through war. Thus, in contrast with the philippics of other folk-nationalists alleging that Christianity had debilitated Germany's racial health, Hitler strove to hide the obvious incongruity of Nazism with the Christian Gospel. He did so through advocacy of a "positive Christianity" that portrayed Jesus as an anti-Semite, whose central message identified the Jews as the enemy of the human race. National Socialism, then, was "nothing other than a practical compliance with the teachings of Christ," as Hitler said in December 1926. He himself would complete the work that Jesus had begun.

Hitler's aversion to attacking mainline religion in Germany was, then, motivated by expedience rather than personal piety. As with other matters, however, Hitler was biding his time in his plans for religion. In October 1941, he declared that "anyone who lives naturally will run into a conflict with the Church." After the war, he would ensure that "the churches promulgate no doctrines that contradict our doctrines." In February 1942, Hitler confided to Himmler and Albert Speer his belief that "the worst cancerous sores are our clergymen of both confessions!. . . . The moment will come when I'll settle accounts with them without further ado." He described his future reckoning with the churches as his "final life's work."

Hitler's inner antipathy toward religion was widely shared by his followers, some of whom, like Alfred Rosenberg, took few pains to conceal their hostility. Rosenberg had early on (1919) called for a state-sponsored repression of the Catholic Church. (His 1930 book *The Myth of the 20th Century* was for this reason placed on the Vatican's *Index of Prohibited Books*.) The official Nazi newspaper *Der Völkische Beobachter*, which Rosenberg edited, wrote that Christianity, "a religion of tolerance, suffering, and enduring," had arisen from the "decaying Roman world empire." Erich Ludendorff, the First World War Prussian general implicated in Hitler's putsch but acquitted at his trial, was smitten with the pagan religious views of his wife Mathilde von Kemnitz. She championed replacing the "Judaized" Christianity of Catholicism and Protestantism with a new Germanic faith, one purified of any Jewish traces.

Hitler's totalitarianism did not brook rival powers within Germany, particularly ones like the Protestant and Catholic churches that elicited fierce devotion from their adherents. He may have been willing to make temporary accommodations with both confessions as he consolidated his power and launched Germany into the Second World War (such as the Concordat with the Vatican signed in July 1933), yet an independent church committed to the highest ideals of the Christian Gospel would not have been tolerated in a victorious postwar Third Reich. The "solution" to what Hitler called the "church problem" (*Kirchenproblem*) would have been no more favorable to the devout than the Nazis' "solutions" to other self-styled "problems" were to their victims; the "Jewish Problem" and the "Gypsy Problem" are two that readily come to mind. Had he won the war, Hitler would have demanded of both confessions' complete subservience to the Nazi state, and this demand would have been enforced at the point of a bayonet. As he menacingly said in August 1942, the Church was a "reptile" that always rose up "whenever state authority weakens. Therefore, it has to be crushed." His promise in *Mein Kampf* to complete the unfinished work of Christ would have been fulfilled by destroying institutional Christianity in Europe.

11

Being Adolf Hitler

Mein Kampf as Anti-Semitic Bildungsroman

Susannah Heschel

The opening chapters of *Mein Kampf* present an invitation: come and join me, the author calls to his readers, in a journey of enlightenment that will reveal the clandestine evil destroying Germany: Jews. While Jews may be visible to the eye, the depth and extent of their wickedness require an awareness that comes with self-cultivation, *Bildung*. Rather than presenting itself in its opening pages as an ideological tract or political platform, *Mein Kampf* asks its readers to join its author in a journey of *Bildung*. Hitler's goal was creating a mass movement that would think of itself as a community, with each person identifying with him, since he viewed himself and his life as the political movement; Nazi politics *was* Hitler, not only in his own mind. He was the figure at the center, with whom each person should be tied in an emotional connection, as emotions, he recognized, are more powerful in uniting people than political platforms. Nowhere were emotions deployed more consistently in *Mein Kampf* than in its anti-Semitic passages about Jews.

A massive body of anti-Semitic literature produced in Germany from the 1870s through 1945 informed readers of alleged Jewish wickedness in nearly every sphere of private and public life. The deleterious effects of Jews were enumerated: crashing the stock market, mocking Christianity, undermining German language and culture, threatening the cleanliness and health of Germans, perverting marriage and sexuality, robbing Germany of its wealth, and stirring its enemies against it in war. Whatever was bad in the world, Bolshevism and capitalism, rape and homosexuality, technology and legalism, was due to the Jews. All that had been enumerated endlessly; *Mein Kampf* was not so much about presenting innovative anti-Semitic ideas or motifs as cultivating "intoxication and irrational."[1] Nor does *Mein Kampf* try to appear intellectually sophisticated, instead quoting various pseudo-scholarly purveyors of race theory, like H. S. Chamberlain's two-volume *Foundations of the Nineteenth Century*.

Mein Kampf's notable literary quality among anti-Semitic texts lies in the way the narrative seeks to engage the reader. The book combines Hitler's account of his own life and a political manifesto (particularly in volume II), yet the autobiographical elements are demonstrably inaccurate, as many historians have shown, while the political manifesto is jumbled and confused, hardly a concrete map of what became Hitler's destructive acts once in power. *Mein Kampf* is constructed literarily for political purposes, and its opening chapters are an effort to win adherents by depicting Hitler's own journey, his intellectual, political, and emotional *Bildung*, to becoming an anti-Semite. The first sixty or so pages of the text are Hitler's Bildungsroman, the fictional story of Hitler's self-discovery written to offer readers a chance to join him in achieving *Bildung*, a view of the supposed reality of Jewish evil and danger not visible behind the veils of deception that allegedly permeate society. The consequences of that achievement are evident from the outset, as anti-Semitic verbiage spills forth from nearly every chapter, with no effort to prove its claims about Jews through scientific evidence or historical fact or even the burgeoning racial theories.

The subfield of affective polarization within political science has identified the central role of negative affect projected onto the out-group in generating a political identification with the in-group.[2] More than political ideology or specific economic concerns, it is affect that generates political polarization within a society; the opposition is turned into the enemy. Hitler first isolated one segment of German society, the Jews, and turned them into Germany's greatest enemy, mobilizing political hostilities, economic resentments, and even religious differences and transforming them into fear, hatred, and repugnance. The transformation from anti-Semitic idea to affect is engineered by *Mein Kampf* as a process of self-discovery to achieve *Bildung* in concert with Hitler himself.

Mein Kampf's power draws from the negative affect it projects onto Jews far more than on a coherent political argument. The book's positive depictions of German Aryans are infrequent, with hazy calls to purity and heroism, while Jews are heavily represented as disgusting, with appeals to primitive emotions, such as smell. Affective polarization of Aryan Germans and Jews is created with heavy attention to repulsiveness of the out-group, Jews. A similar polarization is found in the pro-Nazi writings of German Protestants, who wrote extensively about the repugnance of Jews and Judaism, with far less affirmation of the Aryan Christianity they purportedly were trying to advance.[3] Group cohesion was created through negation; *Mein Kampf*'s anti-Semitic effort is to entice readers to join Hitler in his discovery of the evils and horrors of Jews.

Long viewed as the ideological mandate of the Nazi Party, *Mein Kampf* sold well and also became an important artifact in living rooms, alongside the Bible. The first volume of *Mein Kampf* appeared on July 18, 1925, the second volume on December 11, 1926. By the end of 1932, 228,000 had been sold; after Hitler came to power in January 1933, 4,000 copies were being sold each day.[4] By 1944, 12.5 million copies had been purchased and were being given at civil ceremonies to all newlywed couples at state expense.[5] During the Third Reich, people owned a copy, much as they owned a copy of Martin Luther's German translation of the Bible, even if few read either one cover to cover. Yet the two books, *Mein Kampf* and the *Lutherbibel*, shared commonalities: they speak of morality versus sin; strong political sovereignty against enemies; the importance of purity of blood and illness as a manifestation of wickedness and divine punishment; obedience to authority versus destruction and chaos; transcendent purpose versus distractions from the moral path; ultimate redemption versus utter annihilation.

Both the *Lutherbibel* and *Mein Kampf* sought to unite Germans culturally and politically. By the late 1930s, no doubt influenced by the extraordinary support for Nazi anti-Semitism fostered by the pro-Hitler German Christian movement within the Protestant Church, some Germans came to view the two books as compatible and interchangeable. Some even substituted *Mein Kampf* for the Bible. The Protestant pro-Nazi German Christian movement had rejected the Old Testament as a Jewish book that had no place in the Christian Bible and had begun to revise the New Testament to remove Jewish elements. In early 1939, sixty theology students from the universities of Erlangen, Göttingen, Leipzig, Marburg, Tübingen, and the Theologische Schule of Bethel traveled through Thüringen. They reported that they could find Christian belief only among older people, "Sonst aber war die Stumpfheit gross. Einige Male begegneten wir offener Ablehnung: Die Bibel sei ein Judenbuch, 'Mein Kampf' sei die heutige Bibel." ("Otherwise the obtuseness was enormous. Several times we met with explicit rejection: the Bible is a Jewish book, *Mein Kampf* is the Bible of today.") Many said they had no time to attend church. "In einem Haus, in dem wir glaubten, auf Verständnis zu stossen, erzählte man uns von einer neuen Bibel, die jetzt erschienen sei, in der alles Jüdische ausgemerzt sei, denn anders sei die Bibel nicht mehr zu gebrauchen."[6] ("In a house, in which we thought we might find understanding, we were told about a new Bible that has just appeared, in which everything Jewish was expunged, because otherwise the Bible was no longer usable.")

In the decades after the war, *Mein Kampf* was locked in the "Giftschrank," a so-called poison closet of libraries, unavailable except to scholars. The Norwegian Karl Ove Knausgaard writes, "The book was evil, in some indefinable way. I was unable, too, to have it on my shelf or on my desk, and instead I put it out of sight in the bottom drawer."[7] With the recent publication of a critical edition, two massive volumes of nearly 2,000 pages with over 3,700 notes with extensive annotation and explanation, the book has become a different kind of relic. Quickly becoming an immediate bestseller in Germany, the critical edition is intended to become a scholarly source for better historical understanding. As the historian Anson Rabinbach asks, "Can a mythologized symbol be neutralized by a phalanx of annotations, however erudite?"[8] The critical apparatus of the new edition explains and contextualizes key words and events that are presented to the reader as part of a larger political and cultural world and not simply the product of Hitler's mind. Through its extensive annotations, the critical edition of *Mein Kampf* opens a door to an alternate world, a historical era that ended yet remains alive and even inspiring for a growing and dangerous international movement of anti-Semitism and white nationalism.

Mein Kampf links Hitler's physical movements, from small town to city, rural to urban, to his political and moral awakening. He presents his birth in Braunau am Inn, a rural small town on the Austrian border with Germany, due east of Munich, as symbolically significant for his goal of returning Austria to its glorious German heritage: "One blood demands one Reich."[9] From Braunau, his family moves to Linz, a small city where Hitler spends his childhood, and from there he moves to Vienna in 1907, at the age of eighteen. These moves are narrated not simply as a maturation but as an awakening that stands symbolically for all Germans. Hitler left Linz as a poor rural lad and arrived in Vienna as an impoverished urban worker, "determined to leap into this new world, with both feet, and fight my way through."[10] Poverty in the countryside is one thing; in the city, it becomes dismal, frightful, wretched, sordid, repulsive,[11] and he is horrified by not only the "economic misery" but also the workers' "moral and ethical coarseness" and "the low level of their intellectual development."[12] Within those circumstances, Hitler takes a new interest in politics, turning first to Marxist explanations of poverty and then discovering the true enemy, the Jews. In Linz, there "were few Jews" though there had been a Jewish boy in his school, "but neither I nor the others had any thoughts on the matter."[13] The supposed innocence of Linz has been challenged by historians; the anti-Semitic newspaper *Linzer Fliegendeblätter* was published there regularly starting in 1899.[14] Yet only in his teens, Hitler claims, did he begin to hear about Jews in the course of political discussions: "This filled me with a mild distaste, and I could not rid myself of an unpleasant feeling that always came over me."[15]

"Then I came to Vienna."[16]

Vienna brought not simply a new awareness of politics and the clash of wealth and poverty but awareness of Jews: "Once, as I was strolling through the Inner City, I suddenly encountered an apparition in a black caftan and black hair locks. Is this a Jew? was my first thought."[17] Hitler describes his transformation in religious terms: "For me this was the time of the greatest spiritual upheaval I have ever had to go through. I had ceased to be a weak-kneed cosmopolitan and became an anti-Semite."[18]

The book is flecked with religious references and allusions to biblical language—"Their sword will become our plow," "daily bread"—it performs politics as religion both in its language and as a book. Hitler carefully crafted the opening sentence to include the word "providence" in relation to his birth, presumably to evoke resonances to the birth stories of Jesus and other redeemers and heroes: "Today it seems to me providential that Fate should have chosen Braunau on the Inn as my birthplace."[19] The town, Hitler relates, is "the symbol of a great mission," the site of several martyrs of the fatherland, implying that the redeemer is born where the crucifixion occurred. Throughout, the book tells a principled story: how a savior figure will prevent Germany's moral, political, and economic collapse, much as Jesus redeemed—or at least, tried to redeem—the world from the degeneracy of the Jews.

If Hitler viewed himself as the "Chosen One," as the historian Volker Ulrich writes, or as "a divinely inspired prophet or oracle," as Michael McGuire calls him,[20] what does he expect from his readers? The book was not only a decorative item on a shelf; it was read, if not in its entirety, by huge numbers of people. The many who borrowed the book from a public library, at least in the early years of the Third Reich, is another indication that it was read.[21] Indeed, some university faculties encouraged students to cite *Mein Kampf*; that was true of the theological faculty at the University of Jena during the Third Reich: citing the work of a Jewish author was forbidden and demonstrating an awareness of racial theory was essential. Racial theory was made an essential tool of interpretation. Professor of Practical Theology Wolf Meyer-Erlach insisted that prior to their examinations, theology students had to have read *Mein Kampf* as well as the writings of Alfred Rosenberg (Figure 11.1).[22]

At the same time as it warns of a mortal danger from Jews, *Mein Kampf* promotes unity: "Are we not the same as all other Germans? Do we not all belong together?"[23] It is Hitler who has left his "soft downy bed" and entered the "world of misery and poverty . . . for whom I was later to fight."[24] Immediately, the narrative warns of the "two menaces," Marxism and Jewry.[25] The two are not separate: "Only a knowledge of the Jews provides the key with which to comprehend the inner, and consequently real, aims of Social Democracy."[26] Knowledge of the Jews requires a particular hermeneutic ability, a cultivation of anti-Semitism, because Jews hide themselves and their intentions: "jabbering German with a Jewish accent. It is always the same Jew. . . . For under this cloak of purely social ideas truly diabolic purposes are hidden."[27] At first elusive, anti-Semitism, Hitler comes to realize, is a form of interpretation of reality that requires a transformation of the self. To be an anti-Semite, in other words, is to awaken to the reality of the world that has hitherto been unseen, to achieve insight and understanding, to cultivate the inner intellectual and political resources that pull away the veil concealing

FIGURE 11.1 *Hubert Langziner's portrait of Hitler as "The Standardbearer" (*Der Bannerträger*). He believed he was leading a crusade against the Jews. Courtesy of the United States Holocaust Memorial Museum.*

the horrors perpetrated by the Jews. *Mein Kampf* takes its readers through a journey of self-discovery, with Hitler serving as the model.

One question Hitler tries to answer with *Mein Kampf* is, "How can a German be turned into an anti-Semite?" All that is supposedly dangerous and evil about Jews is presented within the text. While chapter 11 of the first volume, "Nation and Race," tries to present a coherent argument, the most pungent and effective anti-Semitic passages are those that speak of the sexual and medical threats of Jews and are scattered throughout the book. Volume I opens with a friendly voice; the first pages have a calm and casual tone, trying to appeal to a skeptical reader, and only later chapters unleash the torrent of bombastic anti-Semitism that characterized Hitler's speeches and Nazi propaganda after he assumed power.

Mein Kampf is a form of anti-Semitic seduction and awakening, captured metaphorically as Hitler moves from the farms of the rural provinces to the glamorous capital city of the empire, innocent and blissful, with glittering wealth and revolting poverty: "The Court with its dazzling glamour attracted wealth and intelligence."[28] The city is amazing as a political and intellectual center, and as an economic capital, he writes, yet sadly divorced from the vitality of German nationalism and lacking a sense of peoplehood. These early pages of *Mein Kampf* are friendly, welcoming, inviting the reader on a journey with him into his political maturity.

Hitler explains that he wanted to move to Vienna for its culture: to study music, art, and architecture. His goal is the aesthetic cultivation of himself, which he pursues in the company of male friends. The pace of the opening pages is gradual, with observations about his family, friends, and school days. The life in Vienna, by contrast, becomes increasingly fraught, the sentences jangle, and the narrative becomes tense, demanding, and angry in the subsequent chapters.

The dangers of the Jews intensify with each chapter of the book, described in more and more vivid and horrific detail. What is striking is the gradual way the narrative opens, the seductive quality of its style, and articulation of danger. The book speaks with sympathy for the reader, for those who had hoped for more in their lives, addressing them with understanding and empathy. After gaining the confidence of the reader, Hitler defines the root of their problem: the Jews, a destructive force that brings down individuals as well as the collective German people, Europe, and the superior Aryan race.

Back in Linz, he claims, there were no Jews to speak of; historians know well that this is false. Hitler was an innocent from the countryside when he arrived in Vienna, without prejudice against Jews: "Today it is difficult, if not impossible, for me to say when the word 'Jew' first gave me ground for special thoughts. At home I do not remember having heard the word during my father's lifetime."[29] Once in Vienna, he tells us, he sees strange figures and learns they are Jews. Only gradually does he come to realize their power and danger. His slate was clean: it was Jews who led him to anti-Semitism, not any preconceived prejudices. Jews, not politics or prejudice, are the cause of anti-Semitism. Jews function in *Mein Kampf* not only as figures of danger and denigration but also as crucial to Hitler's *Bildung*; they open his eyes, leading to the intellectual climax of *Mein Kampf*: Jews create anti-Semites out of Germans.

Mein Kampf maintains a tension between promise and danger, illustrating, what Horkheimer and Adorno argue, that bourgeois subjectivity shifts between optimism and pessimism. Vienna is the place of promise, a chance for a poor young man to make good. Achieving that promise was elusive, and Hitler contemplates the poverty of low-wage workers and its impact on the family, and for understanding the troubles that he sees, he thanks Providence.[30] Who cares for these German workers? Hitler blames the stupidity, ineptness, and failures of social democracy on the Jews, his initial suggestion of Jewish political responsibility for German suffering.[31]

The danger is that Jews "had become Europeanized and taken on a human look," he writes, and even looked like Germans.[32] Early on, he had believed them to be no more than adherents of a "strange religion."[33] Once in Vienna, however, "I often grew sick to my stomach from the smell of these caftan-wearers. All this could scarcely be called very attractive; but it became positively repulsive when, in addition to their physical uncleanliness, you discovered the moral stains on this 'chosen people.'"[34] Physical repulsion is linked to moral awareness, as Hitler's revulsion leads him to ask: "Was there any form of filth or profligacy, particularly in cultural life, without at least one Jew involved in it?"[35] Hitler evokes hate, disgust, fear, and envy to seduce his readers and win adherents. Anti-Semitism is not merely a political concern but a visceral repulsion that reinforces his belief in the racial opposition between Aryans and Jews, the greatness of Germans and the destructiveness of Jews, whom he links to prostitution, white slavery, and overall cultural decay.

At first annoyed by the anti-Semitism of the press and political parties, Hitler is transformed into an anti-Semite by his "common sense of justice."[36] Anti-Semitism brought him "my greatest transformation of all . . . the greatest inner soul struggles," a "battle between my reason and my sentiments," until "my reason [began] to emerge victorious" so that "with open eyes I saw not only the buildings [of Vienna] but also the people."[37] The transformation is secured by Hitler's immediate shift to a repugnant physical metaphor: "If you cut even cautiously into such an abscess, you found, like a maggot in a rotting body, often dazzled by the sudden light—a kike."[38] The transformation left him "thunderstruck" and "gradually I began to hate them."[39] His anti-Semitism now transforms his views of society and politics, leading to greater sympathy toward the worker, for instance. His transformation has a religious nature: "Hence today I believe that I am acting in accordance with the will of the Almighty Creator: by defending myself against the Jew, I am fighting for the work of the Lord."[40]

Thus, he teaches his bourgeois readers a lesson that they, too, are free of bias and merely responding with natural sensory repugnance to the sight, smell, and behavior of Jews. Anti-Semitism, in other words, is both rational—who wouldn't be repulsed by Jews?—and fixed in the bodily sensations created by emotions. For Hitler, it is precisely the repugnance of Jews that turns good Germans into anti-Semites. Once again, it is Jews who are responsible for anti-Semitism. The thrill the text offers its readers comes by revealing a secret knowledge of danger and redemption. *Bildung* is achieved by awareness that the disgust felt at the sight of Jews has to be understood as a key to moral insight: Jews are not only disgusting but pose a threat of moral degeneracy, which he will further apply to the arts, the disabled, the Slavs, homosexuals, and the Roma/Cinti. Nature is the foundation of society; what is "naturally" repulsive is dangerous.

For the readers, there is pride and glory in attaining a hermeneutic that deciphers history, politics, and the social order as pivoting on Jewish influence. *Bildung* means achieving the insight of an anti-Semitic understanding of society. Anti-Semitism is not only about hating Jews; it can become an all-encompassing identity or "cultural code," in the famous term coined by Shulamit Volkov, and it can also provide a thrill—of violating social convention, blaspheming norms of behavior, having a secret knowledge of Jewish conspiracies, and so forth.[41] Simone de Beauvoir wrote that "the erotic experience is one that most poignantly reveals to human beings their ambiguous condition."[42] *Mein Kampf* offers its readers the exhilaration of insight: the Jews are responsible. Secret knowledge, in turn, stimulates pride, a sense of superiority, the thrill of belonging to a new and revolutionary movement that will change the social order.

Mein Kampf's narrative begins with a description of Jews as odd, distasteful, un-German, marginal figures in Viennese society, and slowly expands to the dangers of Jews—moral, sexual, and political—to culture and society. Hitler's depictions are crucially associated with visceral reactions of disgust aroused by the presence and, subsequently, simply the thought of Jews' existence. Disgust becomes outrage as he turns to metaphors of blood, sex, health, and disease, moving from the danger of Jews to Germans as individuals to their purported menace to Germans as a society and nation: "the inner Judaization of our people."[43]

Images and metaphors about Jews abound in *Mein Kampf*, which a scholar has called "an encyclopaedic myth."[44] What makes their presentation powerful is a narrative that is both personal and sympathetic to the readers. The purpose of the book is simple: transforming an ordinary German into a rabid anti-Semite. Hitler is careful to present his own anti-Semitism not as a result of political indoctrination but rather as a voyage of self-discovery, of opening his eyes to the evil surrounding him. Anti-Semitism requires *Bildung*.

Mein Kampf does not develop new ideas about Jews, but rather presents an amalgamation of notions about Jews found in earlier anti-Semitic literature, presented with a flourish of metaphors and images, invariably drawn in sharp contrast to Aryans. Hitler presents his anti-Semitism drawing from every possible type of argumentation—racial theory, Social Darwinism, philosophy, sexual science, even Christian theology. The anti-Semitic canards of the book are drawn from a range of writers, including Richard Wagner, Paul de Lagarde, Heinrich von Treitschke, Arthur Gobineau, Houston Stewart Chamberlain, Hans F. K. Gunther, Henry Ford, Moeller van den Bruck, Artur Dinter, Julius Streicher, among many others; scholars, philosophers, and demagogues all contribute to the amalgamation, particularly the racism of chapter 11 and beyond.

Contrasts abound. Aryans create and build culture[45] and serve the community,[46] while the Jew is a parasite[47] and liar,[48] an image Hitler develops with a variety of metaphors.[49] Aryans are healthy, while Jews are diseases-ridden. These metaphors are not simply descriptive but create relationships, what Andreas Musolff has called the "inferential structure of Nazi anti-Semitic imagery." Their power lies in the way metaphors draw us as readers into the image, asking us to identify with it and enter its world with our imagination. The metaphor of Jews as spreaders of disease engages readers—all who are not Jewish—to understand themselves as victims who have fallen ill as a result of Jews. The acquired disease is not personal but collective: the defeat of Germany in the First World War; the deposing of the Kaiser and rise of the socialists; the enemies who drew up the humiliating Versailles Treaty—the "Jewish" is surrounding Germany and infecting the country.

Yet the disease is not simply a medical assault on health but an assault against state, culture, race, and even religion. Racial mixing destroys Aryans physically and, in addition, religiously: "To bring about such a development is therefore nothing else but to sin against the will of the eternal creator" ("Sünde treiben wider den Willen des ewigen Schöpfers").[50] The invocation of God, redemption, and other biblically based motifs has been noted by historians as indicating the "redemptive" nature of Nazi anti-Semitism,[51] the creation of a "Holy Reich,"[52] a version of Christian "fall-redemption,"[53] the emergence of "political religion."[54] The religious elements do not constitute a narrative but appear in the text from time to time as a kind of religious affirmation or emphasis of the point being made: Hitler's birth is presented as providential, the Jew is satanic, and anti-Semitism is redemptive.

Christianity itself is nothing more than propaganda, according to Hitler—successful propaganda, to be sure—and is equally subject to the depredations of Jews. Ultimately, Jews penetrate society from the top down, ingratiating themselves with priests and princes. Hitler presents the conversion of Jews to Christianity as their infiltration of the naïve, unsuspecting church: "If the worst came to the worst, a splash of baptismal water could always save the business and the Jew at the same time."[55] Baptism, for Hitler, is yet another Jewish ploy to trick the Church: "Finally he needs only to have himself baptized to possess himself of all the possibilities and rights of the natives of the country. Not seldom he concludes this deal to the joy of the churches over the son they have won and of Israel over the successful swindle."[56]

Entering society from its margins, Jews gradually acquire the building blocks of language, culture, economic power, and character. Yet the acquisition is entirely fraudulent, based on poor imitation, falsehood, and power for himself. Just as Jews speak German with a Jewish accent,[57] what appears benevolent is in fact exploitation.[58] This reaches a climax when Jews deceptively present themselves as leaders of the masses but have only their own interests as the goal.[59]

Mein Kampf's purpose is not only to instruct its readers in the alleged evils of Jews but also to train its readers in the hermeneutics of anti-Semitism: how to become attuned to the dangers inherent in the Jews. To be transformed into an anti-Semite is to cultivate the ability to perceive in the body of a Jew a threat to one's own health. The *Bildung* is thus an instruction in how to transform oneself from a potential victim of Jewish danger into a fighter against its threats. Anti-Semitism becomes a tool of recognition, of removing the scales from the eyes to see clearly the danger of Jews. In that way, like Paul on the road to Damascus (Acts 9:18), *Mein Kampf* offers a conversion experience, encouraging its readers to live in *imitatio Hitler*.

The hermeneutic lesson of *Mein Kampf* is to view the world through the lens of race, based on the superiority of the Germanic, Aryan race. Albrecht Koschorke writes that the book "resembles a political Bidungsroman in the way it amalgamates the unfolding of National Socialist (NS) ideology with a—heavily fictionalized—account of Hitler's own development."[60] Hitler describes himself as an unskilled laborer in Vienna, and threats by union agitators lead to his disgust with Social Democrats and communists. Koschorke calls attention to Hitler's use of "woman"[61] as symbol for "the masses," who would rather bow to a strong man than dominate a weakling" and who therefore is not even aware of her "shameless spiritual terrorization."[62] Perhaps his conflicting view of "the masses" as pathetic weaklings and also as the Aryan master race governed his view of women.

Gender is deployed in the book in multiple ways: Germans have been emasculated by Jews and must rise up and defend German women against rape and racial defilement threatened by Jews; Aryan women who have had sexual relations and borne children of Jewish men receive particular condemnation.[63] At the same time, Hitler insists on the disgust posed by Jews, although disgust is more often associated with women. The conundrum, of course, is that the massive threat of Jews simultaneously suggests the vulnerability of Aryans; they have already been Judaized, he suggests. Surprisingly, the book does not mention homosexuality, though suggesting the penetrability of Germans by Jews carries its own implication. Protecting German blood from Jewish "poisoning" carried gender and sexual implications, popularized in the pornographic images and texts of *Der Stürmer*, portraying Jewish men as rapists and Aryan women as vulnerable targets. Creating "purity" of race combined physical, emotional, sexual, and religious connotations in an erotic package.

Mein Kampf is the first political tract by an authoritarian leader of the twentieth century and points to the overriding importance of emotional arousal and manipulation. A hodgepodge of genres, the text mixes autobiographical anecdotes, historical details, political critique, and sheer ranting, especially in the chapters on race and anti-Semitism. It does not follow a straight narrative and the constant changes in tone are startling and disconcerting—and perhaps that's the point, to throw the reader into a state of confusion and mental chaos. Reports of his war experiences recur and lead Hitler to political assertions and the immediate blaming of the Jews.[64] The volume makes no attempt to demonstrate the truth of any of its claims—if anything, it holds science in contempt. In place of science, it offers its readers a pseudo-gnostic approach: a seductive claim that there are hidden truths that can be known by the few who receive induction into the secrets and who will then have superior status, as if they were high priests of a cult.

Emotion is how hatred of Jews spreads easily and remains so tenacious. The drama of political movements, even more than the political platform of a leader, attracts followers. Fascism is spectacle and passion as much as ideology, just as the performative drama of religious ritual is even more powerful than doctrine. So, too, with anti-Semitism. The passion of hatred, the erotics of terror, and the revulsion of disgust are among the emotions aroused by anti-Semitism that require not only social and political analyses by scholars, but also analyses that elucidate the pleasure, arousal, and satisfaction achieved by experiencing anti-Semitic drama. *Mein Kampf* is an inauguration into a new world, an invitation

Hitler constructs for his readers to join him in a voyage of *Bildung,* from Linz to Vienna, from supposed naivete to mature anti-Semitic awareness of the alleged dangers of the Jews. By now, it is not just the text that has become evil: "Almost all literature is simply text, but not *Mein Kampf. Mein Kampf* is more than text. It is a symbol of human evil."[65]

12

Mein Kampf

Catholic Authority and the Holocaust

Martin Menke

The publication of the critical edition of *Mein Kampf* by the *Institut für Zeitgeschichte* in Munich/Berlin has confirmed the established view that, based on Peter Longerich's and others' research, the elimination of Jews was, from the outset, fundamental to Hitler's vision for National Socialist Germany. Historians agree that the one constant in all Nazi thinking was its hatred of Jews. Whatever one's motives for supporting the Nazis, anti-Semitism was the one element of Hitler's ideology on which everyone could agree and the one article of faith upon which Hitler insisted.[1] In a letter written in 1919, Hitler had identified the "overnight murder" of the Jews as "the best solution, but short of that, mass expulsion."[2] In *Mein Kampf*, Hitler had described Jews as blood leeches, whose mere existence was equivalent to the medieval plague.[3] Hitler also believed that Jews could achieve power only by demoralizing their Gentile opponents by spreading internationalism and Marxism. To eliminate these ideologies and break the power of Jews, these ideologies and the Jews themselves had to be eliminated.[4] Thomas Vordermeyer has shown that Hitler's "rhetoric of annihilation" targeted the Jews, for example, in Hitler's complaint that the prewar *Alldeutsche* movement could not unite against the one common enemy, the Jews.[5]

Hitler understood clearly that to achieve his vision would require the acquiescence and even complicity of the German people. Not only would he have to activate and intensify traditional anti-Semitism, but he would also need to instill in the German people an unquestioning faith in his vision and his leadership, in his goal of eliminating all Jews. Hitler knew this would not be easy. Until his end, one of his most traumatic experiences was the relative ease with which, in 1918, Germans abandoned the war effort and eventually the ruling dynasties of Germany. He accepted the stab-in-the-back myth as truth. Thus, Hitler searched for an authority that inspired, at least in theory, complete and eternal loyalty and even faith.

Hitler found an example of this demand for faith and loyalty in the Catholic Church. To gain genuinely faithful support of Germans, he needed the absolute confidence he imagined the Catholic Church, in particular, to command among its faithful. The Creed of Pius IV (professio fidei Tridentina, 1565) in use for reception into the Catholic Church repeatedly emphasized the importance of obedience to the Church and acceptance of its teachings. While there is no evidence that Hitler himself witnessed this Creed as converts professed it at the time of their conversion, he did serve as an altar boy. The Church's emphasis on the Church as the one true interpreter and teacher of Scripture and dogma was what he envisioned. To gain genuinely faithful support of Germans, he needed that charismatic authority that he attributed to the Christian churches and their "Führer," Jesus Christ.[6]

This argument differs from the view that Hitler openly borrowed the drama and ritual of the Catholic Church. It acknowledges that Hitler detested the Church but warily respected its power over German Catholics. In *Mein Kampf*, he alternatively condemned and praised Catholic teaching and practice and always condemned the German political Catholicism of the Center Party and the Bavarian People's Party. Hitler claimed he was seeking to defend the Catholic faith from the danger posed by the Catholic parties. Ultimately, he wanted the power the Church possessed but without acknowledging how the Church came to exercise this authority, namely through a millennia-old tradition and the faithfuls' commitment. While he was able to inspire fanatical faith and devotion among some Germans, he should have paid more attention to the reality of early twentieth-century Catholicism, which featured declining Mass attendance and declining participation in Catholic community life.

As *Mein Kampf* showed, Hitler was well aware of this challenge that "faith is more difficult to shake than knowledge. Love is less susceptible to change than respect. Hatred is more enduring than animosity. At all times, the driving force in the greatest upheavals on Earth is found less in a fascinating scholarly insight than in fanaticism and in a hysteria that drives the masses forward."[7] To win the people for one's faith, one must not only emphasize one's own struggle to achieve one's goals, but one must also destroy one's enemies, Hitler argued. In other words, for National Socialism to succeed, Germany must annihilate the Jews.[8] Achieving this required the enthusiasm of Nazi true believers and at least the tacit acquiescence of most Germans.[9] Just as Christians believe Jesus is the Messiah who has redeemed the world, and on whose teachings the faith is based, Hitler believed he was the Messiah of a racial state whose salvation for all eternity lay in its racial purity.[10] Hitler not only overestimated the sway the Church held over its members but eventually, Hitler discovered that the faith of the German people in him was even weaker than its faith in Christianity.[11]

To understand how Hitler could develop such an imaginary understanding of Christianity removed from reality as is demonstrated in *Mein Kampf*, one has to understand Hitler's relation to the faith into which he had been baptized. Reading *Mein Kampf*, one might conclude that Hitler was well versed in Scripture and theology. In 1905, at age sixteen, he received the sacrament of confirmation, for which he thanked his godfather, Emanuel Lugert, on the latter's saint's day.[12] Hitler briefly attended the choir school of the Benedictine monastery in Lambach, Upper Austria, and enjoyed the splendid festive liturgy.[13] According to the testimony of his childhood friend August Kubizek, however, by the time Hitler moved to Vienna, he had stopped attending Church services.[14] While Hitler never declared his formal exit from the Catholic Church, by failing to receive communion at least once a year, Hitler had de facto excommunicated himself.[15] Brigitte Hamann noted that "almost all eyewitnesses from his Vienna period mention his hatred for the Catholic Church."[16] Beyond the typical religious formation offered in Austrian public schools, his brief studies at Lambach, and his confirmation preparation, Hitler does not seem to have engaged theology in any meaningful way.[17] As the editors of the new critical edition note, the frequent Bible references, often bungled, may have resulted from the many Scripture tracts sent to the frontlines rather than of systematic study of Scripture.[18] Instead, Hitler was deeply influenced by his contemporary and mentor (if Hitler could concede that role to anyone), Dietrich Eckart. The fact that Hitler dedicated *Mein Kampf* to him demonstrates the importance of Eckart's thinking for Hitler. According to Claus-Ekkehard Bärsch, Eckart was a mystic in the sense that "a mystic believes in his unity with God. He experiences God within himself or recognizes God in humanity."[19] Since the mystic recognizes God within him, he can also perceive God's will.[20] Eckart believed that Judaism is the negation of Germandom as God resides and works within Germans and not within Jews. He summarized his understanding of Germans' role in God's plan with a rhyme, which in English means that Christ is mainly present in the German being; thus, the Anti-Christ hates it. Rarely has there been a more clearly stated claim of national exceptionalism. Hitler himself described it thus, "The eternal nature shall inexorably avenge transgressions against its commandments. Thus I believe I am acting in the spirit of the Almighty Creator. When I fend off Jewry, I am advancing the work of the Lord."[21] Similarly, on the opening day of his 1924 trial, Hitler claimed, "I must categorically state that I refuse to be modest about something I know I can do. When a person believes that he is destined to do something, he cannot escape it; he is obligated to fulfill his destiny."[22] This further illustrates Hitler's "messianic" tendencies as well as his later understanding of himself as the beneficiary of divine providence.[23] It certainly was not a Catholic understanding of God and humanity's relationship to its God. Hitler's relationship with religion was superficial and his sense of its authority largely the product of his imagination.

By the time Hitler returned from the First World War, his personal understanding of providence and salvation evolved into a racist hatred of Jews as the fuel for a new Germany. He would lead this new Germany, and its true glory would begin once Germany had destroyed the Jews. Describing the last German spring offensive of 1918, Hitler wrote, "Once more the songs of the Fatherland of those marching in endless columns trumpeted to heaven, and for the last time, the mercy of the Lord smiled at his ungrateful children." Months later, when Hitler described his reactions and feelings about the November revolution, he made no references to God. Instead, he now referred to "faith in the *Vaterland*."[24] Hitler was not a Catholic, not even a lapsed Catholic. His distance from the Church had become one not just of practice but one of belief.[25]

Nonetheless, in his speeches before 1925 and in *Mein Kampf*, Hitler employed Christian imagery when it served to legitimize his attacks on Jews, communists, even the Catholic Center Party and the Bavarian People's Party.[26] The faith itself and its teaching were trivial to Hitler, like most other ideological value systems: whatever Hitler wanted them to be. Hitler believed established values were transactional and intended to exploit them against his enemies. "Just as religious attitudes are the result of education and only one's religious sensibilities slumber within the individual, the political opinion of the masses is only the end result of a sometimes unbelievably tough and thorough impact on soul and reason."[27] They did not possess any intrinsic significance. According to Christian Dube, once the National Socialists seized power in 1933, Hitler never again referred publicly to Jesus Christ, which would support the notion that Hitler's use of precise Catholic language was utilitarian in nature.

Furthermore, it suggested Hitler himself had assumed the role of the Messiah. It is interesting to note that in the lengthy discussion of the dangers of syphilis and the effect of lax sexual morality, Hitler not once mentioned God, the Ten Commandments, or any other religious teaching.[28] Hitler's fear and his solution to sexual and racial defilement were not religious but moral. Beyond Jesus, however, Dube notes that Hitler intentionally would employ religiously connoted words at the beginning and end of speeches as he did in *Mein Kampf* to achieve an emotional response from his audience.[29]

Hitler's view of religious values makes it easier to understand Hitler's comments on Catholicism and Christianity in *Mein Kampf*. It is not as if Hitler were merely appropriating Catholic images and language to deceive the reader into thinking he was a man of faith. For example, Hitler did not understand or care about ecumenism[19]. Still, in *Mein Kampf*, he repeatedly condemned the differences between Protestants and Catholics as destructive and undermining Germany's ability to restore itself to greatness. Hitler hated the Catholic Church's support for the Hapsburg monarchy and rejected Protestantism for its weakness in combating Jews.[30] For good measure, he blamed the rise of Ultramontanism on the Jews by claiming it was an effort to drive a wedge among the German people.[31]

Given Hitler's view of the churches as weak and corrupted, he must have guessed they would not support the radical measures against Jews which he envisioned. Hitler envisioned a faith committed to racism and a relentless struggle for racial health. He claimed that the churches had lost all commitment to strength and perfection. In *Mein Kampf*, Hitler condemned the churches' opposition to eugenics and the Christian care for the weak. More than that, Hitler used the occasion to describe the churches as ineffective since many church members were using means to prevent births or were giving birth to "physically incapacitated and, of course, mentally degenerate" individuals. From them, one cannot expect an understanding of either church teaching or racial health.[32] Someone who could turn the Golden Rule and the Great Commandment on its head in such a way had no understanding of Christianity.

Ostensibly explaining "true Christianity," Hitler created something entirely new, unrelated to any religious tradition. In a speech of April 1922, Hitler reconceived Jesus not as the teacher of love for one's neighbor and teacher of pacifism but as the furious cleanser of the temple and Jesus the warrior. "The Lord rose at last in his might to seize the scourge to drive out of the temple the brood of vipers and death adders. How terrific was His fight for the world against the Jewish poison."[33] Hitler warned that the movement must "create for these men, seeking and straying masses, a new faith which will not fail them in this hour of confusion, to which they can pledge themselves, on which they can build so that they may, at last, find a place which brings calm to their hearts."[34] In other words, Hitler used Jesus Christ, whom he declared to be Aryan, as a cudgel with which to mount vociferous attacks on Jews and their faith. In *Mein Kampf*, Hitler included the sentence frequently quoted, "Eternal Nature inexorably avenges the infringement of her commands. Hence today, I believe I am acting in accordance with the will of the almighty Creator: by defending myself against the Jew, I am fighting for the mission of the Lord."[35] Not only does this passage illustrate Hitler's use of Christianity to justify anti-Semitism, but it also shows Hitler heretically revised the concept of the transcendent. Not everyone in Hitler's audience would have thought of "eternal nature" as a synonym for "the Lord." Hitler's real thinking became apparent after 1933, when he referred more and more to "providence" and less and less to God. In the passage of *Mein Kampf* in which Hitler discussed Germany's denominational divide, he blamed Jewish interests for exacerbating the acrimony between Catholics and Protestants out of self-interest, as a way to undermine the unity of the German people.[36] Hitler also blamed the churches for grounding their anti-Semitism in religious principles rather than in scientific racism. He seemed to expect the churches to adapt, as if such adaptation would not contradict his own perception that the churches never changed dogma.[37] To him, this was an insufficient basis for his desperate desire to remove all Jews from Germany. His own anti-Semitism, however, often departed far from factual truth. Sometimes one wonders where Hitler's flights of fancy took him. For example, he insisted that Jesus had been Germanic but that Pope Alexander VI, Emperor Wilhelm II, and King Edward VII were Jewish. Hitler justified this statement by explaining that Edward's mother, Queen Victoria, had had an affair with her private physician, a man named Wolf.[38] Barbara Zehnpfennig argued that "the world's subjugation to one's will is purchased with the loss of any experience of reality. In the end, thought and action are mere projections of one's imagination."[39] By this point, Hitler had moved from misinterpretation and mischaracterization of Christianity to outright fiction.

Hitler acknowledged the need for a moral order grounded in faith. Without it, he argued, "the foundations of human existence would be deeply shaken." Thus, he argued, "not only does humanity exist to serve higher ideals, but these higher ideals serve as the foundation of human existence." Hitler's faith, however, was based on race.[40] Evidence of this exclusion of the transcendent was his later claim that "the holiest of human rights and the holiest of obligations is to preserve the purity of the blood." This statement demonstrates Hitler's need to borrow Christian terminology to describe his racial deification, such as the term "holy" to explain beliefs otherwise incomprehensible. According to historian Rainer Bucher, Hitler wanted National Socialist ideology to take the place of Christian faith but with the same unquestioning belief. He claimed that Germans did not need philosophers; they needed simple faith.[41] Furthermore, Bucher points out that Hitler's idea of faith rejected Christianity's universal claims. Hitler's faith was to be purely German.[42]

Hitler's understanding of the relationship between faith and race also illuminates those statements about the Catholic Church in which he claimed to approve of it. There are several passages in which Hitler expresses admiration for the Catholic Church. This admiration, however, stems from a willful misreading of Catholic teaching. Thus, Hitler's compliments usually would not be ones the Church would welcome. To support his exclusive claims to power and legitimacy, he argued that the

> Christian Church could not be satisfied by erecting its own altars. It necessarily had to destroy the pagan altars. Only this fanatical intolerance could give rise to this apodictic faith. In fact, this intolerance was a necessary precondition for [the development of the Christian faith]. Today's individual might painfully note that Christianity introduced spiritual and intellectual terror to antiquity's once free world. Today's individual must admit that this coercion has constricted and controlled the world ever since. This coercion can be broken only by further coercion and terror by further terror.[43]

Similarly, he argued that "in antiquity, the greatness of Christianity did not lie in attempted compromises with comparable philosophical opinions, but in the relentlessly fanatical proclamation and defense of its own teachings."[44]

Here, Hitler distorted history and vastly exaggerated the power of Christianity at any time in antiquity and later. By drawing on the history of early Christianity, Hitler sought to create a historical precedent for his own goals. He sought to justify National Socialism's claims to exclusive ideological authority. Hitler argued that the strength of a religion's hold on its people relied less on the dogma itself than on the authority the dogma permits the faith to exercise over its members.[45] For example, he criticized the all-German movement of Georg Ritter von Schönerer and its Los-von-Rom (Away-from-Rome movement which aimed to create an autonomous German Catholic Church) anti-Ultramontane movement as psychologically unwise, given the hold Catholicism had over most German-speaking Austrians.[46] Hitler went on to warn that any politician seeking to eliminate a particular religion or all religions had better provide a superior replacement.[47] Hitler firmly believed that National Socialism was that perfect replacement but how to convince the people? Not for nothing did the National Socialist Reich Ministry of Propaganda and Popular Enlightenment borrow its name from the age-old Catholic curial office of *Propaganda Fide*, the office responsible for spreading the faith.

While Hitler found his perception of Catholic Church leaders' power over the faithful appealing in its own right, he also recognized the value of Catholicism's claims to tradition and inerrancy. Well known is Hitler's claim that despite proof to the contrary, the Catholic Church has never renounced "even a syllable of its teachings. The Church realizes that its strength lies not in an adaptation to prevailing scientific results. These waver over time. Instead, the Church's strength lies in its stubborn adherence to the long-proclaimed dogma that made the Church's teachings a faith."[48] By claiming this, Hitler ignored the fact that internal theological arguments, perceived heresies, and schism had existed since Christianity's beginnings. Given the lasting contradictions within National Socialism and the ideological infighting among National Socialist leaders, the movement could not have survived without a similar claim to inerrant truth.

For this reason, Hitler always rejected later suggestions that he revise the party program of 1920. Similarly, contrary to the claims of Julius Streicher's rabid anti-Semitic paper *Der Stürmer* and others, in *Mein Kampf*, Hitler praised celibacy not for its sacerdotal significance but because "the constant need to renew the Church's elites contributed to the ongoing strength of the institution."[49] There was no mention of denying the German race potential Aryan offspring or other Social Darwinist thinking. Revealing the worldview that underlay National Socialism's propaganda and educational efforts, Hitler again drew parallels to Christianity. "One's denominational affiliation is merely the result of education, and true religious needs rest deep within the individual. Comparably, the masses' political opinion is only the final result of an often unimaginably harsh and thorough treatment of both soul and reason."[50] Hitler also argued that in life's fundamental decision-making moments, only faith provided moral guidelines. Life's highest ideals stem from life's essential necessities, including faith.[51] Hitler understood the power of faith. Hitler understood the latent power of the Church over even weakly committed Catholics, which is one of the reasons why Hitler hated it so much.

Hitler also explicitly borrowed the Church's attention to liturgical staging as part of the overall effect on the faithful. For example, he argued, "The Church, in its wisdom, had studied the psychological appeal made upon worshipers by their surroundings. While the National Socialist speaker chose the evening for his address, in the Church, the artificially produced twilight incense, burning candles are all designed to have the same effect of casting a secret spell upon the congregation. The movement must similarly study psychology."[52] Thus, while Hitler fabricated a version of Catholic authority removed from reality, his appreciation of Catholic liturgy shaped his thinking about propaganda or what today one might call mass communications.

However, Hitler and his paladins did not trust either the vision of a National Socialist Messiah or modern mass communications. As Götz Aly and Peter Longerich have shown, Germany's new leaders, shared Hitler's fear that the German people lacked sufficient faith in Hitler's racial salvation and even in Germany's destiny.[53] In the Social Darwinist war against the Jews, National Socialist leaders feared that the public would never become sufficiently convinced of the need to annihilate Jews. Judging by Goebbels's diaries, his own relationship with Hitler was one of deep infatuation and fanatic obedience, which made him even more determined to win over the German people. Like Hitler, Goebbels and others believed that Germany had lost the First World War due to a lack of resolute will and faith, combined with Jewish-communist subversion. Aly argued that the regime "purchased" the loyalty of the average German by raising its material standard of living. To win German Gentiles' support once the first wave of enthusiasm (1933–5) had ebbed, first German Jews lost their assets and livelihoods. To maintain support on the home front during the Second World War, the National Socialists systematically plundered the property of foreign Jews and the peoples of the occupied territories in both Eastern and Western Europe.[54] Several events prove the uneven and ultimately unsatisfactory effect of both propaganda and material improvements. In 1938, Gentile Germans complained about the Reich pogrom of November 9 (*Kristallnacht*) because it reminded them of the chaotic days of 1932–3, not because they were concerned for their Jewish neighbors but because they were incensed by the perceived insult to the Führer.

Similarly, in May 1940, *Reichsleiter* Alfred Rosenberg complained to Deputy Führer Rudolf Hess that the propaganda film *The Eternal Jew*, in production based on footage from the Warsaw ghetto, was insufficiently radical.[55] When the film appeared in cinemas, however, Germans reacted contrary to expectations. They rejected the graphic scenes from the ghetto, the perceived brutality of kosher slaughter, for example.[56] Again, the concern was not the fate of Jews but the gory scenes in the film. Germans mostly showed little regard for the future of Jews, but they preferred law and order to National Socialist enthusiasm for radical anti-Semitism. As late as 1943 in Posen, addressing first high-ranking SS officers and later the Gauleiter and other government officials, Heinrich Himmler warned those attending never to make public the extermination of the Jews for fear of shocking the German people. Not only would Germans be appalled at the sight of so many corpses, but Germans would also each point to one Jew or another and demand he or she be spared.[57] In his last documents, written in the *Reichskanzlei* bunker, Hitler acknowledged the failure of the Germans to embrace his vision. He denied having failed. The people had proven too weak to fight for people and race. Hitler explained how the German people had faltered in its racial struggle and, by the law of the survival of the fittest, did not deserve to survive. In the so-called Nero Decree of March 19, 1945, Hitler ordered the enemy to find nothing but scorched earth on German soil, which, if implemented, would have denied the people its basis for survival.[58] In his political testament of April 29, 1945, Hitler identified the causes of Germany's defeat: cowardice and weakness among German leaders against "world Jewry."[59] If the German people had fought more fanatically, had had more determination, the way he had, Germany would have succeeded. In Hitler's mind, the people had possessed insufficient faith in their race and nation, and ultimately, in him.

Beyond anti-Semitism as the object of Hitler's messianic vision, he considered Christianity and especially Catholicism to be a rival source of moral and faith-based authority. After the expected victory in the war, Hitler planned to suppress the churches as a competing source of authority.[60] Contrary to some later interpretations, the war's outcome did not represent a triumphal Christian victory over fascism, far from it. Hitler had given the churches too much credit when he overestimated the faithfuls' support for church teachings and church leaders. Perhaps, if he had recognized that, he might have understood better the challenges facing him in his efforts to gain the people's undying faith in him.

The Catholic response to *Mein Kampf* and to National Socialism reveals the depth of the chasm between Hitler's imagination and the Church's teaching, whose authority he intended to supplant. In 1925 already, Catholic clergy published critiques of Hitler's work.[61] For example, Father Erhard Schlund, OFM, published a detailed analysis of the text.[62] In the *Bayerische Kurier*, Anton Scharnagl published a scathing three-part review of *Mein Kampf*.[63] Thus, as Othmar Plöckinger points out, various Catholic thinkers and Church officials were acquainted with *Mein Kampf*, and each one condemned Hitler's work in no uncertain terms.[64] Beyond this direct criticism, there were Catholic voices that, in however muted form, insisted on the humanity of German Jews. For example, during the political and economic crisis of 1923, Munich archbishop Michael Faulhaber preached a sermon in which he demanded no one be permitted to starve, "not even a Jew."[65] More positively, Jakob Nötges argued that National Socialist racial teaching and Catholic doctrine were incompatible since National Socialist ideology violated the commands of Christian charity (*Nächstenliebe*).[66]

While this defense of Jews is laudable, it is indicative of the ambiguous relationship German Catholics had with Jews. Father Nötges demanded care for Jews as a matter of charity rather than of justice. Similarly, his insistence on the Old Testament's continued validity as part of a revelation stemmed from the then accepted doctrine of Supersessionism, that is, the invalidation of the Jewish covenant with God by the new covenant of the Eucharist. Such distinctions, however, were lost on Hitler.

As the preceding passages show, Hitler did not consider a detailed set of well-formulated and consistent beliefs or even specific dogma necessary for success. Hitler himself had little understanding of the doctrine. He did, however, understand the concept of authority based on fundamental trust and faith rather than on political reasons. The text shows that Hitler believed that power over the people relied primarily on the willingness of Church members to remain faithful. Willingness to accept religious teachings and religious authority is not a question of reasonable arguments and logical conviction but instead of faith and the faithful's trust in their leaders. However, Hitler's logical inconsistency becomes apparent in his criticism of the Austrian hierarchy, when he warns that the elderly in the Church hierarchy will have to adapt to the anti-Semitism of Karl Lueger's Christian party if the bishops wanted to remain relevant.[67] However, Hitler recognized that the pan-German movement's failure stemmed from its inability to accommodate the people's religious needs.[68]

During the Weimar years, Hitler denied both Catholic political parties any role in his messianic vision, the German Center Party and the Bavarian People's Party. He condemned them as un-Christian and as corrupting true faith. Even worse, they cooperated with Jewish interests. In one of his last diatribes against the Bavarian People's Party before the November 1923 putsch, Hitler argued that

> nobody was undertaking any measures against the Jews. We see exactly the same behavior by the Bavarian People's Party and its patent-Christians. Silently they watch as the last crucifix is removed from the schools and as the last harmless Christmas hymn is excised from the songbooks. But when National Socialists claim it is time to do away with these bearers of pestilence, these Jews, the patent-Christians cry crocodile tears. They bear the greatest blame for this poisoning of our people.[69]

There is great irony in this as Christians actively defended their hymns and crucifixes but did little to help either observant Jews or Christians the Nazis considered to be Jews, to whom Christians supposedly were beholden.[70] There was some truth in Hitler's rants. Ideologically, the two Catholic parties were much less anti-Semitic than Church teaching and practice. In April 1922, the Bavarian People's Party leader Count von Lerchenfeld argued that as a human and a Christian, he could not be an anti-Semite. Hitler claimed that just as Christ had agitated against the Jews, he now stirred against those like Lerchenfeld who proclaimed a false faith that protected Jews.[71] In a single speech, Hitler managed to equate himself with Christ, condemn Catholic politicians, and take another swing against Jews. Hitler feared political Catholicism almost as much as the institutional church. In *Mein Kampf*, Hitler principally denied religious denominations the right to become politically active. He accused individual priests of abusing their religion to further their political ambitions.[72]

In the same passages, Hitler warned that

> political parties should have nothing to do with religious problems since these might be foreign perspectives on morals and ethics that could not undermine one's own race. Similarly, religion has no business spouting political nonsense. When religious officials abuse religious institutions or teachings to damage their own unique culture [*Volkstum*], the people must never follow them on their way. They must fight back with equally persuasive weapons.

Hitler had good reason to fear the voice of politically organized German Catholics. Priests played a significant role in both parties. In 1924, the Bavarian People's Party's leader in the Reichstag, Monsignor Leicht, warned that he did not agree with the view held by the National Socialists that "salvation will come from the völkisch movement, perhaps from Mister Hitler or Mister Ludendorff. Neither swastika nor Soviet star can bring salvation, only the cross on which was hung the salvation of the world." Leicht continued, "The NSDAP hat always proclaimed its commitment to the positive Christianity, but that must be some other conception of God. There can only be one God, not a German or a French God; otherwise, there would be more than one God, which contradicts our understanding of God."[73] In two paragraphs, Leicht had rejected Hitler and the National Socialists' promise to bring salvation as well as the notion of a national deity. Such comments must have stung Hitler. He sought not only to break Catholic parties but to condemn all political parties as antithetical to religion.

Finally, Hitler at times used Catholicism to underscore his virulent anti-Semitism but usually in a distorted interpretation of the faith. At Christmas 1921, Hitler needed only a single sentence to use the Feast of Christmas as a means of attacking Jews, socialists, and capitalists. He began that speech, however, in a confusing manner. He proclaimed that "the feast [of Christmas] is one the world would celebrate in unity." So far, so good. However, in the next sentence, he reminded his audience that "the Jews cowardly had nailed the world's liberator to the cross."[74] Using the facts of Good Friday to justify an anti-Semitic Christmas only makes sense if the goal of Hitler's comments was not to celebrate the Nativity or the Resurrection but to attack Judaism.

The failure of the 1923 coup attempt reshaped Hitler's strategic thinking. He lessened the public vitriol against Jews and avoided outright attacks on the Christian religions and their institution, probably as part of a strategy to gain respectability in the political sphere. Upon release from Landsberg prison, he adopted a new strategy of achieving power by subverting political institutions from within. To achieve his goals, he had to assert himself as the Nazi Party's sole leader and as the sole arbiter of its ideology. Despite the Bavarian government's ban on his public speaking, Hitler soon returned to political activity. He sought to solidify his control of the National Socialist Party by improving the organization and insisting on ideological unity. To achieve this, Hitler strictly forbade any religious dissent within the party. This ban won him no support from the bishops. In 1925, Cardinal Faulhaber declared fascism to be unacceptable. He aruged that, because any coup overthrew the divine order, the coup of 1923 was just as much a sin as the Revolution of 1918 had been (Figure 12.1).[75]

Continuing to seek to split the Bavarian People's Party and the Center Party from the Church, Hitler urged the renascent movement to fight the Catholic political parties. He warned his followers to do so on strictly political grounds, such as the Center's cooperation with atheist socialists. Under no circumstances were Hitler's followers to attack the Center Party or the Bavarian People's Party for being Catholic. In *Mein Kampf*, Hitler had vehemently criticized the Christian churches directly and now he needed to distinguish between political parties of the barely stable

FIGURE 12.1 *Cardinal Michael Ritter von Faulhaber in 1937 helped draft the Vatican encyclical* Mit Brennender Sorge *("With burning concern") of Pope Pius XI against racism. Courtesy of Alamy Photos.*

Weimar Republic and the deep-rooted ancient faiths, which he claimed to respect. Attacking the Center and the Bavarian People's Party fed the people's dissatisfaction with the parliamentary republic, but attacking religion would only alienate many Germans. In July 1925, Hitler defended himself against accusations of anti-Catholicism. Again he distinguished between Catholicism and Catholic political parties. According to Hitler, the parties had betrayed the faith. Only National Socialism could preserve Catholicism in Germany.[76] Just before the Reichstag fire, the *Völkische Beobachter* again emphasized that an attack on National Socialism was an attack on Christianity.[77]

Hitler repeatedly stressed the importance of authority and its successful exercise as the basis for Catholicism's continued success. Without such power, the Church would splinter and fail.[78] Hitler recognized he needed the same authority for National Socialism. For Christmas 1925, Hitler issued instructions on the proper National Socialist understanding of the feast. At the time of Christ's birth, the world was just as materially corrupted as it was in 1925, he claimed. Christ, who Hitler claimed to be of Aryan blood, came to change all that. Hitler argued that Jesus was the son of Mary and a German in the Roman legions. "For ourselves, we see in Christ the opportunity to achieve unimaginable greatness. Christ was born in horrible times, preached liberation, and the Jews rejected him. Nonetheless, he built a movement that became a universal faith. National Socialists should use Jesus as a model for the development of National Socialism."[79] Hitler rarely expressed his self-understanding as a modern Messiah so very clearly.

As all of *Mein Kampf* and Hitler's other speeches and writings between 1918 and 1926 show, his arguments are weak and lack logical consistency. There is, however, great clarity that Adolf Hitler despised, feared, and hated all Jews and their faith. No matter whom he was attacking, be it Bolsheviks, trade unions, churches, politicians, and even the former ruling houses, he ultimately considered Jews responsible for the defeat in 1918 and all evils that had befallen Germany since then. The Catholic Church, its faith, and its savior were not religiously meaningful to Hitler. Hitler perceived the Church as a powerful institution whose members obeyed it. To attack that institution without good reason risked losing the support of not only the institution but, more importantly, its followers. Finally, Hitler wanted an organization in which the seemingly unquestioned exercise of authority, the faith in its infallibility, and the faith of the masses in the leader were just as profound as he perceived them to be in the Catholic Church.

As scholars now understand more clearly, *Mein Kampf* was not the rambling outpouring of a madman's mind. Instead, Hitler's thinking reflects a logical reasoning process, even if his premises were wrong and contemptible: Hitler hated Jews. Hitler accused the Christian churches of being too soft and weak, too kind to Jews and other unworthy human life. Furthermore, he blamed the Christian churches for failing to move from religious anti-Semitism to Social Darwinist anti-Semitism. Hitler either was unable to understand or did not care that, were the churches to accept Social Darwinism, they would cease to be Christian. Hitler distorted Christianity beyond all recognition. Unfortunately, the churches condemned Nazi racism and nationalism but did not recognize Nazi anti-Semitism as racist. Despite Hitler's condemnation of the churches, he envied their perceived power and authority over the faithful. He wanted Germans to become as obedient and faithful to National Socialism and to him as he imagined they were to the churches. He wanted this despite recognizing that the churches' claim to authority did not reflect reality. Not only in matters relating to churches, but Hitler's world was one of his imagination and desire, whose relation to the reality of twentieth-century Germany was at times quite tenuous.

Thus, it seems wise to look at the evidentiary record to see what exactly Weimar German Catholics thought and did regarding their Jewish fellow citizens. Concerning anti-Semitism, there were Catholic voices explicitly and implicitly condemning it. Wilhelm Moock, a columnist in the conservative Catholic intellectual journal *Hochland*, pointed to the Jewish people as an exemplary people.

> God made clear to Abraham already that the people of God stands as such above all other peoples and cannot tolerate other notions of a people. People must seek to leave the peoples of nature and join the people of God. The people of Israel is bound together only by religion, yet it has survived centuries of persecution. What is worth preserving in any given people stems from the spirit and mind, not from blood?[80]

The value of the Jewish people, according to Moock, could not be questioned, and he lauded its perseverance.

Similarly, in reporting on events surrounding the Christian burial of a Nazi sympathizer, Philipp Jakob Mayer, Vicar General of Mainz, noted that the local pastor had denied the presence of an SA honor guard. The pastor argued, "National Socialism is unchristian because it preaches racial hatred and the fight against the Jews." The Vicar General added that the National Socialist German party's positions on Jews identified in the party program were incompatible with Catholic teaching.[81] A month later, Cardinal Faulhaber of Munich and Freising reported the matter to the Sacred Council Congregation and explained that the National Socialists "nourished a particular hatred for Jews."[82] Two years later, in a letter to Cardinal Schulte of Cologne, Monsignor Hermann Klens, the clerical leader (General-Präses) of the German Catholic Women's Association, explained that Catholics could not join the patriotic Queen Louise League because the league refused admission to Jewish applicants.[83] Finally, on May 9, 1928, the *Germania*, Germany's leading Catholic newspaper, responded to concerns about antireligious persecution in Mexico raised by Munich rabbi Leo Baerwald. The *Germania*'s editors argued, "We for our part, as a matter of principle, have never failed to condemn exaggerated nationalism as well as anti-Semitism stemming from contemporary religious hatred. In this, we are true to our Church, which has always taken the side of the persecuted."[84] While some of the *Germania*'s claims are questionable in light of the historical record, German Catholicism's flagship newspaper condemned anti-Semitism. Thus, it is clear that, at least at the base, some clergy and Catholic journalists considered the Nazis' anti-Semitism incompatible with Catholic teaching, a condition the Church defines as heresy.

As National Socialism's increasing popularity forced the bishops to issue pastoral statements assessing the new ideology, they did not directly include anti-Semitism among the reasons to condemn the National Socialist movement. Instead, among the many reasons given, they condemned National Socialist racism. For example, the chairmen of the two German bishops' conferences at Fulda and Freising, Cardinals Bertram and Faulhaber, respectively, took the lead in condemning the new movement. "National Socialism elevates race above religion. It rejects the Old Testament and even the mosaic Ten Commandments but denies the pope's primacy in Rome because it is not a German institution."[85]

Already in September 1930, the Center Party's information journal *Das Zentrum* quoted Cardinal Faulhaber as saying that "he was not among those who counted the German people—much less the Aryan race—as history's chosen people. Neither the Aryan race generally nor the Germanic peoples, in particular, are justified in creating their own moral code."[86] Faulhaber's use of racial terms remained problematic, but the cardinal condemned National Socialists for denigrating Christianity's origins in Judaism.

On New Year's Eve 1930, Cardinal Adolf Bertram of Breslau devoted an entire letter to his diocesans to the National Socialist threat.[87] He entitled his reflections "At a serious hour" and described "exaggerated nationalism and the glorification of race as a fateful error."[88] Between February and March 1931, the bishops of the various metropolitan provinces officially condemned the National Socialist ideology and forbade Catholics from becoming party members.[89] Part of the justification for condemning National Socialist ideology stemmed from the fact that "leading Nazi representatives exalt the race higher than religion," which was a severe doctrinal error.[90] Since doctrinal errors are heresies by definition, then based on racism alone, the German hierarchy described National Socialism as heretical. By definition, heresy is remedied not by changing church teaching but by the individual or group recanting its position.

As late as November 1932, Viennese cardinal Innitzer claimed that Christians are patriots because Jews and Jesus Himself were patriots.

> But one must not exaggerate national identity. . . . It is inappropriate to speak of noble and lesser races because such a distinction does not exist. Every nation features advantages and disadvantages. We must not praise our nation's qualities so much that we love only our own and hate others. That contradicts the command to love one's neighbor. It is desirable that

> several nations live in the same state. Then they can learn from each other.[91]

Aside from some confusion between the terms "state" and "nation," Innitzer's admonition confirmed the command to treat Jews well but also revealed the cardinal's belief that Jews constituted a separate race or at least a different nation. What he implicitly conceded to National Socialism was that Jews constituted a different race or nation.

Catholics other than the bishops critically explored the new ideology as well. One of the most prominent early Catholic opponents of the National Socialists was the Capuchin monk Ingbert Naab, who had opposed National Socialist racism ever since the early 1920s. Naab, who would become notorious with a 1932 public protest letter against the National Socialist movement published in Catholic newspapers throughout Germany, in 1931 already published a critique of Hitler.[92] Among Hitler's many failings, Naab criticized Hitler for equating humans with an animal race. According to Hitler, claimed Naab, "there are still 'humans' who are not human. Africans could only learn to do tricks."[93] According to Naab, Hitler's racial teachings served to justify brutal force and had become the Nazis' "dogma above all other dogma." For Naab, "Christianity rejects the inequality of humans in their rights and responsibilities."[94] He could not imagine any common ground between National Socialists and Catholics.

Jesuit priest Father Jakob Nötges provided further evidence of the chasm between National Socialist and Catholic teaching. In 1931, Nötges published a commentary to support the bishops' decision to ban Catholic membership in the NSDAP. Like Naab, Nötges argued that National Socialist racial teaching and Catholic doctrine were incompatible since National Socialist ideology violated the commands of Christian charity (*Nächstenliebe*).[95]

John Connelly, Olaf Blaschke, and others have studied the complicated relationship between Catholics and Jews in the twentieth century that attests to grievous failings on the Church's part.[96] Still, the point is that the Church condemned National Socialist racism and that National Socialist anti-Semitism was race-based. Perhaps the vision of a racially pure National Socialist Germany based on the destruction of an entire group of people was just too alien and too disturbing to penetrate deeply enough among Germans to be successful. Hitler's wish, stated in *Mein Kampf*, to exercise the same authority that the Christian faith possessed even among less faithful members was never fulfilled, which contributed to the dictatorship's collapse.

13

The Apocalypse of Adolf Hitler

Mein Kampf and the Eschatological Origins of the Holocaust

David Redles

Early in *Mein Kampf*, Adolf Hitler presents a largely fictitious retelling of his conversion to anti-Semitism, antiliberalism (social democracy), and anticommunism during his time in Vienna in the first decade of the twentieth century.[1] However, how Hitler chose to recount his conversion is most telling, as it accurately reflects not his time in Vienna as presented in the book but rather his experience in postwar Munich. In *Mein Kampf* Hitler states that his experience in Vienna acquainted him with the evils of the Jewish press, modernist culture, social democracy, and most importantly, communism. According to Hitler, this supposed Jewish control of Viennese culture presaged an even worse future event—global apocalypse:

> At such times I was overcome by gloomy foreboding and malignant fear. Then I saw before me a doctrine, comprised of egotism and hate, which can lead to victory pursuant to mathematical laws, but in so doing must put an end to humanity.[2]

Hitler claimed that he had not thought much about Jews up until this time in Vienna, in part because their "outward appearance had become

Europeanized and had taken on a human look."[3] He further claimed this Jewish culture, as it spread around the world, "was a pestilence, a spiritual pestilence, worse than the Black Death of olden times, and the people was being infected with it!" The Jews were therefore "germ-carriers of the worse sort," who would "poison men's souls." Hitler concluded that Jews seemed "chosen by Nature for this shameful calling."[4] Regarding social democracy, Hitler argued Jews used it with "diabolical craftiness" to seduce their victims, the mass of workers. Hitler claimed this realization led him to study Marxism, which he described as a "plague of nations" created by "veritable devils" which, if it achieves world domination, "must ultimately result in the collapse of human civilization and the consequent devastation of the world." Hitler then returned to the notion of the Jews as a chosen people:

> When over long periods of human history I scrutinized the activity of the Jewish people, suddenly there rose up in me the fearful question whether inscrutable Destiny, perhaps for reasons unknown to us poor mortals, did not with eternal and immutable resolve, desire the final victory of this little nation. Was it possible that the earth had been promised as a reward to this people which lives only for this earth?[5]

Because Marxism was built off of the liberal-democratic notion that all humans are equal, and therefore should be treated equally, Hitler argued that it therefore rejected the "aristocratic principle in Nature." By this he meant the natural "law" that all individuals and races were not created equal and therefore this false notion of human equality rejected the "eternal privilege of power and strength." Once again, Hitler argues that since Marxism essentially rejected Social Darwinism, it literally would be the end of the world:

> As a foundation of the universe, this doctrine would bring about the end of any order intellectually conceivable to man. And as, in this greatest of recognizable organisms, the result of an application of such a law could only be chaos, on earth it could only be chaos, on earth it could only be destruction for the inhabitants of this planet. If, with the help of his Marxist creed, the Jew is victorious over the other peoples of the world, his crown will be the funeral wreath of humanity and this planet will, as it did thousands of years ago, move through the ether devoid of men.[6]

Hitler therefore portrays Jews in *Mein Kampf* as inhuman devils chosen to deliberately poison society by various means, but especially by violating the laws of Nature, determined by the Almighty. This violation would ultimately lead to the end of the world. As a consequence, Hitler claimed he had a mission to prevent this apocalypse, concluding the chapter with "Hence today I believe that I am acting in accordance with the will of the Almighty Creator: by defending myself against the Jew, I am fighting for the work of the Lord."[7] The questions remain: Was Hitler's use of religious metaphors simply a literary choice, or did Hitler really come to believe he was divinely chosen to save the world from Jewish Bolshevism and thereby prevent the end of humanity? And if he did in fact truly believe this scenario, does this then explain the horrifying logic behind the Holocaust? To answer these questions we need to return to Munich, just as the First World War was ending, when the specter of a Bolshevik-style takeover of Germany, purportedly led by Jews, seemed a certainty. The end was near.[8]

Dietrich Eckart: Apocalyptic Prophet of the Millennial Third Reich

On November 8/9, 1918, a socialist revolution, led by the Jewish leader of the Independent Social Democrats Kurt Eisner, broke out in Munich. This mostly nonviolent coup led to the establishment of the Bavarian Free State.[9] On November 11 the armistice was signed, ending the war. Adolf Hitler was at this time in the psychiatric ward of a military hospital in Pasewalk being treated for "war hysteria." He was ultimately diagnosed as a "psychopath with hysterical symptoms."[10]

During this period publicist and writer Dietrich Eckart, the man who one day would become the most influential figure in Hitler's life, was transforming into a virulent exterminatory anti-Semite.[11] The following month Eckart began publishing the anti-Semitic periodical *Auf gut deutsch* (In Plain German).[12] Eckart had become certain that there was a Jewish conspiracy behind, not simply the Eisner socialist republic but the German loss of the First World War. On January 4, 1919, Eckart, working with the semi-secret Thule Society, helped form the German Worker's Party (DAP), the party that would become the National Socialist German Workers' Party (NSDAP or Nazi).[13] Writing in the February 20, 1919, issue of *Auf gut deutsch*, Eckart exclaimed: "This war was a religious war, one can see this clearly; a war between light and darkness, truth and lies, Christ and anti-Christ." In Eckart's mind the Jew was the Anti-Christ or at least his emissary. Eckart concluded that this war between Aryans and Jews could only end with the extermination of one or the other, writing, "when light clashes with darkness, there is no coming to terms! Indeed, there is only struggle for life and death, till the annihilation of one or the other. Consequently, the World War has only apparently come to an end."[14] On February 21, Eisner was assassinated, eventually leading to the establishment of a brief and bloody Bolshevik-styled government. While this so-called Second Revolution was quickly shattered by government forces, greatly aided by right-wing private militias, the specter of Bolshevism terrified and radicalized many citizens of Munich, including Eckart. Later that year Eckart began an article with a prophetic and apocalyptic declaration:

> Signs and wonders are seen—from a flood a new world will be born. These Pharisees however whine about wretched nest eggs! The liberation of humanity from the curse of gold stands before the door! It's not simply a question of our collapse—it's a question of our Golgotha! Salvation is to befall our Germany, not misery and poverty. No other people on Earth are so thoroughly capable of fulfilling the Third Reich than ours! *Veni Creator Spiritus*! [Come Holy Spirit Creator].[15]

For an anti-Semite like Eckart, the linkage of the liberation from the "curse of gold" to the crucifixion is a blaming of Jews for both Germany's postwar economic woes and the death of Jesus. The further linkage of the dawn of the Third Reich with the descent of Holy Spirit is another telling statement. The origins of this idea goes back to the medieval apocalyptic writer Joachim of Fiore, who believed humans were evolving toward salvation along a triune series of fixed stages, what he termed in Latin "*status*."[16] This word is usually translated as stage, age, or state and in German as *Reich* (kingdom, empire, realm). Joachim associated the three *status* with the trinity. The First Reich was of the Father, the Second Reich of the Son, and the Third and Final Reich of the Holy Spirit. This Third Reich would begin during the End Times and would witness the appearance of the final Anti-Christ, whom Joachim portrayed as the dragon from Revelation 12.[17] The Anti-Christ was bound to lose a violent battle with a chosen elect, the "spiritual men," led by a messianic prophet figure referred to as the *Dux* (Leader in English, *Duce* in Italian, and *Führer* in German). The *Dux* would replace the two heads of the Church, the pope and the emperor, and lead humanity into the New Age of the Heavenly Jerusalem. The Anti-Christ defeated thus ushers in the descent of the Holy Spirit, initiating the Third Reich, which Joachim conceived as a New Order on earth and by many of Joachim's followers as the Millennial Kingdom (*Tausendjährige Reich*) of Revelation.[18]

One possible conduit of Joachim's millennialism to Eckart is Henrik Ibsen, whose *Peer Gynt* provided Eckart with his own greatest literary success.[19] Eckart interpreted Ibsen through the lens of Otto Weininger, especially in his *Über die letzten Dinge* (On the Last Things).[20] In Weininger's interpretation Peer represented human genius and the striving for spiritual redemption, while the evil Boyg, a misshapen figure, was the "chief salvation negating principle."[21] Both Weininger and Eckart associated the Boyg with the Jews. For Eckart, therefore, human existence was a perpetual conflict between these opposing forces:

> Truth and lies, Christ and Anti-Christ, "spirit" and "nature," being and presence, reason and madness, love and hate, Baldur and Hodur, Siegfried and Alberich, Parsifal and Klingsor.[22]

Another possible Joachimite influence on Eckart is Ibsen's 1873 play *Emperor and Galilean*. In a key scene the Emperor (Kaiser) Julian the Apostate and his intellectual foil Maximus discuss the coming "Third Reich, where he who is two in one shall rule." When Julian questions who this figure will be, Maximus responds, the Messiah. The following dialogue takes place:

> Julian: Messiah? Neither Kaiser nor Savior?
> Maximus: Both in one and one in both.
> Julian: Kaiser/God, God/Kaiser, Kaiser in the Reich of Spirit and God in Reich of Flesh.
> Maximus: *That* is the Third Reich, Julian!
> Julian: Yes, Maximus, *that* is the Third Reich.[23]

It was in 1919 that Eckart began a search for his Kaiser/God, his German messiah. In the winter of 1919, after hearing Hitler give one of his first speeches for the German Worker's Party, Eckart was certain he had found his messiah. Hitler's discipleship would begin.[24]

Eckart therefore believed that postwar Germany was the End Times, a time that would witness the dawn of the Third and Final Reich. However, the New Age of the Millennial Reich could only be achieved if the Anti-Christ, whom Eckart associated with the Jews, was exterminated. While Eckart, much like Hitler, was anti-Semitic before the war, that anti-Semitism only seems to have become exterminatory in 1919–20. It was not simply the loss of the war that produced this change, but the appearance of a "document" that seemingly proved the Jews really were the Anti-Christ, poised for world domination and, as a consequence, apocalypse.[25]

The Protocols of the Elders of Zion as Eschatological Text

In January 1919, a book appeared in Munich edited by Ludwig Müller von Hausen, the editor of the journal *Auf Vorposten* (On Outpost Duty), who produced it under the pseudonym Gottfried zur Beek. It told a fantastic tale: a group of 300 Jewish elders had gathered in Basel in 1897 as part of a congress meeting of the Jewish Zionist Movement.[26] While the public meetings were about the establishment of a Jewish homeland in Palestine, secret meetings had taken place which discussed the true hidden agenda—detailed plans for Jewish world domination. Entitled *Die Geheimnisse der Weisen von Zion* (The Secrets of the Elders of Zion), the book included a copy of the alleged secret minutes. It quickly became a bestseller.[27] The German version of *The Protocols of the Elders of Zion* (as it came to be known) would reach thirty-nine editions by 1939 and continues to be a source of anti-Semitic propaganda to this day.[28] For the Nazis especially (they acquired the rights to the work in 1929) it proved to be a crucial source that shaped and intensified their millennial view of world history.[29]

The Protocols of the Elders of Zion is a hoax, but for anti-Semites then and now, it is a believed hoax. The forgery was probably concocted in 1903 within the Russian Empire, most likely Ukraine.[30] It combined an obscure nineteenth-century anti-Napoleon III satire, Maurice Joly's *Dialogue aux Enfers entre Machiavel et Montesquieu* (1864), with *The Rabbi's Speech*, a portion of a novel by Hermann Goedsche entitled *Biarritz* (1868).[31] While the hoaxers borrowed the basic structure and language of Joly's work, and thus its critique of modernity, especially Napoleon III's cynical manipulation of democracy and the press, what it took from *The Rabbi's Speech* was its shifting of the blame for the horrors of modernity on to Jews, as well as its apocalyptic inversion of Jewish messianism. *The Rabbi's Speech* is millennial, with references to the imminent coming of a Jewish messianic age that would see the House of David assume leadership of the world in fulfillment of the covenant with Jehovah. The covenant is realized by the Jews through manipulation of the evils of modernity, including capitalism, which is portrayed as centralizing wealth and power in the hands of Jews, and both democracy and socialism, which enables the Jews to manipulate the masses against the aristocratic elites. As described in the text:

> By this means we will be able to make the masses rise when we wish. We will drive them to upheavals, to revolutions; and each of these catastrophes marks a big step forward for our particular interests and brings us rapidly nearer to our sole aim—world domination, as was promised to our father Abraham.[32]

Jewish messianism and millennialism are thereby perverted into a satanic mirror of the desired Christian millennium, a paralleling of millennial desires and fears found later in Nazism.[33]

It was the antimodernism and the apocalyptic anti-Semitism that the Russian religious writer Sergei Nilus seized upon. Nilus was inspired by prophecies of the coming of the Anti-Christ in Russia made in the eighteenth century by the Serafim von Sarov. Nilus elaborated on these prophecies by combining them with the apocalyptic writings of Fedor Dostoevsky and Vladimir Solov'ev, both of whom associated the coming End Times to varying degrees with the Jews.[34] Nilus was convinced he was chosen by heaven to save Russia, and usher in the Third Rome, with Moscow the New Jerusalem of the Apocalypse.[35] The second edition of his book *The Great in the Small: Anti-Christ Considered as an Imminent Political Possibility* contained the *Protocols* as an appendix. Nilus was convinced that the Anti-Christ would be a Jew, and the *Protocols* appeared to support his belief that world Jewry was preparing the ground for his appearance.

For Nilus, therefore, the satanic power behind the dark conspiracy of modernity was the Jew. In 1917, with the Russian Revolution unfolding before his eyes, Nilus published another edition of the *Great and the Small* with the chiliastic title, borrowed from Mt. 24:33, *He is Near, At the Door . . . Here Comes anti-Christ and the Reign of the Devil on Earth*. According to Nilus, the apocalyptic turning point had arrived. Either Russia and the true spirituality of the Orthodox Church would be saved, or the Anti-Christ would rule and the world would end. Nilus had combined fear and rejection of modernity with apocalyptic fear of the Anti-Christ, both of which he associated with Jews.[36] It was this apocalyptic rendering of the *Protocols* that traveled to the West with a number of emigrants fleeing Bolshevik terror, finding its way to Munich, Germany.[37]

With the appearance of the *Protocols* in Munich in 1919, Dietrich Eckart became convinced that the Jews were involved in a conspiracy aimed at achieving world domination. He first mentioned the *Protocols* in the October 10th edition of *Auf gut deutsch*, writing that a British Protestant periodical originating out of Jerusalem had noted that a "Jewish lodge brotherhood 'The Elders of Zion'" had produced a "leaflet" in Russia in 1911. It purportedly claimed that there existed plans for "Jewish world dominion" through the imminent destruction of the Russian and German Imperial empires. Eckart then claimed that a map appeared before the First World War, which showed the exact boundaries that would appear only after the Treaty of Versailles was promulgated after the war. Eckart wrote ironically, "Oh, how wise are you Elders from Zion!" (Figure 13.1)[38]

A little over two months later Eckart returned to the subject of the *Protocols* in an article entitled, "The Midgard Serpent," a reference to the chaos monsters the Nordic god Thor has to defeat in the Icelandic epic, the *Edda*. Eckart began by referring to a section of the story that "describes the desperate struggle of the sons of light with the three monsters of darkness." This battle is Ragnarök, the Nordic apocalypse that results in the destruction of the world and its subsequent rebirth as a new Heaven on Earth. Linking this eschatological struggle with the supposed conflict between Aryans and Jews, Eckart concluded: "We do not need to read it, we experience it today." Eckart then connected this Nordic apocalypse with Revelation 20, which discusses the release of Satan, "the dragon, that ancient serpent," from a thousand years of imprisonment. Eckart associated the "loosing" of Satan with the Jews being released from a thousand years of imprisonment in the "ghettos" of Europe and their subsequent rise in power. According to Eckart, "the Jewish spirit is loosed, or as Christ expressed it, the 'Prince of the World,'" a reference to the Prince of Darkness. Eckart then cites Revelation 12, as Joachim had before him: "for the devil has come down to you in great wrath, because he knows that his time is short!"[39]

This apocalyptic narrative leads Eckart directly into a discussion of Hausen's edition of the *Protocols*, of which Eckart says, "one reads again and again and yet one does not get to the end, because with almost every paragraph one lets the book fall as if paralyzed with unspeakable horror."

FIGURE 13.1 *Dietrich Eckart's Jewish beast of the apocalypse, portrayed as a combination of the Midgard serpent from Ragnarok and "the dragon, that ancient serpent," from Revelation 20. Courtesy of Dietrich Eckart, "The Midgardschlange,"* Auf gut deutsch *(December 30, 1919), 680–1.*

Eckart once again refers to the "Jewish lodge brotherhood 'Elders of Zion'" and the supposed fact that "Russian Jews knew already in 1911 of the collapse of the Czarist empire, but also the German emperorship" and offers as explanation that it was "Bolshevistic chaos with the Jewish world dominion as background." He argues that "whoever wants to become thoroughly acquainted with Jewry should acquire this book."[40]

As the references to Ragnarök and Revelation attest, Eckart believed that the End Times had arrived, and the *Protocols* revealed the Jewish "satanic program" to take over the world.[41] It is for this reason that he concluded in another article, "The hour of decision has come: between existence and non-existence, between Germany and Jewry, between all or nothing, between truth and lies, between inner and outer, between justice and caprice, between sense and madness, between goodness and murder. And humanity once again has the choice!"[42] The appearance of the *Protocols* during the unrelenting chaos of the nascent Weimar Republic only seemed to prove this eschatological narrative to be true, thus legitimating both the conspiracy theory of Jewish world dominance and the apocalyptic anti-Semitism that supported it.[43]

For many anti-Semites, including Eckart and Hitler, the *Protocols* was all the proof they needed that the Jews really were the force of evil in the world. Their long-held fear of a racial apocalypse now found its Eschaton. With the loss of the war and Jewish-Bolshevik Revolution spreading, the End Time was now. The signs of the time could not be more explicit. Hitler, at least, seems to have accepted the *Protocols* in this light.[44] Notes for a speech dated August 12, 1921, entitled "Inflation Protest a Jewish Swindle," linked the hunger created by the German inflation to the supposedly deliberate mass starvation that had recently occurred in Soviet Russia, at the behest purportedly of the Jews. A section called "Hunger in Service of Jewry" has written underneath it, "Elders of Zion." A report on this speech, given a week later, confirms this, noting that "Hitler proves from the book 'The Elders of Zion,' that establishing rule, by whatever means, has always been and will always be the goal of the Semites."[45]

On August 1, 1923, with Germany mired in economic chaos and with a new epidemic of hunger striking millions, Hitler gave a speech entitled "Rising Prices, Republic and Fascist State." His explanation of the chaos did not speak of modern economics nor of the government's floating of worthless monies. The explanation was to be found in the alleged evil machinations of the Jews and their minions, the Bolsheviks and the Freemasons, as revealed in the *Protocols*. Was not the two-pronged attack of "international bank capital" and Soviet-style revolution revealed in this work? Hitler warned his audience: "We stand before a new revolution." Behind it lies the "Soviet star," which

> is the star of David, the true sign of the synagogue. The symbol of that race over the world . . . the dominion of Jewry. The gold star signifies the Jews glistening gold. The hammer, which symbolizes the Soviet crest, represents the Freemasonic element. The sickle the inhuman terror! The hopeless Helots of the German Volk should create the Greater Jewish Paradise!

Jewish banking combined with Bolshevik Revolution and a little help of the Freemasons within Germany were all seen as attempts to take over the world and therefore fulfill the covenant. Hitler continued, "according to the Zionist Protocols, the masses are to be made docile through hunger" and therefore ready "for the second revolution under the Star of David."[46] The *Protocols* therefore became a key element in Hitler's conspiratorial thinking, for it was used to explain the perceived apocalyptic chaos. Using the *Protocols* as a guide, Hitler argued that international Jewish bankers deliberately created the hyperinflation that forced Germans into epidemic hunger, making them pliant for a Jewish-Bolshevik-type revolution, thereby taking another step in the plan to create the Jewish millennial paradise of world dominion. Hitler's conspiratorial mentality, and its peculiar logic, is also seen in his reaction to disclosure that the *Protocols* were a fake. Since he believed that the press was controlled by Jews (part of the plan revealed in the *Protocols*), then accusations of forgery by the press only proved that they were true. Writing in *Mein Kampf*, Hitler stated:

> To what extent the whole existence of this people is based on a continuous lie is shown incomparably by the *Protocols of the Elders of Zion*, so infinitely hated by the Jews. They are based on a forgery, the *Frankfurter Zeitung* moans and screams once every week: the best proof they are authentic. What many Jews may do unconsciously is here consciously exposed. And that is what matters. It is completely indifferent from what Jewish brain these disclosures originate; the important thing is that with positively terrifying certainty they reveal the nature and activity of the Jewish people and expose their inner contexts as well as their ultimate final aims.[47]

We see here Hitler's belief that Jews instinctively strive toward world domination, even if unconscious of this striving.[48] The covenant was now seen as a spiritual and a biological imperative. The *Protocols* revealed the eschatological "ultimate final aims," world domination, and thus world annihilation—apocalypse. Hitler used the *Protocols* like a prophetic text, rereading history as prophecy fulfilled, or in this case, as the working out of the Jewish covenant with Jehovah, increasingly associated not with God but Satan.[49]

The Final Battle of God and Satan: National Socialism versus Jewish Bolshevism

Further insight into the apocalyptic and exterminatory ideas of Eckart and Hitler can be found in an unfinished posthumously published work by Eckart entitled *Bolshevism from Moses to Lenin: A Dialogue between Hitler and Me*.[50] For literary reasons Eckart wrote this piece in a dialogic style to give the reader the sense that they are listening to a private conversation between mentor and protégé, prophet and messiah. Eckart attempts to reveal the hidden history of the Jews and their alleged desire, not simply for world domination but for world annihilation. The German reader of the time was clearly meant to see the loss of the First World War and the subsequent postwar chaos as the product of this same "hidden force." A young Heinrich Himmler would put the brief work on his essential reading list, describing it as "An earthy, witty conversation between Hitler and Eckart that so genuinely and correctly characterizes both of them. It gives a perspective through all time and opens one's eyes to many points that one had not yet seen. I wish that everyone would read this."[51] Ironically he was correct, for it reveals all too clearly the apocalyptic and exterminatory anti-Semitism of the Nazi inner circle.

The work uses a pseudo-scholarly approach, with citations to various standard anti-Semitic statements by a host of literary and historical figures.[52] More importantly, however, and this is typical of Nazi propaganda then and later, *Bolshevism from Moses to Lenin* also utilizes Jewish sources, primarily the Old Testament and the Talmud (questionably analyzed and translated) to seemingly unmask the Jews.[53] For example, the Book of Esther is explained as a Purim festival "murder" of 75,000 Persians, an event which, the authors' claim, "no doubt had the same Bolshevik background." The story of Joseph becomes a deliberate use of hunger to make the *Pöbelvolk* (mob or rabble, meant in the context of racially inferior masses) docile. The Egyptian expulsion of the Jews described in Exodus is used to justify the Nazi desire to expel Germany's Jewish population.[54] Ignoring the bounds of time (a deliberate technique to show the supposed eternal nature of the Jewish drive to world domination and annihilation), Eckart likens the alleged Jewish manipulation of the Egyptian rabble or "Bolshevik horde" to the calls for Liberty, Equality, and Fraternity, which ignited the French Revolution (implying that the Jews used these catchwords of democracy to rile up the mob once again to murder the racial elites—the same implication is later attached to the Russian and German Revolutions).

The Book of Joshua is cited as further proof of the Jewish tendency to "exterminate" Gentiles "root and branch" (this phrasing was, perhaps not ironically, the Nazis' favorite expression for what must be done to solve the Jewish Question). Hitler referred to the destruction of Jericho as an "uninterrupted mass murder of bestial cruelty and shameless rapacity and cold-blooded cunning," a "Hell incarnate."[55] Hitler then cites Isaiah 34, which warns of the Lord's coming bloody vengeance on Edom, where women and children are to be slaughtered. Here the biblical reference is reinterpreted as still more proof of the Jewish eternal desire to exterminate other races: "in all eternity nothing will change . . . so far as the attitude of Jews toward our kings and our leaders is concerned. To destroy them is their eternal aim, and when this can't be accomplished by force, then they will use cunning."[56]

While the Old Testament, "Satan's Bible," or the "Book of Hate," as Hitler refers to it, is presented as a history of the Jewish will to destruction, the New Testament is likewise transformed.[57] Here we find an Aryan Jesus, in Jn 8:44, yelling at "the Jews": "Your father is the devil." Much is made of Jesus whipping the "Children of the Devil."[58] The good work of Jesus the anti-Semite, however, is soon deflected by Schaul turned Saul turned Paul, who Hitler refers to as a "mass murderer turned saint." It is this section on Paul and the origins of "false" Christianity where we get a glimpse as to why Eckart and Hitler became apocalyptic exterminatory anti-Semites.

In their account of the fall of "Aryan" Rome, the last great Aryan civilization until the rise of the Germans, Eckart and Hitler put the blame on the Jews by means, of all things, Christianity. But they clearly distinguished what they term "genuine" Christianity from the "false" Christianity purportedly created by St. Paul of Tarsus. Hitler did not believe Jesus was a Jew but a man of at least half Aryan stock who led a fight against the Jews. According to Eckart, Hitler remarked: "The Hebrews were so firmly convinced of the non-Jewish ancestry of Christ that they counted him among the especially hated Samaritans."[59] Therefore, according to Hitler, Jesus was at least half Aryan and one who fought against the Jews, saying in his wartime table talks: "Jesus fought against the materialism of His age, and, therefore, against the Jews."[60] Hitler went on to say:

> Jesus was most certainly not a Jew. The Jews would never have handed one of their own people over to the Roman courts; they would have condemned Him themselves. It is quite probable that a large number of descendants of the Roman legionaries, mostly Gauls, were living in Galilee, and Jews was probably one of them. His mother may well have been a Jewess.[61]

In Eckart's book, it was Paul who deliberately distorted the message of Jesus to serve the revolutionary aims of the Jews. According to this biblical revisionism, Paul "went to the Greeks and Romans and brought them his 'Christianity': a 'Christianity' with which the Roman Empire became unhinged. 'All men are equal! Brotherhood! Pacifism! No more privileges!' And the Jew triumphed."[62] Thus, according to Eckart, Hitler believed these egalitarian notions were added to Christianity by "the Jew," Paul, deliberately to incite the racially inferior *Pöbelvolk* against the racially superior aristocratic descendants of the ancient Aryans who had founded Greece and Rome, much as they purportedly had done earlier in Egypt and Babylon. In the wartime table talk Hitler is recorded saying much the same thing regarding Paul:

> It was then that the future St. Paul distorted with diabolical cunning the Christian idea. Out of this idea, which was declaration of war on the golden calf, on the egotism and the materialism of the Jews, he created a rallying point for slaves of all kinds against the elite, the masters and those in dominant authority. The religion fabricated by Paul of Taurus, which was later called Christianity, is nothing but the communism of today.[63]

It was for this reason that Hitler remarked three years earlier, on December 13, 1941: "Christ was an Aryan, and St. Paul used his doctrine to mobilize the criminal underworld and thus organize a proto-Bolshevism.

This intrusion upon the world marks the end of a long reign, that of the clear Graeco-Latin genius." In Hitler's mind Bolshevism was simply a revised version of Paul's false Christianity, both of which are designed to incite subhumans against racial superiors: "Of old, it was in the name of Bolshevism. Yesterday, the instigator was Saul: the instigator today, Mardochai. Saul changed his name into St. Paul, and Mardochai into Karl Marx."[64] Therefore Paul

> was the first man to take account of the possible advantages of using a religion as a means of propaganda. If the Jews succeeded in destroying the Roman Empire, that's because St. Paul transformed a local movement of Aryan opposition to Jewry into a supratemporal religion, which postulates the equality of all men amongst themselves, and their obedience to an only god. This is what caused the death of the Roman Empire.[65]

After discussing Paul's false Christianity and the fall of Rome, *Bolshevism from Moses to Lenin* leaps to the Middle Ages, claiming that Charlemagnes's massacre of his fellow Aryan brothers, the Saxons, was done at the behest of the Jews (this follows references to the First World War and the "Jews" bringing the British and the Americans into the war—thus that war, as the Second World War later would be, is conceived as Aryan fratricide orchestrated by the Jews to further their plans at world domination and annihilation). Hitler, according to Eckart, then provides a possible solution to this eternal Jewish Question by citing Giordano Bruno. The Jews are "such a pestilential, leprous and publicly dangerous race that they deserved to be rooted out and exterminated before their birth."[66] For Eckart and Hitler, therefore, the only way to stave off Aryan extermination is the preemptive extermination of the Jews.

Bolshevism from Moses to Lenin concludes with a discussion of the Russian Revolution and the alleged torture deaths of thousands of Russian priests as well as the deliberate death of thirty million Russians by starvation and disease all by the hands of Jewish Bolsheviks.[67] The convergence of the Russian Revolution, the German loss of the First World War (and the subsequent chaos of postwar Weimar), and an obscure reference to *The Protocols of the Elders of Zion* (the Kaiser's Dream) are cited as proof that the final attempt of the Jews at world domination is at hand. But it is not simply slavery at the hands of Jews that is being prophesied here. The continuing references to Jewish extermination of non-Jews is deliberate and from an apocalyptic standpoint, crucial. The pamphlet ends with Hitler discussing the "final goal" to which the Jew is instinctively "pushed":

> Above and beyond world domination—annihilation of the world. He believes he must bring the entire world down on its knees before him

> in order to prepare a paradise on earth. . . . While he makes a pretense to elevate humanity, he torments it into despair, madness and ruin. If he is not commanded to stop he will annihilate all humanity. His nature compels him to that goal, even though he dimly realizes that he must therefore destroy himself. . . . To be obliged to try to annihilate us with all his might, but at the same time to suspect that that must lead irrevocably to his own destruction. Therein lies, if you will: the tragedy of Lucifer.[68]

Even if these are solely the words of Eckart, Hitler expressed exactly the same explanation of Bolshevism and its "Jewish" origins. Indeed, in *Mein Kampf*, the second volume of which was dedicated to Eckart, it is a recurrent theme of Hitler's that the Jews were promised in the Old Testament not eternity in the heavenly New Jerusalem but dominion of the temporal earth. It was to this end that the Jew conspired. It is for this reason, as we saw earlier, that Hitler wondered in *Mein Kampf* if "inscrutable Destiny" had chosen the Jews to rule the "earth" as a "reward" for their destructive nature, in fulfillment with the covenant.[69] Later in the book, Hitler, speaking of these alleged Jewish machinations, states: "for the higher he climbs, the more alluring his old goal that was once promised him rises from the veil of the past, and with feverish avidity his keenest minds see the dream of world domination tangibly approaching." This situation would lead to the fulfillment of the "Jewish prophecy—the Jew would really devour the peoples of the earth, would become their master."[70] Once again, it was for this reason that Hitler concluded that the end result of the "Jewish doctrine of Marxism" would be the literal end of the world:

> If, with the help of his Marxist creed, the Jew is victorious over the other peoples of the world, his crown will be the funeral wreath of humanity and this planet will, as it did thousands of years ago, move through the ether devoid of men.[71]

To combat the destructive internationalism of communism, Hitler pushed for the nationalization of Germans, and ultimately all Aryans, into a racially homogenized *Volksgemeinschaft* (National or Peoples Community, meaning a community of racial comrades). But Hitler argued that to succeed in the nationalization process, Jewish International Bolsheviks had to be destroyed: "The nationalization of the masses will succeed only when, aside from all the positive struggle for the soul of our people, their international poisoners are exterminated."[72]

Hitler continued this theme in his then-unpublished second book. After discussing the supposed parasitic nature of the Jews, a recurring theme in *Mein Kampf* as well, Hitler turned on the supposed Jewish inner compulsion for world domination. Hitler explained:

> His [the Jews] ultimate aim is the denationalization and the chaotic bastardization of other peoples, the lowering of the racial level of the highest, and the domination of this racial mush through the eradication [*ausrottung*] of these people's intelligentsia and their replacement with the members of his own people.

Having taken over individual countries and eventually the world through race poisoning and the policy of extermination, Hitler again concludes, exactly as in *Bolshevism from Moses to Lenin*, that this will result in an apocalypse:

> The Jewish international struggle will therefore always end in bloody Bolshevization—that is to say, in truth, the destruction of the intellectual upper classes associated with the various peoples, so that he himself will be able to rise to mastery over the now leaderless humanity . . . Jewish domination always ends with the decline of all culture and ultimately of the insanity of the Jew himself. Because he is a parasite on the peoples, and his victory means his own end just as much as the death of his victim.[73]

It is following this logic that Hitler wrote in *Mein Kampf*:

> Human culture and civilization on this continent are inseparably bound up with the presence of the Aryan. If he dies out or declines, the dark veils of an age without culture will again descend on this globe. The undermining of the existence of human culture by the destruction of its bearer seems in the eyes of a volkish philosophy the most execrable crime. Anyone who dares to lay hands on the highest image of the Lord commits sacrilege against the benevolent creator of this miracle and contributes to the expulsion from paradise. And so the volkish philosophy of life corresponds to the innermost will of Nature, since it restores that free play of forces which must lead to a continuous mutual higher breeding, until at last the best of humanity, having achieved possession of this earth, will have a free path for activity in domains which will lie partly above it and partly outside it. We all sense that in the distant future humanity must be faced by problems which only a highest race, become master people and supported by the means and possibilities of an entire globe, will be equipped to overcome.[74]

The Aryan/Jewish conflict was conceived as two opposite forces, one of creation and one of destruction, soon to be engaged in the *Endkrieg*, the Final Battle to achieve world domination. For Hitler, if the Aryans, the children of light and of God, reigned supreme, humanity would be saved in the millennial kingdom of the Third Reich. If the children of darkness, of Satan, the Jews, achieved global supremacy, then humanity would cease to exist. Therefore, the Final Battle would come in a fight to the death with Jewish Bolsheviks. In his first important speech after leaving Landsberg prison in 1925, Hitler explained that the Nazi aim was "clear and simple":

> Fight against the satanic power which has collapsed Germany into this misery; Fight Marxism, as well as the spiritual carrier of this world pest and epidemic, the Jews. . . . As we join ranks then in this new movement, we are clear to ourselves, that in this arena there are two possibilities; either the enemy walks over our corpse or we over theirs.[75]

The notion of the satanic power of the Jews was no mere rhetorical device for Hitler. When Hitler stated in *Mein Kampf* that "the personification of the devil as the symbol of all evil assumes the living appearance of the Jew," he meant literally that the Jew was the force of evil and destruction in the world.[76] The Nazis believed themselves involved in a cosmic battle between the forces of good and evil, light and darkness.

Hitler reiterated in a speech to members of the party on May 22, 1926, that "there is going to be a final battle" and that "this final battle will not be fought in the parliaments, but in a trial by violence in which case someone will be left on the ground, either Marxism or ourselves." It was the Nazis' mission to prepare Germany for this impending Armageddon. He continued, using imagery taken from Revelation 12, the same reference used by Joachim of Fiore and Dietrich Eckart earlier, and similarly transforming Satan into the mythical Jewish-Bolshevik: "It is our mission to forge a strong weapon, the will and energy—so that when the hour comes, and the Red dragon rises up, at least some of our people are not despondent and desperate." Later in the speech he returned to this idea that in an ideological war between the Jewish-Bolshevik internationalists and German nationalists, only one or the other will survive:

> Thus, I see the mission of the National Socialist movement in the attempt to oppose this Red Tide, which one day will become brutally violent, with an ideologically resolute national one. We do not want to fight the German Reich, nor the state, but those who strike out. We are convinced that the struggle against Marxism will and must come to a final decision because two world views are fighting with one another.

For Hitler, preparing for this final confrontation was a matter of faith, not simply political ideology:

> That is the great mission of the National Socialist movement, to give our times a new faith and to endeavor to get millions to swear by this faith, so that when the hour of the final decision approaches, the German people will not be completely defenseless against the Jewish international blood stranglers.[77]

Since this war was an ideological one, and therefore in his mind a spiritual one, Hitler pondered in *Mein Kampf*, "can spiritual ideas be exterminated by the sword?" He answered this question by saying one would have to commit to the "complete extermination of even the very last exponent of the idea and the destruction of the last tradition." But, Hitler argued, to "exterminate a doctrine" one need proffer a new "spiritual foundation" to support the effort: "Any attempt to combat a philosophy with methods of violence will fail in the end, unless the fight takes the form of attack for a new spiritual attitude."[78] For Hitler, that new faith was National Socialism. And to grow that faith Hitler explained that the National Socialist movement's "mightiest task" was to expose the machinations of the satanic Jew to the German people: "It must make certain that in our country, at least, the mortal enemy is recognized and that the fight against him becomes a gleaming symbol of brighter days, to show other nations the way to the salvation of an embattled Aryan humanity."[79] Once again, this salvation was only possible with the extermination of Jewish Bolshevism.

Hitler, in an early speech of 1922, *Die "Hecker" der Wahrheit!* (The "Agitator" of Truth!), prophesied on this impending apocalypse, and Germany's choice between slavery and annihilation at the hands of the Jewish Bolsheviks or victory and salvation for Aryan humanity if they followed National Socialism:

> There are only two possibilities in Germany! Do not believe that the Volk will wander everlasting in the midst of compromise! It will devote itself first to the side that has prophesied on the consequences of the coming ruin and has steered clear of it. Either it will be the side of the left: then God help us, that leads us to the final corruption, Bolshevism; or it is the side of the right, which is resolute . . . it allows no compromise. Believe me, the German Volk lost this World War because it had not understood that there is allowed on this earth only victor and slave. And here it is precise; this powerful, great contest can be reduced to but two possibilities: Either victory of the Aryans or its annihilation and victory of the Jews.[80]

It was exactly this apocalyptic imperative that, in Hitler's mind, justified mass extermination. In a speech entitled "Why Are We anti-Semites?" given on April 20, 1923, Hitler returned to his belief that the Jews were "a destroyer of peoples," who attempt to use democracy and Marxism to generate both pacifism and terrorism, and ultimately, destroy morality. Hitler concluded that the Nazis were justified in using the same tactics as the Jews as revealed in the *Protocols*, concluding: "We may be inhuman! But if we save Germany, we have achieved the greatest deed in the world. We may do an injustice! But if we save Germany, then we have removed the greatest injustice in the world. We may be immoral! But if our people are saved, then we have once again broken a path to morality!"[81] Morality therefore during an apocalyptic Holy War was unnecessary and, indeed, potentially catastrophic. Genocide, on the other hand, was justified as fulfillment of a divine mission to save the world. One last question must be address. Does the Holocaust follow logically, albeit horrendously, from these apocalyptic beliefs?

The Holocaust and the Problem of Apocalyptic Expectation

On January 30, 1939, with Europe on the brink of world war, Hitler gave his yearly speech to the Reichstag commemorating his assumption of power, and with it, the dawn of the millennial Third and Final Reich. He once again assumed his role as End Times prophet, linking the coming world war to the Final War against the Jewish Bolsheviks that he had preached and prophesied about since the earlier 1920s. He claimed:

> often in my life I have been known as a prophet and was mostly laughed at. In the time of my struggle for power it was primarily the Jewish *Volk* who responded to my prophecies with laughter . . . I believe that the ringing laughter of Jewry in Germany meanwhile is now stuck in their throats. I will today again be a prophet: if international finance Jewry within and without Europe should succeed in plunging the peoples yet once again in a world war, then it will result not in the bolshevization of the earth and thereby the victory of Jewry, but rather the extermination of the Jewish race in Europe.[82]

The linking of the war with a threat to exterminate the Jews is important. Hitler would return to his prophecy a number of times during the course of the war and after the Final Solution was underway. Not unimportantly, Hitler, and various Nazi publications, misdated the prophecy to September 1, 1939, when the Nazis invaded Poland and began the Second World War. The final struggle against the Jews was inextricably tied to the war against Soviet communism, for it was always considered the same apocalyptic Final Battle. This is why in *Mein Kampf* Hitler wrote: "The fight against Jewish world Bolshevization requires a clear attitude toward Soviet Russia. You cannot drive out the Devil with Beelzebub."[83] Of course, the war in the West was not the apocalyptic conflict Hitler had long foretold, but it had become a necessary step on the way.

However, by 1941 Hitler was ready to move on to the prophesied Final War. Speaking on January 30, 1941, Hitler returned to his early prophecy:

> And I would not want to forget the remark which I had already given at the time, on September 1, 1939, in the German Reichstag. Namely, the remark that if the other world would be plunged into an all-out war by Jewry, then collected Jewry will have played out its role in Europe! They might also still laugh about it today, as they had earlier regarding my

> prophecies. The coming months and years will demonstrate that I will be seen to have been correct here as well.[84]

When the Nazis invaded the Soviet Union several months later in June, initiating the envisioned Armageddon, the new campaign was referred to, not coincidently, as a *Vernichtungskrieg*—a war of extermination. It is, in part, for this reason that the mass murder of Jews entered a new more ferocious scale with Operation Barbarossa. As the mass murders escalated through the end of the year, Joseph Goebbels, writing in *Das Reich* (November 16, 1941), directly tied the genocide in the East to Hitler's prophecy:

> We are experiencing the fulfillment of that prophecy, and it delivers the Jews to the fate which is perhaps severe, but which is more than deserved. Pity, even regret, are totally inappropriate. The Jews are a parasitical race, which lies like a festering mold on the cultures of healthy nations. There is only one remedy: a swift incision, and done away with.[85]

On December 12, 1941, a day after declaring war on the United States and thus truly initiating a world war, Hitler gathered his *Reischsleiter* and *Gauleiter* for a meeting. In his diary attendee Goebbels again referred to Hitler's prophecy:

> Regarding the Jewish question, the Führer is determined to clear the table. He prophesied to the Jews that if they would bring about yet another world war, they would experience their extermination. That was not empty talk. The world war is here. The extermination of Jewry must be the necessary consequence. This question is to be regarded without any sentimentality. We are not to have compassion for the Jews but rather for our people. If the German people yet again have to sacrifice 160,000 dead in the eastern campaign, then the authors of this bloody conflict must pay for it with their lives.[86]

On the same day as this diary entry, Hans Frank, leader of the General Government in Poland and later Commandant at Auschwitz, gave a speech on the extermination of the Jews to those now in charge of the killing operations. He likewise referred to Hitler's prophecy:

> As for the Jews, I will say to you quite openly that one way or another they must be done away with. The Führer once uttered the promise: if the combined forces of Jewry should again succeed in unleashing a world war, then the sacrifice of blood will be made not only the embattled peoples in the war, but also the Jews in Europe will have found their end . . . I would therefore, concerning the Jews, be guided by the expectation that they will disappear. They must be done away with.[87]

Ten days after the Wannsee Conference, on January 20, a meeting that began a more formal and coordinated genocidal process, Hitler gave yet another anniversary speech:

> We are clear to ourselves that the war can end only with either the Aryan peoples exterminated, or that Jewry will vanish from Europe. I have already spoken about it on September 1, 1939, in the German Reichstag—and I am careful not to make rash prophecies—that this war will not go as the Jews envisage it, namely that the European Aryan peoples will be exterminated, rather that the result of this war will be the annihilation of Jewry. For the first time that true old Jewish law will be employed: an eye for an eye, a tooth for a tooth. . . . And the hour will come when the most evil world enemy of all time will have played out its role of the last millennium.[88]

These were not simply public statements cynically calculated to explain the world-historical importance of the struggle to a war-weary populace. Even in private Hitler spoke of his prophecy. Speaking in the presence of Himmler and Heydrich on October 25, 1941, Hitler remarked:

> From the rostrum of the Reichstag I prophesied to Jewry that, in the event of war's proving inevitable, the Jew would disappear from Europe. That race of criminals has on its conscience the two million (German) dead of the First World War, and now hundreds of thousands more.[89]

More than just a self-fulfilling prophecy, Hitler's words from January 30, 1939, became a rationalizing mechanism for others involved in enacting the Final Solution. In a motivational speech to SS leaders in 1942 Himmler paraphrased Hitler's prophecy, saying that "If Jewry should start an international war, perhaps to exterminate the Aryan peoples, so it will not be the Aryan Volk exterminated, rather Jewry."[90] Just as importantly, soldiers at the Eastern Front found righteous justification in identifying their murderous actions, and the suffering engendered by them, to Hitler's prophecy. Corporal Heinrich Sachs wrote to a friend describing the annihilation of the Bolshevik army as a "destiny-intended miracle." In this connection he also mentioned that the Jewish Question was being "solved" with "impressive thoroughness," with the "enthusiastic approval of the indigenous population." He wrote that "as the Führer said in one of his speeches shortly before the outbreak of the war: 'if Jewry should yet once again provoke the nations of Europe in a senseless war, then this will mean the end of this race in Europe!'" Sachs remarked that the "Jew ought have known that the *Führer* was to be taken seriously with his words, and now had to bear the appropriate consequences." Regarding the genocide, Sachs described the murders of the Jews as "inexorably harsh, but necessary, if quiet and peace should finally come among the nations."[91]

The type of paranoid conspiratorial mentality found in *Bolshevism from Moses to Lenin*, in Hitler's *Mein Kampf*, in his speeches, and in his private conversations exhibits an inversion of reality typical of millennial thinking.[92] Once someone is convinced that "Jewish Bolsheviks" are the hidden force of all evil in history, the eternal "wire pullers," all life's difficulties become reducible to a very simple explanation—they result from the machinations of the Jew.

The belief that the Second World War was the long-prophesied apocalyptic war of extermination was a deeply held tenet of Hitler, many Nazis, and Wehrmacht soldiers alike. Acknowledging the importance of such a belief in an imminent apocalyptic struggle between Aryans and Jews does not mean, in a strict intentionalist sense, that the Nazis ever had a set plan or program to exterminate the Jews. But the absolute conviction, the expectation, that the Final Battle was imminent existed ever since the very beginning of Hitler's political career. Once Hitler was in a position to induce the prophesied apocalyptic confrontation, he did so. As Saul Friedänder noted: "a series of radical threats against the Jews were increasingly integrated into the vision of a redemptive final battle for the salvation of humanity."[93] Therefore, Hitler's apocalyptic exterminatory anti-Semitism contains within its own internal logic the *possibility* of its eventual actualization. In other words, if you believe that now is the time, that *the* apocalyptic turning point in world history is at hand, one in which the age-old struggle of good and evil, order and chaos, God and Satan, Aryan and Jew, is to be settled once and for all—and just as importantly, if you believe that you have been divinely chosen to take part in this eschatological battle—it is not surprising that you may find yourself in exactly the prophesied scenario, a war of extermination. The Holocaust, the Final Solution, was not so much a matter of intention on Hitler and the Nazis' part but a matter of apocalyptic expectation.

PART VI

Epilogue

14

Holocaust Education and (Early) Signs of the Erosion of Democracy

Tetyana Hoggan-Kloubert

Introduction

Democracy is threatened well before the authoritarian regimes take power. It begins with rhetoric overstepping the boundaries of human dignity. The lessons from Weimar Republic illustrate that Holocaust education should pay attention to early signals of erosions of (fragile) democracies. Holocaust education aims at, taking Adorno's famous quote, doing everything possible such that Auschwitz will not happen again. This is why Holocaust education has to deal with the historical paths that led to Auschwitz. *Mein Kampf* is one of the historical text documents that makes evident the process of breaking taboos and overstepping the boundaries of human dignity on the road to the barbarism.

The culture of remembrance is an important part of German identity, culture, and politics. The German "dealing with the past" (*Vergangenheitsaufarbeitung*) embraces a sense of responsibility for the past and the commitment to remembering its victims. This responsibility manifests on at least two different levels: (1) on the political level reflected in the special commitment to the state Israel and the principles of humanity in the current politics, for example, in the questions of migration politics,[1] and (2) on an educational level by learning about the past and for the future—reflected in Holocaust education. Holocaust education became a major factor in different educational institutions and programs—the term embraces different pedagogical approaches and praxis—from historical learning to human rights education.[2] Holocaust memory and Holocaust education became a global phenomenon far beyond Germany, with references to the question of universal moral norms in societies,[3] especially through the engagement of supranational organizations like IHRA, UNESCO, OSCE, the European Council, or the EU into the support and proliferation of worldwide learning about the Holocaust. The Holocaust is an important topic in the teaching of history, but it can also be placed under the umbrella of other frameworks, which would benefit from closer links: human rights education, peace education, intercultural education, antiracist education, and democracy education.

Given the strong focus on cultivating memory about the Holocaust and the antecedent developments that led to it, it is not surprising that the new critical edition of Hitler's *Mein Kampf* by the Institute for Contemporary History in Munich/Berlin provoked many discussions—in academia, in educational institutions, and in public discourse—throughout Germany and far beyond. This chapter focuses on the question of how to read this book and discusses Hitler's main propaganda work through the lens of Holocaust education. Acknowledging the antihuman, abhorrent, and insulting nature of Hitler's work, the question of its appropriateness as a "learning material" seems reasonable. In this text, however, I will argue that Holocaust education, conceived and designed also as a pillar of democracy education, *should* engage with primary sources of Nazi propaganda and their implications for attitudes, patterns of thinking, and acting. In their preface to the new edition, the editors state that the debate whether *Mein Kampf* was the announcement of the catastrophe is "the most insistent, even the most agonizing question that Hitler's writing poses."[4] This epilogue certainly does not aim at answering this question but outlines a way of approaching this book with the focus on learning from history for the present—in order to develop oneself as a citizen capable of cocreating democratic societies and, if necessary, protecting freedom and human rights in an increasingly diverse and polarized world.

Mein Kampf is a radical right-wing propaganda work that Hitler wrote to promote himself as a national "leader." It was intended to influence and mobilize the masses. Especially after he took power, this book, which includes Hitler's stylized autobiography and his main ideological writing, became a cult, a domination tool, and the source of propaganda. Nonetheless, *Mein Kampf* is for historical learning first and foremost a source that can be interpreted and analyzed using many different pedagogical approaches.

In reference to different forms of collective memories as developed by Jan Assmann,[5] we speak increasingly about the shift from the so-called communicative or communicated memory (where there are witnesses who can give us oral testimonies about the historical events) to "cultural memory" (where memory is preserved in written sources). This shift is natural, as the generation of witnesses, especially the survivors, passes away. This means that historical-political education on National Socialism, or Holocaust education, will take place without the active participation of the survivors. The methods and tools will be different, so the pedagogical approach will need to be reconceptualized—including all kinds of preserved and available sources of historical information. Testimonials, personal stories, and eyewitness accounts will continue playing a crucial role in Holocaust education, due to the numerous videos and recordings which have been preserved by different initiatives and institutions, for example, in the Visual History Archive of the Shoah Foundation. Written texts and original documents will likely become increasingly important.

Holocaust Education

There are several definitions of Holocaust education. The European Union Agency for Fundamental Rights provides a helpful overview about the corresponding dimensions: "Holocaust education is understood as: Education that takes the discrimination, persecution and extermination of the Jews by the National Socialist as its focus, but also includes Nazi crimes against other victim groups." It embraces "the pedagogical strategies to teach about National Socialist crimes, their precondition and history."[6] Plessow indicates that many scholars have been critical toward using the term "Holocaust education."[7] Even the International Holocaust Remembrance Alliance suggests using the term "Teaching and Learning about the Holocaust."[8] Plessow himself refers to Holocaust education in its wide sense: "including every learning endeavor, concept or activity that focuses on the mass crimes during the National Socialist reign in Germany from 1938 onwards."[9] In this definition he includes primarily European Jewry, but also other persecuted groups. I argue that the content of Holocaust education should begin with Hitler's first documented thoughts on eliminating European Jewry in *Mein Kampf* and thus encompassing the scope of themes around the "early signs of erosion of democracy." This definition is based on the concept of "Education after Auschwitz," as formulated in the 1960s by Theodor Adorno, who famously remarked that "the premier demand upon all education is that Auschwitz not happen again."[10] Yet there is no straightforward path from this moral imperative to any specific programs for Holocaust education. The demand is still there to be sensitive and critical toward words, arguments, implications, and discourses in order to intervene, when necessary.

The understanding of Holocaust education is controversial, as it presupposes that we can and should learn lessons from the Holocaust; it has been challenged and criticized especially by authors who plead for emphasizing the uniqueness of the Holocaust and thus rejecting the universalization of it.[11] Many authors argue that the main purpose of the Holocaust education should be to know the historical content and circumstances, and to remember the victims rather than "instrumentalizing" the Holocaust for any purpose, even the prevention of future atrocities.[12] According to Ofer, Holocaust education should utilize "knowledge for the sake of knowledge," and do so through "a systematic historical analysis," raising "the major issues through readings of primary documents and a comprehensive comparative study."[13] The historian Lucy Dawidowicz criticized Holocaust education because of the instrumental approach to the Holocaust, which discouraged deep understanding by treating Nazi anti-Semitism as the unique example of inhumanity. To conduct Holocaust education in the sense of "peace education," as Dawidowicz described the prevailing tendency, is completely inappropriate for the subject.[14] This debate, which revolves around the question of uniqueness, essentially divides Holocaust scholars into two camps. The first are scholars, like Dawidowicz, who see the Holocaust as a unique event, whose comprehension is possible only within the strictest limits of contextualized inquiry. The second are the scholars advocating for learning from history for the present and future, that is, through dealing with issues of prejudice, bigotry, exclusion, and so on.

The internationalization and globalization of Holocaust memory and Holocaust education involve certainly a risk of de-historicization, that is, abandonment of learning about concrete historical events and their context.[15] I will argue for pursuing both paths—to learn *about* and *from* the Holocaust—and I will follow the notion of Holocaust education as defined in the book *Lessons of the Holocaust* by Michael R. Marrus, where the author stresses that knowledge of the Holocaust "not only deepens understanding of a great watershed in the history of our times but also enlarges our knowledge of the human condition."[16] For that, *Mein Kampf* can be a useful historical document helping to put the Holocaust into a historical context and to understand the dimensions and processes of promoting a unique dehumanizing ideology.

Still, Holocaust education can (and must) lead to a fertile discussion of values. A number of concepts on Holocaust education defend the view that knowledge about the Holocaust, about the unfolding of inhumane thinking turning into inhumane action, can and should increase moral sensitivity toward signs of dehumanization and the early predictors of evil. Archbishop Desmond Tutu writes in his forward to *The Encyclopaedia of Genocide*: "The compelling reason why we should learn about the Holocaust, and the genocides committed against other peoples as well, is so that we might be filled with a revulsion at what took place and thus be inspired, indeed galvanized, to commit ourselves to ensure that such atrocities should never happen again."[17]

The concepts and approaches to Holocaust education, with a grounding in Adorno's notion of education after Auschwitz (as this chapter does), emphasize the need to recognize the signs of totalitarian regimes as the psychological mechanisms of dehumanization and propaganda. A prominent institution pursuing this approach is the organization Facing History and Ourselves (FHAO). This educational curriculum of FHAO focuses on different roles and stances a person can take when faced with dehumanizing occurrences/societal developments: victims, rescuers, bystanders, and perpetrators. The educational programs and learning materials are focused on the question of how to make a moral choice in difficult situations, which is seen as a way of preventing future atrocities.

A focus on the mechanisms by which such evil as Auschwitz was able to be done unhindered will lead us to the book *Mein Kampf*, a book that was kept by nearly every family in Germany and in which Hitler unambiguously described his visions and plans. He already communicated in *Mein Kampf* that the Jews should have been killed with gas during the First World War. Hitler promised from the very first page that all types of policy, domestic as well as foreign, must be based on racial needs—not economic considerations or other principles. Belonging to a nation would be therefore decided by "blood ties." Thus, the Holocaust during the Second World War was not an unpredictable and unexpected event but the consistent practical realization of a terrible ideology. At the same time, we must acknowledge the lack of readiness or capacity to see and anticipate the dangers of the emerging tyranny during the first years of Hitler's dictatorship. American historian on the Holocaust in Europe, Timothy Snyder points out: "The European history of the twentieth century shows us that societies can break, democracies can fall, ethics can collapse, and ordinary men can find themselves standing over death pits with guns in their hands. It would serve us well today to understand why."[18]

Following the appeal of Snyder to be vigilant toward tendencies of possible tyranny, we can ask why the book *Mein Kampf* did not provoke a repudiating reaction of the citizens of the young (and therefore surely fragile) German democracy of the Weimar Republic? One explanation could possibly be the ignorance of the book's content and the dreadful intention of its author. Neil Gregor, however, denounces as myth the claim that the book remained unread despite its being part of each household in the Third Reich. A pervasive claim that "we knew nothing about the content" delineates the climate of concealment, avoidance, and denial in the immediate postwar period.[19] It implies also the denial of responsibility for what had happened, because seemingly nobody knew. Yet the assertion that the Germans consciously, with their eyes open, decided upon tyranny and barbarism, inhumanity, and atrocities would not reflect the reality of those times. According to Alexander Karn,

> Germans who fled the political center beginning in 1930 concluded no deals with the devil, even if they ended up fastened in his clutches later. [. . .] Germans who abandoned the liberal center rarely expressed any desire to see others directly brutalized, but instead they lacked the intellectual tools and the emotional capacity that might have allowed them to make sound predictions about the consequences of their political choices.[20]

In this regard we can turn to an approach reflected in the work of Hannah Arendt, in her famous (and famously misunderstood) notion of the banality of evil. To call evil banal, Susan Neiman says, commenting on Arendt, is to imply "that the sources of evil are not mysterious or profound but fully within our grasp. If so, they do not infect the world at a depth that could make us despair of the world itself. Like a fungus, they may devastate reality by laying waste to its surface. Their roots, however, are shallow enough to pull up."[21] This conclusion highlights the imperative in Holocaust education to focus on early, sometimes even banal, signs of tyranny. Including the critical dealing with *Mein Kampf* into Holocaust education may therefore disclose the origins, context, and methods of the banal evil that led to the atrocities of Auschwitz. Critical dealing with *Mein Kampf* in different learning arrangements could be conceived as a resource for this kind of exercise.

Mein Kampf as a Learning Tool?

Mein Kampf has already been used in various educational settings and also in the challenging "edutainment" format. A cabaret artist Serdar Somuncu, German with Turkish background, became popular through his *Mein Kampf* tour based on reading and commentating Adolf Hitler's manifesto in the form of satire. Somuncu presented 1,400 performances, many of which were to schools, of *Mein Kampf* between 1996 and 2001 to audiences in Germany, Austria, Denmark, Holland, Lichtenstein, and the Czech Republic.[22] The primary critique toward Somuncu's tour was that laughing about *Mein Kampf* indicates a lack of gravity, which should be given to this part of history. Somuncu responded that dealing with *Mein Kampf* involves recognizing the shocking antihuman and anti-Semitic agenda of Hitler, but at the same time revealing the risible passages, the absurdity of the text, and the argumentation.[23] His argument was access to the text contributes to its demystification. For Somuncu, the annotated new edition of *Mein Kampf* is, however, an "absurdity" because it amplifies a "toothless text," which "had already made full-grown Nazis fall asleep" during his readings. As a deterrent, he recommends reading the original text because "the text emanates magical boredom and mental infirmity."[24]

Political cabaret can be considered an informal learning event. However, if we speak about using *Mein Kampf* in Holocaust education, also in formal (schools) and non-formal (different institutions for extra-curricular and adult learning) settings, some didactical considerations should be helpful. I claim that by reading *Mein Kampf* alone (even the newly commented version), it is unlikely that students would grasp the historical significance of it automatically. Furthermore, a possible partial grasping of the content can be problematic, because it can lead to false or distorted understandings.

As shown earlier, surrounding the question of how Holocaust history should be taught and can be learnt, some conflicting conceptions emerge. Research attests that teaching about the Holocaust poses considerable challenges for learners as well as for instructors.[25] Besides the emotional involvement,[26] gap knowledge,[27] and confrontation with violence,[28] it is also a question of the Holocaust's historical contextualization with regard to its predecessors and its aftermath. We need to pay attention to both in the course of Holocaust education by connecting different time dimensions with each other. Totten demonstrated that middle and high school teachers speak often about the Holocaust, without discussing the preconditions and development of it.[29] However, it is the historical knowledge about the rise of the Nazi dictatorship that allows learners to analyze the presuppositions and the consequences of dehumanization; to learn about the fragility of human rights, as well as authoritative abuse of political power toward marginalized peoples and contrarians; how authorities can abuse official power; how propaganda may capture our minds. This lesson will also help us approach the questions of the Holocaust's aftermath, especially with regard to learning from the Holocaust as a vehicle for democracy education, citizenship education, antiracism education, and human rights education.

Access to the text of *Mein Kampf* with a thorough explanation of context and clarification of details and facts (as provided in the new edition) allows the use of the text in different learning situations with varying learning goals. These goals are not limited to the knowledge of historical context, but rather they focus on the reflective connection between different time dimensions: past, present, and future. The knowledge and reflection about the ideology, rhetoric of violence, and inhumanity of the past can increase sensibility toward the possible effects of those on the societies today. In the following sections, I will suggest several possible interconnected aspects in regard to how we can frame the process of learning around *Mein Kampf* with the aim to integrate past, present, and future with each other.

Being Vigilant Advocates of Democracy

The German historian Herman Glaser put this concept into the formula: "Wer in der Demokratie schläft, kann leicht in der Diktatur erwachen" ("Those who sleep in democracy can easily wake up in dictatorship").[30] This sentence could be a helpful lens through which to read *Mein Kampf* while learning about and from the Holocaust.

Holocaust education is often justified by the need to teach students about their role in society as effective citizens. The previously mentioned education after Auschwitz (Adorno) implies the expectation that while dealing with a totalitarian past and its artifacts, the positive or affirmative attitude toward democracy will be developed. Education after Auschwitz is meant by Adorno as "Education towards Autonomy"; the autonomous citizen is characterized by the ability to critically reflect on social conditions and to make (political) judgments and ethical decisions on this basis and to co-shape her lifeworld and society through her actions.[31] This education should equip the citizens in a democracy against antidemocratic, populistic slogans, neo-Nazi refrains, and xenophobic attitudes, through convincing them that democracy is the only form of living together in a society which is morally right, namely the ideal of humanity. UNESCO provided several rationales for why we should teach about the Holocaust, starting with raising awareness of the fact that democracies are fragile: "Teaching how it could gain acquiescence and mobilize its intellectual, social, political and military resources to support and implement policies and actions that resulted in the murder of millions, and enlist groups in other nations, makes it possible to identify important warning signs for all societies" (Figure 14.1).[32]

Referring to the current Holocaust education in the United States, Alfers (2019)[33] diagnosed a shift in topics, especially after the Trump election in 2016. She describes the tendency to focus on the prerequisites that made the Third Reich and Nazi atrocities possible, whereas the concentration on expulsion, deportation, and extermination is, comparatively speaking, diminishing. Since 2016, some historians, famously among them Timothy Snyder, have compared and analyzed current American events in relation to Nazi Germany. In his manifesto "On Tyranny," Snyder warns of the fragility of liberal democracy in the United States and pleads for vigilance for early signs of gradual collapse into authoritarianism and, eventually, tyranny.[34]

In their study, Starratt et al. could observe modest connections between knowledge about the Holocaust and support for democratic and civic values.[35] To analyze through contrast, comparison, assessment of structure of the historical and current rhetoric helps to deepen the understandings

FIGURE 14.1 *Entrance to the Auschwitz concentration camp. Courtesy of the United States Holocaust Memorial Museum.*

of the complexity of issues to stimulate reflection about the correlation of personal choices and societal developments and, finally, to support the development of civic competencies.[36] This approach is, however, a challenging endeavor, because without a necessary context and depth it might lead to superficial learning effects such as simplistic, incorrect connections between past and present.[37] Analyzing and reflecting on the openly antidemocratic authoritarian and tyrannical ideology, as expressed in *Mein Kampf*, and using the background information provided in the comments to the new critical edition, helps to avoid the trap of oversimplification of the historical facts.

The question to put in this context could be: What were the obvious signs of fascistic ideology of Hitler's manifesto and what kept so many German citizens in conformity with Hitler's ideology and the regime? The question of personal choices and personal responsibility for the course of event, as well as awareness of the possible threats of despotic and fascistic rhetoric, can be a possible direction of using *Mein Kampf* as a learning tool. Using the words of Karn:

> The idea behind this philosophy [of Holocaust education, THK] is to teach the past in a manner that equips students to see the ramifications of their choices in contrast to the Germans who, by virtue of their own choices, allowed themselves to be fastened in a system designed to achieve national revitalization and racial purification at any and all costs.[38]

This desire for racial purification appears through Hitler's text and is stated as his obligatory goal for Germany.

If we want education to prevent a future Auschwitz and to recognize the mechanisms by which people were able to commit those atrocities, as Adorno put it, then the integral reflective connection between the past and the present, the precedent and the aftermath, cause and effect, is an indispensable part of such an education. Democracy needs democrats, wrote Adorno; democracy needs to be learned, "again and again, day after day, for a lifetime," wrote German pedagogue Oskar Negt (2004).[39] Democracy is not a self-evident form of living together; it needs to be vigilantly protected.

Identification of Propaganda Tools and Mechanism

Mein Kampf is unambiguously a radical right-wing propaganda book. But does it imply that the German people were victims of National Socialist seduction, which had been set by a refined political propaganda factory?[40] To assume this would mean to place human beings (in general) into the position of tutelage, to deny the capacity to develop their own judgment and the responsibility for one's own views. To use *Mein Kampf* today as a learning tool means to gain awareness of how propaganda could work and influence the attitudes of people, but at the same time to develop agency to resist efforts of propaganda and take responsibility for forming and shaping one's own attitudes and worldview. A learning process with the text *Mein Kampf* can occur when a learner experiences this ideology as a reader and then learns how to free oneself from its propaganda efforts.

I argued before that Holocaust education is not mainly about human rights and peace learning but about the intellectual and emotional ability to analyze, interpret, find, and prove arguments—a general literacy that embraces the possibility to read deeper into texts, the historical as well as modern. In the time of cultural memory,[41] Holocaust education is increasingly using written testimonies, recorded interviews, historical documents, and secondary literature as sources and tools for Holocaust education. These sources are sometimes easily accessible, but often inconsistently and even contradictory in the perspectives and analysis offered. These kinds of sources, however, make it necessary to examine the relevant facts and data. It therefore requires a critical (media)competency in dealing with different information, which is to be directed toward the analysis and reflection about the acquired knowledge—or, using Adorno's term, it progresses "towards autonomy and maturity."

The importance of addressing the question of propaganda in Holocaust education is twofold. First, *Mein Kampf* is a propagandistic book that was important for Hitler's success in installing a regime and in convincing the German people to follow his aggressive plans.[42] George Orwell, while writing a review on *Mein Kampf* in 1940, pointed out that Hitler made promises to the German people of enhancing their power, speaking to their desires of "drums, flags and loyalty-parades," combined with striving for struggle and even "self-sacrifice."[43] He promised the people more than a simple "hedonistic attitude to life," and they followed him, captured by the attraction of this "emotional appeal" to heroism: "Hitler has said to them 'I offer you struggle, danger and death,' and as a result a whole nation 'flings itself at his feet.'"[44] The second reason to deal with propaganda with reference to *Mein Kampf* is that speaking about the tools of persuasive communication and deception can help raise awareness among students about the dangers of this media tool. In *Mein Kampf*, Hitler paid a lot of attention to propaganda, demonstrating the almost limitless possibilities of rhetoric and propaganda in the process of political decision-making.

Certainly, the propaganda techniques and tools are different and more sophisticated today than they were at the time of *Mein Kampf*. "Propaganda comes of age," and attempts to deceive are becoming more diverse and multifaceted, as Martin Choukas stated in his book of the same name in 1965.[45] Modern technology and speed of information dissemination reveal a new level of "adulthood" or "maturity" of propaganda, because today it is possible to communicate any point of view to as many addressees as possible quickly and inexpensively, but also through different communication channels.[46] Snyder points out that the goal of today's propaganda is less about disseminating false content, as much as it is to cause confusion and disorientation. The result, then, is a retreat into the private sphere, distrust of established media, disinterest, and also disenchantment with public and political life. This strategy leads to abandoning the search for truth while also abandoning the attempt to differentiate between truth and lies. He goes even further to say that "Post truth is pre-fascism."[47] Along with idea of Levy and Sznaider,[48] who postulate that Holocaust memories help us differentiate between good and evil, we can argue that books like *Mein Kampf* force us to renew our striving to come closer to the truth (or at least to move away from lies), to differentiate the truth from lies, and to call a lie a lie (and not an "alternative fact").

Dealing with *Mein Kampf* may lead us to these core epistemological questions: How can we gain and assess knowledge and its sources? What kind of knowledge is available to us and how can we perform a critical analysis of it? It can and should hint at the potential relationship between knowledge and attitude, and demands therefore a critical self-reflection: How do I deal with knowledge and how does it impact my world perception? Furthermore, the history of reception of the book may provide a way to reflect on different stages of awareness in the German (and not only German) memory culture. Reading excerpts of the book means exposing oneself to the text, in order to gain in the next step a critical distance to analyze it. Karn suggests thinking in the context of Holocaust education about the inertia of our cognitive structures: "[We] need to wrestle more seriously with the forces of inertia which keep people pent up inside their own cognitive structures, and in that way, beyond the reach of any transformative influence."[49]

At the same time, Holocaust education, as a value-based education, contains an inherent risk to be assertive, intentionally or not. This is why Holocaust education is called upon to be especially vigilant and to put its own methods, approaches, and practices under constant critical scrutiny.[50] An example of a misguided practice was described by Maseth and Proske in 2010. They conducted qualitative research about historical learning in German schools. One of the case studies used by them was a situation in the classroom where students dealt with the excerpts of *Mein Kampf*. The authors note in advance:

> In Germany, Hitler's *Mein Kampf* is considered to be "dangerous for minors" [. . .] The text is "known and notorious" enough that twelfth-grade students are likely to be familiar with its incendiary character. Although the students are expected to have prior knowledge of the text, the way it is used by the teacher suggests the construction of unknowledgeable, impressionable students who must still learn about the inhumane ideology presented in the text. The exercise therefore has a kind of cathartic effect. It is intended to provoke moral outrage on the part of the students, to lead them to condemn the crimes, and to immunize them against the seductive power such ideologies may possess.[51]

As the students were asked to summarize the excerpt, they were using language from the text (words such as "race" and "Aryans"). "Because they lacked critical distance from the text and used Hitler's language uncritically, the teacher accused them of being potential victims of Nazi propaganda." Maseth and Proske see, therefore, the danger of students' becoming overwhelmed or even indoctrinated while dealing with a "primary historical document as morally fraught as *Mein Kampf*."[52] This situation will "pressure the teacher to address students not only from his functional role but also as an individual." Unlike physics class where students' learning can be evaluated as right or wrong and the failure to learn might make one a bad student, in history class the "failure to learn the evils of National Socialism can turn a 'bad student' into a 'bad person.'"[53]

To deal with propagandistic texts means to gain competencies in resisting manipulation and seduction. As citizens in a democracy, we gain tools to deal responsibly with propaganda, populism, and manipulation. Even today in contemporary Germany, there are new voices in the right-wing populist context that argue as far as nationalists did, and there are xenophobic voices in the refugee debate as well as the Pediga movement. It could be supposed the availability of the book could nourish these voices and attitudes. That is why a high sensitivity in dealing with this text is required. At the same time, it should also be presupposed that the citizens in a democracy have the maturity and autonomy to deal with populism and not too easily fall prey to manipulation.

In this line of thought, I want to emphasize again the central components of "Education after Auschwitz," and "Education towards autonomy and maturity," according to Adorno. The loss of autonomy is what Adorno initially seems to problematize as a precondition for barbarism. Individuals deceived by promises of supremacy and power develop a mindset akin a "conformist society."[54] Once the capacity for autonomy has been lost, people tend to blindly acquiesce to the fancies of those in authority and thus follow them without resistance and dissent. Referring again to Snyder's lessons from the historical heritage of tyranny: "Some killed from murderous conviction. But many others who killed were just afraid to stand out. Other forces were at work besides conformism. But without the conformists, the great atrocities would have been impossible."[55] Not having the mindset for dissent, people think that there is no alternative to the status quo. Holocaust education is therefore also learning about searching for tenable alternatives, learning to disagree and to rebut when necessary, learning to resist and exercise agency. Plessow observes a general tendency in Holocaust education to emphasize "an individualization of agency": "Many programs and concepts display a strong belief that in the decision-making of the individual, his or her empowerment lies the road to betterment of societal or fundamental political problems."[56] Autonomous and critical thinking implies sensitivity toward rhetoric, discourses, and language as a tool of naming and marking the world around us.

Paying Attention to the Language—and to Othering

Learning about the Holocaust using the text (and critical analysis) of *Mein Kampf* implies also a closer look at the language and awareness of the meaning and power of words. Words help to shape and categorize worldviews; they shape conclusions drawn about intent, principles, and assumptions of the author. Language served, and continues to serve, as a mediator of political ideology. Using *Mein Kampf* as learning material means in this context to sharpen critical reflection regarding the process of exclusion of the Other—be it on the level of rhetoric as a preliminary stage or on the level of discriminatory actions. The question of dealing with and embracing differences can thus be discussed in the context of individual action, as well as in the social and political realm—and in the realm of ideas and concepts. Hartman et al. speak about Hitler's four core ideologemes: the ideologeme of race, of space, of violence, and of dictatorship.[57] Although developed decades before *Mein Kampf*, and not by Hitler, they were constitutive of his worldview and contained a "catastrophe potential." The barbarism of the political action was caught in words far in advance of its actual enactment.

In his research on *Mein Kampf*, Jäckel argued that Hitler made his plans for the elimination of the Jews quite explicitly.[58] Hitler uses in *Mein Kampf* the metaphor of Germany's "reawakening" under Hitler's rule by "recovering from a disease" and winning the war "against parasites" (i.e., Jews and other ethnic and social groups and nations). Especially clear is the attitude toward Jewish people, who are labeled in the book as "the Jew" or "illness-spreading parasite," among other dehumanizing terms. Hitler postulated his racial thinking more than clearly while asserting that Jews were impure and inferior, and "in order to advance, the [Aryan] race should be purified."[59] Hitler's manifesto written to explain his worldview delivers a clear picture of anti-Jewish ideology: the devaluation of Jews is taken to the extreme, to the idea of "final salvation" (*Erlösungsgedanke*).

The ideology of National Socialism was based on the idea that the German-Aryan race was superior to all others. According to this, the German race was entitled to rule over the other peoples. The web of images and themes used by Hitler (and his followers) was established through the language as a world in which fighting was sacred, and killing (Jewish) people became a question of honor and holy mission. One of the numerous examples in *Mein Kampf* illustrates this strategy: "Today I believe that I am acting in accordance with the will of the Almighty Creator: by defending myself against the Jew, I am fighting for the work of the Lord."[60]

Linguistic tools and euphemisms play a decisive role in making previously unacceptable and ethically wrong concepts sound more tolerable. Karn describes the effect of such discourse on political action: "Nazi mythmaking and a public discourse that glorified ideological combat gave Germans a way of seeing totalitarian infringements and the legal codification of racial discrimination as acceptable and/or necessary trade-offs for their nation's rising international prestige."[61]

Musolff, who did research on the metaphors in *Mein Kampf*, refers to the ubiquitous use of the metaphor of "disease"—a symbol, from which the German "body" suffers[62]—and "'the Jew' is labelled generally as the germ or germ carrier or agent of disease."[63] Musolff points out that Hitler suggested himself in *Mein Kampf* as the healer of the "suffering patient, the German nation": "The nation thus becomes the patient that urgently needs the cure. The healer is present, the diagnosis is clear: the treatment is without alternative."[64]

While dealing with *Mein Kampf*, it seems important to pay attention to the fact that this ideology and rhetoric were widely accepted by Germans (and not only propagated by Hitler). Some research pointed out the danger of Hitlerism, that is, perceiving Hitler as the only perpetrator. For instance, Schwendemann and Marks analyzed the teaching block on National Socialism in a ninth-grade school project.[65] They interviewed students before and after the block and pointed out the attitudes toward Hitlerism after the course: the students were convinced that Hitler himself—and he alone—was responsible for all atrocities in the National Socialist period.

Today, we will obviously read the book through a different lens. It should be said that the text of *Mein Kampf* is not easily accessible to today's readers, especially young ones, as the language has obviously changed over the course of time, and many contemporary allusions, historical examples, and metaphors are no longer understandable; the related issues are no longer relevant to them. However, using this text in educational settings may equip learners with important competencies, which are required in each society. Snyder, while encouraging us to learn from the history, emphasized the attention to the symbols and tokens used: "The symbols of today enable the reality of tomorrow. Notice the swastikas and the other signs of hate. Do not look away, and do not get used to them."[66]

Summing up the suggested frames of using *Mein Kampf* in Holocaust education, I want to add a precaution: *Mein Kampf* was written long before the Holocaust started and can be read to understand the ideology behind the genocide. It can and should be read as a warning sign, an ideology that made atrocities possible. However, not every inhuman ideology has led to a genocide. Analyzing for early signs of the erosion of democracy means exploring the possible signs and using tools for critical inquiry to recognize ideological pitfalls but at the same time being vigilant not to catastrophize development by labeling them with historical comparisons. Notwithstanding, a sensibility toward early signs of the erosion of democracy, combined with a realism and reflexivity, can play an important role in the development of learners who will protect civil liberties and defend oppressed, vulnerable groups—citizens capable of effectively serving as protectors of freedom and human rights in an increasingly diverse and polarized democratic society.

Conclusion

Mein Kampf is an historically important document which can be used to discuss several important questions of the present by understanding the past. It is well suited to provide relevant and revealing insights into fascism and examples about what makes such an inhuman, morally and intellectually repulsive "world view," so attractive for some that they adopt it.

Mein Kampf furthermore can be used as a learning tool within the framework of Holocaust education, pursuing at least two aims: the first is dealing with historical facts through an historical document; the second is shaping critical thinking and contributing to a broadening of historical and political consciousness.

It is an essential document not only for Germany but also for other societies to help understand the roots of an antihuman ideology, and to develop critical and analytical thinking while dealing with propaganda. Thus, discussion about the book is essential at any time, and the relevance of this discussion can be seen in the present moment. The new, critical edition offers a helpful learning tool—even with the risk that neo-Nazis and any other racist groups could also use the book to promote a sinister agenda.

At the same time, the new edition of *Mein Kampf* is a useful source for adults who want to learn on their own and search for well-prepared sources for self-directed learning process. It is a great opportunity for them to deal critically with historical documents. This edition also shows how a critical approach to sources can look like and what it means to question a text, to question a message, and to develop critical reading competency.

A debate continues over whether the Holocaust should be taught in terms of history or human rights. I do not argue that using *Mein Kampf* as a learning tool within Holocaust education should follow only one of the ways: both perspectives are crucial to shape the "Education after Auschwitz." I do, however, provide some arguments why the book *Mein Kampf* can be used as a tool for learning to address global and universal issues of society today. The emphasis on such an approach is placed on critical reflection, forming one's own well-argued opinions on the historical documents.

In educational settings, it is important to help students draw connections between historical events and contemporary issues—without the loss of historical content. The comparison with current tendencies has its challenges and needs to be thoroughly reflected upon. To compare does not imply to catastrophize every event and to equate it with evil. However, while recognizing that evil can be banal, we can pay attention to the accumulation of signs, such as breaking of taboos in rhetoric, growing social acceptance for the violence toward and exclusion of the Other(s), and labeling of minorities. Propaganda is the most popular tool that an authoritarian regime uses, but it is also used in democracies in the form of different PR measures. The propagandists of the past and the PR people of today know how to fight for the minds of the people/voters. Lessons from the past can be helpful in developing caution toward any smear campaign—no matter from which political camp it comes. An analysis of *Mein Kampf* can reveal how one minor political party in Bavaria could evolve into a ruling and hegemonic party that brought us the Second World War and the Holocaust.

Appendix

A résumé of the reception of *Mein Kampf* in Germany (1925–1945)

*Othmar Plöckinger**

Summary

After the Second Word-War the reception of Hitler's *Mein Kampf* was part of the discussion about National-Socialism in Germany. The legend became prevalent that the book was an »unread bestseller«. But investigating the real circumstances in detail another picture emerges. Before 1933 many newspapers and magazines wrote about the book, *Mein Kampf* became essential in the public discussions about National-Socialism and several state-institutions and ministries studied the book. Remarkably anti-Semitism didn't play an important role in all those texts. After 1933 the distribution of *Mein Kampf* did not only rise extraordinary but also was controlled strictly in order to give it the sacrosanct status of »The book of the Germans«. All in all the reception of *Mein Kampf* on public, state and private level was considerable. For that reason a nuanced scientific research to this topic can give a useful contribution to the study of National-Socialism.

Introduction

The last time for decades *Mein Kampf* found some attention was during the trail against the Major War Criminals in Nueremberg in 1945/46. Several passages of the book were used as evidence against the defendants. One of the most interesting disputes developed between a Soviet prosecutor and

*Othmar Plöckinger: "A Résumé of the Reception of Mein Kampf in Germany" (1925–45) (*Francia: Forschungen zur Westeuropäischen Geschichte, 47:2020*).

Albert Speer, Hitler's favourite architect and later Armament Minister. The prosecutor confronted Speer with passages form *Mein Kampf*, which in his opinion showed clearly Hitler's plans of attacking and destroying the Soviet Union. Speer replied that the Soviet diplomats must have read the book as well and nevertheless made the Hitler-Stalin-pact in 1939. Thereupon the Soviet prosecutor ended this dispute with the remark that he doesn't want a further discussion about the question, who read *Mein Kampf* and who didn't.

This episode shows that the question about the readership of *Mein Kampf* was virulent immediately after the war and ever since. And it proves that the book was always subject and instrument of accusation and justification in debates on the historical, political and ethical dimensions of National-Socialism and its legacy. But we have to be aware that this question has some traps which can lead to misinterpretations or even mistakes in the historical analysis. Firstly, it pretends that *Mein Kampf* was the central key to the knowledge and understanding of Hitler's conceptions and the National-socialist ideology in general. Surely, having read *Mein Kampf* made it easier to be aware of what was going on in Germany, but it was not the precondition for that. So heaving read *Mein Kampf* didn't mean full information – and not having read *Mein Kampf* didn't mean having no information. This situation in some respect was characterised by the Austrian Author and Journalist Karl Kraus, when he opened his remarkable and comprehensive text *Die Dritte Walpurgisnacht* (1933/1952) with the legendary sentence: »Mir fällt zu Hitler nichts ein«[1] – and afterwards proved on hundreds of pages, how much he really knew about the National-socialist Germany, including Hitler's book. And secondly – and this concerns mainly Germany –, the question about the readership of *Mein Kampf* includes the assumption that the German people would have rejected Hitler, if they only had read his book. The Jewish German Romanicist Victor Klemperer wrote about this aspect in his famous *Lingua Tertii Imperii*: »Es wird mir immer das größte Rätsel des Dritten Reiches bleiben, wie dieses Buch in voller Öffentlichkeit verbreitet werden durfte, ja musste, und wie es dennoch zur Herrschaft Hitlers und zu zwölfjähriger Dauer dieser Herrschaft kommen konnte, obwohl die Bibel des Nationalsozialismus schon Jahre vor der Machtübernahme kursierte.«[2]

In this respect the question, who and how many people read *Mein Kampf*, was and still is a part of the post-war legend that the Germans were seduced by Hitler as they didn't know, what he really stood for. In this way the comprehensive or partial consent, which Hitler's ideology found in considerable parts of the German society, gets easily out of sight.

So while analysing the reception of *Mein Kampf* we have to bear in mind that we are dealing not only with a book, but with a symbol of the National-socialistic ideology and regime and with the post-war legends of each society. But on the other hand especially these aspects make it necessary and fruitful to ask precisely: Who read the book? Which parts have been read? When and with which purpose was it read?

Therefore at least three different fields of investigation should be considered: The public, the state (including semi-state institutions and organisations) and the private fields. As for Germany, of course these fields can be distinguished clearly only until 1933. Afterwards the situation is quite a different one.

Publishing history and public reception 1925–1933

The first volume of the book was quite a success when it was published in July 1925. Within a few months all 10.000 copies were sold out and a second edition was necessary. The audience was eager to find out what the high traitor from 1923 hat to say about his coup d'état. Therefore the public reaction was quite heavy. Dozens of reviews were published in newspapers and magazines. Some of them were local and regional papers, but also national and international papers as the *Frankfurter Zeitung* or the *Neue Zürcher Zeitung* wrote extensively about the book. Hitler still had the glamour of a radical politician, and therefore several reviewers were disappointed that Hitler didn't write anything about his political rise in Bavaria and his coup in November 1923. Consequently the second volume, published in December 1926, attracted much less public interest[3]. The sales-figures declined continuously and reached its low point in 1928 when no more than 3000 copies. But in 1929 the situation changed. According to the reawakening of the interest in the book the National-socialist publishing-house Eher-Verlag decided not only to have it intensively proofread by Rudolf Heß[4], but to publish a version of *Mein Kampf*, which contained both volumes and was much cheaper than the editions before. It was the »Volksausgabe« which became the widest spread version in Germany, none of the numerous other versions which were to come until 1945 reached its popularity. Only the so-called »Dünndruckausgabe« or »Feldausgabe«, printed on extra-fine and light paper for the use in the Wehrmacht, came close to one million copies. All in all about 12.5 million copies were produced in Germany, two thirds during the war[5].

Looking at the public perception during the Weimar Republic more than 50 reviews were published from 1925 until 1932, and they covered a very wide range of appraisals. We find enthusiastic reviews from party-members like Alfred Rosenberg in the *Berliner Arbeiterzeitung* in 1926, although Rosenberg always had troubles with Hitler's success which was much bigger than his own with his book *Mythus des 20. Jahrhunderts* published in 1930[6]. One of the most exuberant text came from Adolf Bartels, the leading volkisch-antisemitic literature critic, who 1927 saw Hitler's book as the most important political publication in Germany since Bismarck's »Gedanken und Erinnerungen«[7]. We find ambivalent or even hostile reviews in volkisch and nationalist newspapers like the very influential *Deutsche Zeitung*. That newspaper published in 1925 a mainly negative review. It paid some tribute to Hitler's effort in writing a book as he had no higher education and conceded that he has some remarkable skills in propaganda. But the reviewer Otto Bonhard, a main figure in the influential »Alldeutschen Verband«, stated a lot of gaps in knowledge not only in Hitler's so much appreciated field of history but also in »Staatswissenschaft« and »Rassenkunde«. Moreover he found no inventive thoughts in the book whatsoever and criticises that Hitler's seems to think that he, Hitler, has formulated new insights which in realty are well known[8]. This review was very annoying for Hitler, as a lot of liberal and left-wing newspaper refrained from writing own reviews but reprinted with delight parts of this one. Hitler even mentions this humiliating review in the second volume of *Mein Kampf* and tried to defend himself[9].

And we find mocking reviews in socialistic or liberal papers, most of them dealing with Hitler as a figure of the past and not of the future, as the *Frankfurter Zeitung* put it in 1925: »Inzwischen haben aber die konstruktiven Politiker über die Geister des Chaos den Sieg davongetragen. Inzwischen haben sie Deutschland wieder aufgebaut und sind daran, Europa zu sichern. [...] Die Freunde konstruktiver Politik werden das Buch Hitlers zur Hand nehmen und daraus sehen, wie recht sie mit allem hatten, was sie dachten. Die Zeit ist weitergeschritten; Hitler aber ist – vollends nach diesem Selbstbekenntnis – erledigt.«[10]

And Stefan Grossmann, a journalist, writer and assistant of Bert Brecht, summarised his comprehensive review of the book in 1925: »Dieses Buch zeigt Adolf Hitler, wie er ist, arm an Herz, unwissend, eitel, vollkommen phantasielos, und als Milderungsgrund läßt sich nur anführen, daß er offenbar ein unheilbarere Kriegshysteriker ist.«[11]

Surprisingly Jewish magazines dealt only in very exceptional cases *Mein Kampf*, if we leave short notes and references now and then aside. This didn't change till 1933. So there are only a few texts which go deeper into the book and analysed it. The first and most comprehensive one was an article in the »Abwehrblätter« of the »Verein zur Abwehr des Antisemitismus«, which discussed and disproved most of Hitler's anti-Semitic defamations in detail. It is until today one of the best analysis of *Mein Kampf*, although it's end is tragic. The author Johannes Stanjek writes in his closing words: »Man legt Hitlers Buch mit einem Gefühl der Befriedigung beiseite: Solange die völkische Bewegung keine anderen Führer an ihre Spitze zu stellen weiß, solange werden noch manche Wasser ins Meer fließen, bis sie im Land der Dichter und Denker siegen wird.«[12] A shorter follow-up text from Stanjek about the second volume of *Mein Kampf* was entitled consequently: »Hitlers weiterer Feldzug gegen den Verstand«[13].

The second was published in 1930 in the Berlin *Jüdisch-liberale Zeitung* under the title „Die nationalsozialistische Gefahr." Regarding the coming Reichstags-elections in September 1930 the newspaper not only analysed Hitler' anti-Semitism but also quotetd different passages form *Mein Kampf* which showed Hitler's racist point of view towards Engalnd, France and the United States. The quotations were followed by the remark: »Anders als sonst in Menschenköpfen malt sich in diesem Kopf die welt. Soll von solchen Narren die Welt in neues, noch größeres Unheil gestürzt warden? «[14]

Besides that, starting with 1930 Hitler's book became an essential part of the political and journalistic conflicts in Germany. Numerous leaflets, brochures, pamphlets and books were dealing with *Mein Kampf*, be it argumentative or polemical, approving or refusing. Usually all those texts concentrated on a few special aspects and didn't give a comprehensive analysis.

In 1931 there was for an example a broad discussion, whether Hitler is a Christian or not and how the relation between Christianity and National-Socialism has to be seen. Numerous texts against and in favour of Hitler were published, most of them arguing with different passages of *Mein Kampf*. One of the most influential brochures against Hitler was published by Ingbert Naab, a catholic priest, who died in 1935 in his French exile[15]. He analysed and quoted *Mein Kampf* extensively and came to the conclusion »daß wichtige Grundideen und Vorschläge Hitlers mit dem Christentum in absolutem Widerspruch stehen. Darum kann er eben für Christen auch nicht Führer sein.«[16] One of Hitler's most active defenders in this discussion was the physicist and Nobel-Price-Winner Johannes Stark, who – just like Naab – comprehensively quoted *Mein Kampf* in order to prove that Hitler's respects the christian confessions and refuses to interfere in religious matters[17].

But also Hitler's concepts of foreign policy in *Mein Kampf* was analysed for example by the social-democrat Helmuth Klotz in 1931, who was executed in 1943 in Berlin[18]. In his brochure he collected dozens of statements of leading National-Socialists regarding foreign politics in general and their attitude towards different European countries. Hitler's book is one of his central sources and he emphasises Hitler's hostility and aggressivity against France. That's why he hoped his text would be read outside Germany as well and closed his text with the words: »Und eben deshalb wäre ein Deutschland Hitlers der Untergang des neuen Deutschlands, die Katastrophe Europas und der Welt!«[19]

And in 1932 an article, which widely circulated in international communist magazines, the described the threat of France and the Soviet Union, which Hitler exposes in *Mein Kampf*. It's author, the Theodor Neubauer, who was executed in Berlin in spring 1945[20], stated that Hitler might be willing to cooperate with France for a while in order to destroy the Soviet Union: »Antibolschewistische deutsche Außenpolitik endet in der Unterwerfung vor dem französischen Imperialismus, bedeutet Verzicht auf die nationale Befreiung, Verrat an den Volksmassen, die der Tributpolitik geopfert werden.«[21]

Once again surprisingly Hitler's anti-Semitism was discussed in none of this texts on a broader basis: Mostly it was ignored or mentioned only incidentally, sometimes it was seen as a minor matter. And in several texts his anti-Semitism even was judged only as a little bit too radical, but all in all quite reasonable.

State reception 1925–1933

If we look at the reception of *Mein Kampf* on state level we find a similar broad debate. Only a few months after the first volume was published, the Bavarian ministry of interior wrote a study about *Mein Kampf* and analysed in detail Hitler's political attitudes. It stated that Hitler had not changed since 1923 and still was speaking in favour of a violent form of politics. Therefore it refused to lift the ban against Hitler, who wasn't allowed to speak publicly in Bavaria until 1927[22].

This aspect of violence was the topic of a lot of other studies dealing with the political aims and the structure of Hitler's party – and Hitler's book always was a main reference point. Yet until 1930 already five different state-studies had been written and circulated on different governmental levels, including the Reichs-Ministry of the Interior, the Prussian Ministry of the Interior[23], the Berlin Police Presidency and the Reichswehr-Ministry[24]. One of them was written in 1930 by Theodor Heuss, the later first West-German President after the Second World War. Heuss was member of the Reichstag for a liberal Party and dealt with the NSDAP since 1930 more and more intensively[25]. His first study about the NSDAP was made for several groups in the Reichstag an for the Reich Chancery. He described and analysed the structure and the NS-ideology manly in its economic aspects. And he complains Hitler's arbitrary abuse of „Wissenschaft" which has to bow to Hitler's volition, »um ein Weltbild, einen Geschichtsablauf zu ordnen, der notwendig bei dem Verkünder einer neuen Einsicht endigt. Für eine Argumentation, die Thesen und Daten auf ihr Gewicht prüft, ist da gar kein Raum mehr.«[26]

Until 1932 several more state-analyses were made, including the Foreign Ministry in Berlin[27]. The last and most comprehensive one was produced by the Prussian ministry of interior and consisted of almost 400 pages. It was circulated in the highest ranks of the German Government, but was ignored by Chancellor Heinrich Brüning and his minsters on purpose. Using *Mein Kampf* and numerous additional materials from Hitler and other leading National-Socialists the Ministry tried to prove that the NSDAP still was trying to overthrow the Weimar Republic with violence[28].

Ironically the possibility that the NSDAP could seize power in Germany on a legal way never was discussed in all these state-analysis. But in one of the most spectacular cases even the violent aspect of the NSDAP was denied. It was the trial against Hitler (and others) for the preparation of high treason before the Reichsgericht (the Supreme Court) in Leipzig in 1931. Besides other sources the court analysed Hitler's book, but finally dropped the charges. The right-wing Reichs-prosecutor could not find evidence in *Mein Kampf* that Hitler would purpose a violent breach of the Weimar constitution – in contradiction to most of the other analysis of state-institutions[29].

Reception 1933–1945

Of course in 1933 the situation changed completely. That concerned on the one side the distribution of the book. In 1933 almost a million copies were sold without any political pressure or state-driven distribution. Many Germans were eager to find out in detail what the new chancellor stood for beyond his propaganda-speeches[30]. During the following years the sales-figures dropped noticeably what lead the Eher-Verlag to the idea pushing it with different campaigns – one of the most famous was to make the communal authorities to hand it over to bridal couples. Although this campaign was by far not as successful as the Eher-Verlag hoped, it became after 1945 the most common argument for the legend that nobody read the book as it was forced on the Germans. Both are wrong[31].

On the other side both public and state analysis came to an end. The »Parteiamtliche Prüfungskommission zum Schutze des NS-Schrifttums« (PKK) controlled the usage of *Mein Kampf* strictly and made clear in 1937 that analysing or interpreting Hitler's was not allowed: »Wohin aber würden wir kommen, wenn allerorts das Buch des Führers, seine Reden oder das Programm der Partei zum Gegenstand von Untersuchungen, Vergleichen oder gar der Diskussion gemacht würden?«[32] Even the initially very popular collections of various quotes from *Mein Kampf* had to cease. Since 1936 the PKK intensified its control of this kind of publications until in 1939 Hitler himself stopped them completely. His Party-office announced: »Der Führer wünscht nicht, dass sein Werk in Teile zerlegt und nach verschiedensten Gesichtspunkten geordnet herausgebracht wird.«[33] In this way *Mein Kampf* became »Das Buch der Deutschen«, which was put along with the Nibelungenlied and Luther's translation of the Bible. In school-readers three authors became mostly quoted: Goethe, Schiller and Hitler[34]. *Mein Kampf* was ominpresent in books, newspapers, magazines and the radio, it was training material for officers in the Wehrmacht and for members of the SS who in training courses had to deal with a different sections of *Mein Kampf* every week[35].

Thus the book became an important part of the self-dramatization of the Nazi-regime and of its claim of total power on all levels. So we have to note that after 1933 the question, by whom and for which purpose *Mein Kampf* was read, is very difficult to answer. We have to combine several sources to get an impression of the relevance of the book besides propaganda and compulsion.

If we look at the sales-figures, we see that there were two main periods before the war, in which the book was bought to a very high degree. As mentioned above the first one was in 1933, the second one in 1938/39. That is not a coincidence and is underlined by the loan-figures of public libraries in Germany as well: In 1933 and in 1938/39 those figures increased just like the sales-figures. That proves that the Germans had a look at the book mainly during sever crisis: In 1933 many Germans wanted to learn about Hitler's real political goals beyond his countless campaign speeches. And in 1938/39 many Germans were worried about the international confrontation and wanted to learn about the ideological basis of Hitler's foreign policy. Even the exiled Social-democratic Party stated in a report in 1939 that Hitler's book played an important role in discussions between German citizens: »Über die Ziele an sich kann man aus Kreisen der Hitlergegner ähnliches hören wie von überzeugten Nationalsozialisten. Man sagt, dass Hitlers ‚Kampf' über diese Ziele deutlich genug spräche, so dass man sich nicht in Vermutungen darüber zu ergehen brauche.«[36]

After the war the Americans in Bavaria wanted to know a bit more exactly, how many Germans had read the book. Their survey rated about 20 percent of the population or about 12 Million people, and that was a bottom line[37]. For good reasons one can assume that the real number was larger[38].

And large is the number of prominent persons as well, for whom we have evidence that they dealt with the book. There are not only Nazis like Alfred Rosenberg, Joseph Goebbels, Gregor Straßer and Rudolf Heß or followers like Carl Schmitt, Adolf Bartels, Fritz Lenz, Hjalmar Schacht and Ernst von Weizsäcker, but also critics and opponents like Arnold Zweig, Albert Einstein, Karl August Wittfogel and Theodor Wolff. Even victims of the NS-regime dealt with the book. Victor Klemperer was mentioned above. In Prague the German-Czech historian and feminist Käthe Spiegel in 1940/41 was working on a comprehensive analysis of *Mein Kampf*. She analysed several key-words of the National-Socialist ideology in Hitler's book and studied especially the influence of Friedrich Nietzsche and Niccolo Machiavelli. She defined Hitler as utopian who differs from other utopians as he tries to realise his utopia. But Hitler's aims are much more ambitious as the Marxist utopia: »Dem Verfasser [d. i. Hitler] ist es aber nicht um die menschlichen Dinge alleine zu tun, d. h. um die Ordnung unter Menschen. Ihm geht es darüber hinaus darum, die Aufzucht des Menschengeschlechts im bioligischen Sinne zu fördern, den Willen der Natur zu erfüllen, das Werk Gottes wiederum in richtige Bahnen zu lenken!«[39] But she was not able to finish it as she was deported as a Jew in October 1941 to the concentration-camp Litzmannstadt and was killed afterwards[40].

In a few exceptional cases we get insight in the very heart of the perception of the book. Around the world personal copies of *Mein Kampf* survived, including those of Franklin D. Roosevelt and Michail I. Kalinin. For Germany Heinrich Himmler's and Gerhard Hauptmann's copies are still accessible. Gerhard Hauptmann in 1933 worked through his copie, underlined both affirmative and refusing passages and made short comments on various pages. His copy proves that intellectuals by far didn't refuse to read the book[41]. Even more interesting are Heinrich Himmler's copies from 1925/26. He read both volumes after their publication and made numerous notes and underlinings. Besides other topics Himmler found special interest in Hitler's remarks on »Volksgesundheit« and »Rasse«[42]. But nevertheless Himmler was not an uncritical reader in these years. In his diary he summarized his impressions of the first volume of *Mein Kampf*: »Es stehen unheimlich viele Wahrheiten darin. Die ersten Kapitel über die eigene Jugend enthalten manche Schwäche.«[43]

Conclusion

To sum up, we have to leave the legend behind us that Hitler's book was an »unread bestseller.« This legend was part of the German post-war defense-strategy that the German people were seduced by Hitler. Prototypical for this strategy stands Martin Heidegger, who already in 1931 strongly advised his brother to read *Mein Kampf* as the book of a man with an extraordinary political instinct. After the war Heidegger claimed that he never read the book.[44]

So we see that dealing with the reception of *Mein Kampf* means not only dealing with an historical source, but with a current and ongoing challenge. This urges scientists to act carefully and precisely, but also persistently and consequently. It is desirable to find a combination of qualitative and quantitative descriptions, which are complementary to each other. Furthermore we always should have a close look at the motives and circumstances of the reception (or non-reception) of *Mein Kampf*, in order to avoid a restricted view, which easily could be rejected as selective and incomplete. Thus the investigation of the reception of *Mein Kampf* becomes an important contribution and extension to the overall study of National-Socialism and its aftermath until today.

HISTORY 3

Struggle with reality

The first authorized German edition of *Mein Kampf*, a totemic expression of Hitler's identity and a 'swamp of lies, distortions and innuendoes'

ANSON RABINBACH

Adolf Hitler

MEIN KAMPF
A critical edition
Edited by Christian Hartmann, Thomas Vordermayer, Othmar Plöckinger and Roman Töppel
2,000pp. Auftrag des Institut für Zeitgeschichte München – Berlin. €59.
978 3 9814052 3 1

Volker Ullrich

HITLER
Volume I: Ascent 1889–1939
Translated by Jefferson Chase
1,008pp. Bodley Head. £30.
978 1 84792 285 4

On October 29, 1945, the Allied Control Council in Germany issued a decree dissolving the organizations of the National Socialist Party including its leading press agency and publishing house, the Franz Eher Nachfolger GmbH. Since the headquarters of the firm was in Munich, the property of the Eher Verlag was transferred to the Free State of Bavaria, which also assumed legal succession and trusteeship of its assets. A provisional court in Munich (Spruchkammer) initiated criminal proceedings against Max Amann, who had amassed a considerable fortune as the head of Nazi Germany's largest publishing enterprise, sentencing him to ten years imprisonment. In 1948, all copyrights were transferred to the Bavarian State Ministry of Finance, including the copyright to *Mein Kampf*, which belonged to the literary estate of Adolf Hitler. Since German copyright law stipulates that all rights revert to the public domain seventy years after the death of the author, the copyright to *Mein Kampf* expired on December 31, 2015. *Mein Kampf* was never actually banned in the Federal Republic of Germany; it was sold in second-hand bookshops, was obtainable in libraries, and in recent years has been readily available on the internet. Only the publication of the book was proscribed.

In 2010, as the expiry date approached, the Bavarian government sanctioned and contributed half a million euros for a critical and scholarly edition painstakingly prepared by the venerable Institute for Contemporary History (IfZ) in Munich. However, in 2013, protests by members of the Central Council of Jews in Germany gave the Bavarian government pause; how could it ban neo-Nazi rallies and at the same time underwrite Hitler's "bible"? The Institute assured the nervous politicians that the IfZ and not the state of Bavaria bore sole responsibility for the critical edition. Consequently, only this edition can be legally published and disseminated in Germany. All competing editions are banned under a law proscribing "popular incitement". The Bavarian justice minister, Wolfgang Bausback, insisted "that we will continue to do everything we can to prevent the dissemination of this inhuman collection of ideas". Yet this arrangement has not yet been challenged in the courts and a right-wing Leipzig publisher has already tested the waters by producing a facsimile of a 1943 edition.

The heft and price of the new *Mein Kampf* is the best guarantee that it will not become a must-read in racist and extreme nationalist circles. The initial print run of 4,000 copies sold out in days, however, with 15,000 subscribers still awaiting delivery. Sales reached 14,000, securing it a second place on *Der Spiegel*'s bestseller list. In other words, *Mein Kampf*, so long out of print, has become a celebrity book, eagerly acquired by bibliophiles and comparable to prestige editions of Shakespeare or historical-critical editions of the *Leitfiguren* of the German intellectual pantheon. Released from the poison cabinet, *Mein Kampf* has become a desirable commodity.

The critical edition is a sober affair, comprising nearly 2,000 pages with over 3,700 notes in two imposing large-format volumes. The interlaced annotations by a first-rate research team are in reality a second book. The purpose, the Institute's Director, Andreas Wirsching, writes in the foreword, is the "demystification" of "the most comprehensive and in a sense the most intimate testimony of a dictator whose policies and whose crimes completely changed the world". The annotations doggedly track Hitler's biographical elisions, document his sources, correct his countless factual errors, and puncture his exaggerations. Flagging up scores of malapropisms, the editors dissect *Mein Kampf*'s style with a nod to Victor Klemperer's brilliant reflections on the positive connotation given to words like "ruthless", "brutal", and "fanatical", in his famous *LTI: The language of the Third Reich* (1947).

Scholarly diligence aside, the edition is also intended for a broad public. Hitler's book, Wirsching notes, is a symbol that appeals to emotions. Therefore the editors have adopted a mode of presentation designed to "break through" and "end the potential effect of this symbol for all time". Moreover, since *Mein Kampf* was conceived and promoted as prognostication and prophecy, it inevitably raises the question: was it a "draft of what he later did?" To what extent did *Mein Kampf* prefigure and anticipate Hitler's Third Reich and its crimes? To measure the text by its actual effects, they emphasize, is "precisely the aim of this edition with its commentary". If not entirely at cross-purposes, scholarly scruples and political intentions are not entirely compatible. Can a mythologized symbol be neutralized by a phalanx of annotations, however erudite? Can Hitler's typical diatribes on how Jews are the "great masters as liars" be demystified with a long commentary on Arthur Schopenhauer and his appropriation by Dietrich Eckart in 1918? As the Hitler biographer Peter Longerich has observed, the method of "surrounding the text with an army of footnotes that would stand watch like a sentinel over the scandalous writ" is only partially realizable. It can also be argued that the annotations – often more than twice as long as the passages they refer to – dignify Hitler's "world view" by embedding his anti-Semitic clichés in well-established intellectual traditions, however perverse they may have been.

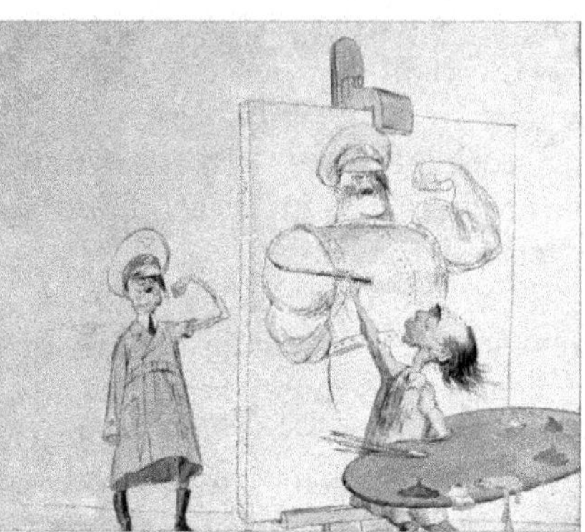

"Es wird nichts so heiss gegessen, wie es gekocht wird", 1941 ("It looks bad, but it'll be all right in the end"), by Kukryniksy (M. W. Kupriyanov, P. N. Krylov and Nikolai A. Sokolov)

As is well known, *Mein Kampf* was initially composed in 1923–4 during the nine months Hitler spent in Landsberg prison serving his reduced (from five years) sentence for high treason. Contrary to popular myth, the first version was not dictated but typed. Prison authorities observed him working diligently on the manuscript for several hours each day. Hitler had already outlined some of its main themes in a series of newspaper articles and accumulated a substantial library supplied by a parade of admiring visitors. He later called Landsberg my "university at state expense". The editors, however, give the unmatriculated Hitler low marks, calling *Mein Kampf* a "swamp of lies, distortions, innuendoes, half-truths and real facts". A typical example is Hitler's claim that during the Weimar Republic "no one" took any interest in the war guilt clause in the Versailles Treaty whereas, from 1918 on, German governments expended considerable resources to refute the accusation.

Anticipating its imminent completion – the original title was "4½ Years of Struggle, Against Stupidity and Cowardice" – the Eher Verlag announced its publication in June 1924. But Hitler failed to keep to successive deadlines, a difficulty compounded by the conditions of his probation and the Bavarian government's ban on the NSDAP and his public utterances. It finally appeared in July 1925 as *Mein Kampf: A reckoning*, the first of two volumes. In all likelihood, the more aggressive title was dropped so as not to endanger Hitler's efforts to lift the ban on his public appearances. The second and more programmatic volume, prepared in his Obersalzburg retreat with the aid of a secretary, followed in December 1926. Until the electoral breakthrough of the National Socialist Party in September 1930, *Mein Kampf* registered lacklustre sales. A 1930 popular edition (*Volksausgabe*) combining the two volumes then went through multiple printings, reaching a total of 12.4 million copies by 1944.

Mein Kampf was neither ignored nor was it merely decorative, as the myth of the book would later have it. It was rarely quoted and apart from minor alterations it remained largely unchanged over the years. Tellingly, there were no authorized abridged versions or compendia of its most quotable passages. Albrecht Koschorke usefully identified the tension between the book as content and as gesture, between intellectual incoherence and its status as the symbolic artefact of the Führer cult. As the totemic expression of the identity of thought

TLS SEPTEMBER 16 2016

and person, of Hitler's singular path to racial and national awakening, its authority was ritualistic, immune to any demystifying critique of its content. In short, it never became the canonical statement of National Socialist doctrine. It was more suitable and more profitable as a present, for example, the "Marriage Edition" given at civil ceremonies to all newly wed couples at state expense. Nonetheless, in his new biography, Volker Ullrich rightly observes that "it must be assumed that convinced National Socialists read at least major parts of it", and the fact that it was borrowed frequently from libraries also speaks to a genuine popular interest.

To call *Mein Kampf* "an unusually egocentric book", as do the IfZ editors, is an understatement. It is worth recalling that its author, who subsequently gave his profession as "political writer", was, at the time, a washed-up local demagogue who led a disastrous *coup d'état* and landed in jail. *Mein Kampf* turns this dismal state of affairs into the story of a "great historical personality", a great theorist, organizer and leader – Hitler remarks on the rarity of this combination – capable of moving the masses.

As a life story, *Mein Kampf* is "highly selective", relying on categories like "fate" and "destiny" to explain the peripatetic career of the young Hitler. As the editors point out, there is little truth in Hitler's self-description as the impoverished, "unrecognized genius" who, as in the classical German novel of self-discovery, emerges from a "struggle within his soul". In fact, it is unlikely that Hitler was actually poor, a labourer, ever read a novel, or underwent a political conversion in Vienna. Though cursorily discussed – perhaps because of his ambiguous status as an Austrian citizen in the German army – his wartime experience as a decorated soldier and his stint as a military education officer in the tumultuous political atmosphere of post-war Munich were far more decisive. In a revealing allusion to Ernst Jünger's *Battle as Inner Experience* (1922), Hitler recalled the war as "his greatest inner experience". In 1926, he wrote to Jünger to tell him that "he had read all of his works".

Though not exactly exploring uncharted territory, the editors provide an illuminating excavation of the political context and sources of what Hitler called his "profession of political faith". *Mein Kampf* took shape as Hitler was engaged in a struggle for supremacy with his political rivals in Munich's right-wing *völkisch* camp. There he met his earliest ideological mentors, Dietrich Eckart, Gottfried Feder and Wilhelm Frick, all of whom confirmed his unshakeable conviction that a "world view is never able to coexist with any other".

Although only a handful of manuscript pages exist and since references are largely absent, the sources for Hitler's "wisdom" cannot, with one or two exceptions, be entirely authenticated. Among those, most important is Feder's *The German State on National and Social Foundations* (1923), for which Hitler wrote a foreword, calling it the "catechism" of the National Socialist movement. Hitler also drew heavily on Alfred Rosenberg's writings – he chose Rosenberg to replace him as party leader during his incarceration – especially his *Traces of the Jews through the Ages* (1920) with its emphasis on the destructive role of Jewish financiers. He borrowed liberally from the "classical" authors of the *völkisch*-nationalist milieu – Houston Stewart Chamberlain, Heinrich Class, Theodor Fritsch, Julius Langbehn, Paul de Lagarde – though without acknowledgement. Henry Ford's *The International Jew: The world's foremost problem* (1920), the editors emphasize, exerted a formative influence on the intellectual world of National Socialism in the early 1920s. Hitler called Ford an "inspiration" and kept his photograph above his desk.

Mein Kampf, however, cannot simply be reduced to Hitler's influences before 1933, nor indeed to the circumstances of its composition in 1924. The editors demonstrate that Hitler's intellectual universe comprised four basic ideas: space, race, violence and dictatorship. A healthy, life-sustaining natural relationship between the size and growth of the population and the size and productivity of its territory, Hitler repeatedly insists, is the core principle of geopolitics. All future wars will be a struggle for existence in which humanitarian considerations are inconsequential. Whether Hitler actually envisioned such a war to revise the hated Versailles order remains, the editors remark, "mostly unclear or undeveloped". Not so, his ruminations on racial eugenics and, even more so, his anti-Semitism: "The Jewish race is everywhere and at all times the incarnation of evil". Here the rhetoric of extermination and elimination is abundant. The "astonishing" parallels between Hitler's early text and his subsequent politics are not confined to his anti-Semitism. The 1933 "Law for the Protection against Hereditarily Diseased Offspring", resulting in the compulsory sterilization of some 400,000 people, is directly prefigured in Hitler's insistence that the state employ "the most modern methods" against those determined to be "incapable of procreation".

The critical edition of *Mein Kampf* does not offer new insights into Hitler's character, a theme which is at the centre of Volker Ullrich's massive three-volume (two have already appeared in German) biography. Ullrich justifies his undertaking on the grounds that previous Hitler biographers have been naive, accepting at face value his apparent lack of an inner life. Ian Kershaw, for example, noted "the emptiness of [Hitler's] existence outside the realm of politics". Rather than accept this self-styled image, Ullrich argues that "we need to look behind the curtain that separated Hitler's public persona and role from the human being". Hitler, Ullrich argues, was not only a gifted orator. He was also "an extraordinarily talented actor". He once called himself "the greatest actor in Europe", and had "an undeniable ability to don different masks to suit various occasions and to inhabit changing roles". This flexibility in drawing on a wide repertoire of roles accounts for the perplexing and contradictory personae that his acquaintances and intimates later remarked on. At the same time, Ullrich insists that he never wavered from the ideological fixations that he had adopted in the early 1920s. First and foremost in this outlook was his fanatical anti-Semitism, which saw the removal of Jews from German society as an absolute necessity. "Indeed, in *Mein Kampf* Hitler had spelled out with exemplary clarity everything he intended to do if he was ever given power." The temptation to see *Mein Kampf* as a blueprint for Nazi policies is a scholarly quagmire that unwittingly affirms Hitler's claim to have been a prophet. This sort of judgement is wisely tempered by the editors of the critical edition: "It would be much too simple to construct a direct road to Auschwitz from Hitler's hateful sermons. But it would be even more problematic to simply ignore such a connection".

NOTES

Introduction

1 Erik Kirschbaum, "German Republication of Hitler's 'Mein Kampf' Causes Furor," *Los Angeles Times*, https://www.latimes.com/world/europe/la-fg-german-republication-of-fuhrer-s-manifesto-causes-furor-20151231-story.html (accessed June 27, 2020).

2 Ibid.

3 Joachim Fest, *Hitler* (New York: Harcourt Brace Jovanovich, 1973), 293.

4 Peter Beyersdorf, *Hitlers "Mein Kampf." Anspruch und Wirklichkeit* (Hollfeld (Ofr.), Beyer, 1974), 96.

5 Dietrich Schwanitz, *Bildung. Alles, was man wissen muß* (Goldmann, 2002), 510.

6 Introduction, Christian Hartmann, Thomas Vordermayer, Othmar Plöckinger and Roman Töppel, *Hitler, Mein Kampf: Eine kritische Edition*, Vol. I (Munich/Berlin: Institute for Contemporary History, 2016), 21.

7 Ibid., 26.

8 Joseph Goebbels, *Die Tagebücher von Joseph Goebbels*, Part I, Volume 2/1, ed. Elke Fröhlich, Anne Munding, Angela Hermann, and Jana Richter (Munich/New York: K. G. Sauer, 1998), 403. While generally panning Hitler's prose style, the editors of the new edition of *Mein Kampf* point out that it "at least partially corresponded to the public taste" of his times. The "literary pope" of folk-national circles, Adolf Bartels, acclaimed both volumes of *Mein Kampf* as an instant classic of right-wing literature, a work originating "from the great depths of the people" that he found "personally captivating." "Introduction," *Hitler, Mein Kampf*, 21, fn. 79.

9 An interesting exception to this generalization is Ian Kershaw, who wrote in his biography of Hitler that he conceived his hatred for the Jews during his Vienna years. Ian Kershaw, *Hitler: Hubris* (New York/London: W. W. Norton & Co., 1998), 66–7.

10 "Introduction," *Hitler, Mein Kampf*, 49.

11 Victor Klemperer, *LTI: Notizbuch eines Philologen* (Stuttgart 2010), 34.

12 Quoted in Roman Töppel, "9 November 1923: Der Hitlerputsch, *Mein Kampf*, und die Verschärfung von Hitlers Judenhass," *Medaon* 12 (2018): 10.

13 Ibid.

14 SS chief Heinrich Himmler had *Mein Kampf* taught in the SS Junker schools, which trained Waffen-SS cadets, as the "foundation of the national socialist world view." Ibid., 11.

Chapter 1

1 This chapter is based on several interviews and discussions between the author and her husband conducted from May 2010 to March 2019 with Werner Hemmrich, the son of the prison guard Franz Hemmrich. Franz Hemmrich met Adolf Hitler for the first time after his admission on November 11, 1923, to the Landsberg prison. Werner Hemmrich has dealt intensively with the history of his father. He partly published the results in the *Landsberger Geschichtsblätter*, a local journal.

2 See Franz Maciejewski, "100 Jahre Ratlosigkeit: Ein deutsches Nachdenken im Schatten des Großen Krieges," *Lettre International* 1122 (Fall 2018): 6.

3 See Birgit Schneider, "Revolution 1918/1919," in *Landsberg in der Zeitgeschichte, Zeitgeschichte in Landsberg* (München: Verlag Ernst Vögel, 2010), 69–70.

4 Ibid., 62–73.

5 Ibid., 83.

6 During the day Count Arco worked on the estate of the Dominican nuns. Franz Hemmrich accompanied him through the city and picked him up in the evening.

7 Schneider, "Revolution 1918/1919," 83.

8 See "Schehle Chronik," Dießen, Lake Ammersee. The chronicle from the period of National Socialism until 1938 is still kept under lock and key by the municipality of Dießen. The author was allowed to read them in 2013.

9 See Karl Filser, "Die Stadt unter nationalsozialistischer Herrschaft," in *Landsberg in der Zeitgeschichte, Zeitgeschichte in Landsberg*, 195.

10 Ibid, 246–9.

11 See Anton Lichtenstern, *Landsberg am Lech, Geschichte und Kultur* (Mering: Holzheu Verlag, 2012), 201.

12 See Father Karl Morgenschweis's unpublished manuscript for German newspapers composed in 1958. The author has a copy in her private archive.

13 See Norbert Frei, *Vergangenheitspolitik, Die Anfänge der Bundesrepublik und die NS-Vergangenheit*, 2nd ed. (München: Verlag C.H. Beck, 1997), 212–23.

Chapter 2

1 At the time, he was *Volksbeauftragter für Heer und Marine* (People's Representative for Army and Navy).

2 Even Dietrich Eckart published his revolution memoirs in a series of articles in 1919 (cf. Othmar Plöckinger, *Unter Soldaten und Agitatoren. Hitlers prägende Jahre im deutschen Militär 1918–1920* [Paderborn: Ferdinand Schöningh, 2013], 265–6).

3 See the full text of the review in Othmar Plöckinger, ed., *Quellen und Dokumente zur Geschichte von "Mein Kampf" 1924–1945* (Stuttgart, Steiner 2016), 210–15.

4 At least, this tribute to the author and journalist Eckart, who died in December 1923, was originally planned for the end of the first volume, but due to the restructuring of the book in spring 1925, it finally was postponed to the end of the second volume.

5 The term "*völkish*" is a complex concept and describes an ideological attitude based on racism, Germanic mythology, and anti-Semitism combined with various other ideological and political elements like antimodernism, neo-paganism, and even vegetarianism. Therefore, the *völkische Bewegung* (*völkish* movement) was not a monolithic block but highly differentiated and its sections were often in fierce conflict with each other.

6 The extent and nature of Hitler's anti-Semitism in his early life have been debated for a long time. Although we may assume that he adopted the widespread Catholic-influenced anti-Semitism in Vienna, there is no evidence that he went beyond conventional anti-Semitic ideas before 1919 (cf. Brigitte Hamann, *Hitlers Wien. Lehrjahre eines Diktators*, 2nd ed. (München/Zürich: Piper, 1996), 333–6; Thomas Weber, *Hitlers erster Krieg. Der Gefreite Hitler im Weltkrieg—Mythos und Wahrheit* (Berlin: Propyläen, 2010), 15–17).

7 For the history and the content of the so-called Gemlich-Letter, see Othmar Plöckinger, *Unter Soldaten und Agitatoren. Hitlers prägende Jahre im deutschen Militär 1918-1920* (Paderborn: Ferdinand Schöningh, 2013), 326–41. It was named after the recipient of the letter, Adolf Gemlich in Ulm (Baden-Wuerttemberg), who, like Hitler, took part in an anti-Bolshevik training program of the *Reichswehr*, the newly formed German army.

8 Cf. Ralf Georg Reuth, *Hitlers Judenhass. Klischee und Wirklichkeit* (München: Piper, 2009), 153–91; Plöckinger, *Soldaten*, 218–48.

9 Formally Hitler didn't change his military affiliation as he still was an Austrian citizen for whom joining the new German army was forbidden (cf. Plöckinger, *Soldaten*, 161).

10 Cf. Plöckinger, *Soldaten*, 178. In *Mein Kampf* Hitler claimed that he gave many speeches in front of various troops, an assertion for which there is no evidence (cf. Plöckinger, *Soldaten*, 173).

11 The party was initially founded as DAP (*Deutsche Arbeiterpartei*—German Workers' Party). The much discussed term "National Socialist" was introduced in spring 1920. Nevertheless, throughout this chapter the party will be referred to as the NSDAP.

12 Cf. Plöckinger, *Soldaten*, 17, 218–48.

13 Cf. Plöckinger, *Soldaten*, 318–19. In *Mein Kampf*, Hitler mentioned *The Protocols* only once, which is minimal in comparison with Nazis like Alfred Rosenberg, Julius Streicher, and others. Cf. Hartmann, *Hitler, Mein Kampf*, 799. (Hereafter, all citations to the critical edition will be abbreviated as "MKI" or "MKII"). The first edition was published under the title *Die Geheimnisse der Weisen von Zion* (*The Secrets of the Elders of Zion*). Cf. Wolfgang Benz, ed., *Handbuch des Antisemitismus: Judenfeindschaft in Geschichte und Gegenwart* 8 (Berlin: De Gruyter Saur, 2008), 6: 552–4.

14 The full name of the publishing house was *Franz Eher Nachf*, but usually it is referred to as *Eher-Verlag*.

15 Cf. Weber, *Presse*, 30–5.

16 *Das deutsche Buch* (1924), Advertisement. All translations from German into English by the author.

17 Cf. Plöckinger, *Quellen*, 26–7.

18 The *Tat-Mythos* (Deed-Myth) was, besides the *Opfer-Mythos* (Victim-Myth), one of the most important features of *völkish* self-perception. As Alfred Rosenberg put it: "Only through the deed do we learn to recognize ourselves." (*Auf gut deutsch*, April 4, 1919). In this respect even *völkish* and conservative critics of Hitler conceded that by the time of his putsch he had done something commendable and unique (cf. *Gewissen*, April 7, 1924).

19 Cf. Thomas Tavernaro, *Der Verlag Hitlers und der NSDAP: Die Franz Eher Nachfolger GmbH* (Vienna: Edition Praesens, 2004), 27–30.

20 Cf. Ernst Piper, *Alfred Rosenberg. Hitlers Chefideologe* (München: Blessing, 2005), 76–81; Volker Ullrich, *Adolf Hitler. Biographie*. vol 1. *Die Jahre des Aufstiegs 18891939* (Frankfurt am Main: S. Fischer, 2013), 124–6; Peter Longerich, *Hitler. Biographie* (München: Siedler, 2015), 77.

21 Of course this approach came to an end in the late 1920s when open ideological discussions were no longer possible within the evolving *Führer-Partei* (leader party). Especially the long-lasting question about a more socialistic or more nationalistic orientation of the party ended with the withdrawal of left-wing members. Otto Strasser, a leading figure among the Nazi left and brother of Gregor Strasser, in 1930 proclaimed the slogan: "The socialists are leaving the party!" (cf. Longerich, *Hitler*, 213–14).

22 Cf. Wiebke Wiede, *Rasse im Buch. Antisemitische und rassistische Publikationen in Verlagsprogrammen der Weimarer Republik* (München: Oldenbourg, 2011), 1–4.

23 *Das Deutsche Buch. Vierter Bericht* (Leipzig: [without publishing house], 1924), preface.

24 Cf. Justus H. Ulbricht, "Agenturen der, Deutschen Wiedergeburt'. Prolegomena zu einer Geschichte völkischer Verlagsarbeit in der Weimarer Republik," 235–44, in: Schmitz, Walter, and Clemens Vollnhals, eds., *Völkische Bewegung—Konservative Revolution—Nationalsozialismus. Aspekte einer politisierten Kultur* (Dresden: Thelem, 2005), 235–40.

25 Cf. Ulbricht, *Publizistik*, 131–6.

26 After 1933, Ernst Boepple had different state posts in cultural fields. After 1939, he was state secretary in Poland and as second deputy of Hans Frank, one of the main culprits of the Holocaust in Poland (cf. Benz, Wolfgang, and Graml, Hermann, and Weiß, Hermann eds. *Enzyklopädie des Nationalsozialismus*, 3rd ed. (Stuttgart: Klett-Cotta, 1998), 824). His *Volksverlag* was not a branch of the *Lehmann-Verlag*, as often stated (cf. Wiede, *Rasse*, 206).

27 Cf. Timothy W. Ryback, *Hitlers Bücher. Seine Bibliothek. Sein Denken* (Köln: Fackelträger, 2010), 166–71.

28 Cf. Udo Kissenkoeter, *Gregor Straßer und die NSDAP*. Stuttgart: Deutsche Verlagsanstalt, 1978, 42.

29 Cf. Börsenverein des deutschen Buchhandels, ed., *Die Verlagserscheinungen des Zentralverlags der NSDAP. Franz Eher Nachf. G.M.B.H. München. Berlin. Wien. 1921-1941*. Leipzig: Börsenverein [1942], 226. By 1941 the *Eher-Verlag* had published some 3,300 books and brochures amounting to 132 million copies.

30 *CV-Zeitung*, May 26, 1922.

31 Cf. *CV-Zeitung*, May 26, 1922, and June 1, 1922. Therefore, the two articles were titled "Das Zitat als politisches Kampfmittel" (The Quote as a Political Weapon).

32 For example, in 1919 Arthur Dinter published his often-quoted book *Lichtstrahlen aus dem Talmud* (Rays of Light from the Talmud) and Alfred Rosenberg in 1920 his book *Unmoral im Talmud* (Immorality in the Talmud). A main basis for this kind of anti-Semitic propaganda was the book *Der Talmudjude* (The Talmud Jew) by August Rohling, first published in 1871 (cf. Hannelore Noack. *Unbelehrbar? Antijüdische Agitation mit entstellten Talmudzitaten. Antisemitische Aufwiegelung durch Verteufelung der Juden* [Paderborn: University Press Paderborn, 2001], 23–7, 79–82).

33 Cf. Benz, ed., *Handbuch*, vol. 2/1, 259–60, and vol. 6, 254–6; Egbert Klautke, "Theodor Fritsch. The "Godfather" of German Antisemitism," 73–88, in: Rebecca Haynes, and Martyn Rady, eds., *In the Shadow of Hitler. Personalities of the Right in Central and Eastern Europe* (London/New York: I.B. Tauris, 2011), 80–1.

34 Fritsch had previously been very skeptical about Hitler and held him responsible for the fragmentation and the numerous conflicts within the *völkish* movement (cf. Massimo Ferrari Zumbini, *Die Wurzeln des Bösen. Gründerjahre des Antisemitismus: Von der Bismarckzeit zu Hitler* (Frankfurt am Main: Vittorio Klostermann, 2003), 626–7).

35 Cf. Benz, ed., *Handbuch*, vol. 6, 257; Zumbini, *Wurzeln*, 340; Klautke, *Fritsch*, 77–8.

36 Institut für Zeitgeschichte, ed., *Hitler*, vol. VI/1, 133. cf. Plöckinger, *Soldaten*, 220.

37 Quoted in Zumbini, *Wurzeln*, 630.

38 Fritsch, ed., *Handbuch*, 13.

39 Fritsch, ed., *Handbuch*, 30.

40 In many cases there were no references to Fritsch's book, not least because several anti-Semitic quotations became a commonplace familiar to every anti-Semite. That was true, for example, for the remark about the 300 Jews who ran Germany, which had been insinuated about the Foreign Minister Walther Rathenau. He was assassinated in 1922. And it was true for the phrase of Arthur Schopenhauer that "the Jew" was the "great master of the lie," a conceit quoted by Dietrich Eckart und Hitler (cf. Dietrich Eckart, *Der Bolschewismus von Moses bis Lenin. Zwiegespräch zwischen Adolf Hitler und mir* (München: Hoheneichen, 1924), 23; MKI, 617). The situation was considerably different with *The Protocols of the Elders of Zion*. The pamphlet was often referred to as proof of the "Jewish world conspiracy", yet seldom were concrete quotations from it ever used.

41 Oddly enough, there was a kind of divergence or ideological identification feature in anti-Semitic literature in the terms used for the Jews: "Jews," "the Jew," "Juda," "Alljuda," "Alljudaan." Hitler mostly used the term "Jews/ Jew." The term "Juda" sometimes appeared in his early speeches, but in the following years he used it less and less as it had an esoteric and mysterious undertone. It cannot be found in *Mein Kampf* and also afterwards he avoids it almost completely. (Julius Streicher, for example, preferred the term "Alljuda.") Finally, the term "Alljudaan" was used to name a "hidden Jewish world-government" and/or a future Jewish state that would dominate the world and in which Germany and other states would be degraded to provinces (cf. Wilhelm Meister, *Judas Schuldbuch. Eine deutsche Abrechnung*, Deutscher Schutz- und Trutzbund, ed., 3rd/4th ed. [Munich: Deutscher Volksverlag, 1919], 117–23).

42 Cf. Plöckinger, *Soldaten*, 261. In 1940 Bang picked up the thread again in his book *Aus Englands Schuldbuch*.

43 "Wilhelm Meister" is the title-figure of a famous novel by Johann Wolfgang von Goethe.

44 Bang published many other books and pamphlets often dealing with the "enslavement of Germany" by international and/or Jewish "financial powers," the Treaty of Versailles, and various treaties in the 1920s relating to German reparation payments.

45 Cf. Uwe Lohalm, *Völkischer Radikalismus. Die Geschichte des Deutschvölkischen Schutz- und Trutzbundes 1919-1923* (Hamburg: Leibniz, 1970),180; Benz ed., *Handbuch*, vol. 2/1, 48–9.

46 Cf. *Münchener Beobachter*, June 21, 1919; *Die Republik*, March 8, 1920; *Völkischer Beobachter*, April 10, 1920; Ino Arndt, *Die Judenfrage in der evangelischen Sonntagspresse* (Doctoral dissertation, University of Tübingen, 1960), 17.

47 Cf. NSDAP-Kassenbuch, Bundesarchiv (Federal Archive) Berlin, NS 26/229.

48 Cf. Heß, ed., *Briefe*, 259. Heinrich Himmler read the book in 1922 (cf. Peter Longerich, *Heinrich Himmler*. Biographie (Munich: Siedler, 2008), 66).

49 Meister, *Schuldbuch*, 15.

50 Meister, *Schuldbuch*, 173.

51 Cf. *Allgemeine Zeitung des Judenthums*, March 5, 1920, 111; *Im deutschen Reich*, May 1920, 151. *Judas Schuldbuch* was called the "most hateful and stupid book of recent times" (*Ost und West. Illustrierte Monatsschrift für das gesamte Judentum*, January–February 1920, 32).

52 Alfred Rosenberg published in 1922 his book *Das Verbrechen der Freimaurerei. Judentum, Jesuitismus, deutsches Christentum* (*The Crime of Freemasonry. Judaism, Jesuitism, German Christianity*) in the publishing house of Julius Lehmann, and Erich Ludendorff in 1927 his brochure *Vernichtung der Freimaurerei durch Enthüllung ihrer Geheimnisse* (*Destruction of the Freemasons by Revealing Their Secrets*) as self-publisher.

53 Cf. Markner, *Wichtl*, 334.

54 *Wiener Morgenzeitung*, August 2, 1921. In 1925, the *CV-Zeitung* published a comprehensive discussion of the book in order to refute the claim that the Freemasons were dominated by Jews (cf. *CV-Zeitung*, February 20, 1925).

55 The book was expanded several times and revised, and in their various forewords Wichtl refers to Freemason Lodges. The book was republished three times after 1933 as well; the last edition was in 1943. Inside the SS, Wichtl was seen as the "teacher in the fight against Freemasonry" (cf. Reinhard Markner, "Friedrich Wichtl (1872-1921)," In *Handbuch der Verschwörungstheorien*, edited by Helmut Reinalter, 334–7. Leipzig: Salier, 2018, 334).

56 Cf. *Münchener Beobachter*, March 15, 1919; *Auf gut deutsch*, March 28, 1919; *Völkischer Beobachter*, December 18, 1919. Even the leading nationalistic newspaper *Deutsche Zeitung* (German Newspaper) published a comprehensive multipart review (cf. *Deutsche Zeitung*, July 31, 1919 [Morgen-Ausgabe] and following).

57 Cf. Plöckinger, *Soldaten*, 302–3.

58 Quoted in Longerich, *Himmler*, 36. It remains unclear whether Himmler referred to the Freemasons or the Jews or both.

59 Copy in Bayerische Staatsbibliothek (Bavarian State Library) Munich, Einbl. XI, 597. The leaflet should not be confused with Drexler's brochure from 1919 (discussed later).

60 Cf. Lohalm, *Radikalismus*, 257; Plöckinger, *Soldaten*, 302–3; Markner, *Wichtl*, 336.

61 Quoted in Plöckinger, *Soldaten*, 303.

62 Friedrich Wichtl, *Weltfreimaurerei, Weltrevolution, Weltrepublik. Eine Untersuchung über Ursprung und Endziele des Weltkriegs*. 7. Aufl. (München: Lehmann, 1920), 255.

63 Cf. Wichtl, *Weltfreimaurerei*, 252–4.

64 Cf. Ullrich, *Hitler*, vol. 1, 128–33; Longerich, *Hitler*, 98–102.

65 Cf. Lohalm, *Radikalismus*, 132–4.

66 Cf. Longerich, *Hitler*, 112–13.

67 Unfortunately, the books of the library were split up among different locations of the Bavarian police library, which were later themselves dissolved. However,

the items of the party library can be reconstructed from the inventory lists created by the police in 1923 (cf. Bayerisches Staatsarchiv [Bavarian State Archive] Munich, Pol. Dir. 6721); Eberhard Jäckel and Axel Kuhn, eds., *Hitler, Sämtliche Aufzeichnungen. 1905-1924* (Stuttgart: Deutsche Verlags-Anstalt, 1980), 518.

68 Rosenberg, *Wesen*, 11.

69 Cf. MKI, 589–91. In some respect Drexler's book was a kind of *Mein Kampf* in miniature (cf. Reignald Phelps, *Anton Drexler—Der Gründer der NSDAP.*, in: Deutsche Rundschau, vol. 87 [December 1961], No. 12, 1135).

70 Anton Drexler, *Mein politisches Erwachen. Aus dem Tagebuch eines deutschen sozialistischen Arbeiters*. 3rd ed. (München: Deutscher Volksverlag, 1923), 51.

71 Cf. Plöckinger, *Feder*, 498–506; see previous discussion.

72 Quoted in Plöckinger, *Geschichte*, 18. Due to political developments and his imprisonment, Hitler did not write the originally planned preface to Feder's book. It therefore remained with a short dedication, which Feder later gladly used, often for advertising purposes (cf. Plöckinger, *Feder*, 514–5).

73 Strangely enough, the publishing house hoped that Hitler would complete the unfinished text after his release from prison (see note of the *Hoheneichen-Verlag* from March 1924 in Eckart, *Bolschewismus*, 50). Quite untypically for this kind of literature, Eckart used endnotes. Almost 150 of them were intended to create the image of a scientific basis for his pamphlet. This method stands in sharp contrast to Hitler, who hardly ever mentioned a concrete source in his speeches and writings, including in *Mein Kampf*.

74 Quoted in Plöckinger, *Quellen*, 198. The review in this newspaper was extremely unpleasant for Hitler as it was taken up and quoted by many others, especially left-wing and liberal newspapers. Hitler was so impressed with the review that he referred to it in the second volume of *Mein Kampf* (cf. MKII, 1191; Plöckinger, *Quellen*, 196–7).

75 Cf. MKI, 488–92, with reference to chapter 6, "War Propaganda," Manheim 176 ff.

76 Cf. Plöckinger, *Soldaten*, 334 f. Jungcurt, *Extremismus*, 47–8. Class's book itself again was strongly influenced by writings of the nineteenth century, in which numerous demands were made that Class also reproduced.

77 Cf. Plöckinger, *Soldaten*, 338.

78 Bayerisches Staatsarchiv (Bavarian State Archive), MInn, 66282.

79 Bry, whose real name was Carl Decke, in 1921 joined the NSDAP and even worked for the *Völkische Beobachter* for a short time. He left the party after the putsch in 1923 and became a conservative critic of the party. He died in 1926 (cf. Hastings, *Catholicism*, 163; Stefan Keppler-Tasaki, *Hans Heinrich Ehrler (1872–1951). Biografie eines Abendländers* (Wien/Köln/Weimar: Böhlau, 2018), 150–1). Die *Jungkonservativen* (Young Conservatives) were a nationalistic movement settled between *völkish*, revolutionary, and conservative attitudes. One of their leading figures was Arthur Moeller van den Bruck, who published in 1923 his famous book *The Third Reich* and

committed suicide in 1925 (cf. André Schlüter, *Moeller van den Bruck. Leben und Werk* [Köln/Weimar/Wien: Böhlau, 2010], 347–64).

80 Carl Christian Bry, *Verkappte Religionen* (Gotha: Leopold Klotz, 1924), 105.

81 It was the magazine of the *Verein zur Abwehr des Antisemitismus* (cf. Plöckinger, *Quellen*, 228).

82 Quoted in Plöckinger, *Quellen*, 238.

Chapter 3

1 The following overview is a combination of lectures I gave on these topics from 2013 to 2019 and an abridged version of a detailed new analysis of the founding years of the Institute, which shall be published in autumn 2021 in *Aufarbeitung des Nationalsozialismus. Ein Kompendium* by Magnus Brechtken (Göttingen: Wallstein, 2021).

Important summaries on the foundation period to date are Hellmut Auerbach, "Die Gründung des Instituts für Zeitgeschichte," in *Vierteljahrshefte für Zeitgeschichte* (VfZ) 18/4 (1970): 529–54; and recently Mathew Turner, Tony Joel, and David Lowe, "'Between Politics and Scholarship': The First Decade of the Institut für Zeitgeschichte, 1949–1958," in *European History Quarterly* 49/2 (2019): 250–71. There has been substantial new material on the 1950s, which requires that the early history is presented in all its complexity anew. Examples of recent contributions include Dieter Krüger, Hans Speidel, and Ernst Jünger, *Freundschaft und Geschichtspolitik im Zeichen der Weltkriege,* edited by Zentrum für Militärgeschichte und Sozialwissenschaften der Bundeswehr (Paderborn: Ferdinand Schöningh, 2016): 185–212; Stefanie Palm, "Auf der Suche nach dem starken Staat. Die Kultur-, Medien- und Wissenschaftspolitik," in Frank Bösch and Andreas Wirsching, eds., *Hüter der Ordnung. Die Innenministerien in Bonn und Ost-Berlin nach dem Nationalsozialismus*, 2nd edition (Göttingen: Wallstein, 2018), 614–23. Klaus-Dietmar Henke, *Geheime Dienste. Die politische Inlandsspionage der Organisation Gehlen 1946-1953* (Berlin: Ch. Links, 2018), 533–77. Rick Tazelaar, *Hüter des Freistaats. Die Bayerische Staatskanzlei zwischen Nationalsozialismus und Nachkriegsdemokratie*, Phil. Diss. (Munich 2020).

2 The foundation document (*Stiftungsurkunde*) had been signed by the minister-president of Bavaria, Hans Ehard, of Hesse, Christian Stock, of Württemberg-Baden, Reinhold Maier, and the president of the Senate of Bremen, Wilhelm Kaisen; each party should have contributed 20,000 Reichsmark; Auerbach, "Die Gründung," 534.

3 The date Heinemann signed the IfZ's constitution was used as an orientation when celebrating the Institute's twenty-fifth anniversary. Director Martin Broszat wrote at the time: "The date for celebrating the Institute of Contemporary History's 25th anniversary—17 October 1975—has been chosen more or less arbitrarily. As the chronology included in this volume shows, its foundation was not a one-off act, but an arduous process that lasted several years. Only the fact that the constitution was successfully drawn up and subsequently signed by then Federal Minister of the Interior Gustav Heinemann on 8 September 1950 justifies the assumption that the Institute was founded in the autumn of 1950." Broszat, "Vorwort," in *25 Jahre Institut für Zeitgeschichte. Statt einer Festschrift* (Stuttgart: DVA, 1975). In 1999 the Institute decided to celebrate its fiftieth anniversary, thus dating its foundation to 1949; Horst Möller and Udo Wengst, eds. *50 Jahre Institut für Zeitgeschichte. Eine Bilanz* (Munich: Oldenbourg, 1999).

4 No women were involved on the decision-making level either in the foundation process or in the development over the first decade. Helene von Bila became the first woman in the foundation's Board (*Stiftungsrat*) in 1966; Beatrice Heuser was in 2004 (!) the first woman on the Academic Advisory Board. As a fully employed researcher (*Wissenschaftliche Mitarbeiterin*), Sonja Noller was the first woman in 1960. Hildegard von Kotze started in 1962 and Ino Arndt in 1963.

5 Christiane Reuter-Boysen, "Anton Pfeiffer (1888–1957)," in *Zeitgeschichte in Lebensbildern*, Bd. 11 (2004): 124–41, here 126–8, 131.

6 Ibid., 129–30.

7 Rainer Pommerin, "Die Mitglieder des Parlamentarischen Rates. Porträtskizzen des britischen Verbindungsoffiziers Chaput de Saintonge," in *VfZ* 36/3 (1988): 578.

8 Ibid.

9 "Kroll is a fanatic whose chief topic of conversation is the simple majority electoral system. He also has a great admiration, however, for the British institutions and was continually in search of information and printed matter concerning British methods. Although his English is not fluent, he has on one occasion had sufficient courage to speak in Hyde Park." Pommerin, "Die Mitglieder," 573.

10 Some exemplary books which provide context include Bernd Faulenbach, *Ideologie des deutschen Weges. Die deutsche Geschichte in der Historiographie zwischen Kaiserreich und Nationalsozialismus* (München: Beck, 1980); Ulrich Heinemann, *Die verdrängte Niederlage. Politische Öffentlichkeit und Kriegsschuldfrage in der Weimarer Republik* (Göttingen: Vandenhoeck & Ruprecht, 1983); Hauke Brunkhorst, *Der Intellektuelle im Land der Mandarine* (Frankfurt/Main: Suhrkamp, 1987). For a summary of the context and wider background, see Magnus Brechtken, "Geschichtswissenschaften im Nationalsozialismus—Einflüsse, Personen, Folgen," *Archivalische Zeitschrift* 96 (2019): 255–76.

11 "Die Amerikaner sagten sich 1947, daß es für ihre deutschen Demokratie-Zöglinge nützlich sein würde, die Hitlersche Politik auf den wissenschaftlichen Seziertisch zu legen. Wohlwollendes Echo aus deutschen Fachkreisen." "Alles Papier zum Thema NS. Hitler auf dem Seziertisch," *Der Spiegel* 17/1949, April 23, 1949, 8.

12 "Alles Papier zum Thema NS. Hitler auf dem Seziertisch," *Der Spiegel* 17/1949, April 23, 1949, 8.

13 James A. Clark, Director ICD (Information Control Division) to Secretary of State Dieter Sattler 29th April 1948, *Akten der Bayerischen Staatskanzlei*; quoted in Auerbach, "Die Gründung," 536.

14 IfZ Archive ID1-1-29-30, Charles D. Winning, Division Director to Fritz Baer, Ministerialrat, Office of the minister president, Bavaria, November 30, 1948 (with translation).

15 When the Institute was established, it received general support but was also watched closely about the way it dealt with the past. In 1951, the American High Commissioner John McCloy advised that "all possible assistance be extended [to] the German Institute for the History of the National Socialist period [. . .] to enable it to gain access to the material it requires"; Glenn C. Wolfe, Director, Office of Administration, HICOG, Staff Announcement Nr. 199, 5.VI.1951, in Library of Congress Central File Box 398, quoted in Astrid Eckert, *Kampf um die* Akten. *Die Westalliierten und die Rückgabe von deutschem Archivgut nach dem Zweiten Weltkrieg* (Stuttgart: Franz Steiner, 2004), 406 (*Struggle for the Files: The Western Allies and the Return of Archives after the Second World War* [Cambridge: Cambridge University Press, 2012]). One result of this support was that Hermann Mau could visit the United States from June 6 to July 25, 1951; see further for more context.

16 One further example is the role of Freiburg historian Gerhard Ritter, who is described as having the best of chances to become the decisive academic leader of the institution ("alle Chancen, federführender Vorstand zu werden"). Ritter himself may have claimed such chances, and perhaps he was the source of these formulations. But neither in 1949 nor later was he regarded as being in such a position by those who had the power of deciding about such role, that is, the members of the *Kuratorium* and particularly its leading representatives from Bavaria and Hesse.

17 Gerhard Ritter, *Europa und die deutsche Frage* (Munich: Münchner Verlag, 1948).

18 Ibid., 199. Cf. Christoph Cornelißen, *Gerhard Ritter. Geschichtswissenschaft und Politik im 20. Jahrhundert* (Düsseldorf: Droste, 2001), 492.

19 Gerhard Ritter, "The Historical Foundations of the Rise of National-Socialism," *in The Third Reich. A Study Published under the Auspices of the International Council for Philosophy and Humanistic Studies with the Assistance of UNESCO* (New York: Weidenfeld & Nicholson, 1955), 381. Ritter had presented this text, an abbreviated version of which was also published in German and Italian, in Arhus on May 10, 1951, completing it in June 1951. See also Cornelißen, *Ritter*, 525, n. 13, referring to BAK N1166/337, letter from Ritter to Maurice Baumont, June 22, 1951; manuscript in BAK N1166/252.

20 Geoffrey Barraclough, *Times Literary Supplement,* April 14, 1950.

21 Gerhard Ritter, "Gegenwärtige Lage und Zukunftsaufgaben deutscher Geschichtswissenschaft. Eröffnungsvortrag des 20. Deutschen Historikertages in München am 12. September 1949," in *Historische Zeitschrift* 170 (1950): 19.

22 Franz Schnabel, cited in Horst Möller, "Das Institut für Zeitgeschichte und die Entwicklung der Zeitgeschichtsschreibung in Deutschland," in Horst Möller and Udo Wengst, eds., *50 Jahre Institut für Zeitgeschichte. Eine Bilanz* (Munich: Oldenbourg, 1999), 5.

23 AVHD, letter Franz Schnabel to Gerhard Ritter of July 15, 1949, cited in Cornelißen, *Ritter,* 534.

24 Cf. The stance of the diplomat Günter Henle (CDU), in Magnus Brechtken, "Mehr als Historikergeplänkel. Die Debatte um ‚Das Amt und die Vergangenheit,'" in *VfZ* 63/1 (2015): 59–91, here 67ff.

25 Hermann Lübbe, "Der Nationalsozialismus im politischen Bewußtsein der Gegenwart," in Martin Broszat ed., *Deutschlands Weg in die Diktatur. Referate und Diskussionen. Ein Protokoll* (Berlin: Siedler, 1983), 341; also in *Historische Zeitschrift* 236 (1983): 579–99 (titled "Der Nationalsozialismus im deutschen Nachkriegsbewußtsein"); Martin Broszat, *Vom Parteigenossen zum Bundesbürger. Über beschwiegene und historisierte Vergangenheiten* (Munich: Fink, 2007), 11–38.

26 The full list of members who convened for the first time at the invitation of the Federal president Heuss on September 11, 1950, in Bad Godesberg were Philip Auerbach, Ludwig Bergsträsser, Hermann Brill, Ludwig Dehio, Konstantin von Dietze, Fritz Hartung, Ernst von Hippel, Erich Kaufmann, Eugen Kogon, Theodor Litt, Gerhard Ritter, Franz Schnabel, Hans Speidel, Bernhard Vollmer, and Wilhelm Winkler.

27 On Bergsträsser's complex career between politics and academic work, see Stephanie Zibell, *Politische Bildung und demokratische Verfassung: Ludwig Bergsträsser (1883-1960)* (Bonn: J.H. Dietz, 2006).

28 Hermann Mau, speech given at the Munich Political-Academic Club on March 12, 1952, IfZ Archive, Ms 49. A central question for all research endeavors was the accessibility of documents from the period before 1945; most of the official German material had been brought to the United States. Mau visited the United States in June and July 1951 for seven weeks to investigate the situation. He was not in any position to negotiate but to learn about the situation and collect information. His report on the journey in which he formulated the impression "that the Americans were ready in principle to return the documents" had quite the opposite effect—they made clear this was not a current question; Eckert, *Kampf um die Akten*, 412, n. 255. On these questions in general, see ibid., 408–14.

29 Despite his short tenure Mau had some impact. He authored a book on the period 1933–45 to which Helmut Krausnick added a few final chapters after Mau's death: Hermann Mau and Helmut Krausnick, *Deutsche Geschichte der jüngsten Vergangenheit 1933-1945. Mit einem Nachwort von Peter Rassow* (Tübingen and Stuttgart: J.B. Metzler, 1953). The small book of 200 pages ran through several editions (30,000 copies until 1961) and was distributed by institutions for political information like the *Bundeszentrale für Heimatdienst* and the Ministry of Defense. Mau also initiated the periodical quarterly *Vierteljahrshefte für Zeitgeschichte*, whose first volume came out in January 1953.

30 Henry Picker, *Hitlers Tischgespräche im Führerhauptquartier 1941-1942,* introduced and published by Gerhard Ritter (Bonn: Athenäum, 1951). On the background of Ritter's motivation and the consequences, see Cornelißen, *Ritter*, 538–45.

31 For a scathing but fitting contemporary comment, see Hannah Arendt, "Bei Hitler zu Tisch," in *Der Monat*, Bd. 37 (1951): 85–90. For the wider context, see Mikael Nilsson, *Hitler Redux. The Incredible History of Hitler's So-Called Table Talks* (London and New York: Routledge, 2021). On the Ritter affair in particular, 58–87. Nilsson analyzes the *Table Talks* as well as the so-called *Monologues* and shows convincingly that "the idea that the table talks contain Hitler's words as they were actually spoken to his entourage in the various military HQs" has been "conclusively disproven. The table talks are not that kind of sources, since they (. . .) were not the product of stenographic notes. Instead they were (as in the case of the nightly monologues) reconstructed entirely from memory," used additional material, and were "sometimes finished long after the date on them." In other words: the table talks are not a source about Hitler's words but a source of what the authors like Picker and Heim wanted to communicate about what they perceived as their understanding. "[T]hey are not Hitler's words" and "cannot, and should not, be quoted as such" (p. 384). Major responsibility for the fact that the public was misled over many decades lies with British historian Hugh Trevor-Roper (Lord Dacre). Nilsson shows in another article "numerous examples of how Trevor-Roper failed to tell his readers vital information about his source material that would most likely have had a negative effect on the credibility of that material, affecting both the original manuscripts' claims to authenticity and the reputation for accuracy of the translations." Trevor-Roper worked closely (and for financial reasons) with François Genoud, a Hitler fan and Nazi sympathizer who sought to influence historiography by "finding" material from the period of Hitler's reign. Trevor-Roper gained financially as an expert evaluator of Hitler documents and Genoud thus gained influence on historiography. "Trevor-Roper's handling of the Hitler diaries," which destroyed his reputation, "was not an oddity in an otherwise spotless past, but rather falls into a pattern that had been well established more than 30 years earlier." Mikael Nilsson, "Hugh Trevor-Roper and the English Editions of Hitler's Table Talk and Testament," in *Journal of Contemporary History* 51/4 (2016): 788–812.

32 The CIA named the working phases of the OG OFFSPRING (1949–50), ODEUM (1950–1), and ZIPPER (1951–6) managed them until 1956 through the "Pullach Operation Base" (POB). Cf. Mary Ellen Reese, *Der deutsche Geheimdienst. Organisation Gehlen* (Berlin: Rowohlt, 1990), 159–71; Kevin C. Ruffner (ed.), *Forging an Intelligence Partnership: CIA and the Origins of the BND, 1949-1956*, vol. 2 (Washington, D.C., 2006); Thomas Wolf, "Die Anfänge des BND. Gehlen Organisationen—Prozess, Legende und Hypothek," in: *VfZ* 64/2 (2016): 191–225.

33 Willi Winkler, "Institut für Zeitgeschichte: Alte Kameraden," *Süddeutsche Zeitung*, April 2, 2018, accessed January 23, 2021, https://www.sueddeutsche.de/kultur/institut-fuer-zeitgeschichte-alte-kameraden-1.3926474-0.

34 BND-Archiv 120002, Blatt 427–37, Wolfgang Langkau (30d), Aktennotiz über die Besprechung von Gehlen (30) mit Kroll (J -1835) am 8. Februar 1950, 10.2.1950. See for a summary and analysis: Henke, *Geheime Dienste*, 543–50.

35 Hermann Foertsch, *Schuld und Verhängnis. Die Fritsch-Krise im Frühjahr 1938 als Wendepunkt der Geschichte der nationalsozialistischen Zeit*

(Stuttgart: DVA, 1951) (*Veröffentlichungen des deutschen Instituts für die Geschichte der nationalsozialistischen Zeit,* Nr. 1). For a critical assessment of Foertsch and his book, see Sebastian Conrad, *Auf der Suche nach der verlorenen Nation. Geschichtsschreibung in Westdeutschland und Japan, 1945-1960* (Göttingen: Vandenhoeck & Ruprecht, 1999), 251–54.

36 According to the files the academic personnel included Gerhard Kroll (1949–51), Anton Hoch (1949–78) (head archivist), Alexander Schönwiese (1949–51), Armand Dehlinger (1950–1), Karl Buchheim (1950–2), Heinrich Stübel (1950–1), Hermann Mau (1951–2) (general secretary), Thilo Vogelsang (1951–78) (head librarian), and Hermann Foertsch (1951–2).

37 Krausnick became general secretary for some months after Mau's death until Paul Kluke arrived. In 1959 Krausnick became Kluke's successor and assumed the title of director in 1961.

38 Overview of German institutes in the field of contemporary history research, in *VfZ* 1 (1953): 196.

39 Register of expert reports at the IfZ.

40 For details on the discussion about the requests and the workload, see Mathew Turner, Tony Joel, and David Lowe, "Between Politics and Scholarship,"260–4.

41 *Gutachten des Instituts für Zeitgeschichte* (Munich: Selbstverlag [self-publishing], 1958).

42 Kluke, "Vorwort," in *Gutachten des Instituts für Zeitgeschichte*, Bd. I (1958): 10. A second volume with a further fifty-nine expert reports was published in 1966 with the Deutsche Verlags-Anstalt, which became the publisher for many books by the IfZ in the next two decades: *Gutachten des Instituts für Zeitgeschichte,* Bd. II (Stuttgart: DVA, 1966).

43 Kluke, "Vorwort," in *Gutachten des Instituts für Zeitgeschichte,* Bd. I (1958): 10.

44 Members of the Advisory Board objected that the reports were being self-published instead of appearing in an established institutional publication series—where they probably would have gained some higher impact. "Head of Department Hübinger expressed his regret that the forthcoming collection of expert reports, which provide an important account of the Institute's internal work, had not been included in the official series of 'Quellen und Darstellungen zur Zeitgeschichte' ('Sources and Accounts of Contemporary History'). Even though he recognised the argument of the supposedly lower cost of self-publishing, being included in the series would have had a beneficial effect on the reports' long-term impact." IfZ Archive ID 3/2, Meeting of the Advisory Board of the Institute for Contemporary History on December 3, 1957, 6. Hübinger was chair of the Advisory Board from 1954 to 1959 and a member of the scientific advisory panel from 1962 to 1979.

45 The thousandth report is dated January 29, 1959, the three thousandth July 2, 1963, that is, just over eleven hundred working days.

46 From an unpublished, typewritten self-description by the director: Helmut Krausnick, *Das Institut für Zeitgeschichte* (March 1962), 9. "As far as the Institute's *financial means* are concerned," Krausnick wrote, "in 1962 the federal subsidies will hopefully reach *300,000 D-Mark*, the state subsidies

227,000 D-Mark. Measured against the amounts of the years before 1956, which scarcely allowed the Institute to pass its test, these subsidies have risen considerably. However, measured against what is supposed to be and could be achieved, they certainly could do with being increased, indeed need to be increased!" Ibid.

47 The publisher was the Walter Verlag, Olten and Freiburg im Breisgau. See the comments by Horst Möller, "Das Institut für Zeitgeschichte 1949-2009," in Horst Möller and Udo Wengst, *60 Jahre Institut für Zeitgeschichte* (Munich: Oldenbourg, 2009), 11.

48 Hans Buchheim, Martin Broszat, Hans-Adolf Jacobsen, and Helmut Krausnick, *Anatomie des SS-Staates. Gutachten des Instituts für Zeitgeschichte*, 2 Vols. (Olten and Freiburg im Breisgau: Walter-Verlag, 1965). Vol. 1: Hans Buchheim, "Die SS—Das Herrschaftsinstrument. Befehl und Gehorsam"; Vol. 2: Martin Broszat, "Nationalsozialistische Konzentrationslager 1933-1945," 7–160; Hans-Adolf Jacobsen,"Kommissarbefehl und Massenexekutionen sowjetischer Kriegsgefangener," 161–279; Helmut Krausnick, "Judenverfolgung," 281–448; 1967 as a two-volume paperback edition in the series dtv dokumente; 2005 in 8th edition as dtv 30145 in one volume; engl.: Helmut Krausnick, Hans Buchheim, Martin Broszat, and Hans-Adolf Jacobsen, eds., *Anatomy of the SS State* (London: Granada, 1968). Buchheim was employed by the IfZ from 1951 to 1966. For a thorough analysis in the context of the Institute's history, see Mathew Turner, *Historians at the Frankfurt Auschwitz Trial. Their Role as Expert Witnesses* (London/New York: I.B. Tauris, 2018).

49 *Anatomie des SS-Staates*, Vol. 1, Preface, 1965 edition, 5.

50 Gerald Reitlinger, *Die Endlösung: Hitlers Versuch der Ausrottung der Juden Europas 1939-1945* (Berlin: Colloquium, 1956) (the English original was *The Final Solution. The Attempt to Exterminate the Jews of Europe 1939-1945* [London: Valentine, 1953]); Léon Poliakov and Josef Wulf, *Das Dritte Reich und die Juden. Dokumente und Aufsätze* (Berlin: Arani, 1955); Wolfgang Scheffler, *Judenverfolgung im Dritten Reich 1933-1945* (Berlin: Colloquium, 1960).

51 *Anatomie des SS-Staates*, Vol. 1, Preface, 1965 edition, 7ff.

52 Magnus Brechtken, "It is my intention to make this the definitive analysis of the great Jewish catastrophe." Raul Hilberg und die Entwicklung der Holocaustforschung, in *Einsicht 08. Bulletin des Fritz-Bauer-Instituts* 4 (2012): 32–7, here 36; Raul Hilberg, *The Politics of Memory. The Journey of a Holocaust Historian* (Chicago: Ivan R. Dee, 1996). For the wider context of why Hilberg's book came out in Germany as late as 1982 and the role some expert opinions by members of the IfZ played in this question, see a summary by René Schlott, "Ablehnung und Anerkennung. Raul Hilberg und das Institut für Zeitgeschichte," in *VfZ* 69/1 (2021): 85–119.

53 A list of all previous publications is available at www.ifz-muenchen.de. Articles in the quarterly journal *Vierteljahreshefte für Zeitgeschichte*, which were published at least five years ago, can be downloaded for free. Since July 2019 the Institute has established a server *Zeitgeschichte open*, where

all publications older than three years will be published in *open access* consecutively: https://open.ifz-muenchen.de (last accessed January 31, 2021).

54 First published in 1953, an English version of Rothfels with an additional commentary on the historiographical context and impact was published in 2016: Hans Rothfels, "Augenzeugenbericht zu den Massenvergasungen," in *VfZ* 1/2 (1953): 177–94; English translation: "Kurt Gerstein's Eyewitness Report on Mass Gassings," in Thomas Schlemmer and Alan E. Steinweis (eds.), *Holocaust and Memory in Europe* (Berlin/Boston: De Gruyter, 2016) (German Yearbook of Contemporary History 1), 63–83; Valerie Hébert, "Hans Rothfels, Kurt Gerstein and the Report: A Retrospective," ibid., 85–105. Another example of important documentation is Helmut Heiber, ed., "Der Generalplan Ost: Dokumentation," in *VfZ* 6/3 (1958): 281–325.

55 Eberhard Jäckel and Axel Kuhn, eds., *Adolf Hitler. Sämtliche Aufzeichnungen 1905–1924* (Stuttgart: DVA, 1980).

56 In their search for new sources Jäckel and Kuhn had selected several texts, which were later identified as forgeries which had been produced by Konrad Kujau, who also invented "Hitler's Diaries." Eberhard Jäckel and Axel Kuhn, "Zu einer Edition von Aufzeichnungen Hitlers," in *VfZ* 29/2 (1981): 304–5. Eberhard Jäckel, Axel Kuhn, and Eberhard Weiß, "Neue Erkenntnisse zur Fälschung von Hitler-Dokumenten," in *VfZ* 32/1 (1984): 163–9.

57 For example (in chronological order): Ernst Deuerlein, ed., *Der Hitler-Putsch. Bayerische Dokumente zum 8./9. November 1923* (Stuttgart: DVA, 1962); Andreas Hillgruber, ed., *Staatsmänner und Diplomaten bei Hitler. Vertrauliche Aufzeichnungen über Unterredungen mit Vertretern des Auslandes*, in zwei Teilen (Frankfurt a.M.: Bernard & Graefe, 1967/1970); Max Domarus, ed., *Hitler. Reden und Proklamationen, 1932–1945*, 2 vols. (Wiesbaden: R. Löwit, 1973); English translation: Max Domarus, ed., *Hitler: Speeches and Proclamations, 1932-1945*, 4 vols. (London/Wauconda, Ill., 1990–8); Manfred Funke ed., *Hitler, Deutschland und die Mächte. Materialien zur Außenpolitik des Dritten Reiches* (Düsseldorf: Droste, 1978); Jäckel and Kuhn, *Hitler. Sämtliche Aufzeichnungen*; Werner Jochmann and Heinrich Heim, eds., *Adolf Hitler, Monologe im Führerhauptquartier 1941–1944. Die Aufzeichnungen Heinrich Heims* (Hamburg: Knaus, 1980); Bayerische Akademie der Wissenschaften, ed., *Akten der Reichskanzlei. Die Regierung Hitler 1933–1945*, 6 vols. (Munich: Oldenbourg, 1983–2012); Lothar Gruchmann, "Hitlers Denkschrift an die bayerische Justiz vom 16. Mai 1923," in *VfZ* 39/2 (1991): 305–28.

58 *Die Tagebücher von Joseph Goebbels*, ed. by Elke Fröhlich. Hrsg. im Auftrag des Instituts für Zeitgeschichte München mit Unterstützung des Staatlichen Archivdienstes Russlands [On behalf of Institut für Zeitgeschichte and with the support of the National Archives Service of Russia] (Munich: Saur, 1993–2008). Part I: "Aufzeichnungen 1923–1941," 9 vols. (Munich: Saur, 1998–2006). Part II: "Diktate 1941-1945," 15 vols. (Munich: Saur, 1993–1996). Part III: "Register 1923–1945" (Munich: Saur, 2007–8).

59 Institut für Zeitgeschichte, ed., *Hitler. Reden, Schriften, Anordnungen Februar 1925 bis Januar 1933. Fünf Bände (in zwölf Teilen), Register, Kartenband,*

Ergänzungsband "Der Hitler-Prozeß 1924" (in vier Teilen) (Munich: Saur, 1992–2003).

60 Gerhard L. Weinberg, ed., *Hitlers Zweites Buch: Ein Dokument aus dem Jahr 1928* (Stuttgart: DVA, 1961) (English translation: *Hitler's Second Book: The Unpublished Sequel to Mein Kampf* [New York: Enigma, 2003]).

61 Gerhard L. Weinberg, Christian Hartmann, and Klaus A. Lankheit, eds., *Außenpolitische Standortbestimmung nach der Reichstagswahl, Juni-Juli 1928* (*Reden, Schriften, Anordnungen*, Bd. II A) (Munich: Saur, 1995).

62 Further detailed information will be provided in the Introduction to the critical edition: Christian Hartmann, Thomas Vordermayer, Othmar Plöckinger, and Roman Töppel, eds., *Hitler, Mein Kampf. Eine kritische Edition*, 2 vols. (Munich: Institut für Zeitgeschichte, 2016), vol. 1, 13–72.

63 On illegal reprints, which have repeatedly been published, see most recently Sven Felix Kellerhof, *Mein Kampf. Die Karriere eines Buches* (Stuttgart: Klett, 2015), 295–308.

64 For the historiographical discourse about the question of how far ideological concepts shaped political action, see, among numerous publications, particularly Eberhard Jäckel, *Hitlers Weltanschauung. Entwurf einer Herrschaft* (Tübingen: Rainer Wunderlich Verlag, 1969); Gerhard Hirschfeld and Lothar Kettenacker, eds., *Der "Führerstaat": Mythos und Realität. Studien zur Struktur und Politik des Dritten Reiches,* with on introduction by Wolfgang J. Mommsen (Stuttgart: Klett-Cotta, 1981); Ian Kershaw, *The Nazi Dictatorship. Problems and Perspectives of Interpretation,* 4th edition (London: Arnold, 2000).

65 Moreover, Neil Gregor argues that the book should be read not only as an autobiography but also as a kind of "novel of education," a veritable *Bildungsroman* of the era: Neil Gregor, "'Mein Kampf' lesen, 70 Jahre später," in *Aus Politik und Zeitgeschichte,* 65 (2015) 43–5, October 19: 3–9. https://www.bpb.de/apuz/213512/mein-kampf-lesen-70-jahre-spaeter.

66 These interpretations were shaped particularly by Hermann Rauschning and the first major Hitler biography by Alan Bullock.

67 See, besides the editions for the period before 1933 mentioned earlier, "Die Edition der Reden Adolf Hitlers von 1933 bis 1945. Ein neues Projekt des Instituts für Zeitgeschichte," in *VfZ* 67/1 (2019): 147–63.

68 For the wider context, see Roman Töppel, "'Volk und Rasse'. In Search of Hitler's Sources," in Elizabeth Harvey and Johannes Hürter, eds., *Hitler—New Research* (Berlin/Boston: De Gruyter, 2018) (*German Yearbook of Contemporary History* 3), 71–110; Eve Rosenhaft, "Hitler's Antisemitism and the Horizons of the Racial State," Ibid., 111–21.

69 See MKII, 1026–7 and 1038–9. In another chapter Hitler talks of "a people of one hundred million," vol. 2, 1550–1.

70 We find these views reflected in many of Hitler's as well as Himmler's speeches.

Chapter 4

1 Peter Longerich, *Hitler: A Biography,* translated by Jeremy Noakes and Lesley Sharpe (Oxford: Oxford University Press, 2018), 949.

2 Ibid.

3 Ibid.

4 Hitler, Manheim 42/MKI 181.

5 Hitler, Manheim 183/MKI 507.

6 Hitler, Manheim 322/MKI 841.

7 Hitler, Manheim 123/MKI 365.

8 Hitler, Manheim 206/MKI 557.

9 Hitler, Manheim 452/MKII 1147.

10 John Adams, "Review of Alex Ross' *Wagnerism: Art and Politics in the Shadow of Music.*" *New York Times,* October 18, 2020.

11 Hitler, Manheim 90/MKI 293.

12 Hitler, Manheim 91/MKI 295.

13 Hitler, Manheim 375/MKII 963.

14 Ibid.

15 Hitler, Manheim 81/MKI 273.

16 Thomas Weber, *Becoming Hitler: The Making of a Nazi* (*Oxford: Oxford University Press,* 2017).

17 Longerich, 32.

18 Hitler, Manheim 510/MKII 1285.

19 Hitler, Manheim 476/MKII 2 1205.

20 Robert Gerwarth, *Hitler's Hangman: The Life of Heydrich* (New Haven: Yale University Press, 2011).

21 Longerich, *Heinrich Himmler*, translated by Jeremy Noakes and Lesley Sharpe (Oxford: Oxford University Press, 2012), 2

22 Hitler, Manheim 457/MKII 1157.

23 Hitler, Manheim 238/MKI 633.

24 Hitler, Manheim 293/MKI 763.

25 Hitler, Manheim 250/MKI 659.

26 Hitler, Manheim 333/MK 1 869.

27 Hitler, Manheim 334/MKI 871.

28 Hitler, Manheim 247/MKI 653.

29 Hitler, Manheim 193/MKI 529.

30 Hitler, Manheim 327/MKI 855.

31 Johann Chapoutot, *Law of the Blood: Thinking as a Nazi*, translated by Miranda Richmond Mouillot (Cambridge MA: Harvard University Press, 2018).

32 Ibid., 400.

33 Ibid.

34 Hitler, Manheim 246/CE 1 649.

35 Ibid.

36 Hitler, Manheim 182–3. Sacha Abamsky, *The House of Twenty Thousand Books* (New York: New York Review of Books, 2015), 74.

37 Toby Thacker, *Joseph Goebbels: Life and Death* (New York: Palgrave Macmillan, 2009), 36.

38 Thacker, 43.

39 Weber, *Becoming Hitler*, 34.

40 Hitler was unimpressed by his rivals for leadership of *völkish* groups, who opposed the Weimar Republic and claimed that they had advocated true German ideas for forty years. He believed that if they had not succeeded in attaining power in all those years, it was time for a new leader to emerge, and he was that leader.

41 Hitler, Manheim 364/MKI 935.

42 Carl Schmitt, *Der Begriff des Politischen* (München: Dunker &Humboldt, 1932).

43 Hitler, Manheim 363/MKI 931.

44 Hitler, Manheim 269/MKI 705.

45 Hitler believed that Germans should not blame England, Italy, or any other country for their defeat, but they should look toward the internal enemy, the Jews, as the cause of their defeat as the Jews weakened the country morally and economically.

46 Hitler, Manheim 193/MKI 529.

47 Ibid.

48 Hitler, Manheim 446/MKII, 1131.

49 Hitler, Manheim 447/MKII 1135.

50 Hitler, Manheim 57/MKI 213.

51 Chapoutot, 409.

52 Ibid., 405.

53 Stephen Fritz, *First Soldier: Hitler as Military Leader* (New Haven: Yale University Press, 2018), 97.

54 Fritz Stern, *Der Traum vom Frieden und die Versuchung der Macht: Deutsche Geschichte Im 20 Jahrhundert (The Dream of Peace and the Temptation of Power: German History in the 20th Century)* (Berlin: Siedler, 1999).

55 Hitler, Manheim 455/MKII 1153.

56 Hitler, Manheim 243/MKI 643.

57 Hitler, Manheim 326/MKI 853.

58 Hitler, Manheim 446/MKII 1131.

59 Hitler, Manheim 447/MKII 1133–5.

60 Hitler, Manheim 325/MKI 847.

61 Rolf Dieter Müller, *Hitler's Wehrmacht 1935-1945*, translated by Janice Anker (Lexington, Kentucky: University Press of Kentucky, 2017), 52.

62 Ibid., 43.

63 Ibid., 147.

Chapter 5

1 Identifying his efforts with revenge against the November criminals who allegedly surrendered to the enemy, Hitler wrote of drawing Germans to a bandwagon that grew more sure of itself as hecklers were increasingly drowned out. Hitler, Manheim 172–3/MKI 481. Hitler exaggerates here but in a direction that reveals his perspective.

2 Hitler, Manheim 46/MKI 189.

3 Hitler, Manheim 553/MKII 1399; Dietrich Orlow, *The Nazi Party 1919–1945: A Complete History* (2013), 33. SA was established in July 1921.

4 In line with his First Order to the SA articulated in *Mein Kampf*, Hitler on the most critical issue about whether SA men could scoff at official police bans made sure that the Storm Troopers painstakingly followed the law, according to his "legal course" strategy for taking power set out in *Mein Kampf*. Stoltzfus, *Hitler's Compromises*, 42–4; The Berlin SA wanted to disregard the police ban in 1927, but Goebbels thought this would be counterproductive and directed the SA away from armed confrontations with the forces of the state for strategic reasons. *Wille und Weg* (later *Unser Wille und Weg*), 1 (1931): 2–5.

5 Hitler, Manheim 267, 87/MKI 701, 285. Für den Politiker aber darf die Abschätzung des Wertes einer Religion weniger durch die ihr etwa anhaftenden Mängel bestimmt werden als vielmehr durch die Güte eines ersichtlich besseren Ersatzes. Solange aber ein solcher Politischer Mißbrauch der Religion anscheinend fehlt, kann das Vorhandene nur von Narren oder Verbrechern demoliert werden. For the politician, however, the appraisal of the value of a religion should be determined less by the defects that may be attached to it than by the quality of a clearly better substitute. But as long as such a political abuse of religion is absent, what exists can only be demolished by fools or criminals.

6 Hitler, Manheim 170–1/MKI 475–7.

7 Hitler, Manheim 44/MKI 183.

8 The police themselves were grateful for the thrashing the Nazis dealt those communist "dogs." *Table Talks*, Trevor Roper, p. 136, 137, entry for November 30, 1941.

9 Eric D. Weitz, *Creating German Communism, 1890–1990: From Popular Protests to Socialist State* (Princeton: Princeton University Press, 1997), 167.

10 Devan Pendas, "Racial States in Comparative Perspective," in *Beyond the Racial State: Rethinking Nazi Germany*, Devin O. Pendas, Mark Roseman, Richard F. Wetzell, eds. (New York and Cambridge: Cambridge University Press: 2017), 116–56, here 133. On gassing Jews, during the First World War, Hitler, Manheim 679/MKII 1719.

11 *Mein Kampf*, Eher-Verlag, 42.

12 Hitler, Manheim 41/MKI 176–7.

13 Hitler, Manheim 170/MKI 475.

14 Hitler, Manheim 172/MKI 479.

15 Hitler, Manheim [393] 530, MKII [1007], 1339.

16 Thomas Childers, *The* Nazi *Voter: The Social Foundations of Fascism in Germany, 1919–1933* (Chapel Hill: University of North Carolina Press, 1983), 14.

17 Timothy S. Brown, *Weimar Radicals: Nazis and Communists between Authenticity and Performance*, (New York: Berghahn Books, 2009), 136.

18 Alan Bullock, *Hitler: A Study in Tyranny* (London: Odhams, 1952), 45, 55, 68, 69, 72; Walter Langer, *The Mind of Hitler: The Secret Wartime Report* (New York: Basic Books, 1972), 142–4.

19 Eric Hofer, *The True Believer: Thoughts on the Nature of Mass Movements* (New York: HarperCollins, 2002 [1951]), 3–16.

20 He did build on the example of Vienna mayor Karl Lueger and his perceptions of Benito Mussolini.

21 "A majority can never replace the Man!," that is, the leader who knows his people well enough to unite them, splintered by an array of political parties. Hitler, Manheim 82/MKI 275. Hitler models the modern hero like Henrik Ibsen's Brand, who saved his village from doom through heroic courage in the face of a lethal storm.

22 Hitler, Manheim 518/MKII 1307.

23 Hitler, Manheim 282–3/MK I 731–3.

24 Ibid.

25 Ibid.

26 Hitler, Manheim 333/MKI 869.

27 Hitler, Manheim 337/MK I 877.

28 Hitler, Manheim 449/MKII 1139.

29 Eberhard Jäckel and Axel Kuhn, eds. *Hitler: Sämtliche Aufzeichnungen: 1905-1924* (Stuttgart: Deutsche Verlags-Anstalt, 1980). Hitler claimed his fundamental views went back to his 1908–13 years in Vienna: "In a few years I created the basis of my knowledge, which I still draw from today. . . . During this time I developed a worldview that became the granite foundation of my current actions." Hitler, Manheim 22/MKI 135. He was drawn to Vienna's mayor Karl Lueger. Georg von Schönerer "taught him about Pan-Germanism and racial anti-Semitism, while Karl Lueger taught him how to control the masses and run a successful political party."

30 A central mission of the SA, as Otto Ohlendorf testified after the war, was to persuade locals to join National Socialism through public debates or going door to door. Testimony, Ohlendorf, October 8, 1947, *The United States of America v. Otto Ohlendorf et al.* Einsatzgruppen Trial Transcript, October 8, 1947, National Archives Microfilm Publication M895, roll 2, 478–9.

31 Hitler, Manheim 546 ff./MKII 1377 ff. Hitler's directives to the SA leader, former Freikorps leader Franz Pfeffer von Salomon From SABE I, November 1, 1926, in Institut für Zeitgeschichte, ed., *Hitler, Reden Schriften, Anordnungen: Februar 1925 bis January 1933*, vol. 2, Part 1, July 1926–July 1927, ed. Bärbel Dusik (Munich: K. G. Saur, 1992), Dokument 44, 83ff.

We are citing both *Mein Kampf* and the full second order (not all of it is in *Mein Kampf*) in

Institut für Zeitgeschichte, ed., *Hitler, Reden Schriften,*

32 Hitler, Manheim 536/MKII 1351. "Sie wollte nicht die Gewalt als das Ziel hinstellen, sondern die Verkünder des geistigen Ziels vor der Bedrängung durch Gewalt schützen."

33 On the SA in church, Victoria Barnett, *For the Soul of the People* (Oxford, 1992) p. 4.

34 Hitler, Manheim 546/MK II 1377.

35 Hitler, Manheim 546–7/MK II 1377–9.

36 Hitler, Manheim 547/MK II 1379.

37 Ibid.

38 Ibid.

39 Hitler, Manheim 547/MKII 1379.

40 Hitler, Manheim 547/MKII 1381.

41 Friedrich, *Hitler's Berlin*, 209.

42 Hitler, Manheim 323/MKI 843.

43 Hitler, Manheim 454–5/MK II 1153.

44 Hitler, Manheim 357/MK I 919–21.

45 Hitler, Manheim 357/MKI 919.

46 Hitler, Manheim 357/MKI 921.

47 Hitler, Manheim 357/MKI 921.

48 Hitler, Manheim 487/MK II 1231.

49 Hitler, Manheim 487/MK II 1233.

50 Hitler, Manheim 487/MK II 1233.

51 Hitler, Manheim 42/MK I 181.

52 Hitler, Manheim 42/MK I 181.

53 Hitler, Manheim 44/MK I 183–5.

54 *Das Reichsgesetzblatt*, I, 1922, 585–93.

55 Quoted in Peter D. Stachura, *Political Leaders in Weimar Germany: A Biographical Study* (New York: Harvester Wheatsheaf, 1993), 187.

56 *Das Reichsgesetzblatt*, I, 1922, 586.

57 Jürgen Erdmann, *Coburg: Bayern und das Reich, 1918–1923* (Coburg: Druck- und Verlagshaus A. Rossteutscher, 1969), 93.

58 Hitler, Manheim 547/MK II 1381.

59 Hitler, Manheim 547–8/MK II 1381.

60 Robert Gerwarth, *November 1918: The German Revolution* (Oxford: Oxford University Press, 2020), 179.

61 Hitler, Manheim 548/MK II 1381–3.

62 https://www.bavariathek.bayern/nc/medien-themen/portale/geschichte-des-bayerischen-parlaments/landtage-seit-1819.html?tx_parlament_pi4%5Blandtag%5D=351&tx_parlament_pi4%5Bkategorie%5D=40&tx_parlament_pi4%5Baction%5D=show&tx_parlament_pi4%5Bcontroller%5D=Landtag&cHash=8fcd299c1d873b94622568c2b08b2928.

http://www.gonschior.de/weimar/Bayern/LT2.html.

https://www.bavariathek.bayern/medien-themen/portale/geschichte-des-bayerischen-parlaments/landtage-seit-1819.html.

63 Liesa Weber, *Handlungsspielräume und Handlungsoptionen von Pfarrern und Gemeindeglidern in der Zeit des Nationalsozialismus* (Göttingen: Vandenhoeck und Ruprecht, 2019), 65.

64 John Angolia, *For Führer and Fatherland: Political and Civil Awards of the Third Reich* (San Jose: R. James Bender Publishing, 1989), 197.

65 Hitler, Manheim 548/MK II 1383–5.

66 Quoted in Erdmann, 97.

67 Hitler, Manheim 548/MK II 1385.

68 Hitler, Manheim 548/MK II 1385.

69 Hitler, Manheim 549-50/MK II 1385–9.

70 Hitler, Manheim 550/MK II 1389.

71 Hitler, Manheim 550/MK II 1389.

72 Quoted in Erdmann, 108.

73 Erdmann, 111.

74 Hitler, Manheim 551/MK II 1391.

75 Hitler, Manheim 551/MK II 1391.

76 Hitler, Manheim 551/MK II 1391.

77 Erdmann, 118–19.

78 Erdmann, 119; Bayerisches Landesamt für Statistik, *Kreisfreie Stadt Coburg: Eine Auswahl wichtiger statistscher Daten*, Statistik kommunal 2018 (Fürth: Bayerisches Landesamt für Statistik, 2019), 6.

79 Hitler, Manheim 552/MK II 1395.

80 Hitler, Manheim 552/MK II 1395.

81 Hitler, Manheim 371 MK I 879.

Chapter 6

1 In 1908, Eugen Fischer studied the "Rehoboth basters" in what is now Namibia, focusing on the offspring of German or Boer fathers and African

women. He continued later with his work on the "Rhineland bastards" in the wake of the First World War, which Hitler discusses in *Mein Kampf*, as noted later in this chapter.

2 His fear of Jewish mastery of the Aryan plays into a type of paranoia seemingly groundless in the 1920s.

3 Hitler, Manheim 624/MKII 1583.

4 Richard Walther Darré popularized the earlier German concept of "Blut und Boden" ("Blood and Soil") in 1930, and it became adopted in the Third Reich as a policy. The Reich's State Hereditary Farm Law of 1933 implemented this ideology, stating that its aim was to "preserve the farming community as the blood-source of the German people" (*Das Bauerntum als Blutquelle des deutschen Volkes erhalten*). See also Clifford R. Lovin, "The Ideological Basis of the Nazi Agricultural Program," *Journal of the History of Ideas*, 28(2) (April–June 1967), 279–88. Also, consider Pauline M. H. Mazumdar, "Blood and Soil: The Serology of the Aryan Racial State," *Bulletin of the History of Medicine, 64(2)* (Summer 1990), 187–219.

5 Hitler, Manheim 134/MKI 391.

6 Hitler, Manheim 3/MKI 93.

7 Editors Elizabeth Harvey and Johannes Hurter in *Hitler—New Research, German Yearbook of Contemporary History* (Oldenbourg: DeGruyter, 2018) point out in detail that many crucial concepts of anti-Semitism were already spread throughout nineteenth-century Germany and that Hitler simply absorbed them. Othmar Plöckinger in his chapter included here indicates that the theme of anti-Semitism permeated much of the existing right-wing literature prior to Hitler's incarceration and was available to him through multiple avenues.

8 Isabel Wilkerson, *Caste: The Origins of Our Discontents* (New York: Random House, 2020).

9 Personal interview with Werner Hemmrich, son of Hitler's prison guard, January 8, 2019. Timothy W. Ryback, *Hitler's Private Library* (New York: Alfred A. Knopf, 2008). According to Werner Hemmrich, son of Hitler's prison guard Franz Hemmrich, his father described the daily activities of Hitler while incarcerated in his memoir, now located at the Institut für Zeitgeschichte in Munich. "Hitler received lots of books from his visitors, who often gave books as gifts to Hitler. He read a great deal." One time Hitler recommended a book to Hemmrich's father; the father said he had no interest in politics, and Hitler gave him a strange look. For his thirtieth birthday Hitler received numerous books on diverse themes (including politics). As we now know, "Hitler," according to Hemmrich, "used some of these as sources for *Mein Kampf*." Interview for our companion documentary documentary on *Mein Kampf*.

10 Benno Mueller-Hill (*Murderous Science*) in the documentary of John J. Michalczyk, *In the Shadow of the Reich: Nazi Medicine* (1996).

11 John Nale, "Arthur de Gobineau on Blood and Race," *Critical Philosophy of Race*, Vol. 2, No. 1, SPECIAL ISSUE: XENOPHOBIA AND RACISM (2014), 107. 106–24.

12 Othmar Plöckinger, personal communication, July 9, 2020.

13 Ryback, 50.

14 Hitler mentions in passing the British political philosopher Houston Stewart Chamberlain in *Mein Kampf* (Hitler, Manheim 269/MK I705).

15 Hitler, Manheim 562/MKII 1427.

16 Hitler, Manheim 86/MKI 285.

17 Hitler, Manheim 91/ MKI 295.

18 See Stefan Arvidsson's *Aryan Idols: Indo-European Mythology as Ideology and Science* (2006), in which he traces the notion of "Aryan" from the nineteenth century through Nazi ideology and beyond.

19 Nordic primarily meant white European. Today, Caucasian is often indicated on forms for a white person. In 1795, a German anthropologist and physician studying skulls believed a female skull from the Caucasian region of Russia was the most symmetrical and ideal, so he believed the white race developed there.

20 Quoted by Edwin Black, *War against the Weak: Eugenics and America's Campaign to Create a Master Race* (New York/London: Four Walls Eight Windows, 2003), 298. Original in K. Holler, "The Nordic Movement in Germany," *Eugenical News*, Vol XVII (1932), 117, 119.

21 Hitler, Manheim 290/MKI 755.

22 Ibid.

23 Hitler, Manheim 294/MKI 765.

24 Hitler, Manheim 296/MKI 769.

25 Hitler, Manheim 295/ MKI 767.

26 Hitler, Manheim 297/ MKI 771.

27 Eberhard Jäckel, ed., *Hitler. Samtliche Aufzeichnungen* 1905-1924, translated by Richard S. Levy. (Stuttgart, 1980), 90, in the *Jewish Virtual Library*, accessed November 20, 2020. https://www.jewishvirtuallibrary.org/adolf-hitler-s-first-anti-semitic-writing, "The Final Aim Must Unquestionably be the Irrevocable *Entfernung* [Removal] of the Jews."

28 Douglas O. Linder, "Famous Trials: October 1923 Interview with Adolf Hitler by George Sylvester Viereck in *The American Monthly*, accessed July 15, 2021, https://famous-trials.com/hitler/2529-1923-interview-with-adolf-hitler.

29 Hitler, Manheim 169/MKI 473.

30 Hitler, Manheim 679/MK II 1719.

31 Richard Weikart, "Progress through Racial Extermination: Social Darwinism, Eugenics, and Pacifism in Germany, 1860–1918," *German Studies Review*, 26(2) (May 2003): 273 [273–94].

32 Joachim Fest, *Hitler* (New York: Vintage Books, 1974), 679–80.

33 Hitler, Manheim 329/ MKI 859.

34 There is an extensive array of research data completed on Nazi doctors including the works of Robert Jay Lifton (*Nazi Doctors*), Benno Müller-Hill (*Murderous Science*), Arthur L. Caplan (*When Medicine Went Mad*). Michael

Kater (*Doctors under Hitler*), John J. Michalczyk (*Medicine, Ethics and the Third Reich*), Robert Proctor (*Racial Hygiene*), among others.

35 Hitler, Manheim 310/ 807.

36 In the novel and in his *Cahiers,* Camus uses the physical phenomenon of the plague in Oran in the 1940s to symbolize the Nazi occupation of a European city.

37 Hitler, Manheim 226/ MKI 605.

38 *Hitler's Table Talk 1941-1944: His Private Conversations*. Trans. Norman Cameron and R. H. Stevens. Introduced and with a new Preface by H. R. Trevor-Roper (New York: Enigma Books, 2000), 332.

39 Roman Töppel, "Volk und Rasse," in Harvey and Hurter, 81.

40 Ibid. Fritsch's publication featured a cover with a venomous snake tattooed with Jewish stars encircling the swastika.

41 Paul Weindling, *Health, Race, and German Politics between Unification and Nazism: 1870-1945* (Cambridge: Cambridge University Press, 1989/1991), 155–87.

42 Hitler, Manheim 435/ MKII 1105.

43 Charles Darwin, *Origin of Species by Means of Natural Selection; or the Preservation of the Favoured Races in the Struggle of Life* (London: W. Clowes and Sons, 1859/1861), 76.

44 Ryback, 90.

45 Hitler, Manheim 132/MKI 387.

46 Hitler, Manheim 283/MKI 733.

47 Hitler, Manheim 96/MK I 305.

48 Hitler, Manheim 296/MKI 769.

49 Hitler, Manheim 332/MKI 869.

50 Hitler, Manheim 394/MKII 1009.

51 Hitler, Manheim 398/MKII 1019.

52 Marie Harm and Hermann Wiehle, *Lebenskunde fuer Mittelschulen-Funfter Tiel, Klasse 5 fuer Jungen* (Halle: Hermann Schroedel Verlag, 1942), 152–7. See also Yuval Noah Harari, *Sapiens: A Brief History of Humankind* (Harper Perennial, 2015), 234–6.

53 Hitler, Manheim 287/MK I, 747.

54 "Adolf Hitler: First Anti-Semitic Writing," September 16, 1919, *Jewish Virtual Library*, accessed December 20, 2020, https://www.jewishvirtuallibrary.org/adolf-hitler-s-first-anti-semitic-writing.

55 Hitler, Manheim 131/MK I 383.

56 Ibid.

57 Ibid.

58 Hitler, Manheim 214/MKI 225–6/ 575, 577.

59 Hitler, Manheim 285/MKI 741.

60 Hitler, Manheim 305/MKI 793.

61 *German History in Documents and Images,* Volume 7. Nazi Germany, 1933-1945 Law for the Prevention of Offspring with Hereditary Diseases (July 14, 1933).

62 Paul Popenoe, "The German Sterilization Law," *Journal of Heredity*, 25(7) July 1934: 257 (257–60), accessed November 28, 2020, https://doi.org/10.1093/oxfordjournals.jhered.a103937. Isabel Wilkerson in *Caste: The Origins of Our Discontent* (New York: Random House, 2020), 80, argues that the Nazi legal system concerning race often looked to America for antecedent racial policies.

63 Hitler, Manheim 404/MKII 1033.

64 Ibid.

65 Hitler, Manheim 405/MKII 1035.

66 Madison Grant, *The Passing of the Great Race: The Racial Basis of European History*, NY: Charles Scribners Sons, 1916), 49. The German translation appeared in 1920, published by the Munich publisher Lehmann, *Untergang der großen Rasse Die Rassen als Grundlage d. Geschichte Europas.*

67 Hitler, Manheim 255/MK I 671.

68 Two films, one American and one German, reveal issues of eugenics principles and show the reasoning for sterilization and euthanasia: *Tomorrow's Children* (1934) by Crane Wilbur describes the plight of a young woman, Alice Mason, whom the court wishes to have sterilized to stop the negative qualities of her family. Herbert Gerdes's 1936 film *Erb Krank* (The Hereditary Defective) graphically indicates how the mentally afflicted have become a burden on the country. In 1937 a full-length film production, "Opfer der Vergangenheit: Die Sünde wider Blut und Rasse" ("Victims of the Past: The Sin against Blood and Race"), became prominently screened in Germany to promote eugenics principles. Another of the six propaganda films dehumanizing mentally challenged patients, the 1937 *Alles Leben ist Kampf* (All Life Is a Struggle) promotes lawful sterilization.

69 Wilkerson, 80. She refers back to the research of Stefan Kühl in *The Nazi Connection: Eugenics, American Racism, and German National Socialism.*

70 Ibid., 115.

71 Ryback, 69.

72 Houston Steward Chamberlain, *Foundations of the Nineteenth Century*, translated from the German by John Lees (London/New York: John Lane Pub. 1913), 492.

73 Hitler, Manheim 316/MKI 825.

74 Hitler, Manheim 286/MKI 743, 747.

75 Florida Constitution in 1885, art. XVI, s. 24.

76 Hitler, Manheim 286/MKI 743, 747.

77 Hitler, Manheim 289/MKI 753.

78 Hitler, Manheim 296/MKI 769.

79 Adolf Hitler, "On National Socialism and World Relations," *German Propaganda Archive* (Calvin University), accessed December 30, 2020, https://research.calvin.edu/german-propaganda-archive/hitler1.htm.

80 Iris Wigger, "'Against the Laws of Civilisation': Race, Gender and Nation in the International Racist Campaign against the 'Black Shame," *Berkeley Journal of Sociology*, 46:114 (2002), 113–31.

81 Robert C. Reinders, "Racialism on the Left: E. D. Morel and the 'Black Horror on the Rhine,'" *International Review of Social History* (13:1), April 1968, 11.

82 Ibid.

83 Hitler, Manheim 430/MKII 1093. Madison Grant note to Charles Davenport, April 2, 1917.

84 See Iris Wigger, *The "Black Horror on the Rhine": Intersections of Race, Nation, Gender and Class in 1920s Germany* (London: Palgrave Macmillan, 2017). Wigger develops the concept of racial mixing in social, political, and psychological terms, commenting at one point on how Edmund Morel reinforced racist beliefs throughout Europe, 46–60. See also Julia Roos, "Racist Hysteria to Pragmatic Rapprochement? The German Debate about Rhenish 'Occupation Children', 1920–30," *Contemporary European History*, 22(2):155–80 (May 2013).

85 Madison Grant, 263.

86 James Whitman, *Hitler's American Model: The United States and the Making of Nazi Race Law* (Princeton, NJ: Princeton University Press, 2018).

87 Hitler, Manheim 325/MKI 851.

88 Hitler, Manheim 624/MKII 1583. See page 1582 of the *Critical Edition* about the French occupation from 1920.

89 Hitler, Manheim 430/MKII 1093.

90 See Sally Marks, "Black Watch on the Rhine: A Study in Propaganda, Prejudice and Prurience," *European Studies Review* (SAGE, London, Beverly Hills and New Delhi), 13 (1983), 297–34. Significant campaigns were waged on the "Black Horror" in the United States and Canada indicating the similar racist attitudes that prevailed globally.

91 *Trials of War Criminals before the Nuernberg Military Tribunals under Control Council* Law, No. 10, Vol. II, "The Medical Case," Nuernberg October 1946–April 1949 (US Government Printing Office, Washington, DC), 129–30.

92 Ibid., "Document Karl Brandt Nr. 51

This is a true and correct copy, certified.

Nuernberg, 5 February 1947

(signature) Dr. Servatius

Defense Counsel"

93 Madison Grant, 44.

94 Ibid., 45.

95 Ibid.

96 Harvard University Law School Nuremberg Trials Project, 117, accessed November 12, 2020, http://nuremberg.law.harvard.edu/documents/2703-extract-from-a-book?q=passing+of+the+great+race#p.1.

Chapter 7

1 Theodor Adorno, *Night Music: Essays on Music 1928–1962*, edited by Rolf Tiedemann, translated by *Wieland Hoban* (London, New York, and Calcutta: Seagull Books, 2009), 275–6.

2 Adolf Hitler, *Mein Kampf*, translated by Ralph Mannheim (Boston: Houghton Mifflin Company, 1971) 303, MKI 785.

3 *Hitler*, Manheim 261/MKI 687.

4 Lion Feuchtwanger's quote in Gil Nicholls, *Adolf Hitler: A Biographical Companion*, ABC-CLIO Inc. (Santa Barbara: CA, 1949), 165.

5 Hitler, Manheim 258/MKI 681.

6 Hitler, Manheim 262/MKI 689.

7 Hitler, Manheim 34/MKI 163.

8 MKI 680, see fn. 163.

9 Ibid. (my translation).

10 MKI 152, n. 59.

11 Hitler, Manheim 70/MKI 245.

12 MKI 680, see fn. 163.

13 Ibid.

14 Hitler, Manheim 58 MK1 213.

15 Hitler, Manheim 259/MKI 681.

16 Hitler, Manheim 303/MKI 785 and 326/MKI 853.

17 MKI 852, fn. 235.

18 MKI 853.

19 Hitler, Manheim 262/MKI 853.

20 Hitler, Manheim 258–9/MKI 681.

21 Hitler, Manheim 255 MKI 669.

22 Hitler, Manheim 290/MKI 755.

23 Igor Golomstock, *Totalitarian Art in the Soviet Union, the Third Reich, Fascist Italy, and the People's Republic of China* (London: Collins Harvill, 1990), 92.

24 Melanie Murphy, "*The Architecture of Doom* (1991): Blueprint for Annihilation," in *Through a Lens Darkly: Films of Genocide, Ethnic Cleansing, and Atrocities* (New York: Peter Lang, 2013), 115.

25 Berthold Hinz, *Art in the Third Reich* (New York: Pantheon, 1980), 82. The "blood and soil" slogan was chanted by white supremacists in the "Unite the Right" rally in Charlottesville, VA, in the summer of 2017.

26 Ibid., 1.

27 Ibid., 24.

28 Golomstock, 80, 104.

29 Hinz, *Art in the Third Reich*, 28.

30 Golomstock, 80.

31 Hinz, 1.

32 Ibid., 40.

33 *Life and Times in Nazi Germany*, edited by Lisa Pines (London: Bloomsbury, 2016), 197.

34 Hinz, 41.

35 Ibid., 43.

36 Golomstock, 61.

37 Arthur Schopenhauer, *The World as Will and Representation*, translated by E. F. J. Payne (New York: Dover Publications, 1969), 257.

38 Michael Meyer, *The Politics of Music in the Third Reich* (New York: Peter Lang, 1991), 92.

39 Ibid.

40 Ibid., 100.

41 Ibid., 101.

42 Ibid., 102.

43 Sam H. Shirakawa, *The Devil's Music Master: The Controversial Life and Career of Wilhelm Furtwängler* (New York/Oxford: Oxford University Press, 1992), 199.

44 Michael H. Kater, *Composers of the Nazi Era* (New York/Oxford: Oxford University Press, 2000), 42.

45 Meyer, 98–9.

46 "Entartete Musik," William Breman Jewish Heritage Museum, accessed January 19, 2021 (https://www.thebreman.org/Exhibitions/Online-Exhibitions/Entartete-Musik).

47 Meyer, 262–3.

48 Ibid., 268–9.

49 Ibid., 270–1.

50 Ibid., 301.

51 Ibid., 302.

52 Pamela Potter "Defining 'Degenerate Music' in Nazi Germany," *The Orel Foundation*, accessed January 19, 2021, http://orelfoundation.org/journal/journalArticle/defining_8220degenerate_music8221_in_nazi_germany.

53 Ibid.

54 Ibid.

55 Meyer, 254.

56 Hinz, 43.

57 Ibid., 42.

58 Adolf Hitler excerpt from speech given on July 19, 1937, dedicating House of German Art, accessed January 10, 2020, https://www.tracesofevil.com/2008/01/munich-war-memorial.html.

Chapter 8

1 Quoted in Hartmann et al., *Hitler,* Mein Kampf*: Eine kritische Edition*, Vol. I (Munich/Berlin: Institute for Contemporary History, 2016), 208, fn. 172. The quotation appears in Eugeni Xammar, *Das Schlangenei. Berichte aus dem Deutschland der Inflationsjahre 1922-1924* (Berlin 2007), 147.

2 Hitler posited his "anti-semitism of reason" in his first recorded statement on the Jews, a letter to his commanding officer, Adolf Gemlich, dated September 16, 1919. In this letter Hitler rejected the pogrom violence that had hitherto characterized efforts to combat the Jews. Instead, he advocated a "legal battle against" the Jews and their "general removal."

3 Lucy S. Dawidowicz, *The War against the Jews, 1933*–1945 (New York: Holt-Rinehart-Winston, 1975).

4 See, for example, Hans Mommsen, "Hitlers Stellung im nationalsozialistischen Herrschaftssystem," in *Der Führerstaat. Mythos und Realität*, ed. Gerhard Hirschfeld and Lothar Kettenacker (Stuttgart: Klett-Cotta, 1981); Hans Mommsen, "Die Realisierung des Utopischen: Die 'Endlösung der Judenfrage' im Dritten Reich," *Geschichte und Gesellschaft* 9 (1983), 381–420; Karl Schleunes, *The Twisted Road to Auschwitz 1933–39* (Champaign, IL: University of Illinois Press, 1990).

5 Quoted in Ian Kershaw, *Hitler 1889–1936: Hubris* (New York/London: W. W. Norton & Co., 1998), 207.

6 Kershaw, *Hitler: Hubris*, 216 ff.; Volker Ullrich, *Hitler: Ascent 1889–1939*, trans. Jefferson Chase (New York: Knopf, 2016), 174.

7 Kershaw, *Hitler,* 236–7.

8 Ibid., 237.

9 Othmar Plöckinger, *Geschichte eines Buches: Adolf Hitlers "Mein Kampf" 1922–1945* (Munich: Oldenbourg Verlag, 2011), 76–7.

10 On the resemblances of *Mein Kampf* to, and its divergences from, the genre of the *Bildungsroman* (novel of development), see the introduction to MKI:30–1.

11 In their introduction to *Mein Kampf*, the editors of the critical edition note at least two such murder fantasies. In one of them, Hitler avers that journalists critical of national enthusiasm in their reporting during the First World War should have been hanged. This musing on what should have been done contrasts with Hitler's future threat to establish a national court that would

convict the "November criminals" and hang them. With the murderous people's court and special courts of the Third Reich, Hitler would later make good his threat. MKI:51, fn. 349. On the people's court and special courts, see the discussion in MKII:1376, fn. 211.

12 Quoted in "Introduction," MKI:52, fn. 360.

13 Portions of Hell's account are reproduced in Gerald Fleming, *Hitler and the Final Solution* (Berkeley/Los Angeles: University of California Press, 1994), 17–18.

14 Quoted in MKI 52, fn. 360.

15 See, for example, the editors' caveat in their introduction to MKI 52.

16 Eckart, to whom volume II of *Mein Kampf* was dedicated, was a close mentor of Hitler's until his death in 1923. The binary structure of Hitler's thought, which couched everything in terms of an urgent, all-important choice between two antipodes, may have been influenced by Eckart's völkisch theorizing. Both Eckart and the nineteenth-century German anti-Semite Paul de Lagarde ruled out any accommodation with the Jews. Eckart wrote that "when the light collides with the darkness, there is no negotiation. There is only the fight for life and death until the annihilation of one or the other." Quoted in Bärsch, "Der Jude als Antichrist," 172. De Lagarde expressed a similar view in 1887, declaring about relations with the Jews that "with trichinae and bacilli one does not negotiate, nor try to educate them. . . . They are exterminated as thoroughly as possible." Quoted in D. M. Terman, "Paranoid Leadership," in *The Leader: Psychological Essays*, ed. C. B. Strozier et al. (New York: Springer, 2011), 158.

17 Hitler, Manheim 206/MKI:557.

18 The literature on Nazi apocalypticism is sizable. Some of the notable works are Claus-E. Bärsch, "Der Jude als Antichrist in der NS-Ideologie: Die kollektive Identität der Deutschen und der Antisemitismus unter religionspolitologischer Perspektive," *Zeitschrift für Religions- und Geistesgeschichte* 47/2 (1995), 160–88; Eric Voegelin, "Religionsersatz: Die gnostischen Massenbewegungen unserer Zeit," *Wort und Wahrheit* 15/1 (1960), 5–18; Harald Strohm, *Die Gnosis under der Nationalsozialismus* (Frankfurt a.M., 1997); David Redles, "The Turning Point: The Protocols of the Elders of Zion and the Eschatological War between Aryans and Jews," in *The Paranoid Apocalypse: A Hundred-Year Retrospective on The Protocols of the Elders of Zion*, ed. Richard Landes and Steven T. Katz (New York: NYU Press, 2012), 112–31; Robert Wistrich, *Hitler's Apocalypse: Jews and the Nazi Legacy* (New York: St. Martin's Press, 1985); Klaus Vondung, "Apocalyptic Violence," in *Apocalyptic Complex: Perspectives, Histories, Persistence*, ed. Nadia Al-Bagdadi, David Marno, and Matthias Riedl (Central European Press, 2018), 35–52. The reader is referred to the chapter by David Redles in this volume.

19 Jeffrey J. Kripal, *Comparing Religions: Coming to Terms* (Malden, MA: Wiley, 2014), 287–8.

20 Michael Burleigh, *The Third Reich: A New History* (New York: Hill & Wang, 2000), 10.

21 Vondung, "Apocalyptic Violence," 38–9.

22 Ibid., 39.

23 Hitler is emphatic in *Mein Kampf* that the Jews are not a religion but a race. See his discussion on this topic, Hitler, Manheim 232/MKI:617 and Hitler, Manheim 307/MKI:795.

24 Hitler, Manheim 139/MKI 403.

25 The phrase "Malthusian catastrophe" refers to demographic theories advanced by Thomas Malthus in *An Essay on the Principle of Population* (1798). The "catastrophe" occurs when a nation's population expands beyond the means of its subsistence. From this premise Malthus inferred that socioeconomic progress was futile because it would inevitably lead to mass starvation. Hitler derived a very different conclusion from Malthus's basic argument. For Hitler, the Malthusian catastrophe could be averted by invading culturally inferior countries and seizing their land, thereby enabling Germany—and other "culturally superior races"—to avert national disaster (Hitler, Manheim 135/ MKI:391).

26 Hitler, Manheim 61/MKI 223.

27 Hitler, Manheim 65/MKI 231.

28 Hitler's scabrous attacks on the Jews are so extreme that in the estimate of one Austrian commentator, they are indicative of an undiagnosed but corrosive mental illness. Stefan Groβmann, *Memoiren*, quoted in MKI:230, fn. 227.

29 Hitler, Manheim 169/MKI 473. One might perceive in such a remark another "murder fantasy."

30 Hitler, Manheim 231/MKI 615.

31 Hitler, Manheim 246/MKI 649.

32 Hitler, Manheim 305/MKI 791.

33 Hitler, Manheim 305/MKI 793.

34 Hitler, Manheim 312/MKI 813.

35 Hitler, Manheim 334/MKI 871.

36 Hitler exhibits here the influence of Georg Ritter von Schönerer (1842–1921), the anti-Semitic Austrian leader of the pan-German movement, who championed the slogan "The people's law breaks the state's law" (*Volksrecht bricht Staatsrecht*). See MKI:304, fn. 161.

37 MKI:304, fn.161.

38 Hitler, Manheim 178/MKI 495.

39 Paul Bang, author of one of the keystone texts of early National Socialism, *Judas's Debt Registry* (*Judas Schuldbuch*, 1919), argued for the existence of a worldwide Jewish conspiracy, the goal of which was to "reduce its victims to helots, slaves to its will, and objects of exploitation." Folk-national ideologues of the 1920s sought to legitimate their attacks with appeals to this sinister image of the Jews as ruthless aggressors—an image that justified measures of self-defense taken against them. See MKI:906, fn. 110.

40 Hitler, Manheim 534/MKII 1347.

41 Hitler, Manheim 581/MKII 1475.

42 Hitler, Manheim 414/MKII 1055.

43 Hitler, Manheim 584/MKII 1483.

44 MKII 1482, fn. 25.

45 Quoted in MKII 1482, fn. 25.

46 Quoted in MKII 1482, fn. 25.

47 Hitler, Manheim 64/MKI 229. Hitler's prose is convoluted here: he writes that social democracy taught him that you can talk while concealing your real thoughts, the goal of which "lies dormant more between [than within the lines]." In the next sentence, he declares that "the time for me had come of the greatest revolution that I had ever inwardly experienced."

48 This excerpt from the court's report is reproduced in MKII 1368, fn. 194.

49 Saul Friedlander, Introduction to *Hitler and the Final Solution*, by Gerald Fleming (Berkeley/Los Angeles: University of California Press, 1994), xxx–xxxi.

50 Fleming, *Hitler and the Final Solution*, 18.

51 Ibid., 19. The importance Fleming attached to Hitler's habit of deliberate dissimulation is reflected in the title of chapter 2 of Fleming's book: "The Art of Dissembling."

52 Saul Friedlander, introduction to *Hitler and the Final Solution*, xxxi. The original German is even more violent; what Hitler threatens is to "plunge a dagger into the heart [of his enemies]" (" . . . dann kriegst du den Stoss ins Herz hinein"). The image here of murdering an opponent by thrusting a knife into his heart was uncannily prefigured by Joseph Goebbels in his 1926 speech "Lenin oder Hitler? Eine Rede" ("Lenin or Hitler? An Address"). There Goebbels wrote that the Nazis wanted to create a state in which the Germans would be formed into a nation. "This people should be readied to plunge the dagger into the middle of the enemy's heart" (the enemy being the Jews). Joseph Goebbels, "Lenin oder Hitler? Eine Rede" (Zwickau, 1926), 24.

Chapter 9

1 *The Goebbels Diaries, 1942-1943,* ed. and trans. Louis B. Lochner (Garden City: Doubleday, 1948), 376–7.

2 Ibid., 377.

3 David M. Crowe, *The Holocaust: Roots, History, and Aftermath* (Boulder: Westview Press, 2014), 241.

4 *Goebbels Diaries, 1942–1943*, 335.

5 Office of United States Chief of Counsel for Prosecution of Axis Criminality, *Nazi Conspiracy and Aggression: Opinion and Judgment* (Washington: US Government Printing Office, 1947), 121–3; Reinhold Pohl, "Reichskommissarriat Ostland: Schleswig-Holstein Kolonies,"

Schleswig-Holsteins und die Verbrechen der Wehrmacht (November 1998), Schutzgebühr 2, 10–12.

6 Robert Cecil, *The Myth of the Master Race: Alfred Rosenberg and Nazi Ideology* (New York: Dodd Mead, 1972), 18.

7 Christian Hartmann et al., *Hitler, Mein Kampf: Eine kritische Edition*, Volume I (Munich and Berlin: Institute for Contemporary History, 2016), 799, 803. See also Hitler, Manheim 307.

8 Wilhelm Marr, *Der Sieg des Judenthums über das Germanenthum* (Bern: Rudolph Costenoble, 1879), 3.

9 Ibid, 3.

10 Ibid., 7–8.

11 Ibid., 10.

12 Ibid., 10–12, 14.

13 Ibid.

14 Ibid.

15 Ibid., 22.

16 Ibid., 37–8, 45.

17 Ibid., 48.

18 Treitschke, one of Germany's most respected historians and editor of the *Preußische Jahrbücher*, wrote these comments while reviewing Heinrich Graetz's *History of* Germany in 1879. In 1880, he published the anti-Semitic portion of his review in the pamphlet, *Ein Wort über unser Juden.*

19 German Historical Institute, Washington, DC, *German History in Documents and Images*, 4. *Forging an Empire, Bismarckian Germany, 1866-1890.* "Heinrich von Treitschke Pronounces 'The Jews Are Our Misfortune'" (November 15, 1879), 1–4, 411. https://ghi.ghi-dc.org/sub_document.cfm ?document_id-1799._Treitschke_Jews are our misfortune_112.pdf, accessed April 2, 2019.

20 Crowe, *The Holocaust*, 159.

21 Ibid., 60.

22 Richard S. Levy, *The Downfall of the Anti-Semitic Political Parties in Imperial Germany* (New Haven: Yale University Press, 1975), 259.

23 Crowe, *The Holocaust*, 70.

24 Nathaniel Deutsch, *The Jewish Dark Continent: Life and Death in the Russian Pale of Settlement* (Cambridge: Cambridge University Press, 2011), 7.

25 Ibid.

26 Robert F. Byrnes, *Pobedonostsev: His Life and Thought* (London: Indiana University Press, 1968), 205.

27 Stephen M. Berk, *Year of Crisis, Year of Hope: Russian Jewry and the Pogroms of 1881–1882* (Westport, CT: Greenwood Press, 1985), 75.

28 Crowe, *The Holocaust*, 72–3.

29 Barry Trachtenberg, *The Revolutionary Roots of Modern Yiddish, 1903–1917* (Syracuse: Syracuse University Press, 2008), 36–7.

30 Hadassa Ben-Itto, *The Lie That Wouldn't Die: The Protocols of the Elders of Zion* (London: Vallentine Mitchell, 2005), 30, 40.

31 Shlomo Lambroza, "The Pogroms of 1903–1906," in John D. Klier and Shlomo Lambroza, eds. *Pogroms: Anti-Jewish Violence in Modern Russian History* (Cambridge: Cambridge University Press, 1992), 225. The "black hundreds," Lambroza notes, "were an amorphous entity that acted as a semi-autonomous arm of the Russian right."

32 Jean-Louis Bredin, *The Affair: The Case of Alfred Dreyfus*, trans. Jeffrey Mehlman (New York: George Braziller, 1986), 28.

33 Frederick Busi, *The Pope of Antisemitism: The Career and Legacy of Edouard-Adolphe Drumont* (Lanham, MD: University Press of America, 1986), 61.

34 Ben-Itto, *The Lie That Wouldn't Die*, 196.

35 Busi, *Pope of Anti-Semitism*, 60.

36 Ibid., 61.

37 Ibid., 64–5.

38 Ibid., 72–3.

39 Gerald Lamprecht, Elenore Lappin-Eppel, and Ulrich Wyrna, *Jewish Soldiers in the Collective Memory of Central Europe: The Remembrance of World War I from a Jewish Perspective* (Wien: Böhlau Verlag, 2019), 308.

40 Zosa Szakowski, "The German Appeal to the Jews of Poland 1914," *The Jewish Quarterly Review*, 59, 4 (April 1969), 311.

41 The American Jewish Committee, *The Jews in the Eastern War Zone* (New York: The American Jewish Committee, 1916), 37–8; Alexander Watson, *Ring of Steel: Germany and Austria-Hungary in World War I* (New York: Basic Books, 2014), 171, 178, 268; S. Ansky, *The Enemy at His Pleasure: A Journal through the Jewish Pale of Settlement during World War I*, ed. and trans. Joachim Neugroschel (New York: Metropolitan Books, 2002), 116–18; Giuseppe Motta, *The Great War against Eastern European Jewry, 1914-1920* (Cambridge: Cambridge Scholars Publishing, 2017), 21; Eric Lohr, *Nationalizing the Russian Empire: The Campaign against Enemy Aliens during World War I* (Cambridge: Harvard University Press, 2003), 138.

42 Raphael Lemkin, *The Jews in Poland*, New York Public Library Archives, Raphael Lemkin Collection, Box 2, Folder I, p. 38; Jürgen Matthaüs, "German *Judenpolitik* in Lithuania during the First World War," *The Leo Baeck Institute Year Book*, 43, 1 (January 1998), 166–7 [155–74].

43 Volker Ullrich, *Hitler: Downfall, 1939-1945*, trans. Jefferson Chase (New York: Alfred A Knopf, 2020), 620.

44 Volker Ulrich, *Hitler: Ascent, 1889-1939*, trans. Jefferson Chase (New York: Vintage Books, 2017), 65–6.

45 Vejas Gabriel Liulevicius, *War Land on the Eastern Front: Culture, National Identity, and German Occupation in World War I* (Cambridge: Cambridge

University Press, 2005), 66–8, 73–5; Lemkin, *The Jews in Poland*, p. 39; Matthäus, "German *Judenpolitik* in Lithuania," 166–7.

46 Irina Atashkevich, *Gendered Violence: Jewish Women in the Pogroms, 1917 to 1921* (Boston: Academic Studies Press, 2018), 9.

47 George Gustav Telberg and Robert Wilson, *The Last Days of the Romanovs* (New York: George H. Doran Company, 1920), 377. The "Jewish Question" is also discussed on 352, 356, 360, 378.

48 *The Protocols of the Learned Elders of Zion*, trans. and ed. Victor E. Marsden (London: The British Publishing Society, 1923), 3.

49 Ibid., 9–12, 15–20, 24.

50 Ibid., 25, 26, 32–3.

51 Ibid., 34, 35–6, 39–40, 40–1, 47–8, 50–2, 52–3, 54.

52 Alfred Rosenberg, *The Track of the Jew through the Ages*, trans. and annotated by Alexander Jacob (Ostara Publications, 2016), 138.

53 *Memoirs of Alfred Rosenberg with Commentaries by Serge Lang and Ernst von Schenck*, trans. Eric Posselt (Chicago: Ziff-Davis Publishing Company, 1949), 16–27.

54 Michael Kellogg, *The Russian Roots of Nazism: White Emigres and the Making of National Socialism, 1917-1945* (Cambridge: Cambridge University Press, 2005), 42–3.

55 Ibid, 65–6.

56 Ibid., 222.

57 Joseph Frank, *Dostoevsky: A Writer in His Times*, ed. Mary Petrusewicz (Princeton; Princeton University Press, 2010), 745–6.

58 Kellogg, *Russian Roots of Nazism*, 108–9.

59 Ibid., 224.

60 Ibid., 113–14; *Memoirs of Alfred Rosenberg*, 20–1.

61 Engelman, *Dietrich Eckart*, 141.

62 Dietrich Eckart, *Totengräber Russlands* (München: Dr. Ernst Böpple, 1920), 1–22, accessed April 10, 2019, https://archive.org/stream/Eckart-Dietrich-Totengraeber-Russlands-1.

63 Michael Makovsky, *Churchill's Promised Land: Zionism and Statecraft* (New Haven: Yale University Press, 2007), 82.

64 Ibid., 85–7.

65 Ibid., 87.

66 Alfred Rosenberg, *Der Staatsfeindliche Zionismus* (Hamburg, 1921), 16–20; Balfour Declaration, British Foreign Office, November 2, 1917, 1.

67 Alfred Rosenberg, *Díe Protokolle der Weisen von Zíon und díe jüdishce Weltpolítík* (München: Hoheneichen Verlag, 1923), 16–17. Rosenberg included these comments in his introduction to the 1933 edition.

68 Hitler, Manheim 639/MKII 1619?

69 Neil Baldwin, *Henry Ford and the Jews: The Mass Production of Hate* (New York: Public Affairs, 2001), 69–72, 88–91.

70 Ibid., 95.

71 Ibid., 97.

72 Robert Lacy, *Ford: The Men and the Machine* (Boston: Little, Brown, 1986), 196; Baldwin, *Henry Ford and the Jews*, 98, 102–3.

73 Henry Ford, *The International Jew*, I (Boring, OR: CPA Book Publisher, 2000), 7–8.

74 Ibid., 7.

75 Ibid., 8.

76 Ibid., 25.

77 Ibid., 158–9.

78 Henry Ford, *Jewish Influence in American Life*, III: *The International Jew* (Boring, OR: CPA Book Publisher, 2000), 88.

79 Ibid., 88. 96–9, 102.

80 Ibid., 103.

81 Ibid., 115.

82 Ibid.,140.

83 Henry Ford, *Aspects of Jewish Power in the United States, IV: The International Jew* (Boring, OR: CPA Book Publisher, 2000), iii.

84 Ibid., p. 67.

85 Ibid., 67–108 *passim.*

86 Ibid., 108–19 *passim.*

87 Ibid., 121–32 *passim.*

88 Ibid.

89 Ibid., 83.

90 Ibid., 203.

91 Ibid., 224.

92 Ibid., 231.

93 Ibid., 231.

94 Ibid., 240.

95 Ibid., 172.

96 Stefan Link, "Rethinking the Ford-Nazi Connection," *Bulletin of the GHI*, 49 (Fall 2011), 140–1 [135–50]; Martin Kitchen, "The Antisemites *Vade Mecum*: Theodor Frisch's *Handbuch der Judenfrage*," *Antisemitism Studies*, 2, Fall 2018, 199, 210, 225 [194–234].

97 Ian Kershaw, *Hitler: 1889-1936 Hubris* (New York: W.W. Norton, 1998), 158, 161; Oron James Hale, "Gottfried Feder Calls Hitler to Order: An Unpublished Letter on Nazi Party Affairs," *The Journal of Modern History*, 30, 4 (December 1958), 361.

98 Link, "Rethinking the Ford-Nazi Connection," 143.

99 Baldwin, *Henry Ford and the Jews*, 210–11, 218–21, 224–5, 232–3, 238–9.

100 Ibid., 328.

101 MKII 1618–19, n. 186.

102 Peter Longerich, *Goebbels: A Biography* (New York: Random House, 2015), 39.

103 Ibid., 39–40.

104 Cecil, *The Myth of the Master Race*, 73–4; *Hitler, Mein Kampf*, 801.

105 Alfred Rosenberg, *Die Protokolle der Weisen von Zion und die jüdische Weltpolitik* (München: Boheneichen Verlag, 1923), 7, 9, 13, 15–16, 17–27; Henry Ford, *The International Jew*, II: *Jewish Activities in the United States* (Borin, OR: CPA Book Publisher, 2000), 65.

106 Alfred Rosenberg, *Der Mythus des 20. Jahrhunderts: Eine Wertung der Seelisch-geistigen Gestaltenkämpfe unserer Zeit* (München: Hoheneichen-Verlag, 1941), 1–19, 113, 214.

107 Office of United States Chief of Counsel for Prosecution of Axis Criminality, *Nazi Conspiracy and Aggression*, I (Washington: US Government Printing Office, 1946), 5.

108 Office of United States Chief of Counsel for Prosecution of Axis Criminality, *Nazi Conspiracy and Aggression: Opinion and Judgment* (Washington: US Government Printing Office, 1947), 121.

109 Ibid., 122–3; Reinhard Pohl, "Reichskommissariat Ostland: Schelswig-Holsteins Kolonie," *Gegewind*, November 1998, 10–12.

110 Kellogg, *Russian Roots of Nationalism*, 225–6.

111 MKI, II, 979.

112 Hitler, Manheim 65/MKI, I, 231.

113 Kershaw, *Hitler, 1889-1936*, 288.

114 *Hitler's Second Book: The Unpublished Sequel to "Mein Kampf" by Adolf Hitler*, ed. Gerhard Weinberg and trans. Krista Smith (New York: Enigma Books, 2003), 231.

115 Ibid., 232.

116 Norman H. Baynes, ed., *The Speeches of Adolf Hitler, April 1922-August 1939*, I (New York: Howard Fertig, 1969), 726–7.

117 Jeremy Noakes and Geoffrey Pridham, eds., *Nazism: A History in Documents and Eyewitness Accounts, 1919–1945*, II: *Foreign Policy, War and Racial Extermination* (New York: Schocken Books, 1988), 1049.

118 Crowe, *The Holocaust*, 159.

119 Ibid., 160–4.

120 *Hitler: Speeches and Proclamations, 1932-1945: The Chronicle of a Dictatorship*, III, *1939–1940*, ed. Max Domarus (Wauconda, IL: Bolchazy-Carducci, 1997), 1909–10.

121 Ibid., 1940.

122 Jürgen Förster, "Hitler's Decision in Favour of War against the Soviet Union," in *Germany and the Second World War*, Volume IV: *The Attack on the Soviet Union*, ed. Hoorst Boog et al., trans. Dean S. McMurry et al. (Oxford: Clarendon Press, 1998), 27, 28.

123 Ibid, 31.

124 Norman Rich, *Hitler's War Aims: Ideology, the Nazi State, and the Course of Expansion* (New York: W. W. Norton, 1973), 212.

125 Förster, "Hitler's Decision," 37.

126 Noakes and Pridham, *Nazism*, II, 1090.

127 Crowe, *The Holocaust*, p. 199.

128 *The Einsatzgruppen Reports: Selections from the Dispatches of the Nazi Death Squads' Campaign against the Jews, July 1941-January 1943*, ed. Yitzhak Arad, et al. (New York: Holocaust Library, 1989), 47, 59, 62.

129 Ibid., 69.

130 Ibid., 77.

131 *Trials of War Criminals before the Nuernberg Military Tribunals under Control Council Law No. 10*, IV: *The RuSHA Case* (Washington, D.C.: US Government Printing Office, 1950), 285–6.

132 Domarus, *Hitler*, IV: *1941-1945*, 3053–7.

133 Karl A. Schleunes, *The Twisted Road to Auschwitz: Nazi Policy toward German Jews, 1933-1939* (Urbana: University of Illinois Press, 1990).

Chapter 10

1 Hitler, Manheim 194–5/MKI 531–2.

2 Stephen Bailey. "The Berlin Strike of 1918," *Central European History*. 13(2):158–74; 1980.

3 Volker Berghahn, *Europe in the Era of Two World Wars: From Militarism and Genocide to Civil Society, 1900-1950* (Princeton: Princeton University Press, 2006), 26–39.

4 Ibid, p. 87; and chapter 4.

5 Paul Hanebrink, *A Specter Haunting Europe: The Myth of Judeo-Bolshevism* (Cambridge: Harvard University Press, 2018), chapter 1, "The Idea of Judeo-Bolshevism."

6 The presence of Jewish wirepullers in politics and other momentous matters is a staple of anti-Semitism.

7 Brigette Hamann, *Hitler's Vienna: A Dictator's Apprenticeship* (New York: Oxford University Press, 1999), 141–4.

8 Hitler, Manheim 193/MKI 526.

9 Hitler, Manheim178/MKI 495.

10 Paul Hanebrink, op. cit.,. 83–5.

11 Hitler sees the SPD as a bad-faith party, which placates its members by demanding in Parliament what it knows it cannot get.

12 Hitler, Manheim 169/MKI 473; Manheim 206/MKI 557.

13 Hitler often but not always attributes horrors of the Russian Revolution specifically to Jews.

14 Hitler, Manheim 63/MKI.

15 Volker Berghahn, op cit.,10–11. Many Germans observed, envied, and desired to emulate the productive American economy whether they would accept the social bargain on which it was based or not. Some managers were eager to implement Taylorized/routinized manufacturing processes.

16 *Mein Kampf* is replete with comments on the obtuseness and unattractiveness of the upper middle class.

17 For a comparison of the two regimes, see Peter Fritzsche and Jochen Hellbeck, "The New Man in Stalinist Russia and Nazi Germany," Michael Geyer and Shelia Fitzpatrick, eds., *Beyond Totalitarianism: Stalinism and Nazism Compared* (Cambridge: Cambridge University Press, 2009), 302-41

18 Hitler, Manheim 410/ MKII 1047.

19 Erik N. Jensen, *Body by Weimar: Athletes, Gender and German Modernity* (Oxford: Oxford University Press, 2010), Introduction, chapter 1 and *passim.*

20 https://encyclopedia.1914-1918online.net/article/langemarck_myth

21 Hitler, Manheim 504–7/ MKII 1269–78 including notes.

22 Christopher Krebs, *A Most Dangerous Book: Tacitus' Germania* (New York: W.W. Norton & Company, 2012), 214–4.

23 Hitler routinely placed people (administrators and other) in competition and then recognized the figure or group who emerged dominant.

24 Derk Pensler, *Shylock's Children: Economics and Jewish Identity in Modern Europe* (Berkeley: University of California Press, 2001), 137.

25 See Despina Stratigakos, *Hitler at Home* (New Haven: Yale University Press,) 2015.

26 Biographical studies of Hitler highlight his love of art and desire for an artistic career. The 2002 film *Max* presents Hitler as lacking the focus, will, and perseverance to pursue an artistic career, moving instead into politics as an easier career path. Hitler was deeply interested in propaganda, including visual effects and ways to reach the mass of mankind, and he was insightful and successful in some of his approaches.

27 Hitler, Mannheim 499-500/MKII 1259.

28 See Daniel Kalder, *Dictator Literature: A History of Despots through their Writing* (Great Britain: Oneworld, 2018).

29 Pensler, *Shylock's Children, passim.*

30 Eliyau Stern, *Jewish Materialism: The Intellectual Revolution of the 1870s* (New Haven: Yale University Press, 2018).

31 Othmar Plöckinger, *Geschichte eines Buches: Adolf Hitlers "Mein Kampf" 1922–1945* (Munich: Oldenbourg, 2006).

32 Pensler, *Shylock's Children*, 8–9

33 Ibid.

34 Holly Case, *The Age of Questions: Or, A First Attempt at an Aggregate History of the Eastern, Social, Woman, American, Jewish, Polish, Bullion, Tuberculosis, and Many Other Questions Over the Nineteenth Century, and Beyond* (Princeton, NJ: Princeton University Press, 2018). Holly Case quotes Mary Gluck: "It is customary to put quotation marks around the Jewish question because it is not so much a question as an exclusionary discourse about Jewish citizenship and national identity" (p. 298). Certainly the Jewish "Question" was not entirely an ill-intended one. Holly Case sees it originating in 1830 in Britain with discussions about the Parliamentary Bill to remove Jewish disabilities. More than most questions, there was a pejorative aura around the Jewish Question, although disparagement of the Ottoman Empire accrues over the course of the century to the Eastern question. The Ottomans seem to be viewed by querists and international actors as ill-governed and disruptive.

35 Ibid, 92; 263, n. 91.

36 Ibid, 7.

37 Hitler, Manheim 220/ MKI 589.

38 Case, Holly, *Age of Questions*, 126.

39 Hitler often said, with will, one can do anything. Hitler, Manheim 356/MKI 957.

40 His feelings toward Mussolini are both admiring and rivalrous.

41 Peter Ross Range, *1924: The Year that Made Hitler* (New York: Back Bay Books, 2016), offers a very clear articulation of this.

42 Timothy Snyder, *Black Earth: The Holocaust as History and Warning* (New York: Tim Duggan Books, 2015), 2.

Chapter 11

1 Jeffrey Herf, "The Engineer as Ideologue: Reactionary Modernists in Weimar and Nazi Germany," *Journal of Contemporary History* 19:4 (October 1984), 645.

2 See, for example, N. Gidron, J. Adams, and W. Horne, *American Affective Polarization in Comparative Perspective* (Cambridge: Cambridge University Press, 2020) and George E. Marcus, W. Russell Neuman, and Michael MacKuen, *Affective Intelligence and Political Judgment* (Chicago: University of Chicago Press, 2000).

3 I have called their efforts to dejudaize Christianity, "theological bulimia," as their focus was constantly on Judaism and its evils rather than Christianity. See Susannah Heschel, "Theology as a Vision for Colonialism: From Supersessionism to Dejudaization," in "German Protestantism" in *Germany's Colonial Pasts: An Anthology in Memory of Susanne Zantop*, eds. Marcia Klotz, Lora Wildenthal, and Eric Ames (Lincoln, NE: University of Nebraska Press, 2005), 148–64.

4 Volker Ulrich, *Hitler: Ascent, 1889-1939* (New York: Vintage, 2017), 175.

5 Marja Vuorinen, "*Mein Kampf* Revisited: Enemy Images as Inversions of the Self," in *Proceedings of the 9th European Conference on Information Warfare and Security*, ed. Josef Demergis (Reading, UK: Academic Publishing, 2010), 320–6.

6 Repertorium des Archivs der Bekennnenden Kirche Schlwswig-Hosltein, Alte Signatur 32; Neue Nummer 184. Nordelbisches Kirchenarchiv Kiel (NEK-Archiv).

7 Karl Ove Knausgaard, *My Struggle: Book 6*, trans. Don Bartlett (New York: Farrar, Straus and Giroux, 2019), 493.

8 Anson Rabinbach, "Struggles with Mein Kampf," *New York Review of Books* (September 16, 2016). Also reviewed in the *Times Literary Supplement* (see Appendix of this volume).

9 Hitler, Manheim 3/MKI, 93.

10 Hitler, Manheim 25/MKI, 143.

11 Hitler, Manheim 28/MKI, 147.

12 Hitler, Manheim 30/MKI, 155.

13 Hitler, Manheim 51/MKI, 201.

14 Ron Rosenbaum, *Explaining Hitler: The Search for the Origins of His Evil* (New York: Random House, 1998), 327.

15 Hitler, Manheim 51–2/MKI, 201.

16 Hitler, Manheim, 52/MKI, 201.

17 Hitler, Manheim 56/MKI, 209.

18 Hitler, Manheim 64/MKI, 229.

19 Hitler, Manheim 3/MKI, 93.

20 Michael McGuire, "Mythic Rhetoric in *Mein Kampf*: A Structural Analysis," *The Quarterly Journal of Speech* 63 (1, 1977):13.

21 Ulrich, *Hitler: Ascent*, 181.

22 Susannah Heschel, *The Aryan Jesus: Christian Theologians and the Bible in Nazi Germany* (Princeton: Princeton University Press, 2008).

23 Hitler, Manheim 7/MKI, 101.

24 Hitler, Manheim 21/MKI, 133.

25 Hitler, Manheim 21/MKI, 133.

26 Hitler, Manheim 51/MKI, 199.

27 Hitler, Manheim 312, 320/MKI, 813/837.

28 Hitler, Manheim 24/MKI, 139.

29 Hitler, Manheim 51/MKI, 199.

30 Hitler, Manheim 29/MKI, 151.

31 Hitler, Manheim 51/MKI, 199.

32 Hitler, Manheim 52/MKI, 201.

33 Ibid.

34 Hitler, Manheim 57/MKI, 229.

35 Ibid.

36 Hitler, Manheim 55/MKI, 207.

37 Ibid.

38 Hitler, Manheim 57/MKI, 213.

39 Hitler, Manheim 63/MKI, 225.

40 Hitler, Manheim 65/MKI, 231.

41 Shulamit Volkov, "Anti-Semitism as a Cultural Code: Reflections on the History and Historiography of Anti-Semitism in Imperial Germany," *Yearbook of the Leo Baeck Institute* 23 (1978): 25–46.

42 Simone de Beauvoir, *The Second Sex*, trans. by Constance Borde and Sheila Malovany-Chevallier (New York: Knopf, 2010), 56.

43 Hitler, Manheim 318/MKI, 833.

44 McGuire, "Mythical Rhetoric," 2.

45 Hitler, Manheim 297/MKI, 771.

46 Ibid., 298/MKI, 773.

47 Ibid., 304/MKI, 791.

48 Ibid., 319/MKI, 835.

49 For example, eternal blood sucker (Ibid., 310).

50 Andreas Musolff, "What Role Do Metaphors Play in Racial Prejudice? The Function of Anti-Semitic Imagery in Hitler's Mein Kampf," *Patterns of Prejudice* 411 (2007):31, fn. 26.

51 Saul Friedlaender, *Nazi Germany and the Jews: Volume 1: The Years of Persecution 1933–1939* (New York: Harper Perennial, 1998).

52 Richard Steigmann-Gall, *The Holy Reich: Nazi Conceptions of Christianity, 1919–1945* (New York: Cambridge University Press, 2004).

53 Musolff, "Metaphors."

54 Claus-Ekkehard Bärsch, *Die politische Religion des Nationalsozialismus: Die religiöse Dimension der NS-Ideologie in den Schriften von Dietrich Eckart, Joseph Goebbels, Alfred Rosenberg und Adolf Hitler* (Munich: W. Fink, 1998).

55 Hitler, Manheim 120/MKI, 357.

56 Ibid., 311/809.

57 Ibid., 312/813.

58 Ibid., 313/817.

59 Ibid., 318–19/833.

60 Albrecht Koschorke, "Ideology in Execution: On Hitler's *Mein Kampf*," *New German Critique* 124, 42 (1, 2015):4.

61 Koschorke, "Ideology in Execution," 41–2.

62 Ibid.

63 Hitler, *Mein Kampf*, 190, 296, 374–6, 400/MKI, 523, 769/MKII, 961–5, 1023.

64 Ibid., 202, 447/549, 1135.

65 Knausgaard, *My Struggle*, 493–4.

Chapter 12

1 Adolf Hitler, "Hitlers 'grundlegende' Rede über den Anti-Semitismus," *Vierteljahrshefte für Zeitgeschichte* 16 (1968): 417.

2 MKI, 208, fn. 172.

3 "Mein Kampf Lesen." Tagung im Erbacher Hof, Mainz, 28.-29.11.2016 (Regionale Fachberatung Rheinland-Pfalz), 2, accessed December 23, 2020: //rfb.bildung-p.de/fileadmin/user_upload/rfb.bildung-rp.de/Evangelische_Religion/Sasse/Materialien/Ausgewaehlte_antisemitische_Passagen_1.pdf.

4 Hitler, "Hitlers 'grundlegende' Rede über den Anti-Semitismus," 409. See also Barbara Zehnpfennig, "Ist Mein Kampf ein unterschätztes Buch?," *Bundeszentrale für politische Bildungsarbeit*, accessed December 23, 2020, https://www.bpb.de/politik/extremismus/rechtsextremismus/216612/hitlers-mein-kampf-ein-unterschaetztes-buch.

5 Thomas Vordermeyer, "Tactical Guidelines in Adolf Hitler's *Mein Kampf*," *Journal of Modern History* 91(2019): 532.

6 Hitler, Manheim 68/MKI 235.

7 Hitler, Manheim 337/MKI 879.

8 Hitler, Manheim 339/MKI 879.

9 Peter Longerich, "*Davon haben wir nichts gewußt!*": *Die Deutschen und die Judenverfolgung 1933-1945* (Berlin, Pantheon: 2007). Hugo Adler documented the large share of the German population that at least were aware of deportations, if perhaps not of the extermination by gas. Hugo Adler, *Der verwaltete Mensch: Studien zur Deportation der Juden aus Deutschland* (Tübingen, Mohr-Verlag,1974).

10 Michael Rissmann, *Hitlers Gott: Vorsehungsglaube und Sendungsbewußtsein des deutschen Diktators* (Pendo: Zürich, 2001), 60.

11 Ian Kershaw, "'Working Towards the Führer.' Reflections on the Nature of the Hitler Dictatorship."

Contemporary European History, 2(1993):103–18.

12 Adolf Hitler, *Sämtliche Aufzeichnungen, 1905-1924*, eds. Eberhard Jaeckel and Axel Kuhn (Stuttgart: Deutsche Verlags-Anstalt, 1980), 43.

13 Hitler, Manheim 6/MKI 99. See also Volker Ullrich, *Adolf Hitler: Die Jahre des Aufstiegs* (Frankfurt am Main: S. Fischer Verlag, 2013), 31. Hitler claimed that he had wanted to become a priest or even abbot until his father came to dislike his "rhetorical talents." Hitler, Manheim 6/MKI 99.

14 August Kubizek, *Adolf Hitler: Mein Jugendfreund* (Graz, 1953), cited in Brigitte Hamann, *Hitler's Vienna: A Dictator's Apprenticeship* (Oxford: Oxford University Press, 1999), 302.

15 Hamann, 250. Hitler complained bitterly and occasionally insightfully about poverty in Vienna. In this discussion, he mentions no Catholic social teaching or God. See also MKI, up to page 161.

16 Hamann, 250.

17 None of Hitler's biographers mention any sort of theological engagement on Hitler's part, nor does there seem to be any evidence that, after leaving school, he ever read a religious text. Other than the Bible, he mentions none in *Mein Kampf.*

18 The editors also noted that "Hitler . . . did not understand the Christian religions and that their message remained alien to him. Hitler himself warned 'Pure Christianity' must lead to 'the destruction of humanity.'" MKI, 340, fn. 230.

19 Claus-Ekkehard Bärsch, *Die politische Religion des Nationalsozialismus: die religiöse Dimension der NS-Ideologie in den Schriften von Dietrich Eckart, Joseph Goebbels, Alfred Rosenberg und Adolf Hitler* (Munich: Wilhelm Fink Verlag 1998), 58.

20 Bärsch, 65, 66.

21 Hitler, Manheim 65/MKI 231.

22 *The Hitler Trial before the People's Court in Munich*. Vol. I, H. Francis Freniere, Lucie Karcic, Philip Fandek, trans. (Arlington, VA: University Publications of America, 1976), 59.

23 *The Speeches of Adolf Hitler: April 1922-August 1939: An English Translation of Representative Passages Arranged under Subjects*. Ed. Norman Baynes, Vol. I (New York: Fertig, 1969), 404.

24 Hitler, Manheim 204/MKI 553.

25 While Derek Hastings has shown that some leading Nazis and certainly many rank-and-file members initially considered party membership and Catholic faith compatible, their faith did not endure. Richard Steigmann-Gall's argument that many party leaders remained Christian is untenable, not only because of their self-excommunication but also because of Hitler's desire to destroy the churches. Derek Hastings, *Catholicism and the Roots of Nazism: Religious Identity and National Socialism* (Oxford: Oxford University Press, 2009) and Richard Steigmann-Gall, *The Holy Reich: Nazi Conceptions of Christianity, 1919-1945* (Cambridge: Cambridge University Press 2003).

26 Rissmann, 82–3.

27 Hitler, Manheim 85/MKI 287.

28 Hitler, Manheim 251–7/MKI 651–6.

29 Manheim, Hitler 379/MKII 973. See also Christian Dube, *Religiöse Sprache in Reden Adolf Hitlers: analysiert an Hand ausgewählter Reden aus den Jahren 1933–1945* (Norderstedt: Books on Demand GmbH, 2004), 197.

30 Hitler, Manheim 108–14/MKI 333–9.

31 Hitler, Manheim, 561/MKII 1423.

32 Hitler, Manheim 402/MKII 1029.

33 Adolf Hitler, *My New Order*, ed. Raoul de Roussy de Sales (New York: Octagon Books, 1973), 67.

34 Hitler, *My New Order*, 68.

35 Hitler, Manheim 65/MKI 231.

36 Hitler, Manheim 561/MKII 1427.

37 Hitler, Manheim 122/MKI 355.

38 *Sämtliche Aufzeichnungen*, 727.

39 Zehnpfennign, Barbara, *Hitlers Mein Kampf: Eine Interpretation* (Paderborn: Wilhelm Fink Verlag. 2006), 275.

40 Paul Hoser, "Hitler und die katholische Kirche: Zwei Briefe aus dem Jahr 1927," *Vierteljahrshefte für Zeitgeschichte* 42(1994)3: 488.

41 Rainer Bucher, *Hitlers Theologie* (Würzburg: Echter, 2008), 41–3.

42 Bucher, *Theologie*, 52–3. Hitler condemned Catholicism's loyalty not only to the universal church embodied in the papacy but also to the supposed cooperation of Habsburg's Catholic hierarchy with Czech nationalist clergy. Hitler, Manheim 108/MKI 333 and 110/335.

43 Hitler, Manheim 479/MKII 973.

44 Ibid.

45 Hitler, *My New Order*.70

46 Ullrich, *Hitler,* 49. See also Ian Kershaw, *Hitler, 1889-1945: Hubris (*New York: W.W. Norton, 1999), 34 and Hitler, Manheim 106/MKI 331.

47 Hitler, Manheim 267/MKI 70.

48 Hitler, Manheim 459/MKII 1163.

49 Hitler, Manheim 432/MKII 1097. See also Claus-Ekkehard Bärsch, "Die Schoah und 'Das Reich, das kommt.' Die politische Religion Joseph Goebbels' und der religiöse Gehalt der Rassedoktrin Adolf Hitlers." *Theologie. Geschichte,* 3(2008), accessed January 14, 2021, http://universaar.uni-saarland .de/journals/index.php/tg/article/viewArticle/164/190.

50 Hitler, Manheim 85/MKI 281.

51 Hitler, Manheim 379/MKI II 973.

52 *The Speeches of Adolf Hitler*, 338.

53 Götz Aly, *Hitlers Volksstaat: Raub, Rassenkrieg und nationaler Sozialismus* (Frankfurt: Fischer Taschenbuch Verlag, 2006) and Peter Longerich, "*Davon haben wir nichts gewußt*": *Die Deutschen und die Judenverfolgung, 1933–1945* (Munich: Pantheon, 2007).

54 See also Christoph Kreutzmüller, *Final Sale in Berlin: The Destruction of Jewish Commercial Activity, 1930–1945* (New York: Berghahn Books, 2015).

55 Rosenberg an Hess, *Akten der Parteikanzlei*, Veröffentlichungen des Instituts für Zeitgeschichte (München, 1983), Microfilm, Nos. 801-00320 - 801-00324, May 1, 1940.

56 Meldung aus dem Reich vom 20. Januar 1941. Doc. No. 155 in *Meldungen aus dem Reich*, vol. 6 (Boberach, 1983), 1917–19.

57 Heinrich Himmler, Speech to SS-commanders in Posen, October 4, 1943, accessed January 3, 2021, https://phdn.org/archives/holocaust-history.org/himmler-poznan/speech-text.shtml.

58 Adolf Hitler, "Nero-Decree of March 19, 1945," accessed January 3, 2021, http://ghdi.ghi-dc.org/docpage.cfm?docupage_id=2382.

59 Adolf Hitler, "Political Will and Testament of April 28, 1945," accessed January 3, 2021, https://jewishvirtuallibrary.org/hitler-s-political-testament-april-1945.

60 Ian Kershaw, *Hitler: A Biography* (New York: W.W. Norton, 2008), 382. See also Rissmann, 51.

61 Othmar Plöckinger, *Geschichte eines Buches: Adolf Hitlers "Mein Kampf," 1922-1945* (Munich: R. Oldenbourg, 2006), 272.

62 Plöckinger, 277–9.

63 Ludwig Volk, *Der Bayerische Episkopat und der Nationalsozialismus, 1930-1934* (Mainz: Matthias-Grünewald-Verlag, 1965), 14.

64 Plöckinger, 277.

65 Michael Kardinal Faulhaber, *Deutsches Ehrgefühl und katholisches Gewissen: Zur religiösen Lage der Gegenwart*, Vol. 1 (München: F. A. Pfeiffer, 1925), 18. While this was a less than ringing endorsement of Jewish rights, Faulhaber later faced criticism that he had been too kind to Jews (Ibid). See also Cornelia Hecht, *Deutsche Juden und Anti-Semitismus in der Weimarer Republik* (Bonn: J.H.W. Dietz Nachf, 2003), and Ulrike Ehret, *Church, Nation and Race: Catholics and Anti-Semitism in Germany and England, 1918–45* (Manchester: Manchester University Press, 2011), in which Ehret puts Catholic-Jewish relations in a longer chronological perspective. For a Catholic-friendly study of Weimar Catholicism and Judaism, see Uwe Mazura, *Zentrumspartei und Judenfrage, 1870/71-1933* (Mainz: Matthias-Grünewald-Verlag, 1994).

66 Jakob Nötges, SJ, *Nationalsozialismus und Katholizismus* (Cologne: Gilde-Verlag, 1931), 157–8.

67 Hitler, Manheim 100/MKI 313.

68 Hitler, Manheim 106/MKI 331.

69 *Sämtliche Aufzeichnungen*, 1000.

70 Wolfgang Benz, "Judenchristen. Zur doppelten Ausgrenzung einer Minderheit im NS-Staat," *Edith Stein Jahrbuch* 3(1997): 307–18. See also Bernhard Stasiewski, ed., *Akten deutscher Bischöfe über die Lage der Kirche 1933-1945*, vol. I (Paderborn: Ferdinand-Schöningh-Verlag, 1968), 53–4.

71 *Sämtliche Aufzeichnungen*, 623.

72 Hitler, Manheim 117/MKI 347. The irony of this becomes apparent in Kevin Spicer, *Hitler's Priests: Catholic Clergy and National Socialism* (DeKalb: Northern Illinois University Press, 2008).

73 *Verhandlungen des Reichstags, Stenographische Berichte*, Vol. 381 (June 5, 1924), 144.

74 *Sämtliche Aufzeichnungen*, 544.

75 Michael Faulhaber, *Deutsches Ehrgefühl und katholisches Gewissen* (Munich: Dr. Franz A. Pfeiffer Verlagsgesellschaft, 1925), 18.

76 *Reden, Schriften, Anordnungen, Februar 1925 bis Januar 1933*, 114.

77 *Völkischer Beobachter* (Berlin edition), Nr. 53, 22. Februar 1933.

78 *Reden, Schriften, Anordnungen, Februar 1925 bis Januar 1933*, 92.

79 Ibid., 237.

80 Wilhelm Moock, "Christentum und Nation," *Hochland* 30 (1932).

81 *Akten deutscher Bischöfe über die Lage der Kirche, 1918-1933*, Vol. II. (Paderborn: Ferdinand-Schöningh-Verlag, 2007), 853, Nr. 489, Meyer an Ordinariat München, Mainz, 24. Dezember 1929.

82 *Akten 1918-1933*, Vol. II, 1003, Nr. 492, Faulhaber an die Konzilskongregation, München, 25. Januar 1930.

83 *Akten 1918-1933*, Vol. II, 1180, Nr. 565, Klens an Schulte, Düsseldorf, 3. Februar 1932.

84 Walter Hannot, *Die Judenfrage in der katholischen Tagespresse Deutschlands und Österreichs 1923-1933* (Mainz: Matthias-Grunewald-Verlag, 1990), 121.

85 *Akten, 1918-1933*, 795-797, Nr. 3*a, Anlage zu Nr. 3*, 2. Entwurf Faulhabers für Pastorale Anweisungen (München, 18. Dezember 1930).

86 Bundesarchiv Berlin, R 8007/2 Wahldienst der Zentrumspartei 28.7.-14.9 1930: Wahldienst 58 (Artikeldienst der Deutschen Zentrumspartei Nr. 305), September 9, 1930: "Katholisches gegen 'germanisches' Moralgesetz: Kardinal Faulhaber gegen das völkische Rasseideal der Nationalsozialisten."

87 On Bertram to 1933, see Sascha Hinkel, *Adolf Kardinal Bertram: Kirchenpolitik in Kaiserreich und Weimarer Republik* (Paderborn: Ferdinand-Schöningh-Verlag, 2010), 117.

88 Bistumsarchiv Görlitz, Nachlaß Adolf Kardinal Bertram, Vol. 3, Hirtenbriefe zu verschiedenen Anlässen, 1914-1940: "Die Stellung der katholischen Kirche zu Radikalismus und Nationalismus: Ein offenes Wort zu ernster Stunde am Jahresschlusse 1930."

89 *Akten deutscher Bischöfe über die Lage der Kirche 1933-1945*, Vol. I, 1933–4, Veröffentlichungen der Kommission für Zeitgeschichte series A, vol. 5 (Mainz: Matthias-Grunewald-Verlag, 1968), 806ff, Nrs. 6*-13*, Pastorale Anweisungen und Kundgebungen, 10. Februar-19. März 1931.

90 Cardinal Faulhaber, who crafted one early version of the statement, had written, "Nazism exalts race over religion," but he had encountered opposition from other bishops who wished to weaken the generalization. *Akten 1933-1945*, 795, Nr. 3*, 2. Entwurf Faulhaber für Pastoral Anweisung, München, 18. Dezember 1930.

91 IfZ, ED 414, NL Herbert Frank *Salzburger Chronik*, Nr. 262, 14.11.1932.

92 Ingbert Naab, O.Min.Cap., "Das Dritte Reich ist da!" *Der Gerade Weg*, June 19, 1932, trans. in Neil Gregor, *Nazism* (Oxford, 2000), 38–40.

93 Ingbert Naab, O.Min.Cap., *Ist Hitler ein Christ?* (Munich: Zeichenring Verlag, 1931), 10–13. On Naab, see *Bibliographisch-Biographisches Kirchenlexikon* at http://www.bautz.de/bbkl/n/naab.shtml. On the proper respect for African clergy, see Pius XI, *Rerum Ecclesiae: Encyclical of Pope Pius XI on Catholic Missions* (February 28, 1926), No. 26.

94 Naab, 17.

95 Jakob Nötges, SJ, *Nationalsozialismus und Katholizismus* (Cologne: Gilde-Verlag, 1931), 157–8.

96 John Connelly, *From Enemy to Brother: The Revolution in Catholic Teaching on the Jews, 1933-1965* (Cambridge: Harvard University Press, 2012), 28, and Olaf Blaschke, "Die Anatomie des katholischen Anti-Semitismus. Eine Einladung zum internationalen Vergleich." Ed. Aram Matthioli, *Katholischer Anti-Semitismus im 19. Jh.* (Zürich: Oldenbourg Wissenschaftsverlag, 2000), 10.

Chapter 13

1 Hitler, Manheim 3–65/MK I 89–231. For an accurate account of Hitler's time in Vienna, see Brigitte Haman, *Hitler's Vienna: A Dictator's Apprenticeship* (Oxford: Oxford University Press, 1999).

2 Hitler, Manheim 51/MKI 199.

3 Hitler, Manheim 52/MKI 201.

4 Hitler, Manheim 58/MKI 213.

5 Hitler, Manheim 64/MKI 229.

6 Hitler, Manheim 65/MKI 231.

7 Hitler, Manheim 65/MK1 231.

8 That Weimar Germany was interpreted by many in apocalyptic ways is discussed in David Redles, *Hitler's Millennial Reich: Apocalyptic Belief and the Search for Salvation* (New York: New York University Press, 2005), esp. 14–45. See also Klaus Vondung, *The Apocalypse in Germany*, translated by Stephen D. Ricks, (Columbia, MO: University of Missouri Press, 2000); and Jürgen Brokoff, *Die Apokalypse in der Weimar Republik* (Munich: Wilhelm Fink Verlag, 2001).

9 On Eisner, see Albert Earle Gurganus, *Kurt Eisner: A Modern Life* (Rochester, NY: Camden House, 2018).

10 Bernhard Horstmann, *Hitler in Pasewalk* (Düsseldorf: Droste Verlag, 2004), 28. On Hitler during this postwar period, see Othmar Plöckinger, *Unter Soldaten und Agitatoren: Hitlers Prägende Jahre im Deutschen Militär 1918–1920* (Paderborn: Ferdinand Schöningh, (2013); and Thomas Weber, *Becoming Hitler: The Making of a Nazi* (New York: Basic Books, 2017).

11 On Eckart, see Margarete Plewnia, *Auf dem Weg zu Hitler: Der völkische Publizist Dietrich Eckart* (Bremen: Schünemann, 1970); and Ralph Max Engelman, "Dietrich Eckart and the Genesis of Nazism," PhD dissertation, University of Michigan, Ann Arbor, 1971).

12 Volker Ullrich, *Hitler: Ascent, 1889-1939* (New York: Knopf, 2016), 106.

13 Discussed in Nicholas Goodrick-Clarke, *The Occult Roots of Nazism* (New York: New York University Press, 1992), 149–50; Hermann Gilbhard, *Die Thule Gesellschaft: Vom Okkulten Mummerschanz zu Hakenkreuz* (Munich: Kiessling Verlag, 1994), 148–54.

14 Dietrich Eckart, "Immer lächen, und doch ein Schurke!" *Auf gut deutsch* (February 7, 1919), 83.

15 Dietrich Eckart, "Luther und der Zins," *Auf gut deutsch* (July 5: 1919), 386–7.

16 On the influence of Joachim through the ages, see Matthias Riedel, *Joachim von Fiore: Denker der vollendeten Menschheit* (Würzberg: Königshausen & Neumann, 2004); Bernard McGinn, *The Calabrian Abbot: Joachim of Fiore in the History of Western Thought* (New York: Macmillan, 1998); and Marjorie Reeves, *The Influence of Prophecy in the Later Middle Ages: A Study in Joachism* (Southbend, IN: Notre Dame University Press, 1993) and *Joachim of Fiore and the Prophetic Future* (New York: Harper & Row, 1977).

17 Joachim's use of the dragon from Revelation is discussed in Pavlína Cermanová, "Gog and Magog: Using Concepts of Apocalyptic Enemies in the Hussite Era," in Wolfram Brandes, Felicitas Schmieder, and Rebekka Voss, eds., *Peoples of the Apocalypse: Eschatological Beliefs and Political Scenarios* (Berlin: de Gruyter, 2016), 239–56.

18 The connection of Joachim's concept of the Third Reich to the Nazis is discussed in David Redles, "Nazi End Times: The Third Reich as Millennial Reich," in Karolyn Kinane and Michael A. Ryan, eds., *End of Days: Essays on the Apocalypse Antiquity to Modernity* (Jefferson, NC: McFarland, 2009), 173–96. See also Matthias Riedl, "Longing for the Third Age: Revolutionary Joachism, Communism, and National Socialism," in Matthias Riedl, ed., *A Companion to Joachim of Fiore* (Leiden: Brill, 2018), 267–318; Stefan Heep, "The Long Way of Political Theology to Religious 'Germanism' or How National Socialism Could be Perceived as Fulfillment of Christianity," in *Politics, Religion & Ideology* (2020), vol. 21, No. 3, 311–36; Thomas Flanagan, "The Third Reich: Origins of a Millenarian Symbol," *History of European Ideas*, 8(3) (1987): 283–95; and Buchard Brentjes, *Der Mythos vom Dritten Reich: Drei Jahrtausende Traum von der Erlösung* (Hannover: Fackelträger-Verlag, 1997).

19 Eckart composed a free translation of Peer Gynt that was first produced in 1914, and it became the second most performed work at the Royal Playhouse during the war. Dietrich Eckart, *Henrik Ibsens Peer Gynt: in freier Übertragung für die deutsche Bühne eigerichtet* (Munich: Hoheneichen, 1917). For the view that Ibsen's work may have influenced Hitler as well, see Steven F. Sage, *Ibsen and Hitler: The Playwright, the Plagiarist, and the Plot for the Third Reich* (New York: Carroll & Graf, 2006).

20 Otto Weininger, *Über die letzten Dinge* (Vienna: W. Braumüller, 1904).

21 Ibid, 35.

22 My translation of the German, as found in Englemann, "Dietrich Eckart," 70. The latter three associations were inspired by antithetical characters in Richard Wagner's operas, taken from Nordic mythology and Christian Grail legends, which similarly presented a world of opposing forces locked in a struggle for redemption.

23 Quoted in Michael Hesemann, *Hitlers Religion: Die fatale Heilslehre des Nationalzozialismus* (Munich: Pattloch, 2004), 174.

24 See Frank Jacob, "Dietrich Eckart and the Formulation of Hitler's Antisemitism," in Frank Jacob and Sarah K. Danielsson, eds., *Intellectual Anti-Semitism: Comparative Studies from a Global Perspective* (Würzburg: Verlag Königshausen & Neumann, 2018), 83–94.

25 See Claus-Ekkehard Bärsch, "Der Jude als Antichrist in der NS-Ideology," *Zeitschrift für Religions- und Geistesgeschichte* 47(2) (1995): 160–88 and "Antijudaism, Apokalyptik und Satanologie: Die religiösen Elemente des nationalsozialistischen Antisemitismus," *Zeitschrift für Religions- und Geistesgeschichte* 40(2) (1988): 112–33.

26 On the origins of this myth, see Michael Hagemeister, "Die 'Protokolle der Weisen von Zion' und der Basler Zionistenkongress von 1897," in Heiko Haumann, ed., *Der Traum von Israel: Die Ursprünge des modernen Zionismus* (Weinheim: Beltz Athenäum Verlag, 1998): 250–73.

27 Gottfried zur Beek, ed., *Die Geheimnesse der Weisen von Zion* (Charlottenberg: Verlag Auf Vorposten, 1919). Müller von Hausen had received a copy of the *Protocols* from Piotr Shabelskii-Bork, a former Russian officer who had fled to Germany from Bolshevik Russia. Shabelskii-Bork was closely associated with Fyodor Vinberg, a fellow Russian refugee who published a version of the *Protocols* in *Luch Sveta* (*Ray of Light*), a yearbook that presented the combat against the Jewish Elders as a religious mission. According to Vinberg, if the Germans and Russians joined together to defeat the Jews, there would be peace on earth. For more on this and other aspects of the *Protocols*, see Norman Cohn, *Warrant for Genocide: The Myth of the Jewish World Conspiracy and Protocols of the Elders of Zion* (London: Serif, 1996). A useful historiography concerning the *Protocols*, including a few corrections to Cohn's work, is Ronald S. Green, "Scholars Contending with Delusional Ideology: Historians, Antisemitic Lore, and *The Protocols*," *SHOFAR* 18 (2000): 82–100. See also Evan Horn and Michael Hagemeister, eds., *Die Fiktion von der jüdischen Weltverschwörung: Zu Text und Kontext der "Protokolle der Weisen von Zion"* (Göttingen: Wallstein Verlag, 2012).

28 On some of the modern uses of this pernicious forgery, see Dina Porat, "*The Protocols of the Elders of Zion*: New Uses of an Old Myth," in Robert S. Wistrich, ed., *Demonizing the Other: Antisemitism, Racism, and Xenophobia* (Amsterdam: Harwood Academic, 1999), 322–34.

29 For more on the apocalyptic nature of the fake source, see David Redles "The Turning Point: *The Protocols of the Elders of Zion* and the Eschatological War between Aryans and Jews," in Richard Landes and Steven T. Katz, eds., *The Paranoid Apocalypse: A Hundred-Year Retrospective on* The Protocols of the Elders of Zion (New York: New York University Press, 2012), 112–31.

30 The possible origin of the document, based on a close analysis of available copies, is discussed in Cesare G. De Michelis, *The Non-Existent Manuscript: A*

Study of the Protocols of the Sages of Zion (Lincoln: University of Nebraska Press, 2004), esp. 73–86.

31 Maurice Joly, *Dialogue aux enfers entre Machiavel et Montesquieu ou La politique de Machiavel au XIXe siècle, par un contemporain* (Brussels: A. Mertens, 1864). Goedsche's book, written under the name Sir John Retcliffe the Younger, was entitled *Biaritt*z (Berlin: C.S. Liebrecht, 1868). The "Rabbi's Speech" section was later republished as a supposedly factual document as *Die Geheimnisse des Judenfriedhofes in Prag* (Praha: Orbis, 1942).

32 Quotations from *The Rabbi's Speech* as found in appendix one of Cohn's, *Warrant for Genocide*, 279–84.

33 I talk about this process at length in *Hitler's Millennial Reich*. See also James M. Rhodes, *The Hitler Movement: A Modern Millenarian Revolution* (Stanford: Hoover Institute Press, 1980); and Robert Ellwood, "Nazism as a Millennialist Movement," in Catherine Wessinger, ed., *Millennialism, Persecution, and Violence* (Syracuse: Syracuse University Press, 2000), 241–60.

34 See the work of Michael Hagemeister, "Eine Apokalypse unserer Zeit: Die Prophezeiungen des heiligen Serafim von Sarov über das Kommen des Antichrist und das Ende der Welt," in Joachim Hösler and Wolfgang Kessler, eds., *Finis Mundi: Endzeiten und Weltenden im östlichen Europa* (Stuttgart: Franz Steiner Verlag, 1998): 41–60; "Sergej Nilus und die 'Protokolle der Weisen von Zion," *Jahrbuch für Antisemitismusforschung* 5 (1996): 127–47; and "Trilogie der Apokalypse: Vladimir Solov'ev, Serafim von Sarov und Sergej Nilus über das Kommen des Antichrist und das Ende der Weltgeschichte," in Wolfram Brandes und Felicitas Schmieder, eds., *Antichrist: Konstruktionen von Feindbildern* (Berlin: Akademie Verlag, 2010), 255–75.

35 That this belief in Moscow as the Third Rome merged with a growing sense of Russia's special mission is discussed in David G. Rowley, "'Redeemer Empire': Russian Millenarianism," *American Historical Review* (1999), 1582–602. This sense of salvific mission would pass on to Russian Bolshevism, connecting the concept of the Third Rome to the third and final stage of Marxist revolutionary theory. See Peter J. S. Duncan, *Russian Messianism: Third Rome, Revolution, Communism and After* (New York: Routledge, 2000).

36 Discussed in Cohn, *Warrant for Genocide*, 99–100.

37 On the passage of the *Protocols* to Germany and later to the Nazis, see Michael Kellogg, *The Russian Roots of Nazism: White Émigres and the Making of National Socialism* (Cambridge: Cambridge University Press, 2005).

38 Dietrich Eckart, "Tagebuch," *Auf gut deutsch* (October 10, 1919), 512–13. The map in question is most likely the one that appears as an appendix to Hausen's translation of the *Protocols* entitled "The Kaiser's Dream." Eckart noted in the above article that this supposed prewar map labeled the Russian territory "Russian Desert," exactly as the "Kaiser's Dream" map does. This map actually first appeared in the English periodical *Truth* in 1890 and was meant as a satire of the then German Kaiser's imperial ambitions. Hausen and Eckart claimed that it was a true document that betrayed Jewish desires to redraw the map of Europe through organizing a world war between the

European empires. The origins of the "Kaiser's Dream" is discussed in Cohn, *Warrant for Genocide*, 154.

39 Dietrich Eckart, "Die Midgardschlange," *Auf gut deutsch* (December 30, 1919), 680–1. This article is directly preceded by two images. One labeled "Before the World War" shows a woman wearing a crown and holding a sword, representing the European monarchies, standing upon a snake with a stereotypical Jewish head. The second image is labeled "After the World War" and shows the woman now being strangled by the "Jewish" snake, the crown, and sword on the ground.

40 Ibid., 681, 683.

41 Ibid., 692.

42 Dietrich Eckart, "Die Schlacht auf den Katalaunischen Feldern" *Auf gut deutsch* (February 20, 1920), 86.

43 On the Jewish-Bolshevik conspiracy myth, see Lorna Waddington, *Hitler's Crusade: Bolshevism, the Jews and the Myth of Conspiracy* (London: I.B. Taurus, 2012); and Paul Hanebrink, *A Specter Haunting Europe: The Myth of Judeo-Bolshevism* (Cambridge, MA: Belknap), 2018.

44 For analysis of Hitler's early speeches and their indebtedness to the *Protocols*, see Günter Schubert, *Anfänge nationalsozialistischer Außenpolitik* (Köln: Verlag Wissenschaft und Politik, 1963), 33–5. Also instructive is Alexander Stein, *Adolf Hitler: Schüler der "Weisen von Zion"* (Karlsbad: Verlagsanstalt Graphia, 1936).

45 Eberhard Jäckel and Axel Kuhn, eds., *Hitler: Sämtliche Aufzeichnungen, 1905-1924* (Stuttgart: Deutsche Verlag-Anstalt, 1980), 452, 458.

46 Adolf-Viktor von Koerber, ed., *Hitler: Sein Leben, Seine Reden* (Munich: Deutscher Volksverlag, 1923), 71–2. Interestingly, Sergei Nilus earlier had interpreted the Jewish star as the sign of the Anti-Christ.

47 Hitler, Manheim 307–8/MKI 799–803.

48 This notion that the *Protocols*, even if a forgery, nonetheless reveal a truth is explored in Randall L. Bytwerk, "Believing in 'Inner Truth': *The Protocols of the Elders of Zion* in Nazi Propaganda, 1933-1945," *Holocaust and Genocide Studies* 29(2) (2015): 212–29.

49 This had been done as well by Alfred Rosenberg in his *Die Spur des Juden im Wandel der Zeiten* (Munich: Deutsche Volksverlag, 1920).

50 Dietrich Eckart, *Der Bolschewismus von Moses bis Lenin: Zwiegspräche zwischen Adolf Hitler und mir* (Munich: Hoheneichen-Verlag, 1924). Some scholars dismiss the value of this work as it was solely written by Eckart: see Margarete Plewnia, *Auf dem Weg zu Hitler: Der völkische Publizist Dietrich Eckart* (Bremin: Schüneman, 1970, esp. 94–112, and Shaul Esh, "Eine neue literarische Quelle Hitlers? Eine methodolgische Überlegung," *Geschichte in Wissenschaft und Unterricht* 15 (1964): 487–93. Ralph Max Engelman, in his dissertation "Dietrich Eckart and the Genesis of Nazism" (University of Michigan, 1971), agrees that the source was composed solely by Eckart but states, I think correctly, that "everything we know about Eckart and Hitler lends credence to the document as a representation of the relationship and

ideas they shared" (236). While the words are Eckart's, I will cite "Hitler" as I believe these words truly reflect Hitler's ideas, formed under the tutelage of his mentor.

51 This portion of Himmler's recommended reading list can be found in Manfred Messerschmidt, *Die Wehrmacht im NS-Staat: Zeit der Indoktrination* (Hamburg: R.v. Decker, 1969), 241.

52 These include classical writers like Strabo and Cicero, early Church fathers such as Aquinas and Chrysostom, as well as later religious and philosophical thinkers like Martin Luther, Giordano Bruno, Schopenhauer, and many others.

53 This built on the work of Alfred Rosenberg, who in the pages of Eckarts' *Auf gut Deutsch* and in his *Die Spur des Juden im Wandel der Zeiten* attempted to fuse the Talmud and *The Protocols of the Elders of Zion* in order to "expose" the Jews. This tendency to use Jewish sources to "reveal" their true nature continued after the Nazis assumed power. Discussed by Paul Lawrence Rose in "Talmudic Scholarship in the Stab-Rosenberg's 'Institute for Research into the Jewish Question,'" paper delivered at the 113th annual meeting of the American Historical Association, held January 7–10, 1999, Washington, DC.

54 Eckart, *Der Bolschewismus*, 7–8.

55 Ibid., 9. Hitler is referring to Josh. 6:21, "Then they utterly destroyed all in the city, both men and women, young and old, oxen, sheep and asses, with the edge of the sword."

56 Ibid.

57 The Talmud is similarly used to "reveal" the "true" Jewish nature (for instance, misreading Jebamoth 60 b as demanding the preserving of three-year-olds for the sexual pleasure of rabbis). Ritual murders of non-Jewish children also make their appearance here with striking resonance to contemporary American fears of child sex abuse and sacrifices found in QAnon conspiracy theories, a modern-day Blood Libel. Sirach 36:2-12 is used to again reveal the Jewish instinct for exterminating *goyim*, as is Schulchan Aruch, Orach Caijim 480; "Pour out, oh Lord your fury over the *goyim*, who do not know you and over the kingdoms which do not invoke your name. Pursue them in wrath and extinguish them beneath God's heaven." For Eckart this is an invocation that all nonbelievers are to be "exterminated." Hitler responds, "Some religion! This wallowing in filth, this hate, this malice, this arrogance, this hypocrisy, this pettifogging, this incitement to deceit and murder—is that a religion? Then there has never been anyone more religious than the devil himself. It is the Jewish essence, the Jewish character, period!"

58 Ibid., 24 The reference is to Jn 8:43. By the time of the writing of the Gospel of John the distinction between Christian and Jew (increasingly a dreaded Other) begins already to shape the developing Christian anti-Jewish narrative. The growing myth of Jewish culpability in the death of Jesus played an increasingly important role in Christian anti-Semitism. See John Dominic Crossan, *Who Killed Jesus: Exposing the Roots of Anti-Semitism in the Gospel Story of the Death of Jesus* (New York, 1995). It is not surprising that the Gospel of John is reported to have been Hitler's favorite Gospel. For background on the Christian myth of the Satanic Jew, see Joshua Trachtenberg, *The Devil and the*

Jews: The Medieval Conception of the Jew and Its Relation to Modern Anti-Semitism (New Haven: Yale University Press, 1943) and Andrew Gow, *The Red Jews: Anti-Semitism in an Apocalyptic Age, 1200-1600* (New York: E. J. Brill, 1995).

59 Eckart, *Der Bolschewismus*, 18.

60 H. R. Trevor-Roper, ed., *Hitler's Table Talk: 1941-1944*, translated by Norman Cameron and R. H. Stevens (New York: Enigma Books, 2008), 548. Entry for November 29–30, 1944. This English edition of the table talks was translated from the French edition published by Swiss Hitler admirer François Genoud. That edition has some material not found in, or at least poorly translated from, the German editions based on the notes of Henry Picker, *Hitlers Tischgespräche im Führerhauptquartier* (Munich: Propyläen, 2009) and Heinrich Heim, *Adolf Hitler: Monologe im Führerhauptquartier, 1941-1944*, edited by Werner Jochmann (Munich: Orbis Verlag, 2000). I have consulted both German editions to verify the English translations that I have used in this chapter. Mikael Nilsson covers the difficult history of the table talks in *Hitler Redux: The Incredible History of Hitler's So-Called Table Talks* (London: Routledge, 2021), and while he presents ample evidence to urge the historian to use the talks with caution, I believe he goes too far in largely dismissing them as a legitimate source. The main contention he makes is that we cannot use the talks as verbatim sources, but they never were that anymore than Eckart's *Bolshevism from Moses to Lenin* was. The point, as I have made before, is to think of these sources as a kind of gospel, meaning various individuals' attempts to capture Hitler's thinking in private, where he expressed views that he often kept hidden from the public. See my "The Hitler Gospels and Old Guard Testimonials: Reconstructing a Mythical World," appendix to *Hitler's Millennial Reich*, 191–201.

61 Ibid. See also 60. On the influence of the Aryan Jesus concept on National Socialism, see Martin Leutzsch, "Karrieren des arischen Jesus in den Anfängen der nationalsozialistischen Bewegung," in Uwe Puschner and Clemens Vollnhals, eds., *Die völkisch-religiöse Bewegung im Nationalsozialismus: Eine Beziehungs- und Konfliktgeschichete* (Göttingen: Vandenhoeck & Ruprecht, 2012), 195–217; and Peter M. Head, "The Nazi Quest for the Aryan Jesus," *Journal for the Study of the Historical Jesus* 2(1) (2004): 55–89.

62 Eckart, *Der Bolschewismus*, 28.

63 Trevor-Roper, *Hitler's Table Talk*, 548. That Eckart reports Hitler's thoughts on the Aryan Jesus and the Jewish Paul in 1923 and Hitler is recorded saying exactly the same thing some twenty years later in the wartime table talks points to the validity and usefulness of both sources.

64 Ibid., 63. This monolog ends with this chilling conclusion from Hitler: "By exterminating this pest, we shall do humanity a service of which our soldiers can have no idea."

65 Ibid., 61–2. For this reason, the historical debate on whether Hitler saw himself as pro-Christian or anti-Christian is essentially misguided, as Hitler clearly considered all forms of Christianity after Paul as infected with Jewish thought and in need of purging. He considered Jesus an anti-Jewish racial socialist, one with whom Hitler himself identified.

66 Eckart, *Der Bolschewismus*, 30. The massacre of the innocents in the Children's Crusade is likewise transformed into a Jewish-designed massacre rather than a Turkish victory (which also conveniently ignores the thousands of Jews killed by millennial obsessed crusaders).

67 This is another interesting charge, as the Nazis later would determine that some thirty to forty million Slavs would have to be starved for German resettlement to be successful. See Gerhard L. Weinberg, "Germany's War for World Conquest and the Extermination of the Jews," *Holocaust and Genocide Studies* 10 (1996): 126. See also Alex J. Kay, "The Purpose of the Russian Campaign Is the Decimation of the Slavic Population by Thirty Million," in Alex J. Kay, Jeff Rutherford, and David Stehel, eds., *Nazi Policy on the Eastern Front, 1941: Total War, Genocide, and Radicalization* (Rochester, NY: University of Rochester Press, 2012), 101–29.

68 Eckart, *Der Bolschewismus*, 49–50.

69 Hitler, Manheim 64/MKI 229.

70 Hitler, Manheim 313, 452/MKI 817, MKII 1147.

71 Hitler, Manheim 65/MKI 231. Later in the book Hitler stated about the Jew: "his striving for world domination will end by his own dying out." Hitler, Manheim 662/MKII 1677.

72 Hitler, Manheim 338/MKI 879.

73 Adolf Hitler, *Hitler's Second Book: The Unpublished Sequel to Mein Kampf*, trans. Krista Smith (New York: Enigma Books, 2003), 231. For a detailed discussion of the origins of this book and why it was not published, see the introduction by the book's editor, Gerhard L. Weinberg.

74 Hitler, Manheim 383–4/MKII 981–2.

75 Adolf Hitler, *Die Rede Adolf Hitlers in der ersten grossen Massenversammlung bei Wiederaufrichtung der Nationalsozialistischen Deutschen Arbeiterpartei* (Munich: Ehrer, 1925), 8.

76 Hitler, Manheim 324/MKI 845.

77 Clemmons Vollnhals, ed., *Hitler: Reden, Schriften, Anordnungen, Februar 1925 bis Januar 1933* (Munich: K. G. Saur, 1992), vol. 1, 450, 454,457.

78 Hitler, Manheim 170–2/MKI 475–9.

79 Hitler, Manheim 640/MKII 1623.

80 von Koerber, *Hitler*, 29.

81 Hitler, *Adolf Hitler Reden*, 56.

82 Max Domarus, *Hitler Reden und Proklamationen, 1932-1945* (Neustadt: Verlagsdruck. Schmidt, 1962–3), vol. 3, 1058. Although it lies beyond the confines of this paper, Hitler's messianic belief in himself as a prophet and savior was more than just propaganda; it was an absolute conviction. And just as importantly, he was accepted in that role by millions of Germans. For more, see Redles, *Hitler's Millennial Reich*, 108–59. See also Ludolf Herbst, *Hitlers Charisma: Die Erfindung eines deutschen Messias* (Frankfurt am Main: Fischer, 2010).

83 Hitler, Manheim 662/MKII 1679.

84 Domarus, *Hitler*, vol. 4, 1663.

85 Quoted in Hermann Graml, *Antisemitism in the Third Reich*, trans., Tim Kirk (Cambridge: Blackwell, 1992), 186.

86 Joseph Goebbels, *Die Tagebücher von Joseph Goebbels*, ed., Elke Fröhlich (Munich: K. G. Saur, 1996), pt. 2, vol. 2, 498–9. Entry December 13, 1941.

87 Hans Frank, *Das Diensttagebuch des deutschen Generalgouverneurs in Polen 1939-1945*, eds. Werner Präg and Wolfgang Jacobmeyer (Stuttgart: Deutsche Verlags-Anstalt, 1975), 457–8.

88 Domarus, *Hitler*, vol. 4, 1828–9.

89 Trevor-Roper, *Hitler's Table Talk*, 69.

90 Heinrich Himmler, *Geheimreden 1933 bis 1945 und andere Ansprachen*, Bradley F. Smith and Agnes F. Peterson, eds. (Frankfurt am Main: Proyläen Verlag, 1974), 200.

91 Quoted in *Deutsche Soldaten sehen die Sowjet-Union*, collected and edited by Wolfgang Diewerge (Berlin: W. Limpert, 1941), 38.

92 As Richard Hofstadter noted regarding the importance of paranoia in modern millennial thinking, conspiracy becomes "the motive force in historical events. History *is* conspiracy, set in motion by demonic forces of almost transcendent power, and what is felt to be needed to defeat it is not the usual methods of political give-and-take, but an all-out crusade." In Richard Hofstadter, *The Paranoid Style in American Politics and Other Essays* (Chicago: University of Chicago Press, 1979), 9.

93 Saul Friedländer, *Nazi Germany and the Jews* (New York: HarperCollins, 1997), 314.

Chapter 14

1 See, for example, Chad Hoggan and Tetyana Kloubert, "Migration and Human Dignity: Rhetoric and Practice in Germany," in *Advancing the Global Agenda for Human Rights, Vulnerable Populations and Environmental Sustainability: Adult Education as Strategic Partner*, ed. Mary Alfred, Petra Robinson, and Elizabeth Roumell (Charlotte: Information Age Publishing, 2021), 49–65.

2 Elisabeth Meilhammer and Eva Matthes, "Holocaust education in der Migrationsgesellschaft Einleitung zu diesem Heft," *Bildung und Erziehung*, Vol. 73, No. 3, (2020), 203–11, here 10–11.

3 Daniel Levy and Natan Sznaider, *The Holocaust and Memory in the Global Age* (Philadelphia: Temple UP, 2006); A. Assmann, "The Holocaust—A Global Memory? Extensions and Limits of a New Memory Community," in *Memory in a Global Age. Discourses, Practices and Trajectories*, ed. Aleida Assmann and S. Conrad (Houndmills: Palgrave Macmillan, 2010), 97–117; Jan Assmann, "Communicative and Cultural Memory," in *Cultural Memory Studies: An International and Interdisciplinary Handbook*, ed. A. Erll and A. Nünning (Berlin: De Gruyter, 2008), 109–18.

4 Christian Hartmann, Thomas Vordermayer, and Othmar Plöckinger, Roman Töppel, E. Raim et al., *Hitler,* Mein Kampf. *Eine kritische Edition* (Munich: Institut für Zeitgeschichte, 2016), 44.

5 Jan Assmann, 109–18.

6 "Discover the Past for the Future. The Role of Historical Sites and Museums in Holocaust Education and Human Rights Education in the EU," FRA, Publications Office of the European Union, 2011, accessed February 22, 2021, https://fra.europa.eu/sites/default/files/fra_uploads/1792-FRA-2011-Holocaust-Education-Summary-report_EN.pdf.

7 Oliver Plessow, "A Quarter Century of Globalization, Differentiation, Proliferation, and Dissolution? Comments on Changes in Holocaust Education Since the End of the Cold War," in *Holocaust Education Revisited. Holocaust Education—Historisches Lernen—Menschenrechtsbildung*, ed. A. Ballis and M. Gloe (Wiesbaden: Springer VS, 2019), 21–42.

8 Monique Eckmann and Doyle Stevick, "General Introduction," in *Research in Teaching and Learning about the Holocaust*, ed. M. Eckmann, D. Stevick, J. Ambrosewicz-Jacobs, and International Holocaust Remembrance Alliance (Berlin: Metropol & IHRA, 2017), 17–32.

9 Plessow 2019, 4.

10 Theodor Adorno, *Can One Live after Auschwitz?: A Philosophical Reader* (Stanford: Stanford University Press [1966]/2003).

11 Thomas D. Fallace, *The Emergence of Holocaust Education in American Schools* (Houndmills: Palgrave Macmillan, 2008), 97; Michael Gray, *Contemporary Debates in Holocaust Education* (Houndmills: Palgrave Macmillan, 2014), 61–76; Eva Matthes and E. Meilhammer, *Holocaust Education Im 21. Jahrhundert-Holocaust Education in the 21st Century*, ed. E. Matthes and E. Meilhammer (Bad Heilbrunn: Klinkhardt, 2015), 9–28.

12 Nicolas Kinloch, "Parallel Catastrophes? Uniqueness, Redemption and the Shoah," *Teaching History* 104: 8–14.

13 Dalia Ofer, "History, Memory and Identity: Perceptions of the Holocaust in Israel," *Jews in Israel: Contemporary Social and Cultural Patterns,* ed. U. Rebhun and C. Waxman (Hanover and London: Brandeis University Press, 2004), 394–417.

14 Lucy Dawidowicz, "How They Teach the Holocaust," *What Is the Use of Jewish History?*, ed. N. Kozody (New York: Schocken Books, 1992), 65–83.

15 Tetyana Kloubert, "Holocaust Education in post-sozialistischen Ländern," *Holocaust Education in the 21st Century*, ed. E. Matthes, and E. Meilhammer (Bad Heilbrunn: Klinkhardt, 2015), 214–29.

16 Michael R. Marrus, "Lessons of the Holocaust and the Ceaseless, Discordant Search for Meaning," *Holocaust Scholarship*, ed. C. R. Browning, S. Heschel, M. R. Marrus and M. Shain (Palgrave Macmillan, London, 2015), 170–86.

17 Israle Charny, "Genocide Early Warning System (GEWS)," *Encyclopaedia of Genocide* lvii, ed. I. W. Charny, R. P. Adalian, S. L. Jacobs, E. Markusen, and M. I. Sherman (Santa Barbara: ABC-CLIO, 1999), 257–9.

18 Timothy Snyder, *On Tyranny: Twenty Lessons from the Twentieth Century* (London: Penguin Random House UK, 2017), 11–12.

19 Neil Gregor, "*Mein Kampf* lesen, 70 Jahre später, " *Aus Politik und Zeitgeschichte* 65, no. 43–5 (2007): 3–9.

20 Alexander Karn, "Toward a Philosophy of Holocaust Education: Teaching Values without Imposing Agendas," *The History Teacher* 45, no. 2 (2012): 221–40.

21 Susan Neiman, *Evil in Modern Thought: An Alternative History of Philosophy* (Princeton: Princeton University Press, 2004), 302.

22 Kathrin Bower, "Serdar Somuncu: Reframing Integration through a Transnational Politics of Satire," *The German Quarterly* 85, no. 2 (2012): 193–213.

23 Ibid.

24 See Interview with Serdar Somuncu, "Der Kommentar überhöht den Text," Interview by Liane von Billerbeck, *Deutschlandfunk Kultur*, December 30, 2015, accessed February 22, 2021, https://www.deutschlandfunkkultur.de/serdar-somuncu-zu-hitlers-mein-kampf-der-kommentar.1008.de.html?dram:article_id=341124.

25 David H. Lindquist, "Guidelines for Teaching the Holocaust: Avoiding Common Pedagogical Errors," *The Social Studies* 97, no. 5 (2006): 215–21.

26 Daniel Mönch, "Gedenkstättenbesuche als emotionales Erlebnis. Welche Rolle weisen Geschichtslehrkräfte den Emotionen ihrer Schülerinnen und Schüler zu?" *Holocaust Education Revisited. Holocaust Education—Historisches Lernen—Menschenrechtsbildung*, ed. A. Ballis and M. Gloe (Wiesbaden: Springer VS, 2019), 87–108.

27 Angela Boone, "The Continuing Knowledge Gap in Holocaust Aftermath Education in the Netherlands," *Holocaust Education Revisited. Holocaust Education—Historisches Lernen—Menschenrechtsbildung*, ed. A. Ballis and M. Gloe (Wiesbaden: Springer VS, 2019), 109–22.; H. Knothe and M. Broll, ". . . und es war wirklich stecknadelruhig." Zwischen Faktenwissen und Betroffenheit. Was meinen Lehrkräfte, wenn sie von gelingendem Unterricht zu Nationalsozialismus und Holocaust sprechen? *Holocaust Education Revisited. Holocaust Education—Historisches Lernen—Menschenrechtsbildung*, ed. A. Ballis and M. Gloe (Wiesbaden: Springer VS, 2019), 123–40.

28 Christian Wevelsiep, "Narrative zwischen Gewalt und Leiden, " *Holocaust Education Revisited. Holocaust Education—Historisches Lernen—Menschenrechtsbildung,* ed. A. Ballis and M. Gloe (Wiesbaden: Springer VS, 2019), 261–87.

29 Samuel Totten, "Holocaust Education," *Educating about Social Issues in the 20th and 21st Centuries: A Critical Annotated Bibliography*, ed. S. Totten and J. E. Pederson (Charlotte, NC: Information Age Publishing, 2012), 223–50.

30 Hermann Glaser, "Zur Mentalitätsgeschichte des Nationalsozialismus—Ein Weg, um den Erfolg von *Mein Kampf* zu verstehen, " *Aus Politik und Zeitgeschichte* 65, no. 43–5 (2015): 25–31.

31 Adorno, 19.

32 United Nations Educational, Scientific, and Cultural Organization, *Education about the Holocaust and Preventing Genocide: A policy Guide* (Paris: UNESCO, 2017), 23.

33 Sandra Alfers, "Holocaust Survivor Testimony in the Age of Trump. An American Perspective," *Holocaust Education Revisited. Holocaust Education—Historisches Lernen—Menschenrechtsbildung,* ed. A. Ballis and M. Gloe (Wiesbaden: Springer VS, 2019), 45–62.

34 Snyder, 11–12.

35 Gerene K. Starratt, Ivana Fredotovic, Sashay Goodletty, and Christopher Starratt, "Holocaust Knowledge and Holocaust Education Experiences Predict Citizenship Values among US Adults," *Journal of Moral Education* 46, no. 2 (2017): 177–94.

36 Dennis J. Barr, Beth Boulay, Robert L. Selman, Rachel McCormick, Ethan Lowenstein, Beth Gamse, and Leonard M. Brielle, "A Randomized Controlled Trial of Professional Development for Interdisciplinary Civic Education: Impacts on Humanities Teachers and their Students," *Teachers College Record* 117, no. 2 (2015): 1–52; UNESCO 2017.

37 Veronica Boix-Mansilla, "Historical Understanding: Beyond the Past and into the Present," *Knowing, Teaching, and Learning History: National and International Perspectives* ed. P. N. Stearns, P. Seixas, and S. Wineburg (New York, NY: New York University Press, 2000), 390–418; D. Van Straaten, A. Wilschut, and R. Oostdam, "Making History Relevant to Students by Connecting Past, Present, and Future: A Framework for Research," *Journal of Curriculum Studies* 48, no. 4 (2016): 479–502.

38 Karn, 235.

39 Oskar Negt, "Politische Bildung ist die Befreiung der Menschen," *Positionen der politischen Bildung 2. Ein Interviewbuch zur außerschulischen Jugend- und Erwachsenenbildung*, ed. K. P. Hufer and I. Scheurich (Schwalbach/Ts.: Budrich, 2004), 196–213.

40 Bodo von Borries, "The Third Reich in German History Textbooks since 1945," *Journal of Contemporary History* 38 (2003): 45–62.

41 As opposed to the communicative memory, based on a dialogue with living witnesses, see Jan Assmann, "Communicative and Cultural Memory."

42 See the chapters "Kriegspropaganda," "Der Kampf der ersten Zeit—die Bedeutung der Rede," "Propaganda und Organisation."

43 George Orwell, "Review of *Mein Kampf* by Adolf Hitler," *Worldview* 18, no. 7–8 ([1940]1975), accessed December 11, 2021, https://carnegiecouncil-media.storage.googleapis.com/files/v18_i007-008_a010.pdf.

44 Ibid.

45 Michael Choukas, *Propaganda Comes of Age* (Washington DC.: Public Affairs Press, 1965).

46 Tetyana Kloubert, "Mündigkeit in 'postfaktischer' Zeit: Facetten eines Leitmotivs der Demokratiebildung heute," *Hessische Blätter für Volksbildung,* 3 (2018): 217–26.

47 Snyder, 71.

48 Levy and Sznaider.

49 Karn, 233.

50 Meilhammer & Matthes, 206.

51 W. Meseth and M. Proske, "Mind the Gap: Holocaust Education in Germany, between Pedagogical Intentions and Classroom Interactions," *Prospects* 40 (2010): 201–22.

52 Ibid., 213.

53 Ibid., 213.

54 Adorno, 17.

55 Snyder, 50.

56 Plessow, 35.

57 Hartman et al., 45.

58 E. Jäckel, *Hitler's World View. A Blueprint for Power* (Cambridge, MA: Harvard University Press, 1981), 58.

59 Ibid.

60 Adolf Hitler, "Indem ich mich des Juden erwehre, kämpfe ich für das Werk des Herrn," *Hitler, Mein Kampf. Eine kritische Edition*, ed. C. Hartmann, T. Vordermayer, O. Plöckinger, R. Töppel, E. Raim, et al. (Munich: Institut für Zeitgeschichte, [1925/27]/2016), 66.

61 Karn, 232.

62 A. Musolff, "What Role Do Metaphors Play in Racial Prejudice? The Function of Antisemitic Imagery in Hitler's *Mein Kampf*," *Patterns of Prejudice* 41, no. 1 (2007): 21–43.

63 Bazillus, Bazillenträger, Erreger, Musolff 2007, 37.

64 Musolff, 26–7.

65 W. Schwendemann and S. Marks, "Unterrichtsthema Nationalsozialismus in der Hauptschule—Ergebnisse einer Pilotstudie," *Im Gespraech. Hefte der Martin-Buber-Gesellschaft* 4 (2002): 62–77.

66 Snyder, 32.

Appendix

1 Karl Kraus, *Die Dritte Walpurgisnacht* (München, 1967), p. 9.

2 Victor Klemperer, *LTI. Lingua Tertii Imperii. Die Sprache des Dritten Reiches*, 3. ed. (Leipzig, 1991), pp. 28–9.

3 The phenomenon that the first volume was more popular than the second still persisted after 1933 although the merging of the two volumes into one smoothened it.

4 Heß mainly corrected stylistic deficiencies, erratas and – to a high degree – the headlines of each page. But although more or less comprehensive stylistic changes have been carried out continuously, there have been no major

contentual changes in *Mein Kampf* from 1925 until 1945. The most important one concerned an passage about the structure of the NSDAP – in 1930 the »Germanic democracy« was replaced by the »unconditional authority of the leader« which should dominate the party (cf. Othmar PLÖCKINGER, *Geschichte eines Buches. Adolf Hitlers »Mein Kampf« 1922–1945*, 2. ed. (München, 2011), pp. 192–4; Christian HARTMANN, Thomas VORDERMAYER, Othmar PLÖCKINGER, Roman TÖPPEL (ed.), *Hitler, Mein Kampf. Eine kritische Edition.* 2 vols. (München and Berlin, 2016), vol. 1, p. 286 f.).

5 For the publication-history of *Mein Kampf* cf. PLÖCKINGER, Geschichte eines Buches (as in n. 4), p. 173–91 For the time until November 1933 the records of the Eher-Verlag have survived so that for this period the figures are very detailed and accurat, cf. Othmar PLÖCKINGER (ed.), *Quellen und Dokumente zur Geschichte von »Mein Kampf«. 1924–1945* (Stuttgart, 2016), pp. 137–60.

6 Cf. PLÖCKINGER (ed.), *Quellen und Dokumente* (as in n. 5), pp. 267–73.

7 Cf. PLÖCKINGER (ed.), *Quellen und Dokumente* (as in n. 5), p. 287.

8 Cf. PLÖCKINGER (ed.), *Quellen und Dokumente* (as in n. 5), pp. 196–200.

9 Cf. HARTMANN et al. (ed.), *Hitler, Mein Kampf*, Bd. II, p. 1196 f.

10 PLÖCKINGER (ed.), *Quellen und Dokumente* (as in n. 5), p. 250.

11 PLÖCKINGER (ed.), *Quellen und Dokumente* (as in n. 5), p. 242. The review was published in the conservative Austrian newaspaper *Neue Freie Presse* and in the left-liberal German Magazin *Tage-Buch*.

12 Cf. PLÖCKINGER (ed.), *Quellen und Dokumente* (as in n. 5), p. 238

13 Cf. PLÖCKINGER (ed.), *Quellen und Dokumente* (as in n. 5), p. 282.

14 Jüdisch-liberale Zeitung, 10. Jg., Nr. 34, 20.8.1930.

15 Cf. Klaus SCHOLDER, *Die Kirchen und das Dritte Reich*, vol. 1 (Frankfurt, Berlin and Wien, 1977), p. 170.

16 PLÖCKINGER (ed.), *Quellen und Dokumente* (as in n. 5), p. 379.

17 Cf. PLÖCKINGER (ed.), *Quellen und Dokumente* (as in n. 5), pp. 356–8.

18 Cf. Herbert LINDER, *Von der NSDAP zur SPD. Der politische Lebensweg des Dr. Helmuth Klotz (1894–1943)* (Konstanz, 1998), p. 333 f.

19 PLÖCKINGER (ed.), *Quellen und Dokumente* (as in n. 5), p. 442.

20 Cf. Hermann WEBER, Andreas HERBST, *Deutsche Kommunisten. Biographisches Handbuch. 1918 bis 1945*, 2. ed. (Berlin, 2008), p. 630 f.

21 PLÖCKINGER (ed.), *Quellen und Dokumente* (as in n. 5), p. 528.

22 Cf. PLÖCKINGER (ed.), *Quellen und Dokumente* (as in n. 5), 307 f. The ban on speaking against Hitler was extended afterwards to a great number of other German states including Prussia (cf. Othmar PLÖCKINGER, *Der Redner Hitler im Urteil seiner Zeitgenossen*, in: Josef KOPPERSCHMIDT (ed.), Hitler der Redner (München, 2003), pp. 217–41, here: pp. 221–4).

23 Cf. Robert M.W. KEMPNER (ed.), *Der verpaßte Nazi-Stopp. Die NSDAP als staats- und republikfeindliche, hochverräterische Verbindung. Preußische Denkschrift von 1930* (Frankfurt a. M. u. a., 1983.

24 Cf. PLÖCKINGER, *Geschichte eines Buches* (as in n. 4), pp. 214–21.

25 In 1932 he published the wide-spread and influencial book *Hitlers Weg* in which he tried to give an overall analysis of Hitler and the NSDAP (cf. Theodor HEUSS, Hitlers Weg. Eine historisch-politische Studie über den Nationalsozialismus (Stuttgart, Berlin and Leipzig, 1932), reprint: Hildesheim u. a. 2008).

26 PLÖCKINGER (ed.), *Quellen und Dokumente* (as in n. 5), p. 344. Hitler's description of the Jewish history Heuss saw as »groteskeste Schmeichelei in der zentralen Bewertung ihrer historischen Rolle.« (ibid.)

27 Especially when analysing topics like »Lebensraum«, allience-system, Bolshevism or France the Foreign Ministry refered to *Mein Kampf* (vgl. PLÖCKINGER, *Geschichte eines Buches* (as in n. 4), p. 222).

28 Cf. PLÖCKINGER, *Geschichte eines Buches* (as in n. 4), pp. 222–4.

29 Cf. PLÖCKINGER (ed.), Quellen und Dokumente (as in n. 5), pp. 460–5.

30 Many libraries as well bought one or even more copies of the book as the demand was quiet strong. But nevertheless this explains only a small part of the high sales-figures in 1933 (cf. PLÖCKINGER (ed.), *Quellen und Dokumente* (as in n. 5), pp. 137–60.; PLÖCKINGER, *Geschichte eines Buches* (as in n. 4), pp. 184–8, 420–9).

31 Cf. PLÖCKINGER, *Geschichte eines Buches* (as in n. 4), pp. 432–40.

32 Cit. in: PLÖCKINGER, *Geschichte eines Buches* (as in n. 4), p. 417. The PKK furthermore was enraged that about 80% of the controlled quotations taken from *Mein Kamp* and Hitler's speeches were wrong.

33 Cit. in: PLÖCKINGER, *Geschichte eines Buches* (as in n. 4), p. 414.

34 Cf. PLÖCKINGER, *Geschichte eines Buches* (as in n. 4), p. 418; Karin LAUF-IMMESBERGER, *Literatur, Schule und Nationalsozialismus* (St. Ingbert, 1987), p. 83.

35 Cf. PLÖCKINGER, *Geschichte eines Buches* (as in n. 4), 407–11; SS-Leithefte, 2. Jg., H. 1, 22.2.1936 (and following volumes).

36 Cf. PLÖCKINGER, *Geschichte eines Buches* (as in n. 4), 440.

37 Cf. Sven Felix KELLERHOFF, *»Mein Kampf«. Die Karriere eines Buches* (Stuttgart, 2015), pp. 226–9.

38 On the one hand the datas were based on volontary declarations, on the other hand the survay was made in catholic Bavaria, but evangelic parts of Germany tenendcial were more affirmative to National-Socialism.

39 Wiener Library London, 521/1, p. 203

40 Cf. Gerhard OBERKOFLER, *Spiegel Käthe*, in: Österreichisches Biographisches Lexikon, vol. 13 (Wien 2007–2010), p. 19.

41 Cf. Hans SARKOWICZ, Alf MENTZER, *Literatur in Nazi-Deutschland. Ein biografisches Lexikon* (Hamburg and Wien, 2000), pp. 181–3.

42 Cf. Othmar PLÖCKINGER, *Heinrich Himmlers Privatexemplar von »Mein Kampf« als zeitgeschichtliche Quelle*, in: Zeitschrift für Religions- und Geistesgeschichte, 61. Jg., Heft 2 (2009), pp. 171–8, here: p. 174 f.

43 Cit. in: Ibid., p. 171.

44 Cf. PLÖCKINGER (ed.), *Quellen und Dokumente* (as in n. 5), pp. 465–7.

BIBLIOGRAPHY

Adler, Hugo. *Der verwaltete Mensch: Studien zur Deportation der Juden aus Deutschland*. Tübingen: Mohr-Verlag, 1974.

Adorno, Theodor. *Can One Live after Auschwitz?: A Philosophical Reader*. Stanford: Stanford University Press, 1966/2003.

Adorno, Theodor. *Night Music: Essays on Music 1928–1962*, edited by Rolf Tiedemann, trans. Wieland Hoban. London: Seagull Books, 2009.

Alfer, Sandra. "Holocaust Survivor Testimony in the Age of Trump: An American Perspective." In *Holocaust Education Revisited. Holocaust Education—Historisches Lernen Menschenrechtsbildung*, edited by Markus Gloe and Anja Ballis, 45–62. Wiesbaden: Springer VS, 2019

Aly, Götz. *Hitlers Volksstaat: Raub, Rassenkrieg und nationaler Sozialismus*. Frankfurt: Fischer Taschenbuch Verlag, 2006.

The American Jewish Committee. *The Jews in the Eastern War Zone*. New York: The American Jewish Committee, 1916.

Angolia, John. *For Führer and Fatherland: Political and Civil Awards of the Third Reich*. San Jose: R. James Bender Publishing, 1989.

Ansky, S. *The Enemy at His Pleasure: A Journey through the Jewish Pale of Settlement during World War I*, edited and trans. Joachim Neugroschel. New York: Metropolitan Books, 2002.

Arad, Yitzhak, Shmuel Krakowski, and Shmuel Spector, eds. *The Einsatzgruppen Reports: Selections from the Dispatches of the Nazi Death Squads' Campaign against the Jews, July 1941–January 1943*. New York: Holocaust Library, 1989.

Arndt, Ino. *Die Judenfrage in der evangelischen Sonntagspresse* (Doctoral diss., University of Tübingen, 1960).

Arvidsson, Stefan. *Aryan Idols: Indo-European Mythology as Ideology and Science*. Chicago: University of Chicago Press, 2006.

Assmann, Aleida. "The Holocaust—A Global Memory? Extensions and Limits of a New Memory Community." In *Memory in a Global Age: Discourses, Practices and Trajectories*, edited by Aleida Assmann and Sebastian Conrad, 97–117. Houndmills: Palgrave Macmillan, 2010.

Assmann, J. "Communicative and Cultural Memory." In *Cultural Memory Studies: An International and Interdisciplinary Handbook*, edited by A. Erll and A. Nünning, 109–18. Berlin: De Gruyter, 2008.

Atashkevich, Irina. *Gendered Violence: Jewish Women in the Pogroms, 1917 to 1921*. Boston: Academic Studies Press, 2018.

Bailey, Stephen. "The Berlin Strike of 1918." *Central European History* 13, no. 2 (1980): 158–74.

Baldwin, Neil. *Henry Ford and the Jews: The Mass Production of Hate*. New York: Public Affairs, 2001.

Balfour, Arthur James. "Balfour Declaration." British Foreign Office. November 2, 1917.

Barnes, James J., and Patience P. Barnes. *Hitler's "Mein Kampf" in Britain and America: A Publishing History 1930–1939*. Cambridge: Cambridge University Press, 1980.

Barnett, Victoria. *For the Soul of the People*. Oxford: Oxford University Press, 1992.

Bärsch, Claus-Ekkehard. "Antijudaism, Apokalyptik und Satanologie: Die religiösen Elemente des nationalsozialistischen Antisemitismus." *Zeitschrift für Religious- und Geistesgeschichte* 40, no. 2 (1988): 112–33.

Bärsch, Claus-Ekkehard. "Der Jude als Antichrist in der NS-Ideologie." *Zeitschrift für Religious- und Geistesgeschichte* 47, no. 2 (1995): 160–188.

Bärsch, Claus-Ekkehard. *Die politische Religion des Nationalsozialismus: die religiöse Dimension der NS-Ideologie in den Schriften von Dietrich Eckart, Joseph Goebbels, Alfred Rosenberg und Adolf Hitler*. Munich: Wilhelm Fink Verlag, 1998.

Baynes, Norman H., *The Speeches of Adolf Hitler, April 1922–August 1939*. New York: Howard Fertig, 1969.

Beek, Gottfried zur. *Die Geheimnisse der Weisen von Zion*. Charlottenberg: Verlag Auf Vorposten, 1919.

Ben-Itto, Hadassa. *The Lie That Wouldn't Die: The Protocols of the Elders of Zion*. London: Vallentine Mitchell, 2005.

Benoist-Méchin, Jacques. *Eclaircissements Sur "Mein Kampf." La Doctrine d'Adolf Hitler*. Paris: Albin Michel, 1940.

Benz, Wolfgang. "Judenchristen. Zur doppelten Ausgrenzung einer Minderheit im NS-Staat." *Edith Stein Jahrbuch* 3 (1997): 307–18.

Benz, Wolfgang, Hermann Graml, and Hermann Weiß, ed. *Enzyklopädie des Nationalsozialismus* 3rd edition. Stuttgart: Klett-Cotta, 1998.

Benz Wolfgang, *Handbuch des Antisemitismus. Judenfeindschaft in Geschichte und Gegenwart* 8, Berlin: De Gruyter Saur, 2008.

Berghahn, Volker. *Europe in the Era of Two World Wars: From Militarism and Genocide to Civil Society, 1900–1950*. Princeton: Princeton University Press, 2006.

Berk, Stephen M. *Year of Crisis, Year of Hope: Russian Jewry and the Pogroms of 1881–1882*. Westport: Greenwood Press, 1985.

Bessel, Richard. *Germany after the First World War*. Oxford: Clarendon Press, 1993.

Beyersdorf, Peter. *Hitlers "Mein Kampf": Anspruch und Wirklichkeit*. Hollfeld: R.J. Beyer, 1974.

Black, Edwin. *War against the Weak: Eugenics and America's Campaign to Create a Master Race*. New York: Four Walls Eight Windows, 2003.

Blaschke, Olaf. "Die Anatomie des katholischen Anti-Semitismus. Eine Einladung zum internationalen Vergleich." In *Katholischer Anti-Semitismus im 19*. Jh, edited by Aram Matthioli, 77–110. Zürich: Oldenbourg Wissenschaftsverlag, 2000.

Boix-Mansilla, V. "Historical Understanding: Beyond the Past and into the Present." In *Knowing, Teaching, and Learning History: National and International Perspectives*, edited by P. N. Stearns, P. Seixas, and S. Wineburg, 390–418. New York: New York University Press, 2000.

Boone, Angela. "The Continuing Knowledge Gap in Holocaust Aftermath Education in the Netherlands." In *Holocaust Education Revisited—Historisches Lernen—Menschenrechtsbildung*, edited by Markus Gloe and Anja Ballis, 109–122. Wiesbaden: Springer VS, 2019.

Brechtken, Magnus. *Aufarbeitung des Nationalsozialismus. Ein Kompendium*. Göttingen: Wallstein, 2021.

Bredin, Jean-Louis. *The Affair: The Case of Alfred Dreyfus*, trans. Jeffrey Mehlman. New York: George Braziller, 1986.

Brentjes, Burchard. *Der Mythos vom Dritten Reich: Drei Jahrtausend Traum von der Erlösung*. Hannover: Fackelträger-Verlag, 1997.

Brokoff, Jürgen. *Die Apokalypse in der Weimar Republik*. Munich: Wilhelm Fink Verlag, 2001.

Brown, Timothy S. *Weimar Radicals: Nazis and Communists between Authenticity and Performance*. New York: Berghahn Books, 2009.

Brunkhorst, Hauke. *Der Intellektuelle im Land der Mandarine*. Frankfurt/Main: Suhrkamp, 1987.

Bry, Carl Christian. *Verkappte Religionen*. Gotha: Leopold Klotz, 1924.

Bucher, Rainer. *Hitlers Theologie*. Würzburg: Echter, 2008.

Bullock, Alan. *Hitler: A Study in Tyranny*. Old Saybrook: Konecky and Konecky, 1952/1962.

Burleigh, Michael. *The Third Reich: A New History*. New York: Hill & Wang, 2000.

Busi, Frederick. *The Pope of Antisemitism: The Career and Legacy of Edouard-Adolphe Drumont*. Lanham: University Press of America, 1986.

Byrnes, Robert F. *Pobedonostsev: His Life and Thought*. London: Indiana University Press, 1968.

Campbell, Francis Stuart. *Menace of the Herd*. Milwaukee: The Bruce Publishing Company, 1943.

Case, Holly. *The Age of Questions: Or, a First Attempt at an Aggregate History of the Eastern, Social, Woman, American, Jewish, Polish, Bullion, Tuberculosis, and Many Other Questions Over the Nineteenth Century, and Beyond*. Princeton: Princeton University Press, 2018.

Cecil, Robert. *The Myth of the Master Race: Alfred Rosenberg and Nazi Ideology*. New York: Dodd Mead, 1972.

Cermanová, Pavlína. "Gog and Magog: Using Concepts of Apocalyptic Enemies in the Hussite Era." In *Peoples of the Apocalypse: Eschatological Beliefs and Political Scenarios*, edited by Wolfram Brandes, Felicitas Schmieder, and Rebekka Voss, 239–56. Berlin: De Gruyter, 2016.

Chamberlain, Houston Steward. *Foundations of the Nineteenth Century*, trans. John Lees. London: John Lane Company, 1913.

Chapoutot, Johann. *Law of the Blood: Thinking and Acting as a Nazi*, trans. Miranda Richmond Mouillot. Cambridge: Harvard University Press, 2018.

Charny, I. "Genocide Early Warning System." In *Encyclopedia of Genocide*, edited by I. W. Charny, R. P. Adalian, S. S. Jacobs, E. Markusen, and M. I. Sherman, 257–59. Santa Barbara: ABC-CLIO, 1999.

Childers, Thomas. *The Nazi Voter: The Social Foundations of Fascism in Germany, 1919–1933*. Chapel Hill: University of North Carolina Press, 1983.

Choukas, Michael. *Propaganda Comes of Age*. Washington D.C.: Public Affairs Press, 1965.

Churchill, Winston. *The Second World War* 1. New York: Houghton Mifflin Books, 1986.

Cohn, Norman. *Warrant for Genocide: The Myth of the Jewish World Conspiracy and Protocols of the Elders of Zion*. London: Serif, 1996.

Connelly, John. *From Enemy to Brother: The Revolution in Catholic Teaching on the Jews, 1933–1965*. Cambridge: Harvard University Press, 2012.

Crossan, John Dominic. *Who Killed Jesus: Exposing the Roots of Anti-Semitism in the Gospel Story of the Death of Jesus*. New York: Harper Collins, 1995.

Crowe, David M. *The Holocaust: Roots, History, and Aftermath*. Boulder: Westview Press, 2014.

Darwin, Charles. *Origins of Species by Means of Natural Selection: Or the Preservation of the Favoured Races in the Struggle of Life*. London: W. Clowes and Sons, 1859/1861.

Das Deutsche Buch. Vierter Bericht. Leipzig: [without publishing-house], 1924.

Dawidowicz, Lucy. "How They Teach the Holocaust." In *What Is the Use of Jewish History?*, edited by Neal Kozody, 65–83. New York: Schocken Books, 1992.

Dawidowicz, Lucy. *The War against the Jews, 1933–1945*. New York: Holt-Rinehart-Winston, 1975.

De Beauvoir, Simone. *The Second Sex*, trans. Constance Borde and Sheila Malovany-Chevallier. New York: Knopf, 2010.

De Michelis, Cesare G. *The Non-Existent Manuscript: A Study of the Protocols of the Sages of Zion*. Lincoln: University of Nebraska Press, 2004.

Deutsch, Nathaniel. *The Jewish Dark Continent: Life and Death in the Russian Pale of Settlement*. Cambridge: Cambridge University Press, 2011.

Domarus, Max. *Hitler: Speeches and Proclamations, 1932–1945: The Chronicle of a Dictatorship, III,* 1939–1940. Wauconda: Bolchazy-Carducci, 1997a.

Domarus, Max. *Hitler: Speeches and Proclamations, 1932–1945: The Chronicle of a Dictatorship, IV*. Wauconda: Bolchazy-Carducci, 1997b.

Domarus, Max. *The Essential Hitler: Speeches and Commentary*, edited by Patrick Romane. Wauconda: Bolchazy-Carducci, 2007.

Drexler, Anton. *Mein politisches Erwachen. Aus dem Tagebuch eines deutschen sozialistischen Arbeiters 3*rd edn. München: Deutscher Volksverlag, 1923.

Dube, Christian. *Religiöse Sprache in Reden Adolf Hitlers: analysiert an Hand ausgewählter Reden aus den Jahren 1933–1945*. Norderstedt: Books on Demand GmbH, 2004.

Duncan, Peter J. S. *Russian Messianism: Third Rome, Revolution, Communism and After*. New York: Routledge, 2000.

Eckart, Dietrich. *Der Bolschewismus von Moses bis Lenin: Zwiegspräche zwischen Adolf Hitler und mir*. Munchen: Hoheneichen-Verlag, 1924.

Eckart, Dietrich. *Totengräber Russlands*. München: Dr. Ernst Böpple, 1920. Available online: https://archive.org/stream/Eckart-Dietrich-Totengraeber-Russlands-1.

Eckmann, Monique, and Doyle Stevick. "General Introduction." In *Research in Teaching and Learning about the Holocaust*, edited by Doyle Stevick, Jolanta Ambrosewicz-Jacobs, and Monique Eckmann, 17–32. Berlin: Metropol & IHRA, 2017.

Ellwood, Robert. "Nazism as a Millennialist Movement." In *Millennialism, Persecution, and Violence*, edited by Catherine Wessinger, 241–60. Syracuse: Syracuse University Press, 2000.

Engelman, Ralph M. *Dietrich Eckart and the Genesis of Nazism*. Ann Arbor: University Microfilms International, 1979.

Ensor, R. C. K. *Hitler's Self-Disclosure in "Mein Kampf."* Oxford: Oxford University Press, 1939.

Erdmann, Jürgen. *Coburg: Bayern und das Reich, 1918–1923*. Coburg: Druck-und Verlagshaus A. Rossteutscher, 1969.

Evans, Richard J. *The Coming of the Third Reich*. New York: Penguin Books, 2004.

Fallace, T. D. *The Emergence of Holocaust Education in American Schools*. Houndmills: Palgrave Macmillan, 2008.

Faulenbach, Bernd. *Ideologie des deutschen Weges. Die deutsche Geschichte in der Historiographie zwischen Kaiserreich und Nationalsozialismu*. München: Beck, 1980.

Faulhaber, Michael. *Deutsches Ehrgefühl und katholisches Gewissen*. Munich: Dr. Franz A. Pfeiffer Verlagsgesellschaft, 1925.

Feder, Gottfried. *Der Deutsche Staat auf nationaler und sozialer Grundlage. Neue Wege in Staat, Finanz und Wirtschaft*. München: Deutschvölkische Verlagsbuchhandlung, 1923.

Fest, Joachim C. *Hitler*. New York: Harcourt Brace Jovanovich, 1973.

Filser, Karl. "Die Stadt unter nationalsozialistischer Herrschaft." In *Landsberg in der Zeitgeschichte, Zeitgeschichte in Landsberg*. München: Verlag Ernst Vöge, 2010.

The First Day, February 26, 1924. In *The Hitler Trial before the People's Court in Munich*, Volume I, trans. H. Francis Freniere, Lucie Karcic, and Philip Fandek. Arlington: University Publications of America, 1976.

Flanagan, Thomas. "The Third Reich: Origins of a Millenarian Symbol." *History of European Ideas* 8, no. 3 (1987): 283–95.

Fleming, Gerald. *Hitler and the Final Solution*. Berkeley: University of California Press, 1994.

Foertsch, Hermann. *Schuld und Verhängnis. Die Fritsch-Krise im Frühjahr 1938 als Wendepunkt der Geschichte der nationalsozialistischen Zeit*. Stuttgart: Deutsche Verlags Anstalt, 1951.

Ford, Henry. *Aspect of Jewish Power in the United States, IV: The International Jew*. Boring: CPA Book Publisher, 2000.

Ford, Henry. *Jewish Influence in American Life, III: The International Jew*. Boring: CPA Book Publisher, 2000.

Ford, Henry. *The International Jew I*. Boring: CPA Book Publisher, 2000.

Ford, Henry. *The International Jew II: Jewish Activities in the United States*. Boring: CPA Book Publisher, 2000.

Förster, Jürgen. "Hitler's Decision in Favor of War against the Soviet Union." In *Germany and the Second World War IV: The Attack on the Soviet Union*, edited by Research Institute for Military History, trans. Dean S. McMurray, Ewald Osers, and Louise Willmont. Oxford: Clarendon Press, 1998.

Frank, Joseph. *Dostoevsky: A Writer in His Times*, edited by Mary Petrusewicz. Princeton: Princeton University Press, 2010.

Fredotovic, Starratt, I. S. Goodletty, and C. Starratt. "Holocaust Knowledge and Holocaust Education Experiences Predict Citizenship Values among US Adults." *Journal of Moral Education* 46, no. 2 (2017): 177–94.

Frei, Norbert. *Vergangenheitspolitik, Die Anfänge der Bundesrepublik und die NS Vergangenheit*, 2nd ed. München: Verlag C.H. Beck, 1997.
Friedländer, Saul. "Introduction." In *Hitler and the Final Solution*, edited by Gerald Fleming, xxx–xxxi. Berkeley: University of California Press, 1994.
Friedländer, Saul. *Nazi Germany and the Jews: Volume 1: The Years of Persecution 1933–1939*. New York: Harper Perennial, 1998.
Friedrich, Thomas. *Hitler's Berlin: Abused City*, trans. Stewart Spencer. New Haven: Yale University Press, 2012.
Fritsch, Theodor. *Handbuch der Judenfrage. Eine Zusammenstellung der wichtigsten Tatsachen zur Beurteilung des jüdischen Volkes*. 29. Aufl. Leipzig: Hammer-Verlag, 1923.
Fritz, Stephen. *First Soldier: Hitler as Military Leader*. New Haven: Yale University Press, 2018.
Gerwarth, Robert. *Hitler's Hangman: The Life of Heydrich*. New Haven: Yale University Press, 2011.
Gerwarth, Robert. November 1918*: The German Revolution*. Oxford: Oxford University Press, 2020.
Gilbhard, Hermann. *Die Thule Gesellschaft: Vom okkulten Mummerschanz zu Hakenkreuz*. München: Kiessling Verlag, 1994.
Glaser, Hermann. "Zur Mentalitätsgeschichte des Nationalsozialismus—Ein Weg, um den Erfolg von Mein Kampf zu verstehen." *Aus Politik und Zeitgeschichte* 65, no. 43–5 (2015): 25–31.
Goebbels, Joseph. "*The Goebbels Diaries,*" *1942–1943*, March 1993, edited by and trans. Louis B. Lochner, 376–77. Garden City: Doubleday, 1948.
Golomstock, Igor. *Totalitarian Art in the Soviet Union, the Third Reich, Fascist Italy, and the People's Republic of China*. London: Collins Harvill, 1990.
Goodrick-Clarke, Nicholas. *The Occult Roots of Nazism*. New York: New York University Press, 1992.
Gordon, Harold J. Jr. *Hitler and the Beer Hall Putsch*. Princeton: Princeton University Press, 1972.
Gordon, Noam, James Adams, and Will Horne. *American Affective Polarization in Comparative Perspective*. Cambridge: Cambridge University Press, 2020.
Gow, Andrew. *The Red Jews: Anti-Semitism in an Apocalyptic Age, 1200–1600*. Leiden: Brill, 1995.
Graml, Hermann. *Antisemitism in the Third Reich*, trans. Tim Kirk. Cambridge: Blackwell, 1992.
Grant, Madison. *The Passing of the Great Race: The Racial Basis of European History*. New York: Charles Scribner's Sons, 1916.
Grawe, Lukas. "Langemarck Myth." In *International Encyclopedia of the First World War*, edited by Ute Daniel, Peter Gatrell, Oliver Janz, Heather Jones, Jennifer Keene, Alan Kramer, and Bill Nasson. Berlin: Freie Universität Berlin, 2019. Available online: https://encyclopedia.1914-1918-online.net/article/langemarck_myth.
Gray, Michael. *Contemporary Debates in Holocaust Education*. Houndmills: Palgrave Macmillan, 2014.
Gregor, Neil. *How to Read Hitler*. New York: W. W. Norton & Company, 2005.
Gurganus, Albert Earle. *Kurt Eisner: A Modern Life*. Rochester: Camden House, 2018.

Hackett, Francis. *What "Mein Kampf" Means to America*. 2nd ed. New York: Reynal & Hitchcock, 1941.

Hagemeister, Michael. "Die 'Protokolle der Weisen von Zion' und der Basler Zionistenkongress von 1897." In *Der Traum von Israel: Die Ursprünge des modernen Zionismus*, edited by Heiko Haumann, 250–73. Weinheim: Beltz Athenäum Verlag, 1998.

Hagemeister, Michael. "Eine Apokalypse unserer Zeit: Die Prophezeiungen des heiligen Serafim von Sarov über das Kommen des Antichrist und das Ende der Welt." In *Finis Mundi: Endzeiten und Weltenden im östlichen Europa*, edited by Joachim Hösler and Wolfgang Kessler, 127–47. Stuttgart: Franz Steiner Verlag, 1998.

Hagemeister, Michael. "Sergej Nilus und die 'Protokolle der Weisen von Zion." *Jahrbuch für Antisemitismusforschung* 5 (1996): 127–47.

Hagemeister, Michael. "Triologie der Apokalypse: Vladimir Solov'ev, Serafim von Sarov und Sergej Nilus über das Kommen des Antichrist und das Ende der Weltgeschichte." In *Antichrist: Konstruktionen von Feindbildern*, edited by Wolfram Brandes und Felicitas Schmieder, 255–275. Berlin: Akademie Verlag, 2010.

Hale, Oron James. "Gottfried Feder Calls Hitler to Order: An Unpublished Letter on Nazi Party Affairs." *The Journal of Modern History* 30, no. 4 (December 1958): 358–62.

Hamann, Brigitte. *Hitler's Vienna: A Dictator's Apprenticeship*. Oxford: Oxford University Press, 1999.

Hamann, Brigitte. *Hitlers Wien. Lehrjahre eines Diktators*. 2. Aufl. München/Zürich: Piper, 1996.

Hanebrink, Paul. *A Specter Haunting Europe: The Myth of Judeo-Bolshevism*. Cambridge, MA: Belknap, 2018.

Hannot, Walter. *Die Judenfrage in der katholischen Tagespresse Deutschlands und Österreichs 1923–1933*. Mainz: Matthias-Grunewald-Verlag, 1990.

Hanser, Richard. *Putsch! How Hitler Made Revolution*. New York: Peter H. Wyden, 1970.

Hant, Claus. *Young Hitler*. London: Quartet Books, 2010.

Hartmann, Christian, Thomas Vordermayer, Othmar Plöckinger, and Roman Töppel. Hitler, *Mein Kampf: Eine kritische Edition* I. Munich/Berlin: Institute for Contemporary History, 2016.

Hartmann, Christian, Thomas Vordermayer, Othmar Plöckinger, and Roman Töppel. Hitler, *Mein Kampf. Eine kritische Edition* 2. München/Berlin: Institut für Zeitgeschichte, 2016.

Harvey, Elizabeth, and Johannes Hurter. *Hitler: New Research, German Yearbook of Contemporary History*. Oldenbourg: De Gruyter, 2018.

Hastings, Derek. *Catholicism and the Roots of Nazism: Religious Identity and National Socialism*. Oxford: Oxford University Press, 2010.

Hauner, Milan. "Did Hitler Want World Domination?" *Journal of Contemporary History* 13, no. 1 (1978): 15–32.

Heß, Rudolph. "Rudolf Heß." In *Briefe 1908–1933*, edited by Wolf Rüdiger. München/Wien: Langen-Müller, 1987.

Heep, Stefan. "The Long Way of Political Theology to Religious 'Germanism' or How National Socialism Could be Perceived as Fulfillment of Christianity." *Politics, Religion & Ideology* 21, no. 3 (2020): 311–36.

Heinemann, Ulrich. *Die verdrängte Niederlage. Politische Öffentlichkeit und Kriegsschuldfrage in der Weimarer Republik*. Göttingen: Vandenhoeck & Ruprecht, 1983.

Herbst, Ludolf. *Hitlers Charisma: Die Erfindung eines deutschen Messias*. Frankfurt am Main: Fischer, 2010.

Heschel, Susannah. *The Aryan Jesus: Christian Theologians and the Bible in Nazi Germany*. Princeton: Princeton University Press, 2008.

Heschel, Susannah. "Theology as a Vision for Colonialism: From Supersessionism to Dejudaization." In *Germany's Colonial Past: An Anthology in Memory of Susanne Zantop*, edited by Marcia Klotz, Lora Wildenthal, and Eric Ames, 148–64. Lincoln: University of Nebraska Press, 2005.

Hesemann, Michael. *Hitlers Religion: Die fatale Heilslehre des Nationalzozialismus*. Munich: Pattloch, 2004.

Hilberg, Raul. *The Politics of Memory: The Journey of a Holocaust Historian*. Chicago: Ivan R. Dee, 1996.

Hinkel, Sascha. *Adolf Kardinal Bertram: Kirchenpolitik in Kaiserreich und Weimarer Republik*. Paderborn: Ferdinand-Schöningh-Verlag, 2010.

Hinz, Berthold. *Art in the Third Reich*. New York: Pantheon, 1980.

Hitler, Adolf. *Die Rede Adolf Hitlers in der ersten grossen Massenversammlung bei Wiederaufrichtung der Nationalsozialistischen Deutschen Arbeiterpartei*. München: Ehrer, 1925.

Hitler, Adolf. "Hitlers 'grundlegende' Rede über den Anti-Semitismus." *Vierteljahrshefte für Zeitgeschichte* 16 (1968): 417.

Hitler, Adolf. *Hitler's Table Talk 1941–1944: His Private Conversations*, trans. Norman Cameron and R. H. Stevens. New York: Enigma Books, 2000.

Hitler, Adolf. *Mein Kampf*, trans. Ralph Manheim. Boston: Houghton Mifflin, 1971.

Hitler, Adolf. *Mein Kampf: Zwei Bände in einem Band Ungekürzte Ausgabe*. München: Franz Eher Nachfolger Verlag, 1943.

Hitler, Adolf. *My New Order*, edited by Raoul de Roussy de Sales, 67. New York: Octagon Books, 1973.

Hitler, Adolf. *Reden, Schriften, Anordnungen: Februar 1925 bis Januar 1933*. Berlin: De Gruyter, 1991.

Hitler, Adolf. *Hitler. Reden, Schriften, Anordnungen 5*, edited by Clemens Vollnhals. München: K.G. Saur, 1992.

Hitler, Adolf. *Sämtliche Aufzeichnungen, 1905–1924*, edited by Eberhard Jaeckel and Axel Kuhn. Stuttgart: Deutsche Verlags-Anstalt, 1980.

Hofstadter, Richard. *The Paranoid Style in American Politics and Other Essays*. Chicago: University of Chicago Press, 1979.

Hoggan, Chad and Tetyana Kloubert. "Migration and Human Dignity: Rhetoric and Practice in Germany." In *Advancing the Global Agenda for Human Rights, Vulnerable Populations and Environmental Sustainability: Adult Education as Strategic Partner*, edited by Mary Alfred, Petra Robinson, and Elizabeth Roumell. Charlotte: Information Age Publishing, 2021.

Horstmann, Bernhard. *Hitler in Pasewalk*. Düsseldorf: Droste Verlag, 2004.

Hoser, Paul. "Hitler und die katholische Kirche: Zwei Briefe aus dem Jahr 1927." *Vierteljahrshefte für Zeitgeschichte* 42, no. 3 (1994): 488.

Humbert, Manuel. *Hitlers "Mein Kampf", Dichtung Und Wahrheit*. Paris: Pariser Tageblatt, 1936.

Jablonsky, David. *The Nazi Party in Dissolution: Hitler and Verbotzeit 1923-1925*. London: Frank Cass, 1989.

Jäckel, Eberhard, and Axel Kuhn. *Hitler: Sämtliche Aufzeichnungen, 1905-1924*. Stuttgart: Deutsche Verlag-Anstalt, 1980.

Jäckel, Eberhard. *Hitler's Weltanschauung: A Blueprint for Power*. Middletown: Wesleyan University Press, 1972.

Jäckel, Eberhard. *Hitler's World View: A Blueprint for Power*. Cambridge: Harvard University Press, 1981.

Jensen, Erik N. *Body by Weimar: Athletes, Gender and German Modernity*. Oxford: Oxford University Press, 2010.

Joly, Maurice. *Dialogue aux enfers entre Machiavel et Montesquieu ou La politique de Machiavel au XIXe siècle, par un contemporain*. Brussels: A. Mertens, 1864.

Jungcurt, Uta. *Alldeutscher Extremismus in der Weimarer Republik. Denken und Handeln einer einflussreichen bürgerlichen Minderheit*. Berlin/Boston: De Gruyter, 2016.

Kalder, Daniel. *Dictator Literature: A History of Despots through Their Writing*. Great Britain: Oneworld, 2018.

Karn, Alexander. "Toward a Philosophy of Holocaust Education: Teaching Values without Imposing Agendas." *The History Teacher* 45, no. 2 (2012): 221–40.

Kater, Michael H. *Composers of the Nazi Era*. Oxford: Oxford University Press, 2000.

Kay, Alex J. "The Purpose of the Russian Campaign Is the Decimation of the Slavic Population by Thirty Million." In *Nazi Policy on the Eastern Front, 1941: Total War, Genocide, and Radicalization*, edited by Alex J. Kay, Jeff Rutherford, and David Stehel, 101–29. Rochester, NY: University of Rochester Press, 2012.

Kellogg, Michael. *The Russian Roots of Nazism: White Emigres and the Making of National Socialism, 1917–1945*. Cambridge: Cambridge University Press, 2005.

Keppler-Tasaki, Stefan. *Hans Heinrich Ehrler (1872–1951). Biografie eines Abendländers*. Wien/Köln/Weimar: Böhlau, 2018.

Kershaw, Ian. "'Working towards the Führer.' Reflections on the Nature of the Hitler Dictatorship." *Contemporary European History* 2 (1993): 103–18.

Kershaw, Ian. *Hitler: 1889–1936 Hubris*. New York: W.W. Norton, 1998.

Kershaw, Ian. *The Nazi Dictatorship. Problems and Perspectives of Interpretation*. 4th ed. London: Arnold, 2000.

Kershaw, Ian. *Hitler: A Biography*. New York: W. W. Norton, 2008.

Kinloch, Nicolas. "Parallel Catastrophes? Uniqueness, Redemption and the Shoah." *Teaching History* 104 (2001): 8–14.

Kissenkoetter, Udo. *Gregor Straßer und die NSDAP*. Stuttgart: Deutsche Verlagsanstalt, 1978.

Kitchen, Martin. "The Antisemites *Vade Mecum*: Theodor Frisch's *Handbuch der Judenfrage*." *Antisemitism Studies* 2, no. 2 (Fall 2018): 194–234.

Klautke, Egbert. "Theodor Fritsch. The 'Godfather' of German Antisemitism," *In the Shadow of Hitler: Personalities of the Right in Central and Eastern Europe*, edited by Rebecca Haynes and Martyn Rady, 73–88. London/New York: I.B. Tauris, 2011.

Klemperer, Victor. *LTI: Notizbuch eines Philologen*. Leipzig: Reclam, 2010.

Kloubert, Tetyana. "Holocaust Education in Post-Sozialistischen Ländern." *Holocaust Education in the 21st Century*, edited by Eva Matthes and Elisabeth Meilhammer, 214–29. Bad Heilbrunn: Klinkhardt, 2015.

Knausgaard, Karl Ove. *My Struggle: Book 6*, trans. Don Bartlett. New York: Farrar, Straus, and Giroux, 2019.

Knothe, Holger, and Mirko Broll. " . . . und es war wirklich stecknadelruhig." Zwischen Faktenwissen und Betroffenheit. Was meinen Lehrkräfte, wenn sie von gelingendem Unterricht zu Nationalsozialismus und Holocaust sprechen?" In *Holocaust Education Revisited—Historisches Lernen—Menschenrechtsbildung*, edited by Anja Ballis and Markus Gloe, 123–40. Wiesbaden: Springer VS, 2019.

Koschorke, Albrecht. "Ideology in Execution: On Hitler's *Mein Kampf*." *New German Critique 124* 42, no. 1 (2015): 4.

Krebs, Christopher. *A Most Dangerous Book: Tacitus' Germania from the Roman Empire to the Third Reich*. New York: W. W. Norton & Company, 2012.

Kreutzmüller, Christoph. *Final Sale in Berlin: The Destruction of Jewish Commercial Activity, 1930–1945*. New York: Berghahn Books, 2015.

Kripal, Jeffrey J. *Comparing Religions: Coming to Terms*. Malden: Wiley, 2014.

Krüger, Dieter, Hans Speidel und Ernst Jünger. *Freundschaft und Geschichtspolitik im Zeichen der Weltkriege, herausgegeben vom Zentrum für Militärgeschichte und Sozialwissenschaften der Bundeswehr*. Paderborn: Ferdinand Schöningh, 2016.

Kubizek, August. "Adolf Hitler: Mein Jugendfreund." In *Hitler's Vienna: A Dictator's Apprenticeship*, edited by Brigitte Hamann, 114. Oxford: Oxford University Press, 1999.

Kubizek, August. *The Young Hitler I Knew*. Barnsley: Greenhill Books, 2006.

Lacy, Robert. *Ford: The Men and the Machine*. Boston: Little, Brown, 1986.

Lambroza, Shlomo. "The Pogroms of 1903–1906." In *Pogroms: Anti-Jewish Violence in Modern Russian History*, edited by John D. Klier and Shlomo Lambroza, 194–207. Cambridge: Cambridge University Press, 1992.

Lamprecht, Gerald, Elenore Lappin-Eppel, and Ulrich Wyrna. *Jewish Soldiers in the Collective Memory of Central Europe: The Remembrance of World War I from a Jewish Perspective*. Wien: Böhlau Verlag, 2019.

Lemkin, Raphael. "The Jews in Poland." New York Public Archives, Raphael Lemkin Papers, Box 2, Folder I: 38.

Lemkin, Raphael. "The Jews in Poland." New York Public Archives, Raphael Lemkin Papers, Box 2, Folder 9: 166–67.

Levy, Daniel, and Nathan Sznaider. *The Holocaust and Memory in the Global Age*. Philadelphia: Temple University Press, 2006.

Levy, Richard S. *The Downfall of the Anti-Semitic Political Parties in Imperial Germany*. New Haven: Yale University Press, 1975.

Lichtenstern, Anton. *Landsberg am Lech, Geschichte und Kultur*. Mering: Holzheu Verlag, 2012.

Lindquist, David H. "Guidelines for Teaching the Holocaust: Avoiding Common Pedagogical Errors." *The Social Studies* 97, no. 5 (2006): 215–21.

Link, Stefan. "Rethinking the Ford-Nazi Connection." *Bulletin of the GHI* 49 (Fall 2011): 135–50.

Liulevicius, Vejas Gabriel. *War Land on the Eastern Front: Culture, National Identity, and German Occupation in World War I*. Cambridge: Cambridge University Press, 2005.

Lohalm, Uwe. *Völkischer Radikalismus. Die Geschichte des Deutschvölkischen Schutz- und Trutzbundes*. 1919–1923. Hamburg: Leibniz, 1970.

Lohr, Eric. *Nationalizing the Russian Empire: The Campaign against Enemy Aliens during World War I*. Cambridge: Harvard University Press, 2003.

Longerich, Peter. *"Davon haben wir nichts gewußt!": Die Deutschen und die Judenverfolgung* 1933–1945. Berlin, Pantheon: 2007.

Longerich, Peter. *Heinrich Himmler*. München: Siedler, 2008.

Longerich, Peter. *Heinrich Himmler*, trans. Jeremy Noakes and Lesley Sharpe. Oxford: Oxford University Press, 2012.

Longerich, Peter. *Hitler. Biographie*. München: Siedler, 2015.

Longerich, Peter. *Goebbels: A Biography*. New York: Random House, 2015.

Longerich, Peter. *Hitler: A Biography*, trans. Jeremy Noakes and Lesley Sharpe. Oxford: Oxford University Press, 2018.

Lovin, Clifford R. "The Ideological Basis of the Nazi Agricultural Program." *Journal of the History of Ideas* 28, no. 2 (1967): 279–88.

Maciejewski, Franz. "100 Jahre Ratlosigkeit: ein deutsches Nachdenken im Schatten des Großen Krieges." *Lettre International* 6 (2018): 122.

Maier, Charles S. *The Unmasterable Past: History, Holocaust, and German National Identity*. Harvard University Press, 1997.

Makovsky, Michael. *Churchill's Promised Land: Zionism and Statecraft*. New Haven: Yale University Press, 2007.

Marcus, George E., W. Russell Neuman, and Michael MacKuen. *Affective Intelligence and Political Judgment*. Chicago: University of Chicago Press, 2000.

Markner, Reinhard. "Friedrich Wichtl (1872–1921)." In *Handbuch der Verschwörungstheorien*, edited by Helmut Reinalter, 334–37. Leipzig: Salier, 2018.

Marr, Wilhelm. *Der Sieg des Judenthums über das Germanenthum*. Bern: Rudolph Costenoble, 1879.

Marrus, Michael R. "'Lessons' of the Holocaust and the Ceaseless, Discordant Search for Meaning." In *Holocaust Scholarship*, edited by C. R. Browning, S. Heschel, M. R. Marrus, and M. Shain, 170–86. London: Palgrave Macmillan, 2015.

Maser, Werner. *Hitler's Mein Kampf*. London: Faber and Faber, 1970.

Matthaüs, Jürgen. "German *Judenpolitik* in Lithuania during the First World War." *The Leo Baeck Institute Year Book* 43, no. 1 (January 1998): 155–74.

Mazumdar, Pauline M. H. "Blood and Soil: The Serology of the Aryan Racial State." *Bulletin of the History of Medicine* 64. no. 2 (1990): 187–219.

Mazura, Uwe. *Zentrumspartei und Judenfrage, 1870/1-1933*. Mainz: Matthias-Grünewald-Verlag, 1994.

McGinn, Bernard. *The Calabrian Abbot: Joachim of Fiore in the History of Western Thought*. New York: Macmillan, 1986.

McGuire, Michael. "Mythic Rhetoric in *Mein Kampf*: A Structural Analysis." *The Quarterly Journal of Speech* 63, no. 1 (1977): 13.

Meister, Wilhelm. *Judas Schuldbuch. Eine deutsche Abrechnung. Herausgegeben vom Deutschen Schutz- und Trutzbund*, 3./4. Aufl. München: Deutscher Volksverlag, 1919.

Meilhammer, Elisabeth, and Eva Mathes. "Holocaust education in der Migrationsgesellschaft Einleitung zu diesem Heft." *Bildung und Erziehung* 73/3 (2020): 203–11.

Messerschmidt, Manfred. *Die Wehrmacht im NS-Staat: Zeit der Indoktrination*. Hamburg: R.V. Decker, 1969.

Meyer, Michael. *The Politics of Music in the Third Reich*. New York: Peter Lang, 1991.

Michaelis, Meir. "World Power Status or World Dominion? A Survey of the Literature on Hitler's 'Plan of World Dominion' (1937–1970)." *Historical Journal* 15, no. 2 (1972): 331–60.

Michalczyk, John J. *Medicine, Ethics and the Third Reich: Historical and Contemporary Issues*. Sheed and Ward, 1994.

Mommsen, Hans. "Hitler's Stellung im nationalsozialistischen Herrschaftssystem." In *Der Führerstaat. Mythos und Realität*, edited by Gerhard Hirschfeld and Lothar Kettenacker, 43–72. Stuttgart: Klett-Cotta, 1981.

Mönch, Daniel. "Gedenkstättenbesuche als emotionales Erlebnis. Welche Rolle weisen Geschichtslehrkräfte den Emotionen ihrer Schülerinnen und Schüler zu?" *Holocaust Education Revisited—Historisches Lernen—Menschenrechtsbildung*, edited by Anja Ballis and Markus Gloe, 87–108. Wiesbaden: Springer VS, 2019.

Möller, Horst and Udo Wengst. *50 Jahre Institut für Zeitgeschichte. Eine Bilanz*. Munich: De Gruyter Oldenbourg, 1999.

Motta, Giuseppe. *The Great War against Eastern European Jewry, 1914–1920*. Cambridge: Cambridge Scholars Publishing, 2017.

Müller, Rolf Dieter. *Hitler's Wehrmacht 1935–1945*, trans. Janice Anker. Lexington, Kentucky: University Press of Kentucky, 2017.

Murphy, Melanie. "The Architecture of Doom (1991): Blueprint for Annihilation." In *Through a Lens Darkly: Films of Genocide, Ethnic Cleansing, and Atrocities*, edited by John J. Michalczyk and Raymond G. Helmick, 115–120. New York: Peter Lang, 2013.

Musolff, Andreas. "What Role Do Metaphors Play in Racial Prejudice? The Function of Anti-Semitic Imagery in Hitler's *Mein Kampf*." *Patterns of Prejudice* 411 (2007): 31.

Negt, Oskar. "Politische Bildung ist die Befreiung der Menschen." In *Positionen der politischen Bildung 2. Ein Interviewbuch zur außerschulischen Jugend- und Erwachsenenbildung*, edited by Klaus-Peter Hufer and Imke Scheurich, 196–213. Schwalbach/Ts.: Budrich, 2004.

Neiman, Susan. *Evil in Modern Thought: An Alternative History of Philosophy*. Princeton: Princeton University Press, 2004.

Nicholls, David. *Adolf Hitler: A Biographical Companion*. Santa Barbara: ABC-CLIO, 1949.

Noack, Hannelore. *Unbelehrbar? Antijüdische Agitation mit entstellten Talmudzitaten. Antisemitische Aufwiegelung durch Verteufelung der Juden*. Paderborn: University Press Paderborn, 2001.

Noakes, Jeremy, and Geoffrey Pridham. *Nazism: A History in Documents and Eyewitness Accounts, 1919–1945*, II: *Foreign Policy, War and Racial Extermination*. New York: Schocken Books, 1988.

Nötges, Jakob, S. J. *Nationalsozialismus und Katholizismus*. Cologne: Gilde-Verlag, 1931.

Ofer, Dalia. "History, Memory, and Identity: Perceptions of the Holocaust in Israel." In *Jew in Israel: Contemporary Social and Cultural Patterns*, edited by Uzi Rebhun and Chaim Waxman, 394–417. Hanover: Brandeis University Press/University Press of New England, 2004.

Office of United States Chief of Counsel for Prosecution of Axis Criminality. *Nazi Conspiracy and Aggression*, I. Washington: US Government Printing Office, 1946.

Office of United States Chief of Counsel for Prosecution of Axis Criminality. *Nazi Conspiracy and Aggression: Opinion and Judgement*. Washington: US Government Printing Office, 1947.

Orlow, Dietrich. *The Nazi Party 1919–1945: A Complete History*. New York: Enigma Books, 2013.

Orwell, George. "Review of *Mein Kampf* by Adolf Hitler." *Worldview* 18, no. 7–8 ([1940]1975): 27.

Pendas, Devan. "Racial States in Comparative Perspective." In *Beyond the Racial State: Rethinking Nazi Germany*, edited by Devin O. Pendas, Mark Roseman, and Richard F. Wetzell, 116–56. Cambridge: Cambridge University Press, 2017.

Pensler, Derek. *Shylock's Children: Economics and Jewish Identity in Modern Europe*. Berkeley: University of California Press, 2001.

Phelps, Reginald. "Anton Drexler—Der Gründer der NSDAP." *Deutsche Rundschau* 87, no. 12 (December 1961): 1134–43.

Pines, Lisa, ed., *Life and Times in Nazi Germany*. London: Bloomsbury, 2016.

Piper, Ernst. *Alfred Rosenberg. Hitlers Chefideologe*. München: Blessing, 2005.

Plessow, Oliver. "A Quarter Century of Globalization, Differentiation, Proliferation, and Dissolution? Comments on Changes in Holocaust Education since the End of the Cold War." In *Holocaust Education Revisited. Holocaust Education—Historisches Lernen—Menschenrechtsbildung*, edited by Markus Gloe and Anja Ballis, 21–42. Wiesbaden: Springer VS, 2019.

Plewnia, Margarete. *Auf dem Weg zu Hitler: Der völkische Publizist Dietrich Eckart*. Bremen: Schünemann, 1970.

Plöckinger, Othmar. *Geschichte eines Buches. Adolf Hitlers "Mein Kampf" 1922–1945*. Munich: Oldenbourg Verlag, 2011.

Plöckinger, Othmar. *Quellen und Dokumente zur Geschichte von "Mein Kampf". 1924–1945*. Stuttgart: Franz Steiner, 2016.

Plöckinger, Othmar. "Gottfried Feders Einfluss auf die wirtschafts- und staatspolitischen Vorstellungen der frühen NSDAP und auf Hitlers 'Mein Kampf'', *Vierteljahrsschrift für Sozial- und Wirtschaftsgeschichte* 105, no. 4 (2018): 497–527.

Plöckinger, Othmar. *Unter Soldaten und Agitatoren. Hitlers prägende Jahre im deutschen Militär 1918–1920*. Paderborn: Ferdinand Schöningh, 2013.

Pohl, Reinhold. "Reichskommissarriat Ostland: Schleswig-Holstein Kolonies." In: Gesellschaft für politische Bildung e.V. (ed.), *Schleswig-Holsteins und die Verbrechen der Wehrmacht*, 10–12. Brodersdorf: Druck WDA, 1998.

Porat, Dina. "The Protocols of the Elders of Zion: New Uses of an Old Myth." In *Demonizing the Other: Antisemitism, Racism, and Xenophobia*, edited by Robert S. Wistrich, 322–34. Amsterdam: Harwood Academic, 1999.

The Protocols of the Learned Elders of Zion, Chapter 1–24, edited by and trans. Victor E. Marsden. London: The British Publishing Society, 1923.

Range, Peter Ross. *1924: The Year that Made Hitler*. New York: Back Bay Books, 2016.

Redles, David. *Hitler's Millennial Reich: Apocalyptic Belief and the Search for Salvation*. New York: New York University Press, 2005.

Redles, David. "Nazi End Times: The Third Reich as Millennial Reich." In *End of Days: Essays on the Apocalypse from Antiquity to Modernity*, edited by Karolyn Kinane and Michael A. Ryan, 173–96. Jefferson, NC: McFarland, 2009.

Redles, David. "The Turning Point: *The Protocols of the Elders of Zion* and the Eschatological War between Aryans and Jews." In *The Paranoid Apocalypse: A Hundred-Year Retrospective on The Protocols of the Elders of Zion*, edited by Richard Landes and Steven T. Katz, 112–13. New York: New York University Press, 2012.

Reeves, Marjorie. *Joachim of Fiore and the Prophetic Future*. New York: Harper & Row, 1977.

Reeves, Marjorie. *The Influence of Prophecy in the Later Middle Ages: A Study in Joachism*. South Bend: Notre Dame University Press, 1993.

Reuth, Ralf Georg. *Hitlers Judenhass. Klischee und Wirklichkeit*. München: Piper, 2009.

Rhodes, James M. *The Hitler Movement: A Modern Millenarian Revolution*. Stanford: Hoover Institute Press, 1980.

Rich, Norman. *Hitler's War Aims: Ideology, the Nazi State, and the Course of Expansion*. New York: W.W. Norton, 1973.

Riedel, Matthias. *Joachim von Fiore: Denker der vollendeten Menschheit*. Würzberg: Königshausen & Neumann, 2004.

Riedel, Matthias. "Longing for the Third Age: Revolutionary Joachism, Communism, and National Socialism." In *A Companion to Joachim of Fiore*, edited by Matthias Riedelm, 267–318. Leiden: Brill, 2018.

Rissmann, Michael. *Hitlers Gott: Vorsehungsglaube und Sendungsbewußtsein des deutschen Diktators*. Pendo: Zürich, 2001.

Ritter, Gerhard. *Europa und die deutsche Frage*. München: Munchner Verlag, 1948.

Ritter, Gerhard. "The Historical Foundations of the Rise of National-Socialism." In *The Third Reich. A Study Published under the Auspices of the International Council for Philosophy and Humanistic Studies with the Assistance of UNESCO*, edited by Maurice Baumont, John H. E. Fried, and Edmond Vermeil, 381–416. New York: Praeger, 1955.

Rofthfels, Hans. "Kurt Gerstein's Eyewitness Report on Mass Gassings." In *Holocaust and Memory in Europe*, edited by Thomas Schlemmer and Alan E. Steinweis, 63–84. Berlin/Boston: De Gruyter Oldenbourg, 2016.

Rosenbaum, Ron. *Explaining Hitler: The Search for the Origins of His Evil*. New York: Random House, 1998.

Rosenberg, Alfred. *Die Spur des Juden im Wandel der Zeiten*. Munich: Deutsche Volksverlag, 1920.

Rosenberg, Alfred. *Der Staatsfeindliche Zionismus*. Hamburg: Deutschvölkische Verlagsanstalt, 1922.

Rosenberg, Alfred. *Díe Protokolle der Weisen von Zion und díe jüdische Weltpolítík*. München: Hoheneichen Verlag, 1923.

Rosenberg, Alfred. *Wesen, Grundsätze und Ziele der Nationalsozialistischen Deutschen Arbeiterpartei. Das Programm der Bewegung*. München: Deutscher Volksverlag, 1923.

Rosenberg, Alfred. *Der Mythus des 20. Jahrhunderts; Eine Wertung der Seelisch-geistigen Gestalten Kämpfe unserer Zeit*. München: Hoheneichen-Verlag, 1941.

Rosenberg Alfred. Memoirs with Commentaries by Serge Lang and Ernst von Schenck, trans. Eric Posselt. Chicago: Ziff-Davis Publishing Company, 1949.

Rosenberg, Alfred. *The Track of the Jew through the Ages*, trans. Alexander Jacob. Burlington: Ostara Publications, 2016.

Ryback, Timothy W. *Hitler's Private Library: The Books That Shaped His Life*. New York: Alfred A. Knopf, 2008.

Ryback, Timothy W. *Hitlers Bücher. Seine Bibliothek. Sein Denken*. Köln: Fackelträger, 2010.

Sage, Steven F. *Ibsen and Hitler: The Playwright, the Plagiarist, and the Plot for the Third Reich*. New York: Carroll & Graf, 2006.

Santillan-Castrence, Pura. "Adolf Hitler's *Mein Kampf*." *The Philippine Social Science Review—University of the Philippines* 2 (1939).

Schleunes, Karl A. *The Twisted Road to Auschwitz: Nazi Policy toward German Jews, 1933–1939*. Urbana: University of Illinois Press, 1990.

Schlüter, André. *Moeller van den Bruck. Leben und Werk*. Köln/Weimar/Wien: Böhlau, 2010.

Schmitt, Carl. *Der Begriff des Politischen*. München: Dunker & Humboldt, 1932.

Schneider, Birgit. "Revolution 1918/1919." In *Landsberg in der Zeitgeschichte, Zeitgeschichte in Landsberg*, 69–70. München: Verlag Ernst Vöge, 2010.

Schopenhauer, Arthur. *The World as Will and Representation*, trans. E. F. J. Payne. New York: Dover Publications, 1969.

Schubert, Günter. *Anfänge nationalsozialistischer Außenpolitik*. Köln: Verlag Wissenschaft und Politik, 1963.

Schwanitz, Dietrich. *Bildung: Alles, was man wissen muß*. Munich: Goldmann, 2002.

Shirakawa, Sam H. *The Devil's Music Master: The Controversial Life and Career of Wilhelm Furtwängler*. Oxford: Oxford University Press, 1992.

Shirer, William L. *The Rise and Fall of the Third Reich: A History of Nazi Germany*. New York: Simon & Schuster, 1960.

Snyder, Timothy. *Black Earth: The Holocaust as History and Warning*. New York: Tim Duggan Books, 2015.

Snyder, Timothy. *On Tyranny: Twenty Lessons from the Twentieth Century*. London: Penguin Random House, 2017.

Spicer, Kevin. *Hitler's Priests: Catholic Clergy and National Socialism*. DeKalb: Northern Illinois University Press, 2008.

Stachura, Peter D. *Political Leaders in Weimar Germany: A Biographical Study*. New York: Harvester Wheatsheaf, 1993.

Stasiewski, Bernhard, ed. *Akten deutscher Bischöfe über die Lage der Kirche, 1918–1933*, Volume II. Paderborn: Ferdinand-Schöningh-Verlag, 2007.

Steigmann-Gall, Richard. *The Holy Reich: Nazi Conceptions of Christianity, 1919–1945*. Cambridge: Cambridge University Press 2003.

Stein, Alexander. *Adolf Hitler: Schüler der "Weisen von Zion."* Karlsbad: Verlagsanstalt Graphia, 1936.

Steinweis, Alan E. *Studying the Jew: Scholarly Antisemitism in Nazi Germany*. Cambridge: Harvard University Press, 2006.

Stern, Eliyau. *Jewish Materialism: The Intellectual Revolution of the 1870s*. New Haven: Yale University Press, 2018.

Stern, Fritz. *Der Traum vom Frieden und die Versuchung der Macht: Deutsche Geschichte Im 20 Jahrhundert*. Berlin: Siedler, 1999.

Stoltzfus, Nathan. *Hitler's Compromises: Coercion and Consensus in Nazi Germany*. New Haven: Yale University Press, 2016.

Stratigakos, Despina. *Hitler at Home*. New Haven: Yale University Press, 2015.

Strohm, Harald. *Die Gnosis unter der Nationalsozialismus*. Frankfurt: Suhrkamp, 1997.

Szakowski, Zosa. "The German Appeal to the Jews of Poland 1914." *The Jewish Quarterly Review* 59, no. 4 (April 1969): 311–20.

Tavernaro, Thomas. *Der Verlag Hitlers und der NSDAP. Die Franz Eher Nachfolger GmbH*. Wien: Edition Praesens, 2004.

Tazelaar, Rick. *Hüter des Freistaats. Die Bayerische Staatskanzlei zwischen Nationalsozialismus und Nachkriegsdemokratie*. Munich: Phil. Diss., 2020.

Telberg, George Gustav, and Robert Wilson. *The Last Days of the Romanovs*. New York: George H. Doran Company, 1920.

Terman, D. M. "Paranoid Leadership." In *The Leader: Psychological Essays*, edited by C. B. Strozier, Daniel Offer, and Oliger Abdyli, 158. New York: Springer, 2011.

Thacker, Toby. *Joseph Goebbels: Life and Death*. New York: Palgrave Macmillan, 2009.

Toland, John. *Adolf Hitler*, volumes 1 and 2. New York: Doubleday, 1976.

Totten, Samuel. "Holocaust Education." In *Educating about Social Issues in the 20th and 21st Centuries: A Critical Annotated Bibliography*, edited by Samuel Totten and John E. Pederson, 223–50. Charlotte: Information Age Publishing, 2012.

Trachtenberg, Barry. *The Revolutionary Roots of Modern Yiddish, 1903–1917*. Syracuse: Syracuse University Press, 2008.

Trachtenberg, Joshua. *The Devil and the Jews: The Medieval Conception of the Jew and Its Relation to Modern Anti-Semitism*. Philadelphia: Jewish Publication Society, 1943.

Trials of War Criminals before the Nuremberg Military Tribunals under Control Council Law No. 10, IV: The RUSHA Case. Washington, D.C.: US Government Printing Office, 1950.

Ulbricht, Justus H. "Agenturen der 'Deutschen Wiedergeburt'. Prolegomena zu einer Geschichte völkischer Verlagsarbeit in der Weimarer Republik." In *Völkische Bewegung—Konservative Revolution—Nationalsozialismus. Aspekte einer politisierten Kultur*, edited by Walter Schmitz and Clemens Vollnhals, 235–44. Dresden: Thelem, 2005.

Ulbricht, Justus H. "Völkische Publizistik in München. Verleger, Verlage und Zeitschriften im Vorfeld des Nationalsozialismus." In *München—Hauptstadt der Bewegung: Bayerns Metropole und der Nationalsozialismus*, edited by Richard Bauer, 131–36. Wolfratshausen: Ed. Minerva, 2002.

Ullrich, Volker. *Adolf Hitler. Biographie. Die Jahre des Aufstiegs 1889–1939. vol 1*. Frankfurt am Main: S. Fischer, 2013.

Ullrich, Volker. *Hitler: Ascent, 1889–1939*, trans. Jefferson Chase. New York: Vintage Books, 2017.

Ullrich, Volker. *Hitler: Downfall, 1939–1945*, trans. Jefferson Chase. New York: Alfred A. Knopf, 2020.

Viereck, George Sylvester. "Hitler: The German Explosive." *American Monthly* (October 1923): 235–38.

Volk, Ludwig. *Der Bayerische Episkopat und der Nationalsozialismus, 1930–1934*. Mainz: Matthias-Grünewald-Verlag, 1965.

Voegelin, Eric. "Religionsersatz: Die gnostischen Massenbewegungen unserer Zeit." *Wort und Wahrheit* 15, no. 1 (1960): 5–18.

Volkov, Shulamit. "Anti-Semitism as a Cultural Code: Reflections on the History and Historiography of Anti-Semitism in Imperial Germany." *Yearbook of the Leo Baeck Institute* 23 (1978): 25–46.

Vondung, Klaus. "Apocalyptic Violence." In *Apocalyptic Complex: Perspectives, Histories, Persistence*, edited by Nadia Al-Bagdadi, David Marno, and Matthias Riedl, 35–52. Plymouth: Central European University Press, 2018.

Vondung, Klaus. *The Apocalypse in Germany*, trans. Stephen D. Ricks. Columbia: University of Missouri Press, 2000.

Vuorinen, Marja. "*Mein Kampf* Revisited: Enemy Images as Inversions of the Self." In *Proceedings of the 9th European Conference on Information Warfare and Security*, edited by Josef Demergis, 320–6. Reading: Academic Publishing, 2010.

Waddington, Lorna. *Hitler's Crusade: Bolshevism, the Jews and the Myth of Conspiracy*. London: I. B. Taurus, 2012.

Waite, Robert G. L. *The Psychopathic God: Adolf Hitler*. New York: Basic Books, 1977.

Watson, Alexander. *Ring of Steel: Germany and Austria-Hungary in World War I*. New York: Basic Books, 2014.

Weber, Horst J. *Die deutsche Presse, insbesondere die völkische, um den Hitlerprozeß. Ein Beitrag zur Lehre von der Parteipresse*. Leipzig: Diss., 1930.

Weber, Leisa. *Handlungsspielräume und Handlungsoptionen von Pfarrern und Gemeindeglidern in der Zeit des Nationalsozialismus*. Göttingen: Vandenhoeck und Ruprecht, 2019.

Weber, Thomas. *Hitlers erster Krieg. Der Gefreite Hitler im Weltkrieg—Mythos und Wahrheit*. Berlin: Propyläen, 2010.

Weber, Thomas. *Hitler's First War: Adolf Hitler, the Men of the List Regiment, and the First World War*. Oxford: Oxford University Press, 2010.

Weber, Thomas. *Becoming Hitler: The Making of a Nazi*. Oxford: Oxford University Press, 2017.

Weikart, Richard. "Progress through Racial Extermination: Social Darwinism, Eugenics, and Pacifism in Germany, 1860–1918." *German Studies Review* 26, no. 2 (2003): 273–94.

Weininger, Otto. *Über die letzten Dinge*. Vienna: W. Braumüller, 1904.

Weitz, Eric D. *Creating German Communism, 1890–1990: From Popular Protests to Socialist State*. Princeton: Princeton University Press, 1997.

Wevelsiep, Christian. "Narrative zwischen Gewalt und Leiden." In *Holocaust Education Revisited. Holocaust Education—Historisches Lernen—Menschenrechtsbildung*, edited by Markus Gloe and Anja Ballis, 261–87. Wiesbaden: Springer VS, 2019.

Whitman, James. *Hitler's American Model: The United States and the Making of Nazi Race Law*. Princeton: Princeton University Press, 2018.

Wichtl, Friedrich. *Weltfreimaurerei, Weltrevolution, Weltrepublik. Eine Untersuchung über Ursprung und Endziele des Weltkriegs*. 7th ed. Munich: Lehmann, 1920.

Wiede, Wiebke. Rasse im Buch. *Antisemitische und rassistische Publikationen in Verlagsprogrammen der Weimarer Republik*. Munich: Oldenbourg, 2011.

Wiendling, Paul. *Health, Race, and German Politics between Unification and Nazism: 1870–1945*. Cambridge: Cambridge University Press, 1989/1991.

Wiener Library. "The Story of *Mein Kampf*." *Wiener Library* Bulletin 6 (December 1952): 31.

Wigger, Iris. *The 'Black Horror on the Rhine': Intersections of Race, Nation, Gender and Class in 1920s Germany*. London: Palgrave Macmillan, 2017.
Wilkerson, Isabel. *Caste: The Origins of Our Discontents*. New York: Random House, 2020.
Weinberg, Gerhard. *Hitler's Second Book: The Unpublished Sequel to "Mein Kampf" by Adolf Hitler*, trans. Krista Smith. New York: Enigma Books, 2003.
Wistrich, Robert. *Hitler's Apocalypse: Jews and the Nazi Legacy*. New York: St. Martin's Press, 1985.
Xammar, Eugeni. *Das Schlangenei. Berichte aus dem Deutschland der Inflationsjahre 1922-1924*. Berlin: Berenberg Verlag, 2007.
Zehnpfenning, Barbara. *Hitlers* Mein Kampf: *Eine Interpretation*. Paderborn: Wilhelm Fink Verlag. 2006.
Zentralverlags der NSDAP. *Die Verlagserscheinungen des Zentralverlags der NSDAP. Franz Eher Nachf*. G.M.B.H. München. Berlin. Wien. 1921–1941. Leipzig: Börsenverein, 1942.
Zumbini, Massimo Ferrari. *Die Wurzeln des Bösen. Gründerjahre des Antisemitismus: Von der Bismarckzeit zu Hitler*. Frankfurt am Main: Vittorio Klostermann, 2003.

CONTRIBUTORS

Editors

John J. Michalczyk is Professor and Director of Film Studies in the Art, Art History and Film department of Boston College, and author and/or editor of ten books, including *Filming the End of the Holocaust, Confront! Resistance in Nazi Germany* and *Nazi Law: From Nuremberg to Nuremberg*. Since 1992 he has been a documentary filmmaker, whose works include *The Cross and the Star: Jews, Christians and the Holocaust*; *Nazi Medicine: In the Shadow of the Reich*; *Creating Harmony: The Displaced Jewish Orchestra from St. Ottilien*; *Writing on the Wall: Remembering the Berlin Wall*; and *Nazi Law: Legally Blind*.

Michael S. Bryant is Professor of History and Legal Studies at Bryant University in Smithfield, Rhode Island, specializing in the impact of the Holocaust on the law, human rights, German criminal law, and international humanitarian law. He is the author of five books: *Confronting the Good Death: Nazi Euthanasia on Trial, 1945-53* (2005); *Eyewitness to Genocide: The Operation Reinhard Death Camp Trials, 1955-66* (2014); *Nazi Crimes and Their Punishment, 1943-1950: A Short History with Documents* (Passages: Key Moments in History) (Hackett, 2020) *A World History of War Crimes: From Antiquity to the Present* (2015; 2nd edition, 2021); and (with Michael Bazyler, Kristen Nelson, and Sermid al-Saraf) *Comparative Law: Global Legal Traditions for the 21st Century* (2021).

Susan A. Michalczyk is Professor at the Boston College Morrissey College of Arts and Science and author, editor, and documentary filmmaker. She has been a partner with her husband, John Michalczyk, in both teaching and film production for over twenty-five years, focusing on issues of social justice and human rights. Coproducer and scriptwriter, she has worked on films such as *Nazi Medicine: In the Shadow of the Reich*; *Creating Harmony: The Displaced Persons' Orchestra from St. Ottilien; Writing on the Wall: Remembering the Berlin Wall*; *Nazi Law: Legally Blind*; and the recent documentary, *Mein Kampf: Prelude to the Holocaust*, a companion piece to this book.

Authors

Paul Bookbinder is a longtime faculty member in the history department at the University of Massachusetts/Boston, who teaches and writes about Hitler, the Weimar Republic, Nazi Germany, and the Holocaust. His most recent publication is a book chapter, "Our Enemies Have No Rights: Carl Schmitt and the Two-Tiered System of Justice," in *Nazi Law: From Nuremberg to Nuremberg*, edited by John J. Michalczyk.

Magnus Brechtken was Assistant Professor at the Universities of Bayreuth (1994–5) and Munich (1995–2002) and spent several years of research in Britain, France, Poland, and the United States. After his Habilitation in 2002 he became DAAD-Langzeitdozent and Associate Professor and Reader at the University of Nottingham. In 2012, he was appointed deputy director of the Munich Institute for contemporary history. He is also Professor at the University of Munich. His publications include "*Madagaskar für die Juden*": *Antisemitische Idee und politische Praxis 1885-1945*; *Scharnierzeit 1895–1907. Persönlichkeitsnetze und internationale Politik in den deutsch-britisch-amerikanischen Beziehungen vor dem Ersten Weltkrieg*; *Life Writing and Political Memoir*; and *Albert Speer—Eine deutsche Karriere.*

David M. Crowe is Presidential Fellow at Chapman University and Professor Emeritus of history and law at Elon University. His recent publications include *The Holocaust: Roots, History, and Aftermath*, second edition, *Stalin's Soviet Justice: "Show" Trials, War Crimes Trials, and Nuremberg*, "The Tokyo and Nuremberg IMT Trials: A Comparative Analysis," in *70 Years On: The International Military Tribunal for the Far East*, "The German Plunder and Theft of Jewish Property in the General Government," in *Nazi Law: From Nuremberg to Nuremberg*, and "MacArthur, Keenan and the American Quest for Justice at the IMFTE," in *Transcultural Justice at the Tokyo Tribunal: The Allied Struggle for Justice, 1946-48.* He is currently writing *Raphael Lemkin: The Life of a Visionary.*

Barbara S. Gawlick is Professor of Music at Boston College. She received her MA in Dalcroze/Eurhythmics from the Music Academy in Lodz in her native Poland and her DMA from the New England Conservatory of Music. Her expertise lies in music education methods, policy, and advocacy. She directs the Boston College Music Outreach program, which provides free concerts and music instruction in underserved communities in Greater Boston.

Ralf Yusuf Gawlick is Professor of Music at Boston College and a German-American composer of Romani-Kurdish descent. His works include solo, chamber, orchestral, film, electroacoustic, and choral music, traversing a wide range of styles and often exploring aspects of his complex international heritage. His music, published by several firms, has been performed internationally (in venues including Vienna's Musikverein and New York's Carnegie Hall) and is recorded on the Musica Omnia label in composer-supervised performances by the works' dedicatees.

Susannah Heschel is the Eli M. Black Distinguished Professor and Chair of the Jewish Studies Program at Dartmouth College. The author of *Abraham Geiger and the Jewish Jesus*, *The Aryan Jesus: Christian Theologians and the Bible in Nazi Germany*, and *Jüdischer Islam: Islam und jüdisch-deutsche Selbstbestimmung*, she and Umar Ryad have coedited *The Muslim Reception of European Orientalism*. She is a Guggenheim Fellow and has held fellowships at the National Humanities Center and the *Wissenschaftskolleg zu Berlin*, and has received research grants from the Ford Foundation and the Carnegie Foundation.

Tetyana Kloubert is Akademische Rätin (Associate Professor) at the University of Augsburg, Germany. She researches civic education and adult learning in Western and Eastern Europe and the United States, focusing in particular on the distinction between education and indoctrination, on education for migrants and refugees, and on dealing with the totalitarian past. She received her PhD (2013) and habilitation (2019) from the University of Augsburg (Germany) and her two MAs from the University of Jena (Germany) and National University of Chernivtsi (Ukraine).

Martin Menke is Professor of history at Rivier University in Nashua, New Hampshire. He has published several articles on the Weimar-era German Center Party and its relationship to nationalism generally and to the NSDAP in particular, including "The Complexities of Ludwig Kaas: New Research on the Ermächtigungsgesetz," *From Weimar to Hitler: Studies on the Dissolution of Weimar Democracy and the Establishment of the Third Reich, 1932-1934*. He is currently at work on a monograph on German Center Party decision-making, 1917–33.

Melanie Murphy is Associate Professor of history and member of the International Studies Faculty at Emmanuel College, Boston, Massachusetts, where she teaches European, Middle Eastern, and World History. She has written on culture and politics under communism and fascism, as well as on literature and political identity, and contributed a chapter on homosexuality and the law to *Nazi Law: From Nuremberg to Nuremberg* (2018).

Othmar Plöckinger is a high school teacher of history, German literature, and mathematics in Salzburg, as well as a freelance historian and lecturer at the University of the Bundeswehr in Munich. His main research is the early history and ideology of National Socialism. He is one of the editors of the critical German edition of *Mein Kampf* and scientific advisor for the recently published French edition. Last summer, his new anthology dealing with the linguistic aspects of *Mein Kampf* in translation was published.

David Redles is Professor of history at Cuyahoga Community College in Cleveland, Ohio. He is author of *Hitler's Millennial Reich: Apocalyptic Belief* *and the Search for Salvation* (2005) and coauthor, along with Jackson Spielvogel, of *Hitler and Nazi Germany*, ninth edition (2020). He also contributed chapters to *The Paranoid Apocalypse: A Hundred-Year Retrospective on the Protocols of the Elders of Zion* (2011); *The Fundamentalist Mindset: Psychological Reflections on Religion, Violence, and History* (2010); *End of Days: Essays on the Apocalypse from Antiquity to Modernity* (2009); and *War in Heaven, Heaven on Earth: Theories of the Apocalyptic* (2005).

Karla Schönebeck, author and journalist, has been dealing with National Socialism and its contemporary effects for many years. Her main focus is on intergenerational, interreligious, and intercultural dialogue. She initiated with the University of Music and Performing Arts the international Wolf Durmashkin Composition Award (WDCA) for young artists. She has organized public workshops, discussions, and exhibitions such as "Music and the Holocaust" and "From Lithuania to Landsberg." Her most recent project is organizing an exhibition, "Liberation Concert: Humanity, Dignity, Hope."

J. Ryan Stackhouse is an historian of modern Europe specializing in Nazism. His forthcoming book *Enemies of the People: Hitler's Critics and the Gestapo* (CUP, 2021) has been described as "the most important study on Gestapo policing in any language to date." Ryan loves to share what he learns on *The Third Reich History Podcast* and interviews experts about the many faces of authoritarianism on the New Books Network.

Nathan Stoltzfus is Dorothy and Jonathan Rintels Professor of Holocaust Studies at Florida State University and author or editor of seven books. The most recent are *Hitler's Compromises: Coercion and Consensus in Nazi Germany* and *Resistance of the Heart: Intermarriage and the Rosenstrasse Protest in Nazi Germany.* In 1996, he was Fraenkel Prize cowinner, a New Statesman Book of the Year, and prize winner of Munich's Besten Liste for nonfiction. He also co-edited *Women Defying Hitler: Resistance and Rescue under the Nazis* as well as *The Power of Populism and the People.*

Timothy W. Ryback is author of *Hitler's Private Library: The Books That Shaped His Life* and *Hitler's First Victims: A Quest for Justice*, as well as *The Last Survivor: Legacies of Dachau.* Ryback has written on culture and politics, in particular the legacies of National Socialism, for numerous publications, including *The Atlantic Monthly*, *The New Yorker*, *The New York Times*, *The Wall Street Journal*, and *The Financial Times.* Ryback is Director of the Institute for Historical Justice and Reconciliation in the Hague, and former deputy secretary general of the Académie Diplomatique Internationale, in Paris. He previously served as vice president of the Salzburg Global Seminar, in Austria. Ryback has a PhD from Harvard University, where he taught in the Concentration of History and Literature, the university's oldest interdisciplinary academic program.

INDEX